CONFLICTING WORLDS
New Dimensions of the American Civil War

T. Michael Parrish

Lee *in the* Shadow *of* Washington

 Richard B. McCaslin

Louisiana State University Press   *Baton Rouge*

Designer: Barbara Neely Bourgoyne
Typeface: Sabon
Typesetter: Coghill Composition Co., Inc.
Printer and binder: Thomson-Shore, Inc.

Library of Congress Cataloging-in-Publication Data

McCalsin, Richard B.
    Lee in the shadow of Washington / Richard B. McCaslin.
        p.   cm. — (Conflicting worlds)
    Includes bibliographical references and index.
    ISBN 0-8071-2696-9
    1. Lee, Robert E. (Robert Edward), 1807–1870.   2. Lee, Robert
E. (Robert Edward), 1807–1870—Sources.   3. Generals—Confederate
States of America—Biography.   4. Confederate States of America.
Army—Biography.   5. United States. Army—Biography.   6.
Washington, George, 1732–1799—Influence.   I. Title.   II. Series
E467.1.L4 M47   2001
973.7'3'092—dc21

The paper in this book meets the guidelines for permanence and durability of the Committee on Production Guidelines for Book Longevity of the Council on Library Resources. ⊗

Contents

Illustrations

Acknowledgments

The production of this study involved countless visits to archives far from my office at High Point University in North Carolina. Many of Lee's papers have been published, but quite a few have not. The staffs at the following archives and libraries have my undying gratitude for their patient support: the Center for American History, University of Texas at Austin; Eleanor S. Brockenbrough Library, Museum of the Confederacy, Richmond; Georgia Historical Society, Savannah; Howard-Tilton Library, Tulane University, New Orleans; Jesse Ball Dupont Library, Stratford Hall, Stratford, Va.; Library of Congress, Washington, D.C.; Louisiana State Museum, New Orleans; New Jersey Historical Society, Newark; Southern Historical Collection, University of North Carolina, Chapel Hill; United States Military Academy Library and Archives, West Point, N.Y.; United States Army Military History Institute, Carlisle, Pa.; University of South Carolina Library, Columbia; University of Virginia Library, Charlottesville; Virginia Historical Society, Richmond; Library of Virginia, Richmond; Washington and Lee University Library, Lexington, Va.; Washington University Library, St. Louis, Mo.; and William G. Perkins Library, Duke University, Durham, N.C. For their assistance, reams of helpful advice, and occasional free lunches, I thank all of them. They know this project would never have been completed without their support.

Closer to home, I relied greatly on the assistance of several institutional staffs. At the Herman and Louise Smith Library of High Point University, reference librarians David L. Bryden and Pat Sager provided crucial support. Jackie Hedstrom and others at the Neal F. Austin Public Library in High Point endured my countless questions and hurried interruptions with good grace and correct information. I thank all of you.

I cheerfully assume all responsibility for the faults of this work, but it would be wrong of me to do the same for either the initiative to begin this project or the push that completed it. Brooks Simpson prodded me into accepting the burden of yet another study of Lee and accepted my initial proposal. Later, Michael Parrish was kind enough to provide a tremendous amount of archival material, thus greatly enhancing the final product. This project would never have begun without the support of one friend and scholar, and it would never have been completed without the other. I hope they are satisfied with the result.

I have been fortunate enough to enjoy the company of many other friends who happen to be great scholars. I am grateful to all of you, but most especially to Frederick C. Schneid, George L. Simpson, and Peng Deng of the Department of History and Political Science at High Point University. All three of you provide invaluable advice and support. Three faithful student workers, Amy Townsend, Christina Mercurio, and Amy Davis, also have my gratitude for their patience with tedious tasks.

My wife Jana and daughter Christy have patiently endured my preoccupation with history for many years now. They have been joined by my grandson Caleb, who wonders why Poppa taps on the computer so much. Of course, he wants to join in the fun, and maybe he will. I hope this study is worthy of their support.

Lee *in the* Shadow
of Washington

Introduction

Robert E. Lee spent his fifty-fourth birthday, January 19, 1861, in his room at Fort Mason, Texas, reading Edwin Everett's biography of George Washington. Why did he read this? Because Lee lived within the shadow of Washington, who had been presented to him from birth as a role model. When Lee like Washington faced a call for revolution, he read the most recent work about Washington for answers. Called to lead, Lee like Washington made himself the principal military leader in an effort to found a new nation. Lee wore a colonel's uniform as Washington had done; rode a horse bearing the name of one of his idol's mounts, Traveller; and packed one of Washington's swords in his baggage. Crushed by defeat, Lee became president of Washington College and devoted the rest of his life to enhancing his idol's legacy.

Three issues dominate the voluminous historiography of Lee: his decision regarding secession, his military campaigns, and his conduct in defeat. Many authors have briefly noted Lee's focus on Washington, but few have fully explored Washington's influence on Lee's actions. Raised with Washington as his model, Lee obeyed the call to lead his people in a revolution as Washington had done. Like Washington, Lee made his army the focus of the war and tried to be an inspirational leader. The key to winning the war for Lee, as for Washington, was to force his foe to negotiate before his own support dissipated. To this end, Lee assumed the primary burden of winning the war, and he invoked the legacy of the Revolution to motivate his dwindling army. Defeat crushed Lee because it meant that he had failed to meet the standard set by a man he revered.

Remarks about Lee's devotion to Washington are common when authors explain his support for secession. John F. C. Fuller, recalling that Lee married the daughter of Washington's adopted son, writes that Lee's role as the "representative of the family which had founded American liberty" was crucial in his decision. Gene Smith concurs that "In a sense he was Washington's heir." Philip Van Doren Stern asks, "Could the kind of act of separation that was justified in 1776 be wrong in 1861?" Clifford Dowdey answers by noting that Lee's "greatest hero," Washington, "had been the greatest revolutionary of them all." Nancy and Dwight Anderson assert that Lee "through kinship and kindred spirit . . . was a Washington" and "believed that he was doing as Washington would have done." Thomas L. Connelly and Drew G. Faust concur with the Andersons that many Southerners, including Lee, insisted they were defending the heritage of the Revolution in 1861.[1]

Such remarks concerning Lee's motivation in the secession crisis raise as many questions as they answer. How did Lee come to have such a strong interest in Washington? Did this manifest itself at other times? This work attempts to demonstrate that Lee's whole life was saturated with the legacy of Virginia's Revolutionary generation. Members of Lee's family had been leaders of that generation, particularly his father, Henry Lee III, renowned as Light-Horse Harry. Lee's father, however, provided a poor role model, and he and his wife Anne pressed Washington upon young Lee as a better example. The result was that Lee retained a focus on Washington throughout his life, not just during the secession crisis.

---

1. John F. C. Fuller, *Grant and Lee: A Study in Personality and Generalship* (Stevenage, U.K., 1933), 102 [1st quote]; Gene Smith, *Lee and Grant: A Dual Biography* (Norwalk, Conn., 1984), 87 [2nd quote]; Philip Van Doren Stern, *Robert E. Lee, The Man and the Soldier: A Pictorial Biography* (New York, 1963), 123 [3rd quote]; Clifford Dowdey, *Lee* (Boston, 1965), 135 [4th and 5th quotes]; Nancy S. and Dwight Anderson, *The Generals: Ulysses S. Grant and Robert E. Lee* (New York, 1988), 213, 229–30 [6th and 7th quotes]; Thomas L. Connelly, *The Marble Man: Robert E. Lee and His Image in American Society* (Baton Rouge, 1977), 96; Drew G. Faust, *The Creation of Confederate Nationalism: Ideology and Identity in the Civil War South* (Baton Rouge, 1988), 14.

Lee's close ties to the Revolutionary generation and his devotion to Washington as a role model became the key difference between him and Virginians who stayed with the Union. As Burton J. Hendrick explains, "The mere fact that Lee was a Virginian did not automatically make him a follower of the Confederacy." More than half of the Virginians who graduated from West Point before the Civil War stayed with the Union. Among them was Maj. George H. Thomas, who had shared a tent with Lee in Texas; Lee's living mentor, Winfield Scott, also stayed with the Union army, and Lee's cousins Samuel P. Lee and John F. Lee remained in the Union navy and army respectively. The crucial factor in Robert E. Lee's decision was George Washington. When Lee followed Virginia into the war, he acted within the legacy with which he was raised. The Andersons admit, "The notion of that past was home to Lee in ways no physical place could ever be." Because of this, Fuller says, "Deep in *Lee's* soul it was the voice of his ancestors that was speaking" in 1861. Gamaliel Bradford adds that Lee "felt, with the most earnest conviction, that he was fighting for the ideas of Washington and Jefferson, and that in his place they would have done as he did."[2]

Most authors not only leave unanswered the question of why Lee was so devoted to Washington, but they also fail to explore how this bond affected Lee's conduct in the war. Lee not only looked to Washington for guidance in the secession crisis, but sought to emulate his example as a commander. Lee was thrust into a role far beyond that of his father—he became like Washington a leader of a revolution, as he believed it to be. Thomas L. Connelly has outlined the debate within the Confederacy about whether the fate of the new nation lay in the hands of Lee, but he admits, like Lee staff member Charles Marshall before him, that one thing is certain: from the time Lee took charge in Virginia, he assumed that the success of his cause lay with him as it had with Washington. Contrary to the assertion of historians such as Louis H.

2. Burton J. Hendrick, *The Lees of Virginia: Biography of a Family* (Boston, 1935), 429–32 [1st quote]; Robert W. Winston, *Robert E. Lee: A Biography* (New York, 1941), 60; John Bigelow, "Robert E. Lee and Secession: A Study of Loyalty" (Typescript, 1936, John Bigelow Papers, Library of Congress, Washington, D.C.), 67; Anderson and Anderson, *Generals,* 86 [2nd quote]; Fuller, *Grant and Lee,* 97 [3rd quote]; Gamaliel Bradford, *Lee the American* (Boston, 1912; rev. ed., Cambridge, Mass., 1929), 38 [4th quote]; Francis MacDonnell, "The Confederate Spin on Winfield Scott and George Thomas," *Civil War History* 44 (Dec. 1998): 255–66.

Manarin that "Any effort to compare [Lee] with any other general not of his time would be futile and full of so many exceptions that it would be valueless," an analysis of Lee's effort as an emulation of Washington provides useful insights into his decisions.[3]

The "essence" of Washington's strategy, which was dictated by his limited means, was a "strategy of attrition." His focus was not the British army, which he could never hope to eliminate, but the British public's will to continue the war. The key was to convince the British "that the struggle was either hopeless or too burdensome to pursue." At the same time, Washington realized that "the crucial battlefields were in the minds of individual Americans." To sustain their support, his troops had to "seek an impressive record," or the cause was lost.[4] Fortunately for him and his cause, patriot troops, with foreign assistance, outlasted British popular support for the war, and he triumphed.

Lee faced the same great challenge that taxed Washington, and he conducted himself during his revolution in a similar manner. As James M. McPherson has written, "Confederate armies did not have to invade and conquer the North; they needed only to hold out long enough to force the North to the conclusion that the price of conquering the South and annihilating its armies was too high, as Britain had concluded in 1781." Believing this, Lee made his army the primary focus of the war and campaigned in a fashion that "bore a striking resemblance to the American strategy in the Revolutionary War." Lee knew that Southerners needed "resounding victories and an early peace" before their morale and economy crumbled. Unlike Jefferson Davis, however, who believed "the war could be won simply by not losing," Lee worried that "it could be lost simply by not winning."[5] This pushed Lee to seek decisive victories more aggressively than Washington.

3. Connelly, *Marble Man,* 13–26; Charles Marshall, *An Aide-de-Camp of Lee,* ed. Frederick Maurice (Boston, 1927), 66–67; Louis H. Manarin, "Lee in Command: Strategical and Tactical Policies . . ." (Ph.D. diss., Duke University, 1965), viii [quote].

4. Russell Weigley, *The American Way of War* (New York, 1973; reprint, Bloomington, Ind., 1977), 3 [1st and 2nd quotes], 5, 7–8, 11–12, 14 [3rd quote], 21, 38–39; Holmes M. Alexander, *Washington and Lee: A Study in the Will to Win* (Boston, 1966), 27, 33–34, 36, 38–39, 47–48; James T. Flexner, *Washington: The Indispensable Man* (New York, 1974), 64 [4th quote], 179 [5th quote].

5. James M. McPherson, "American Victory, American Defeat," in Gabor S. Boritt, *Why the Confederacy Lost* (New York, 1992), 19–20 [1st quote]; Emory M. Thomas, *The Confederacy as a Revolutionary Experience* (New York, 1970), 45 [2nd and 3rd quotes], 48; Steven E. Woodworth, *Davis and Lee at War* (Lawrence, Kans., 1994), 157 [4th and

Lee's emulation of Washington has occasionally been noted by writers who have analyzed his martial efforts. Shortly after the Civil War, John E. Cooke wrote that "It is very easy to talk about a 'second Washington' without meaning much," but he pointed out that the "enemy had then, as now, to be worried out." Many years later, Emory M. Thomas wrote that with the Maryland raid in 1862, "In his quaint, modest way, Lee was staking his claim to become the Father of a new country—the nineteenth-century George Washington." Thomas focuses on Lee's attempt to dictate civil policy to Davis, but he also refers to Lee's assumption that he could win the war as commander of the Confederacy's primary army. Gary W. Gallagher agrees that Lee's army became the keystone of the Confederacy, declaring that "Lee and his soldiers ascended to a position comparable to that occupied by George Washington and his Continental army during the American Revolution."[6]

Lee's focus on winning the war almost single-handedly has led some writers to assert that Lee lacked a strategic vision. Not having fully considered Lee's focus upon George Washington, they declare that the problem was a misguided determination to defend Virginia. Fuller wrote that Lee's localism led to a neglect of the west that proved fatal to the Confederacy. Connelly later agreed that Lee was unrealistic in thinking that his offensive success in Virginia would offset losses elsewhere. In a study of Confederate commanders coauthored with Archer Jones, Connelly asserts that Lee "either had no unified view of grand strategy or else chose to remain silent on the subject." He was paralyzed by "localistic and provincial" thinking focused on Virginia, and thus he could not "perceive Confederate strategic problems in their entirety." Connelly finds the strongest evidence of Lee's tunnel vision in his insisting upon support for his army to the detriment of those in the west, where defeat led directly to the Confederacy's fall.[7]

5th quotes]; James M. McPherson, *Battle Cry of Freedom: The Civil War Era* (New York, 1988), 337; Joseph L. Harsh, *Confederate Tide Rising: Robert E. Lee and the Making of Southern Strategy, 1861–1862* (Kent, Ohio, 1998), 7, 59–60.

6. John E. Cooke, *Wearing of the Gray* (New York, 1867; reprint, Bloomington, Ind., 1959), 357–58 [1st and 2nd quotes]; Emory M. Thomas, *Robert E. Lee: A Biography* (New York, 1995), 256 [3rd quote]; Gary W. Gallagher, *The Confederate War* (Cambridge, Mass., 1997), 8, 58–59 [4th quote], 63, 65, 72, 85–92, 139–40.

7. Fuller, *Grant and Lee*, 255–56; Thomas L. Connelly, "Robert E. Lee and the Western Confederacy: A Criticism of Lee's Strategic Ability," *Civil War History* 15 (June 1969):

Lee in fact did have a strategic vision. With the strong support of President Davis, he made his army the primary tool to force the North to negotiate. In so doing, Lee was not guilty of localism; instead, he believed that he had to convince the North to quit just as Washington had wearied the British. Lee knew about Saratoga and Gen. Nathaniel Greene's campaigns in the southern colonies (in which Lee's own father played a prominent role), but he had read that Washington sustained the war with his army and dealt the telling blow at Yorktown. If Lee suffered from tunnel vision, it was due to his attempt to play the same role as Washington, not to an overdeveloped sense of loyalty to his home state. Did he thus kill the Confederacy? Historians such as Joseph L. Harsh, Stephen W. Sears, Albert Castel, Charles P. Roland, and Gallagher rightly agree that the best chance for victory lay in the east and that Lee's efforts "lengthened the life of the Confederacy." Gallagher further points out that Lee's aggressive strategy was best suited for winning the attention of Europe, a fact Lee did not stress because he feared Southerners relied too much on the hope of foreign intervention.[8]

Lee's efforts provided the best chance not only of breaking Northern will but also of sustaining Southern morale. Gallagher asserts that "Lee pursued a strategy attuned to the expectations of most Confederate citizens." Lee not only provided them with hope through his victories, but he also met their assumptions about revolutionary leadership. Faust declares that the "nationalist movement with which the Confederates most frequently identified was . . . the American War of Independence." They believed that they, and not the North, were the true heirs of the Revolution. Washington's image adorned the Confederacy's seal and a postage stamp. Ragged Confederates took great pride in their appearance, assuming they more closely resembled Washington's Continentals than did their Union counterparts. The Confederates had all heard sto-

---

127–29, 131; Thomas L. Connelly and Archer Jones, *The Politics of Command: Factions and Ideas in Confederate Strategy* (Baton Rouge, 1983), 33 [1st quote], 38–42, 46 [2nd quote], 194 [3rd quote].

8. Harsh, *Confederate Tide Rising,* 21; Frederick Maurice, *Robert E. Lee, the Soldier* (Boston, 1925), 82; John J. Bowen, *The Strategy of Robert E. Lee* (New York, 1914), 88; Alan T. Nolan, *Lee Considered: General Robert E. Lee and Civil War History* (Chapel Hill, 1991), 72–73; Gary W. Gallagher, "Introduction," in Gary W. Gallagher, ed., *Lee the Soldier* (Lincoln, Nebr., 1996), xxvii [quote]; Gary W. Gallagher, "Another Look at the Generalship of R. E. Lee," in Gallagher, *Lee the Soldier,* 277–78.

ries about the patriots and never tired of telling them. Davis knew this and insisted on being inaugurated on the birthday of Washington, "the man most identified with the establishment of American independence," in 1862. Steven E. Woodworth has asserted that most Confederates hailed Davis as Washington's heir, but this is not supported by the evidence. In the midst of their own revolution, they looked for a military leader and embraced Lee as the successor of Washington.[9]

Some authors, most notably Thomas and Paul D. Escott, have asserted that Confederates initially looked to the Revolution for inspiration, but wartime circumstances compelled them to begin thinking of their struggle as unique. There were no parallels in the Revolution for such radical measures of self-preservation as conscription and impressment. This shift of perspective may have been necessary for some of the embattled Confederates, but Lee consistently invoked the memory of Washington and his troops as inspiration. Contrary to the rebuke of Sir Garnet J. Wolseley, Lee never forgot "he was the great Revolutionary Chief engaged in a great Revolutionary war."[10]

Lee's reliance on Washington as a model may have been his best option, but it did not bring victory. The 1864 campaign was reminiscent of the Yorktown campaign, but tragically for Lee, it was his Confederates rather than the enemy who became trapped in a siege like the British. As Thomas notes, "The South had attempted to duplicate the strategy of Washington, only to find themselves at the last in the position

---

9. Gallagher, *Lee the Soldier*, 277 [1st quote]; Faust, *Confederate Nationalism*, 14 [2nd quote], 25; Emory M. Thomas, *The Confederate Nation, 1861–1865* (New York, 1979), 221–22; Harsh, *Confederate Tide Rising*, 60–62; Anderson and Anderson, *Generals*, 340; James D. Richardson, comp., *The Messages and Papers of Jefferson Davis and the Confederacy, 1861–1865*, 2 vols. (Washington, D.C., 1896–1899; reprint, New York, 1981), 1:129 [3rd quote]; James I. McPherson, *What They Fought For* (Baton Rouge, 1994), 9–11, 25; Gallagher, *Confederate War*, 59, 65, 146; Henry A. White, *Robert E. Lee and the Southern Confederacy, 1807–1870* (New York, 1897), 347; Thomas, *Lee*, 256; Woodworth, *Davis and Lee*, 5. Both Northerners and Southerners, of course, revered the memory of the Revolution, and both sides embraced that legacy as justification for their own actions during the Civil War. See Reid Mitchell, *Civil War Soldiers* (New York, 1988), 1–22, 93; and James M. McPherson, *For Cause and Comrades: Why Men Fought in the Civil War* (New York, 1997), 18–21, 104–6, 110–13.

10. Thomas, *Confederate Nation*, 222–24; Paul D. Escott, *After Secession: Jefferson Davis and the Failure of Confederate Nationalism* (Baton Rouge, 1978), 169–71, 175–81, 190–91; Garnet J. Wolseley, "General Lee," in Gallagher, *Lee the Soldier*, 107 [quote].

of Lord Cornwallis." The North during the Civil War was not analogous to Britain in the Revolution. The Federal government had more
resources and did not face the logistical problems the British had
encountered. Union forces were more numerous and were more easily
reinforced than the British had been, allowing them to attack upon several fronts at once. The Union's larger navy blockaded the coast more
effectively than the British and by the war's end controlled most inland
waterways as well. Northern diplomacy precluded European aid, which
had been crucial to the colonies. Finally, Northerners' will to maintain
the Union far exceeded the desire of Englishmen to keep their distant
colonies. Russell Weigley concluded correctly that "soldiers never
fought more bravely to rescue so mistaken a strategic design" than did
Lee's army. Some authors argue that Lee might have undertaken a guerrilla war, but he could not have done so any more than Washington
could. Southern expectations and military traditions—many founded on
cherished concepts about Washington's efforts—and fears about slave
control constricted the options considered by Lee and his fellow Confederates.[11]

Lee's failure cannot be attributed entirely to the Union's nationalism
and material superiority. While pursuing a strategy focused upon himself as the principal leader, Lee used aggressive tactics that reflected
influences other than Washington. John H. Chamberlayne in a postwar
speech declared that Lee was "the pupil of Scott, the follower of Washington, [and] the son of Light Horse Harry." More than a hundred years
later, John M. Dederer agreed that two sources for Lee's audacity were
his experience in the Mexican War under Winfield Scott and the exploits
of his own father, but he added a more trenchant observation. Lee's tactics, which focused on annihilating rather than defeating his foe,
reflected a close study of Napoleon. As William R. Cox, who served
under Lee, wrote, his commander "manifested the patience of Washington," but he also "showed the elan in battle . . . so characteristic of
Napoleon." This remark was echoed by Thomas, who wrote that Lee
and other Confederates "harkened back in substance to the example of

11. Thomas, *Revolutionary Experience*, 51 [1st quote]; Flexner, *Washington*, 110,
179; Weigley, *American Way of War*, 117 [2nd quote]; Gallagher, *Confederate War*,
123–52.

George Washington and the Continental Army," but spoke the "language" of Napoleon and his contemporaries.[12]

Lee's use of Napoleonic tactics brought him victories, but at a terrible cost. Even Connelly and Jones, who condemn Lee's "obsession with the war effort in Virginia," admit that his use of Napoleonic principles, including his concentration of force, brought great success. A fundamental tenet of Napoleonic warfare was to retain the initiative. To do this repeatedly against a more numerous foe cost Lee dearly. Many, including President Davis and officers who served under Lee, were quick to note that Lee attacked aggressively at every opportunity. Some had the temerity to criticize him, but few, except perhaps Lt. Gen. James Longstreet, challenged Lee during the war.[13]

Many scholars attribute Lee's failure to his insistence upon maintaining the offensive. Fuller echoes Longstreet when he declares that Lee's aggression not only lessened his own impact but fatally damaged the overall strategy of the South. Connelly repeats that Lee's "penchant for the offensive" drained the Confederacy, costing it more than it could afford. Alan T. Nolan agrees that Lee's aggressive defensive strategy was "misplaced" because he could never defeat the Federal armies. This idea is more fully explored by Grady McWhiney and Perry D. Jamieson in their study of Confederate assaults, which provides interesting data but perhaps goes too far in its musing that Lee's Celtic heritage led him astray. Weigley supports the contention that Lee's tactics excessively drained Southern resources, adding that Lee unfortunately shared Napoleon's "passion for the strategy of annihilation and the climactic, decisive battle" in a time when technology made such battles both costly and futile. Finally, Weigley points out that Napoleon suffered heavy

12. John H. Chamberlayne, "Address on the Character of General Robert E. Lee," *Southern Historical Society Papers* 3 (1877): 32 [1st quote]; John M. Dederer, "The Origins of Robert E. Lee's Bold Generalship: A Reinterpretation," *Military Affairs* 49 (July 1985): 117–20; Charles A. Culberson, comp., *The Greatest Confederate Commander* (Washington, D.C., 1907), 14 [2nd and 3rd quotes]; Thomas, *Revolutionary Experience,* 45–46 [4th and 5th quotes]; Harsh, *Confederate Tide Rising,* 72–73.

13. Connelly and Jones, *Politics of Command,* xi–xii [quote], 174; Walter H. Taylor, *Four Years with General Lee* (New York, 1877; reprint, New York, 1962), 90; Walter H. Taylor, *General Lee: His Campaigns in Virginia, 1861–1865* (Norfolk, Va., 1906), 180; Robert Stiles, *Four Years under Marse Robert* (New York, 1903), 191; Jefferson Davis, *The Rise and Fall of the Confederate Government,* 2 vols. (New York, 1881), 2:152; Helen D. Longstreet, *Lee and Longstreet at High Tide* (Gainesville, Ga., 1904), 84.

losses, but he had a large populace from which to draft replacements, an advantage that Lee did not share.[14]

In defense of Lee's tactics, it must be noted that not only did his aggression suit the mind-set of the Confederacy, but he was following the advice of many military experts of his own time as well as the present. He understood the limits of Southern resources and morale—he had to win before either was depleted. For this reason, he attacked whenever an opportunity arose. McWhiney and Jamieson admit that experts throughout the Civil War emphasized offensives. Antoine Henri de Jomini, interpreter of Napoleon for many of them, wrote that an assault was the most effective way to win. This belief was still held more than a century later. A 1982 U.S. Army manual asserts that "the entire art of war consists of a well-planned and exceptionally circumspect defense followed by a rapid, audacious attack." Lee had seen assaults succeed in Mexico, and as far as he knew, no decisive victory had ever been won by staying on the defensive. He was not alone: despite heavy casualties, assaults remained popular during the Civil War because nothing was more decisive if successful.[15]

Lee's drive to be a successful leader like Washington in fact led him to modify his Napoleonic tactics. This is seen in his fieldworks, which Jomini disparaged and "would doubtless have appeared a little odd and old-fashioned" to Napoleon. Lee altered his tactics as circumstances demanded, but his strategy remained constant: he and his army would

14. Gallagher, *Confederate War,* 121–23; Fuller, *Grant and Lee,* 267; Connelly, "Lee and the Western Confederacy," 191 [1st quote]; McPherson, *Battle Cry,* 337, 472–75; Nolan, *Lee Considered,* 73–79 [2nd quote], 80–85; Grady McWhiney and Perry D. Jamieson, *Attack and Die: Civil War Military Tactics and the Southern Heritage* (Tuscaloosa, Ala., 1982), passim; Weigley, *American Way of War,* 79 [3rd quote], 97, 127. For a good summary of the historical criticism of Robert E. Lee's leadership during the Civil War, see Edward H. Bonekemper III, *How Robert E. Lee Lost the Civil War* (Fredericksburg, Va., 1997).

15. McWhiney and Jamieson, *Attack and Die,* 144; Gallagher, *Confederate War,* 9–11, 115–16, 131–32, 138; Harsh, *Confederate Tide Rising,* 60–62; Weigley, *American Way of War,* 41–42, 146–47; Richard E. Beringer et al., eds., *Why the South Lost the War* (Athens, Ga., 1986), 150 [quote] and Appendix II; Edward Hagerman, "The Tactical Thought of Robert E. Lee and the Origins of Trench Warfare in the American Civil War, 1861–1862," *Historian* 38 (Nov. 1975): 22–25, 28–30; Edward Hagerman, "From Jomini to Dennis Hart Mahan: The Evolution of Trench Warfare and the American Civil War," *Civil War History* 13 (Sept. 1967): 198–99, 205–6.

win the war. However, his focus on emulating Washington proved fatal when he was forced into the trenches at Richmond. Like Washington, he did not defy civilian control, and Davis wanted him to defend the capital. Lee protested, but he remained and his army withered away. He had conducted an aggressive, mobile defense for two years and realized that entering the trenches was dangerous, but he accepted that Davis wished to defend the city. Lee, unlike Napoleon, would not seize control of the Confederacy. He was, according to Charles P. Roland, "too American to play Napoleon."[16] He reached past Napoleon to Washington, who inhabited a chronologically more distant but emotionally closer place in history for Lee.

Because Lee made his army the focus of the Confederate war effort, his surrender meant the defeat of the Confederacy. This left Lee at a loss. During the war, Lee had striven to be like Washington the revolutionary. Now he had to overcome defeat and somehow emulate Washington as a statesman. Seeking to become in some measure the creative force that the post-Revolution Washington had been, Lee became president of a small college that bore Washington's name. There he labored to recover Washington relics that had been lost to invading Federals, especially those who had occupied Arlington. Lee's words often focused on Washington as he struggled to justify his decisions and provide a model for Reconstruction. Unwilling to write his own history, he edited a second edition of his father's Revolutionary memoirs. After his death, the College put Lee's name alongside Washington's in its title. Lee became, as Stephen Vincent Benet wrote, "The shape who stands at Washington's left hand."[17] Lee probably would have been pleased with that epitaph but concerned that some would think he was equal to Washington.

Some authors, most notably Connelly, have argued that it was after Lee's death that a "Lee cult" deliberately "implanted a Washington

16. Fuller, *Grant and Lee,* 244–45; Connelly and Jones, *Politics of Command,* 12; Paddy Griffith, *Battle Tactics of the Civil War* (New Haven, Conn., 1989), 191 [1st quote]; Edward Hagerman, *The American Civil War and the Origins of Modern Warfare* (Bloomington, Ind., 1988), 122–25; Hagerman, "Tactical Thought of Lee," 23–24; Hagerman, "From Jomini to Mahan," 200, 202–4; Charles P. Roland, *Reflections on Lee: A Historian's Assessment* (Mechanicsburg, Pa., 1995), 98 [2nd quote].

17. Gallagher, *Confederate War,* 95–96; William A. Bryan, *George Washington in American Literature, 1775–1865* (New York, 1952), 188–92; Stephen Vincent Benet, *John Brown's Body* (New York, 1941), 188 [quote].

symbolism" in the process of transforming Lee into a Lost Cause hero of almost mythical proportions. The defeated Southerners, casting about for a "justification for secession," created for Lee a bond with Washington that provided a "needed symbolism" to link the Lost Cause to the Revolution.[18] If this book does nothing more, it will belie that argument. Comparisons of Lee with Washington began before the Civil War and continued throughout that conflict. Lee rarely used historical references, but when he did, he referred to Washington. He surrounded himself with Washington relics, and he married into Washington's family. Defeated Confederates did not have to stretch to create a link between the two men; Lee had done that for them. More important, the comparisons survived the Lost Cause movement and continued as Lee became a national, rather than regional, hero, demonstrating the enduring impact of Lee's efforts to emulate his idol.

Today, the images of Lee and Washington remain linked in the capital city of the state that both men led into revolution. Lee's equestrian statue stands two miles from that of Washington on the capitol lawn in Richmond. Just inside the room in the capitol where Lee accepted command of Virginia's forces, and where his own father served as a legislator, is a life-size bronze statue of Lee in uniform. It provides an interesting contrast to the image of Washington in civilian garb that stands outside the chamber under the interior dome designed by another Virginian, Thomas Jefferson. It is the supreme irony of this juxtaposition of images that Washington won his revolution and established an indelible image as a statesman while Lee, trapped by defeat, has not been allowed to shed the military garb of a defeated cause. Having lived his life in Washington's shadow, Lee never escaped the revolutionary image he imposed upon himself.

18. Thomas L. Connelly, "The Image and the General: Robert E. Lee in American Historiography," *Civil War History* 19 (March 1973): 56–58 [quotes]; Gaines M. Foster, *Ghosts of the Confederacy* (New York, 1986), 100–101; Gallagher, *Confederate War,* 171.

1

Mystic Chords of Memory
A Revolutionary Heritage

Abraham Lincoln, in his first inaugural address, declared that the "mystic chords of memory" that bound Americans to the Founding Fathers should bind them to support the Union. Many years later Charles F. Adams, in an essay for the centennial of Robert E. Lee's birth, quoted Oliver Wendell Holmes in saying that a "child's education begins about two hundred and fifty years before it is born." About Lee, Adams added, "it is quite impossible to separate any man—least of all, perhaps, a full-blooded Virginian—from his prenatal traditions and living environment."[1] Virginia was the home of many Founding Fathers, but unfortunately for Lincoln it was their Revolutionary tradition that most influenced Lee. His exposure to people and places that recalled the Revolution and exalted George Washington led Lee to play a role similar to Washington's for the Confederacy in the Civil War.

Lee's father, Henry Lee III, provided an immediate link to the Revolution and Washington. The younger Lee would have agreed with John Adams when he said that during the Revolution the Lee clan had "more men of merit in it than any other family." In his introduction to a second

---

1. Mortimer J. Adler et al., eds., *The Annals of America*, 18 vols. (Chicago, 1968), 9:250–55 [1st quote]; Charles F. Adams, *Lee's Centennial* (Boston, 1907), 18 [2nd and 3rd quotes]; Philip A. Bruce, *Robert E. Lee* (Philadelphia, 1907), 11.

edition of his father's memoirs of the Revolution, Robert E. Lee would later write proudly about five Lee brothers, his cousins, who served with Washington: Richard Henry, Francis Lightfoot, Thomas Ludwell, William, and Arthur Lee. The first three worked with Washington in the legislature before the Revolution and with William became involved with Washington in a business venture. These four brothers also joined Washington in signing a petition in Westmoreland County against the Stamp Act. Richard Henry and Thomas Ludwell Lee later served on the council that declared Virginia's independence. Thomas Ludwell Lee then joined the Committee of Public Safety created to govern Virginia, while Richard Henry and Francis Lightfoot Lee sat by Washington in the Continental Congress. There Richard Henry Lee introduced the independence resolution that was signed on July 4, 1776, and he and Francis Lightfoot Lee endorsed the declaration penned by Thomas Jefferson. Meanwhile, Arthur and William Lee served as diplomatic agents for the colonial cause.[2]

The successful conclusion of the Revolution did not bring an end to the Lees' prominence or their ties to George Washington. Arthur returned to the Virginia House of Representatives and became a congressman for the Confederation. Francis Lightfoot Lee served in the Virginia Senate. Richard Henry once again played the most prominent role. He was elected president of the Confederation Congress but declined to attend the Constitutional Convention and opposed ratification. This fight split the Lees: Francis Lightfoot campaigned for the Constitution with the support of Washington. Those who favored the Constitution

---

2. Burton J. Hendrick, *The Lees of Virginia: Biography of a Family* (Boston, 1935), 96–97, 118–20, 137–56, 162–75, 195–96, 214, 218–19, 236–37, 241–51, 254–61, 293–95, 306–7, 312, 316–18; Paul C. Nagel, *The Lees of Virginia: Seven Generations of an American Family* (New York, 1990), 6, 45, 77, 79–80, 82–84, 94–96, 105–7, 125, 134–35, 180, 183–86, 191–95, 197; Casenove G. Lee, *Lee Chronicle: Studies of the Early Generations of the Lees of Virginia,* ed. Dorothy M. Parker (New York, 1957), 73; Henry A. White, *Robert E. Lee and the Southern Confederacy, 1807–1870* (New York, 1897), 7–9; William P. Snow, *Lee and His Generals: Their Lives and Campaigns* (New York, 1867; reprint, New York, 1982), 10; James T. Flexner, *Washington: The Indispensable Man* (New York, 1974), 57–59, 74; Stanley F. Horn, ed., *The Robert E. Lee Reader* (Indianapolis, 1949), 16 [quote]; Robert E. Lee to Samuel Tyler, Mar. 17, 1870, Robert E. Lee Letterbooks, De Butts-Ely Collection, Library of Congress, Washington, D.C. [hereinafter LC]; Henry Lee III, *Memoirs of the War in the Southern Department of the United States,* ed. Robert E. Lee (New York, 1869), 14–15.

triumphed, but Richard Henry penned the Tenth Amendment, successfully pressed for the Bill of Rights, and was elected to the United States
Senate. Interestingly, two of his daughters married Washingtons.[3]

Robert E. Lee was impressed with the services of the five Lee brothers
for the Revolution and the young republic, but he was most proud of
his father's ties to Washington. Even the circumstances of Henry Lee III's
birth were closely intertwined with the life of Washington, according to
one cherished family story. Henry Lee II was also a burgess like his three
nephews who served with Washington. He outdid them in one way,
however: he married his cousin, Lucy Grymes, after allegedly wooing
her from Washington. Some later argued that Washington's courtship of
Lucy was a yarn spun by Washington Irving in his biography of General
Washington, but Robert E. Lee enjoyed the association. He answered
one query by writing, "I believe there are grounds for the belief that
Genl Washington in early life was pleased with the beauty of Miss Sue
Grimes." He, like Irving, got her name wrong but valued the link
between the families. Apparently Henry Lee II's triumph caused no hard
feeling. He and Washington often rode together for exercise, while Lucy
and Martha Washington became good friends. The Lees' first son,
named Henry Lee III for his father, knew General Washington's wife as
"Aunt Martha."[4]

Henry Lee III's immediate family worked closely with their more dis-
tinguished cousins and Washington during the Revolution. Richard and
John Lee, Henry Lee II's brothers, became burgesses and signed the
Stamp Act petition like their Westmoreland County neighbors. Henry
Lee II served with Richard Henry and Thomas Ludwell Lee in the con-
vention that declared Virginia's independence. After the war began,

3. Hendrick, *Lees of Virginia*, 347, 350, 355–65, 431; Casenove G. Lee, *Lee Chroni-
cle*, 73–74; White, *Southern Confederacy*, 13; Nagel, *Lees of Virginia*, 130–33, 135–38;
Thomas Boyd, *Light-Horse Harry Lee* (New York, 1931), 168–69; Fitzhugh Lee, *General
Lee* (New York, 1894; reprint, Wilmington, N.C., 1989), 80.

4. White, *Southern Confederacy*, 2–6; Henry Lee III, *Memoirs*, 14–16; Hendrick, *Lees
of Virginia*, 76, 97, 330–31; Casenove G. Lee, *Lee Chronicle*, 85; Robert E. Lee to W.
[Carnar], Sept. 18, 1867, Robert E. Lee Papers, Virginia Historical Society, Richmond
[hereinafter VHS]; Armistead L. Long, *Memoirs of Robert E. Lee* (New York, 1886), 20;
Robert W. Winston, *Robert E. Lee: A Biography* (New York, 1941), 6–7; Noel B. Gerson,
Light-Horse Harry: A Biography of Washington's Great Cavalryman, General Henry Lee
(New York, 1966), 1, 3–4, 34.

Henry Lee II commanded the militia in his county, sending troops to General Washington. Among these were two of his sons, Charles Lee and Henry Lee III. Charles became a naval officer and then a Virginia legislator. Later he was chosen by Washington, upon the advice of Henry Lee III, to be Attorney General. A third son of Henry Lee II, Richard Bland Lee, became a congressman in 1789.[5]

Of the Lees, Robert E. Lee's father, Henry Lee III, became Washington's closest ally both during and after the Revolution. Lee joined Washington's army in the fall of 1776 as a cavalry captain. Their friendly alliance belied any differences between the Lees and General Washington. If there remained any resentment about the courtship of Henry Lee III's mother, it was ignored, as were lingering hints of a feud over Mount Vernon, where Henry Lee III and his parents often visited. The estate had come to Washington only after a fraudulent patent and several lawsuits wrested it from the Lees. Henry Lee III never mentioned this, and apparently he never acknowledged the strain that the Revolution placed on the friendship of Richard Henry Lee with Washington.[6]

Robert E. Lee could recount as well as anyone of his era how loyalty and hard fighting transformed Henry Lee III into "Light-Horse Harry," Washington's trusted cavalry commander. Lee fought well at Brandywine, and he and his troops served as Washington's guard at Germantown. After a promotion to major, he became the chief cavalry officer of Washington's army and then won a gold medal from Congress for a raid on Paulus Hook. Washington himself had hesitated to authorize the latter expedition, but when jealous officers tried to have Lee court-martialed after the operation for exceeding his authority and not achieving all that he could, Washington stated that all was done at his order. Friends and foes alike noticed that Lee was one of the few who could banter with the stiff Washington.[7]

5. Hendrick, *Lees of Virginia,* 134–35, 331; White, *Southern Confederacy,* 8–9; Casenove G. Lee, *Lee Chronicle,* 86; Fitzhugh Lee, *General Lee,* 7–8; Nagel, *Lees of Virginia,* 79–80, 97, 159–60; Gerson, *Light-Horse Harry,* 14–16, 201.

6. Casenove G. Lee, *Lee Chronicle,* 65, 86; Hendrick, *Lees of Virginia,* 49–50, 303, 332; Gerson, *Light-Horse Harry,* 19–23; Margaret Sanborn, *Robert E. Lee: A Portrait* (Philadelphia, 1966), 4; Emory M. Thomas, *Robert E. Lee: A Biography* (New York, 1995), 123; Nancy S. and Dwight M. Anderson, *The Generals: Ulysses S. Grant and Robert E. Lee* (New York, 1988), 12.

7. Boyd, *Harry Lee,* 26–29, 40–60; Winston, *Lee,* 7; Fitzhugh Lee, *General Lee,* 9; Gerson, *Light-Horse Harry,* 24–89; Charles Royster, *Light-Horse Harry Lee and the Legacy of the American Revolution* (New York, 1981), 21.

After Paulus Hook, Light-Horse Harry became a lieutenant colonel in command of a legion. His continued success brought an invitation from Washington to join his staff, which Lee declined. Instead, he and his troops joined Gen. Nathaniel Greene in the southern colonies. Following a generally successful campaign, Lee took a message from Greene to Washington. He arrived during the siege of Yorktown and stood with Washington as the British surrendered. Lee resigned only a few months after Yorktown and returned to Virginia, where he married Matilda Lee, the niece of the civilian Lee brothers who served in the Continental Congress and other Revolutionary councils. She was escorted by her uncle, Richard Henry Lee, at the wedding, and Washington attended.[8]

Light-Horse Harry's postwar life proved as tragic as his Revolutionary exploits were brilliant. His first two sons—the second of whom was named for Washington, his godfather—died in childhood, and a third boy survived only a year after Matilda died in 1790. He served in Congress and as governor of Virginia during this period, but his work drew few accolades. His poor management of his business affairs prompted his father to leave him only "some of his lesser lands" in his will. Matilda also bequeathed her ancestral home where they lived, Stratford Hall, to her surviving children, Henry Lee IV and Lucy Grymes Lee, but Light-Horse Harry convinced the trustees to allow him to sell almost all of that property. Tenants tended the remaining land, while the house itself deteriorated without servants or money to maintain its vast rooms.[9]

Throughout his decline, Lee remained a friend of Washington, even when they disagreed. Light-Horse Harry was among those who supported the Constitution in the Virginia convention, where he spoke in favor of the new compact at the behest of Washington. The political

8. Boyd, *Harry Lee*, 61, 32–34, 73–76, 78, 80–86, 134–43; Casenove G. Lee, *Lee Chronicle*, 72, 283–85; Fitzhugh Lee, *General Lee*, 9; Sanborn, *Portrait*, 4–5; Winston, *Lee*, 8; Hendrick, *Lees of Virginia*, 87–88, 336, 340–43, 345; Royster, *Light-Horse Harry Lee*, 25, 37–38, 40–44; Anderson and Anderson, *Generals*, 13; Gerson, *Light-Horse Harry*, 63–64, 92–149.

9. Connie H. Wyrick, "Stratford and the Lees," *Journal of the Society of Architectural Historians* 30 (Mar. 1971): 77–78; Gerson, *Light-Horse Harry*, 150, 152, 154, 165, 168–69; Fitzhugh Lee, *General Lee*, 16–17; Sanborn, *Portrait*, 7–8, 15–16; Winston, *Lee*, 12; Anderson and Anderson, *Generals*, 13; Boyd, *Harry Lee*, 156, 161–63; Thomas, *Lee*, 24–25 [quote], 27; Royster, *Light-Horse Harry Lee*, 65, 92.

dilemma that would confront Robert E. Lee was foreshadowed in a conflict that strained the friendship of his father with Washington. When Washington strongly endorsed Alexander Hamilton's proposal to assume state debts, an expansion of federal power, Lee angrily protested. He wrote, "To disunite is dreadful to my mind; but, dreadful as it is, I consider it a lesser evil than Union on the present conditions." The younger Lee did not fail to notice that his father supported the central government, but not at the expense of local autonomy.[10]

Washington did try to help Lee. He considered appointing him to command the army but decided that would distress many who had held higher ranks during the Revolution. President Washington's letter explaining his decision was treasured by the Lees and published in Henry Lee IV's laudatory account of Light-Horse Harry's Carolina campaign. Dejected, Lee considered joining the revolutionary army of France. He wrote to his wartime friend the Marquis de Lafayette, but Lafayette was jailed, and Lee abandoned the idea on the advice of Washington. When the Whiskey Rebellion erupted in 1794, Lee commanded federal forces and earned the gratitude of Washington, who according to family lore rode with him into Pennsylvania, but he caught no rebels and lost his governor's seat when it was declared vacant. Robert E. Lee later asserted that his father "retired" as governor, but in truth he was forced to do so. Washington knew about his friend's business failures, and even rebuked Lee for giving him a bad check. Nonetheless, in 1798, when the threat of a war with France led to Washington's appointment as general-in-chief, he made Lee a major general.[11]

According to Robert E. Lee, his father returned once more to the Virginia legislature in 1798 at Washington's request. There he joined Washington in supporting the Alien and Sedition Acts, and he denounced

10. Henry Lee III, *Memoirs,* 45–46 [quote]; Edgar E. Hume, "Light-Horse Harry and His Fellow Members of the Cincinnati," *Virginia Magazine of History and Biography* 15 (Apr. 1935): 271; White, *Southern Confederacy,* 13; Royster, *Light-Horse Harry Lee,* 98–100; Boyd, *Harry Lee,* 168–78; Gerson, *Light-Horse Harry,* 154–61, 164–66, 171.

11. Henry Lee III, *Memoirs,* 45, 48 [quote]; Boyd, *Harry Lee,* 202, 210–12, 223–35, 249; Henry Lee IV, *The Campaign of 1781 in the Carolinas* (Philadelphia, 1824; reprint, Spartanburg, S.C., 1975), xliv–xlvi; Thomas, *Lee,* 24–26; Sanborn, *Portrait,* 10–11, 13–14; Gerson, *Light-Horse Harry,* 176–78, 188–97, 202–3; Anderson and Anderson, *Generals,* 13, 15–17; Fitzhugh Lee, *General Lee,* 11; Royster, *Light-Horse Harry Lee,* 130, 134, 149.

efforts at nullification. Writing in the aftermath of his own unsuccessful challenge to Federal authority, Robert E. Lee noted that his father's support for George Washington was limited by his continued devotion to state sovereignty. The elder Lee, during the arguments over the Alien and Sedition Acts, stated that if the measures were actually unconstitutional, then a state legislature would have the right to oppose them. Furthermore, according to Robert E. Lee, his father declared "that the State of Virginia was his country, whose will he would obey, however lamentable the fate to which it might subject him." In spite of these assertions, Washington was pleased with Light-Horse Harry Lee and supported his bid for a congressional seat by voting for him with a grand flourish in the public polling.[12]

Elected to Congress, Light-Horse Harry performed a last sad duty for his former commander. Washington died in 1799, and Lee wrote the memorial resolution adopted by Congress. Overcome with emotion, Lee asked his friend John Marshall to read the missive for him. Lee himself later presented a longer eulogy. When he read the final line, which immortalized Washington as "first in war, first in peace, and first in the hearts of his countrymen," he earned a place alongside the first President in the pantheon of Revolutionary heroes. This distinction was not nearly enough to sustain a failing political career without Washington. After the inauguration of Thomas Jefferson, with whom he had fallen out over nullification, Light-Horse Harry quit elective politics.[13]

The death of Washington removed any impediments to Lee's downward spiral. He briefly became a major general again in 1807 during clashes with the British, but his scorn for Jefferson did not allow the opportunity to continue. He installed a chain on the door of Stratford to thwart his creditors, but in 1809 he was declared bankrupt and jailed for more than a year. During that time he began writing his memoir, but sales proved disappointing. He opposed the War of 1812 and was badly injured and disfigured by a mob while defending the office of a friend, a

12. Thomas, *Lee*, 27–28; Sanborn, *Portrait*, 17–19; Boyd, *Harry Lee*, 253, 256; Gerson, *Light-Horse Harry*, 203–14; Henry Lee III, *Memoirs*, 50 [quote]-52; White, *Southern Confederacy*, 17; Fitzhugh Lee, *General Lee*, 11; Royster, *Light-Horse Harry Lee*, 149; Winston, *Lee*, 13–14, 393; Hendrick, *Lees of Virginia*, 385.

13. Boyd, *Harry Lee*, 253, 256; Gerson, *Light-Horse Harry*, 209–14; Royster, *Light-Horse Harry Lee*, 149; Hendrick, *Lees of Virginia*, 385; Anderson and Anderson, *Generals*, 13.

Baltimore editor who published antiwar editorials. Robert E. Lee proudly recounted that President James Madison visited his family and offered to make his father a general, but by then his health was ruined. Instead, with Madison's support Lee went to Barbados to begin a fruitless search for a cure to his injuries. In 1818, Light-Horse Harry Lee died while traveling home for the first time since his exile. His illness had compelled him to seek asylum on Cumberland Island at Dungeness, the home of Nathaniel Greene. General Greene was dead, but his daughter and her husband had provided for Light-Horse Harry until he died, and they buried him at Dungeness.[14]

Even in exile, Light-Horse Harry provided a vivid link to George Washington for young Robert E. Lee. Robert was not ashamed of his father because he was not fully aware of his more sordid behavior. He was only six years old when he last saw his father, and he was eleven when Light-Horse Harry died. For Robert E. Lee, the primary sources of information about his father were his family, who did not talk much about his decline, and his memoirs, which included little about the post-Revolution period. When he did learn the truth, it shook him. Charles C. Jones's biography of Light-Horse Harry came to him in the summer of 1870. Lee was too ill to write to his brother Charles Carter Lee about the volume, so his wife Mary Custis Lee did so. She wrote that this "very circumstantial account of the last days of Genl. Harry Lee . . . differs so much & so painfully from what we know that Robert is much concerned to know its truth." Robert E. Lee was especially concerned to read of his father's "want of self control & great instability of temper." This was "not at all consistent" with what he had learned, and he wanted to deny the "allegations" if they were untrue. Carter, who along with Robert in 1861 had welcomed a decision by Virginia legislators to bring their father home for burial as a hero, provided no satisfactory reply.[15]

Light-Horse Harry did his utmost to instill in his sons the idea that Revolutionary ideals were best embodied in Washington. Washington

14. Thomas, *Lee*, 29–30, 32–33, 36; Boyd, *Harry Lee*, 288, 292, 295–97, 330–31; White, *Southern Confederacy*, 22; Henry Lee III, *Memoirs*, 53; Gerson, *Light-Horse Harry*, 237; Clifford Dowdey, *Lee* (Boston, 1965), 34–35.

15. Mary Custis Lee to Charles Carter Lee, Aug. 1, 1870, Ethel Armes Papers, LC; Fitzhugh Lee, *General Lee*, 16; Henry Lee III, *Memoirs*, passim.

was his "father figure," whom he always revered "with extraordinary devotion." He told stories of the Revolution to Charles Carter Lee and read to him from family papers and books stored at Stratford. Carter dutifully repeated these tales to his younger brother, and when Robert was older, he read them himself. Likewise, the elder Lee wrote to Carter while he was in exile, providing a stream of advice. He never wrote to Sydney Smith Lee, his second son, or Robert, but he apparently expected Carter to convey his messages to his brothers, adding in one missive an instruction for Carter to "Hug my dear Robert for me." Later, Robert E. Lee studied these notes, absorbing his father's focus upon Washington as a role model.[16]

Most of Light-Horse Harry's advice from exile focused on the examples of great writers and of Washington, who he believed was the most wonderful man he knew. His sons were "to avoid all frivolous authors; such as novel writers" and instead "adhere to history and ethical authors of unrivalled character," foremost among whom was John Locke, of whom he wrote, "Do not only study, but consult him as the Grecians did the Delphic oracle." He also urged them to read Greek and Roman, especially the meditations of Marcus Aurelius. Later in life, Robert E. Lee would repeat this same advice to his own children, and one of the few books that he kept in his office was the meditations of Marcus Aurelius. The ultimate role model, though, was "the great Washington," as Light-Horse Harry referred to his commander. Typical of his remarks was that "'A man ought not only to be virtuous in reality, but he must always appear so,' thus said to me the great Washington."[17]

Such sentiments echoed the lessons imparted to Light-Horse Harry's

16. Gerson, *Light-Horse Harry*, 171, 244; Thomas, *Lee*, 24 [1st and 2nd quotes], 34; Boyd, *Harry Lee*, 218 [3rd quote]; Ethel Armes, *Stratford Hall: The Great House of the Lees* (Richmond, 1936), 315; Henry Lee III to Charles Carter Lee, Aug. 15, 1813, Armes Papers, LC; Jennings C. Wise, *Robert E. Lee: Unionist* (Harrisburg, Pa., 1927), 3; Paul D. Casdorph, *Lee and Jackson: Confederate Chieftains* (New York, 1992), 14–16.

17. Henry Lee III, *Memoirs*, 61–63 [quotes], 75; Gerson, *Light-Horse Harry*, 242; Robert E. Lee to Agnes Lee, Sept. 5, 1857, Mrs. Mason Barret Collection, Howard-Tilton Library, Tulane University, New Orleans; Robert E. Lee, Jr., *Recollections and Letters of General Robert E. Lee* (New York, 1904), 247–48; Robert A. Brock, ed., *Gen. Robert Edward Lee: Soldier, Citizen, and Christian Patriot* (Richmond, 1897), 123–24, 130; Douglas S. Freeman, *R. E. Lee: A Biography*, 4 vols. (New York, 1934), 1:32.

sons by their mother. Light-Horse Harry married Anne Hill Carter on June 18, 1793, at Shirley, her family's plantation upon the James River southeast of Richmond. She was then twenty years of age; he was thirty-seven and the governor of Virginia. Their union brought together two powerful families with close ties to Washington. Anne's great-grand-father, Robert "King" Carter, was prominent in colonial politics and, ironically, feuded with the Lees, but his son Robert joined with the Lees and Washingtons in land ventures and became one of Matilda Lee's godfathers. When Light-Horse Harry placated Anne's father, Charles Hill Carter, by abandoning the idea of joining the revolution in France, Carter gave his blessing to the marriage, as Washington had done.[18]

Secure in her own heritage, Anne produced many children for Light-Horse Harry but named none of them for Lees. The first was Algernon Sydney, a name that Robert E. Lee wrote was selected to honor a "great martyr of liberty" who was, "according to family tradition, of the kindred of the Lees." The boy died at the age of sixteen months. Anne's second son was named Charles Carter, in honor of her own father. A daughter was next: Ann Kinloch, named for a Carter relative. Anne delivered her third son while traveling with her husband. He was named Sidney Smith, for the family who took her in when she was in labor. Anne's health began to decline and she became an invalid, but she had two more children. Robert Edward, born at Stratford on January 19, 1807, was named for two of Anne's brothers. The last child was a daughter, Catherine Mildred, named for Anne's sister.[19]

Light-Horse Harry's failings left the daily care of his children in Anne's hands. When her father died in 1806, he left Anne a trust designed to prevent incursions by her husband. The next year, she inherited most of her sister Mildred's estate, again with provisions excluding Light-Horse Harry. This gave her the means to provide financially for her children as she worked on their character. She lavished attention on her youngest son, Robert. A devout Episcopalian, she ensured that he

18. Thomas, *Lee*, 23–25, Sanborn, *Portrait*, 9, 11–12, 321; Henry Lee III, *Memoirs*, 49; Boyd, *Harry Lee*, 211–13; Dowdey, *Lee*, 5–6; Anderson and Anderson, *Generals*, 13–14; Hendrick, *Lees of Virginia*, 58–63, 66–68; Casenove G. Lee, *Lee Chronicle*, 58–63, 66; Mrs. Roger A. Pryor, "The Ancestors of General Robert E. Lee," in Brock, *Lee*, 85; Nagel, *Lees of Virginia*, 34–35.

19. Henry Lee III, *Memoirs*, 50 [quotes]; Fitzhugh Lee, *General Lee*, 17; Thomas, *Lee*, 26, 28–29; White, *Southern Confederacy*, 1; Sanborn, *Portrait*, 3.

learn his catechism and attend church regularly, although he was not confirmed until he was forty-six years of age, alongside two of his daughters. She also selected a role model. Her husband had been a disappointment and was not emphasized as a primary focus, though Anne apparently never spoke ill of him, and she wore a locket containing a lock of his hair until her death. Instead, many biographers agree that she chose a hero from her childhood, a fellow Episcopalian with whom she was personally acquainted: Washington. Because Robert was "his mother's child," for him General Washington, who died eight years before his birth, became "a man of [his] own time [whom] . . . he had happened not to know."[20]

Anne came by her devotion to Washington honestly. For her father, the best role model was Washington. From his children he "insisted first on reverence to God and next on allegiance to the memory of Washington." Anne enjoyed telling her children about Washington, particularly her reaction upon meeting him. Robert may have heard these stories repeated when he attended the school for young Carter males at the home of Anne's sister in Fauquier County. He studied there until he was enrolled in an Alexandria school for which Washington had been a trustee. Certainly the parallels between Washington's life and his own were clear: both were products of their father's second marriages and were left fatherless at a young age. Anne even had relics of Washington to show her children. Allegedly a portrait of Washington that he had given to Anne's maternal grandfather hung in the parlor, and Anne constantly wore a locket that contained Washington's image. It was a gift from the president, who had engraved upon it "George Washington to his dear Anne." The only known picture of Anne shows her wearing this pin.[21]

20. Thomas, *Lee,* 29, 34, 44–45, 160–61; Dowdey, *Lee,* 30 [1st quote], 34 [2nd quote]; Sanborn, *Portrait,* 31; Anderson and Anderson, *Generals,* 13–14, 16.

21. Dowdey, *Lee,* 11–12, 14 [1st quote]; Hendrick, *Lees of Virginia,* 383; Thomas, *Lee,* 34, 38; Sanborn, *Portrait,* 12, 39, 43; Edwin Wildman, *Famous Leaders of Character in America* (Boston, 1922), 18; Frederick T. Hill, *On the Trail of Grant and Lee* (New York, 1932), 7–8; Freeman, *Lee,* 1:36; Flexner, *Washington,* 5; William F. Chaney, *Duty Most Sublime: The Life of Robert E. Lee as Told through the "Carter Letters"* (Baltimore, 1996), 18; Eugene E. Prussing, *The Estate of George Washington, Deceased* (Boston, 1927), 170–72; Francis A. MacNutt, "A Lee Miscellany: Portrait of Mrs. Anne Hill (Carter) Lee," *Virginia Magazine of History and Biography* 33 (Jan. 1925): 370–71 [2nd quote]; J. Anderson Thomson, Jr., and Carlos M. Santos, "The Mystery in the Coffin:

From birth, Robert E. Lee's surroundings also contributed to his focus on the Revolution, especially Washington. Stratford, where he was born, is in the same county, Westmoreland, as Washington's birthplace. Throughout Lee's life, he would mistakenly believe that he was born in the same room as several Revolutionary Lees, who were in fact born before the home was built. He did, though, wear the same long gown as they, sewn by their mother, at his christening. In addition to the image of Washington that hung in the parlor, Lee was surrounded "by portraits, parchments, and other tokens, which recalled the already ancient origin and position of his forefathers." Pictures of four generations of Lees hung at Stratford. Among them were Richard Lee I, a colonial politician whose stand with his fellow Virginians against Oliver Cromwell's rule was greatly admired by his Confederate descendant; Richard Lee II, another member of the colonial council and militia leader whose opposition to the national government led to difficulties; Thomas Lee, the first native Virginian to serve as governor, a business associate of Washington, and the builder of Stratford; Arthur Lee; and Light-Horse Harry.[22]

Anne and her children left Stratford while Light-Horse Harry was in jail. Henry Lee IV reached his twenty-first birthday and so became the

---

Another View of Lee's Visit to His Father's Grave," *Virginia Magazine of History and Biography* 103 (Jan. 1995): 90; John M. Dederer, "In Search of the Unknown Soldier: A Critique of the Mystery in the Coffin," *Virginia Magazine of History and Biography* 103 (Jan. 1995): 109–10.

22. Casenove G. Lee, *Lee Chronicle*, 55–56, 72–73, 85, 93; Pryor, "Ancestors," 94; Hendrick, *Lees of Virginia*, 12–14, 17–20, 23–25, 33, 39, 41–43, 439; Snow, *Lee and His Generals*, 17; Fitzhugh Lee, *General Lee*, 3–6; Dowdey, *Lee*, 8; Henry Lee III, *Memoirs*, 12–14; Freeman, *Lee*, 1:168; Sanborn, *Portrait*, 7; Armes, *Stratford Hall*, 43, 56–57, 62, 218, 309; Robert E. Lee to Samuel Tyler, Mar. 17, 1870, Lee Letterbooks, De Butts-Ely Collection, LC; Gerson, *Light-Horse Harry*, 1; Edward Lee Childe, *The Life and Campaigns of General Lee*, trans. George Litte (London, 1875), 23 [quote]; James D. McCabe, *Life and Campaigns of Robert E. Lee* (Atlanta, 1866), 15; J. William Jones, ed., *Personal Reminiscences, Anecdotes, and Letters of Gen. Robert E. Lee* (New York, 1874), 357–58; Philip Van Doren Stern, *Robert E. Lee, the Man and the Soldier: A Pictorial Biography* (New York, 1963), 26–27. Many authors, including Lee family members, assert that Robert E. Lee was born in the same room at Stratford as several Revolutionary cousins, but the most recent study of the family, by Paul C. Nagel, confirms that the building of the home did not begin until after the birth of Thomas Lee's eldest sons, Richard Henry and Francis Lightfoot Lee. In fact, Nagel surmises that none of Thomas Lee's children were born at Stratford. See Nagel, *Lees of Virginia*, 10, 12, 22–27, 30–32, 38–43, 46, 49.

outright owner of the estate. Robert E. Lee, who was just three years of age, later asserted that his father moved them "for the purpose of educating his children." Whatever the reason, Anne relocated to a house in Alexandria, waited until her husband was released, then settled with him and her children across the street from a house once owned by Washington. They soon moved again to a town house owned by William H. Fitzhugh, a descendant of both King Carter and Richard Lee II and a cousin to Anne. His father, William F. Fitzhugh, had worked with Lees and Washingtons in their business ventures and was a military aide to Washington. This move put the wanderers "within what was almost a compound of homes owned by Lee family members." Nearby lived three of Light-Horse Harry's brothers: Richard Bland, Charles, and Edmund Jennings Lee.[23]

Alexandria was saturated with the memory of Washington. Washington had drawn the first plans for the town, directed the digging of its wells, and donated an engine to the Friendship Fire Company. As a vestryman, Washington purchased the chandelier for Christ Church. His pew was there, where Lee's family attended services and heard the gospel read from Washington's Bible. Some recalled that Washington drilled his company for the French and Indian War in the square. The Carlyle House, where Edward Braddock's ill-fated expedition had organized, still stood, as well as the Masonic lodge to which Washington had belonged. Veterans of the Revolution were always ready to talk about their commander, and a tavern proudly recalled that it had been his headquarters. Many other businesses also kept the memory of his patronage alive, and a small museum displayed mementoes. As historian Joseph L. Harsh later noted, "It was impossible to walk the streets of Alexandria . . . without encountering the ghost of Washington at every corner."[24]

Young Lee's interest in Washington was reinforced by visits to family.

---

23. Henry Lee III, *Memoirs*, 53 [1st quote]; Thomas, *Lee*, 31–32 [2nd quote]; Anderson and Anderson, *Generals*, 19; Dowdey, *Lee*, 34; Snow, *Lee and His Generals*, 12; Hendrick, *Lees of Virginia*, 365, 399, 431; Nagel, *Lees of Virginia*, 160, 197–98, 235.

24. Sanborn, *Portrait*, 35–37; Anderson and Anderson, *Generals*, 23; Hendrick, *Lees of Virginia*, 406; Freeman, *Lee*, 1:21, 29; Flexner, *Washington*, 196; Maurine W. Redway, *Marks of Lee on Our Land* (San Antonio, 1972), 14; Joseph L. Harsh, *Confederate Tide Rising: Robert E. Lee and the Making of Southern Strategy, 1861–1862* (Kent, Ohio, 1998), 72 [quote].

Anne often took her children to Shirley, managed by her nephew Hill Carter after her father's death. This became a habit that Lee continued as an adult, visiting at least once a year. Among Shirley's treasures was a full-length portrait of Washington by Charles Willson Peale, which hung in the dining room. Anne and her children also visited Ravensworth, where the Fitzhughs lived, as well as the homes of other Carter relatives. Lees were not excluded; Anne often stayed with Richard Bland Lee, her brother-in-law, though she visited with dwindling frequency at Stratford. Henry Lee IV became a major in the War of 1812 and a legislator, but he deteriorated like his father. He married a wealthy orphan, but their daughter was killed by a fall from the front steps, his wife found solace in morphine, and he had an affair with her sister. His decline climaxed with the sale of Stratford to pay his debts to his adulterous sister-in-law, who ironically bought the estate with her husband and lived there for fifty years. Reviled as "Black Horse Harry," Henry Lee IV reconciled with his wife, but her addiction and his decline continued.[25]

Anne and her children were more comfortable at Arlington, the home of George Washington Parke Custis; his wife Mary, the sister of Anne's sponsor, William H. Fitzhugh; and their daughter, Mary Anna Randolph Custis. As the adopted son of Washington, Custis had devoted his life to sustaining the memory of President Washington. He was actually one of four children of John Parke Custis, Martha Washington's son by her first marriage. Widowed and remarried to Washington, Martha had taken John to Mount Vernon. According to family lore recounted by Robert E. Lee, John was raised as General Washington's stepson and became a "man of worth and probity, highly esteemed by Genl. Washington." During the Revolution, he served as an aide to Washington until he died of camp fever at Yorktown. In truth, John was a "monster" whose death did not greatly sadden Washington, but two of his children—George and Eleanor Parke Custis (nee Nelly)—went to live at Mount Vernon. The boy became devoted to Washington and stayed by

25. Sanborn, *Portrait,* 13, 39; Sally N. Robins, "Mrs. Lee During the War," in Brock, *Lee,* 339; Hendrick, *Lees of Virginia,* 378–79, 401; Thomas, *Lee,* 35–36, 39–40, 59; Winston, *Lee,* 18–20; Dowdey, *Lee,* 37; Freeman, *Lee,* 1:23; Nagel, *Lees of Virginia,* 206–15; Anderson and Anderson, *Generals,* 16.

his side constantly, even when the older man took the oath of office as president.[26]

John Parke Custis had bought the site of Arlington. He named the place Mount Washington, but his son renamed it for an older Custis residence when he settled there in 1802. There was an old house, but Custis built a new one. It was not completed before he died in 1857, but he and his wife Mary, who was also a great-granddaughter of Richard Lee II, filled it with Washington relics as a "virtual national shrine to the Father of the Country." These included wartime mementoes such as pistols, swords, camping gear, and a pair of flags, British and Hessian, given to Washington by Congress for his victory at Yorktown. Household treasures included Martha's tea table, bookcases built under Washington's direction that still held many of his books, and the bed on which he had died. Some of Martha's dresses were preserved, as well as some of General Washington's clothing. Other items included watches and documents, especially a "treasure chest" filled with letters that originally held a part of Martha's dowry for her second wedding. China given to her by English admirers was displayed. Beside it was a set with the seal of the Society of the Cincinnati, bought for Washington by Light-Horse Harry. Also from Mount Vernon were knife boxes, silver candlesticks and wine coolers, vases, a candelabrum, and a tea service made for President Washington in 1789.[27]

26. *Arlington House: A Guide to Arlington House, the Robert E. Lee Memorial, Virginia* (Washington, D.C., 1990), 12, 16; Robert E. Lee to Emily Miller, June 19, 1868 [1st quote], Robert E. Lee Letterbooks, Robert E. Lee Papers, VHS; Karl Decker and Angus McSween, *Historic Arlington: A History of the National Cemetery from Its Establishment to the Present Time* (Washington, 1892), 19–20; Thomas, *Lee,* 39; Sanborn, *Portrait,* 39; Flexner, *Washington,* 43 [2nd quote], 165; Rose M. E. MacDonald, *Mrs. Robert E. Lee* (Boston, 1939), 8.

27. Decker and McSween, *Historic Arlington,* 28–29, 40, 41; Robert E. Lee to Emily Miller, June 19, 1868, Lee Letterbooks, Lee Papers, VHS; Anderson and Anderson, *Generals,* 43, 245; *Arlington House,* 13, 14, 17; Jones, *Personal Reminiscences,* 367; Mary Custis Lee De Butts, ed., *Growing Up in the 1850s: The Journal of Agnes Lee* (Chapel Hill, N.C., 1984), xii, xvii; Sanborn, *Portrait,* 38; Earl S. Miers, *Robert E. Lee: A Great Life in Brief* (New York, 1956), 19 [1st quote]; Stern, *Pictorial Biography,* 58–59 [2nd quote]; MacDonald, *Mrs. Lee,* 7; Winston, *Lee,* 36–37; John E. Cooke, *A Life of Gen. Robert E. Lee* (New York, 1871), 32; Judith W. Maguire, *General Robert E. Lee, the Christian Soldier* (Richmond, 1873), 53–54; Benson J. Lossing, "Arlington House," *Harper's Monthly*

Many Washington relics were used daily at Arlington. A lantern from Mount Vernon illuminated the foyer. Washington's coach was used until it fell apart. The Cincinnati china dwindled from several hundred pieces to fifty due to use and donations of the dishes to friends of the family. A pair of Washington's tents sheltered groups of visitors. Washington's punch bowl often served as the center of festivities for male guests, such as the receptions for the marriages of Sydney Smith Lee and of his brother Robert to Custis' daughter Mary. Allegedly it was given to Washington by William F. Fitzhugh, Custis' father-in-law. Music for such events was provided by Nelly, who played a harpsichord given to her by Washington when she married his nephew Lawrence Lewis.[28]

Some of the most prized Washington relics at Arlington were family portraits. Of course, there were some of Custis, but most were of relatives, such as his sister Nelly and their father, John Parke Custis. Elsewhere hung images of Custis' grandfather and grandmother, Daniel Parke Custis and Martha Dandridge Custis Washington. The most cherished pictures were those of George Washington by Charles Willson Peale and James Sharpless. Peale painted Washington in 1772 in the uniform of a militia colonel. Sharpless completed his portrait in 1796, the last to be done of the first president from life.[29]

Custis made his own artistic contributions to the Washington iconography. As "the child of Mt. Vernon, the last link that bound Washington to his countrymen," he lauded Washington in paintings, speeches, and publications. He painted five battle scenes that featured Washington: Monmouth, Trenton, Princeton, Germantown, and Yorktown. The last of these focused on the two flags in his possession. Custis also wrote

7 (Sept. 1853): 439–43; Eleanor L. Templeman, "Cincinnati Export Porcelain: The Washington and Lee Services," *Art and Antiques* 5 (Jan. 1982): 75–76.

28. Winston, *Lee,* 36–37; Sanborn, *Portrait,* 38; Anderson and Anderson, *Generals,* 46, 173; Decker and McSween, *Historic Arlington,* 21, 31, 40; Long, *Memoirs of Lee,* 38; Cooke, *Life of Lee,* 32; Lossing, "Arlington House," 439, 441, 444–45; Templeman, "Cincinnati Porcelain," 76; MacDonald, *Mrs. Lee,* 39–40, 123; Flexner, *Washington,* 379–80; George G. Shackelford, "Lieutenant Lee Reports to Captain Talcott on Fort Calhoun's Construction on the Rip Raps," *Virginia Magazine of History and Biography* 60 (July 1952): 479–80.

29. Brock, *Lee,* 95, 145–49, 151, 154, 156; Decker and McSween, *Historic Arlington,* 15–18, 39–40; Jones, *Personal Reminiscences,* 367; Maguire, *Lee, Christian Soldier,* 53–54; Lossing, "Arlington House," 435–39; Flexner, *Washington,* 53; MacDonald, *Mrs. Lee,* 11, 15; *Arlington House,* 34.

four plays, memoirs such as *Conversations with Lafayette,* and a series of articles and speeches that was later published by his daughter. Wealthy from inheritances and rental income, Custis had time to talk with a stream of visitors, both distinguished and common. Among his many listeners was Robert E. Lee, who was "entranced" with Arlington and its many relics of Washington, his "lifetime hero." Custis was not content with merely sanctifying Arlington; in 1815 he erected the first monument at Washington's birthplace.[30]

In addition to Custis, there were other living links to the first president at Arlington. At least three slaves at Arlington had served previously at Mount Vernon. One, an elderly female named Carolina Branham, enjoyed talking about Martha and George Washington. She praised Martha for her "beauty & good management," but she claimed President Washington should not be the focus of such a fuss, for "he was only a man!" However, she spoke with pride of being the one to open the gate for him whenever he came home, and she had been at his bedside when he died. When they played together as children, Robert E. Lee and Custis' daughter Mary spoke to the slaves who had worked at Mount Vernon, enjoying stories about General Washington and Martha. When Lee and Mary married in the parlor at Arlington in 1831, Carolina attended. She lived until just before Christmas, 1855, after years of regaling all of Lee's children with the same stories of Mount Vernon that she had told their father.[31]

The Washington relics of Arlington provided tangible links to the role model pressed on Lee by his mother and father. Most physical connections to Lee's own family heritage had been lost in the decline of his father. Much of Stratford's furniture was sold to settle debts when Light-Horse Harry was arrested, and most of what remained was left behind when the family moved. The library amassed by generations of Lees was either scattered or denied to the youngest Lee by the degeneration of Black Horse Harry. Even military mementoes were lost. In

30. Winston, *Lee,* 36; Decker and McSween, *Historic Arlington,* 41; *Arlington House,* 16–17, 31, 39; Thomas, *Lee,* 39, 61; Hendrick, *Lees of Virginia,* 406; Thomas Connelly, *The Marble Man: Robert E. Lee and His Image in American Society* (Baton Rouge, 1977), 7; Lossing, "Arlington House," 445–54.

31. De Butts, *Journal of Agnes Lee,* 80–81 [quotes]; Stern, *Pictorial Biography,* 49; Connelly, *Marble Man,* 171–72; Mary P. Coulling, *Lee Girls* (Winston-Salem, N.C., 1987), 57; Freeman, *Lee,* 1:109.

response to an inquiry in 1866, Lee recalled that when he was a teenager, soon after his father's death, he was shown two of Light-Horse Harry's swords but he confessed that he did not know what had happened to them. When Lee sought tangible evidence of the past, especially the Revolution, the Washington relics at Arlington provided that link.[32]

Because of Custis' prominence, Anne and her children became acquainted with others who had strong ties to the Revolution and Washington. Probably the most exciting encounter was in October 1824, when General Washington's tents sheltered a gathering in honor of Lafayette. Custis gave a long speech as usual and then escorted the French hero to Washington's tomb at Mount Vernon. There before a crowd that may have included Robert E. Lee and his future wife Mary, Custis gave Lafayette a ring with a lock of Washington's hair. Preserved among the Lee papers were notes from Lafayette to Light-Horse Harry written during the Revolution, all of which conveyed friendship and admiration. Lafayette did not forget his manners; he visited his comrade's widow and was honored with a parade, in which Robert E. Lee marched as a "marshal."[33]

Under the tutelage of his mother, with the influence of his absent father and surrounded by reminders of Washington, Robert E. Lee became as reserved and deliberate as Light-Horse Harry had been boisterous and impetuous. Lee, like so many of his generation, internalized an idealized image of Washington as a model of stoic virtue. Washington "was in all respects the perfect character" in biographies written prior to 1855. He was a "plaster saint" with "no vices" and "no temper." Writers of the period insisted that the key to Washington's greatness was his self-discipline, which triumphed over a "naturally impulsive, passionate, and aggressive" nature. Lee absorbed this and struggled to control a temper that associates later likened to that of Washington. In a memorial service for Lee in 1871, James P. Holcombe asserted that his personality "reflected, as in the mirror of youth, the severe and majestic image of Washington." Like his father's failings, Lee ignored or was

32. Boyd, *Harry Lee,* 303; Robert E. Lee to Thomas J. Massie, June 1, 1866, Lee Letterbooks, De Butts-Ely Collection, LC.

33. Sanborn, *Portrait,* 51; Anderson and Anderson, *Generals,* 23; Decker and McSween, *Historic Arlington,* 33; Henry Lee IV, *Campaign of 1781,* i–iv in Appendix; Winston, *Lee,* 22; MacDonald, *Mrs. Lee,* 23 [quote]; Hume, "Cincinnati," 273.

unaware of Washington's flaws. For him, like many others of his generation, General Washington was a perfect idol.[34]

Lee's interest in Washington, a fellow Episcopalian, even shaped the paradigm of his faith. Lee's beliefs led him to live a moral and virtuous life; Washington's life provided a blueprint for such an effort. Lee's fatalistic expressions of faith were deeply rooted in his generation's conception of Washington. For Lee and his contemporaries, it was a "convention of Washington iconography that he was but acting as the agent of a power greater than himself." The first president thereby became a model for religious fatalism for Lee and many other Americans of his era. Interestingly, Lee became a vestryman for St. John's Episcopal Church while he lived in New York, but he returned to Alexandria to be confirmed with two of his daughters in Christ Church, where Washington had served on the vestry.[35]

Lee's character was firmly grounded in the perception of Washington that had been presented to him throughout his youth, and his family connections to General Washington provided him with an opportunity to join the Virginia gentry. Lee's father bequeathed no substantial estate, so joining the landed elite seemed almost impossible. Education offered an opportunity, and Lee's eldest brother, Carter, took that route, graduating from Harvard College. Anne's second son, Sydney Smith Lee, chose the military, and President James Monroe appointed him as a midshipman. Soon after his seventeenth birthday, Lee decided upon the United States Military Academy. With a letter from William H. Fitzhugh, who of course mentioned Light-Horse Harry's career in the Revolution, Lee secured an appointment. Carter Lee and Henry Lee IV also wrote on Robert's behalf, as well as eight members of Congress. Custis' sister Nelly introduced Lee to Andrew Jackson. Escorted by the "belle

34. Gamaliel Bradford, *Lee the American* (Boston, 1912; rev. ed., Cambridge, Mass., 1929), 225; Holmes M. Alexander, *Washington and Lee: A Study in the Will to Win* (Boston, 1966), 74–75; Thomas, *Lee,* 41, 45; Edward H. O'Neill, *A History of American Biography, 1800–1935* (Philadelphia, 1935), 163 [1st–4th quotes]; George B. Forgie, *Patricide in the House Divided* (New York, 1979), 24, 39 [5th quote]; Jones, *Personal Reminiscences,* 491 [6th quote]; Bertram Wyatt-Brown, *Southern Honor: Ethics and Behavior in the Old South* (New York, 1982), 98; Lester H. Cohen, *The Revolutionary Histories: Contemporary Narratives of the American Revolution* (Ithaca, N.Y., 1980), 226–28.

35. Forgie, *Patricide,* 22–23 [quote], 26–28; Sanborn, *Portrait,* 226; Thomas, *Lee,* 159–61.

of Mount Vernon," Lee even got a note from Jackson urging his entry to West Point.[36]

Lee entered West Point, redolent with memories of Washington and the Revolution, in 1825. Washington's "log headquarters" stood on campus. Two daughters of a Revolutionary veteran lived there and provided board to senior cadets. Barracks used in the Revolution remained until they burned in 1827, while the ruins of Fort Putnam, a Revolutionary War post, loomed over the school. Lee helped to enhance the Revolutionary aura. When asked his residence, he responded that he resided in Westmoreland County, stressing his heritage. One of the first reviews in which he marched was for Lafayette. Lee also served on a committee that arranged for a statue of Taddeus Kosciuszko, the Polish engineer who served with Light-Horse Harry under Greene and whose cottage stood nearby. Lee even found a fellow Virginian who shared his zeal: Joseph E. Johnston, whose father served with Light-Horse Harry in the Revolution and at the Virginia constitutional convention. Years later, outraged at being ranked fourth and not first among Confederate generals, Johnston railed against such attempts to "tarnish [his] fair fame," the symbols of which included his father's sword, "delivered to [him] from his venerable hand without a stain of dishonor."[37]

The West Point that Lee entered had been reformed into an engineering school with a curriculum that included little about history. In the fourth year, there was an omnibus course on history, grammar, philosophy, and geography in which Chaplain Thomas Picton monotonously recited platitudes. The engineering course for the fourth year was of more interest. The cadets studied S. François Guy de Vernon's *Treatise on the Science of War and Fortification,* translated by John M. O'Con-

36. Thomas, *Lee,* 35, 38–39; Long, *Memoirs of Lee,* 28; Thomas, *Lee,* 41–43; Anderson and Anderson, *Generals,* 23–24; Sanborn, *Portrait,* 37, 50; Charles D. Rhodes, *Robert E. Lee the West Pointer* (Richmond, 1932), 10–11; Hill, *Grant and Lee,* 10 [quote]; Freeman, *Lee,* 1:39–43.

37. Dowdey, *Lee,* 42; Anderson and Anderson, *Generals,* 38; Gerson, *Light-Horse Harry,* 103, 107, 116, 123–24, 133–36, 160; Stephen E. Ambrose, *Duty, Honor, Country* (Baltimore, 1966), 154 [1st quote]; Stern, *Pictorial Biography,* 39; Winston, *Lee,* 25; Hume, "Cincinnati," 276; Varina H. Davis, *Jefferson Davis, Ex-President of the Confederate States of America: A Memoir by His Wife,* 2 vols. (New York, 1890), 2:151–52 [2nd and 3rd quotes]; John J. Bowen, *The Strategy of Robert E. Lee* (New York, 1914), 31–32; James M. McPherson, *Battle Cry of Freedom: The Civil War Era* (New York, 1988), 365–66; Freeman, *Lee,* 1:49, 52, 70–71.

nor. Through this, they were exposed to the ideas of Antoine Henri de Jomini, a summary of which O'Connor included. For cadets such as Lee who were interested in military history, this brief material became an important focal point, a status enhanced by later exposure to other works by Jomini, whose military concepts were "essentially identical" to those of his commander, Napoleon Bonaparte.[38]

Lee was fascinated with Napoleon and read avidly about him, but he also continued to study the Revolution. In the fall of his second year, having excelled in French, he borrowed a set of memoirs on Napoleon and two other books on the emperor from the West Point library. During the spring of 1827, he read a biography of John Paul Jones and the memoirs of Joseph Fouche, the minister of police for Napoleon, along with another work on Napoleon's campaigns and volumes of Rousseau's and Molière's writings. That fall he borrowed four volumes of Voltaire's works and the memoirs of Alexander Garden, a major in the Revolution, which included stories about Light-Horse Harry. In the spring of 1828, he took works by Hamilton, Rousseau, and Montesquieu, as well as Machiavelli's *Art of War,* another study of Jones, a book on the signers of the Declaration of Independence, and a work on cavalry by Charles E. de Warnery, a Prussian general during the Napoleonic era. During his final year at West Point, Lee read Guillaume Henri Dufour's work on fortifications, William Wirt's biography of Patrick Henry, and both volumes of *Memoir of the Life of Richard Henry Lee.*[39]

38. Thomas, *Lee,* 48; Ambrose, *Duty, Honor, Country,* 90, 96; Casdorph, *Lee and Jackson,* 30; Russell Weigley, *The American Way of War* (New York, 1973; reprint, Bloomington, Ind., 1977), 82–83; Richard E. Beringer et al., eds., *Why the South Lost the War* (Athens, Ga., 1986), 333 [quote]; Archer Jones, "Military Means, Political Ends," in Gabor S. Boritt, ed., *Why the Confederacy Lost* (New York, 1992), 50; Edward Hagerman, *The American Civil War and the Origins of Modern Warfare* (Bloomington, Ind., 1988), 5–6; Edward Hagerman, "The Tactical Thought of Robert E. Lee and the Origins of Trench Warfare in the American Civil War, 1861–1862," *Historian* 38 (Nov. 1975): 23–24; Edward Hagerman, "From Jomini to Dennis Hart Mahan: The Evolution of Trench Warfare and the American Civil War," *Civil War History* 13 (Sept. 1967): 200; Freeman, *Lee,* 1:77.

39. Thomas L. Connelly and Archer Jones, *The Politics of Command: Factions and Ideas in Confederate Strategy* (Baton Rouge, 1973), 13–15; Charlotte Wilson, "Robert E. Lee at West Point" (B.A. Thesis, West Virginia University, 1941), 19–21, 23–25; United States Military Academy, Library Circulation Records, 1824–1829, United States Military Academy Library and Archives, West Point, N.Y.; William A. Bryan, *George Washington in American Literature, 1775–1865* (New York, 1952), 27–28; Holmes M. Alexander,

Young Lee thrived at West Point. He became a cadet staff sergeant, the highest rank open to a freshman, at the end of his first year. A year later, he ranked second in his class and was promoted to cadet adjutant, the highest rank in the cadet corps. As was customary, he got a furlough for his excellent work. He spent the time with his mother, who lived with his brother Carter and sister Mildred. Anne suffered with tuberculosis, but they made time to visit relatives. One stop was Kinloch, the Fauquier County home of Edward C. Turner, son of Thomas Turner, a cousin who served as Robert's guardian after the death of Light-Horse Harry. There Robert renewed his acquaintance with Mary Anna Randolph Custis. Upon his return to West Point, Lee studied diligently, graduating second in his class as one of six members who had no demerits.[40]

Because of his high standing, Lee became a second lieutenant in the engineers. Like his classmates, he got a furlough after his graduation in June 1829. He arrived at the Fitzhughs' home, Ravensworth, in time to be with his mother when she died on July 26. He spent the rest of the summer with relatives and friends, and he often encountered Mary. That fall he went to his first post: Cockspur Island at Savannah, where Fort Pulaski, named for a Revolutionary hero, was being constructed. The work was brutal and interrupted only by visits to Savannah. There Lee enjoyed the company of Jack Mackay, a friend from West Point, his three sisters, and several other young ladies. Lee may well have been flattered by the attention of the latter, but he did not forget the only daughter of Washington's adopted son. When his work halted for the summer in 1830, he went to Virginia. He found Mary at Chatham, the home of her late grandfather, William F. Fitzhugh. Allegedly Washington had met and courted Martha at Chatham. Lee was fascinated with General Washington's tie to Chatham, and he may have proposed to Mary there that summer, though some historians say that he did so at Arlington.[41]

Washington and Lee, 73; Anderson and Anderson, *Generals,* 39; Freeman, *Lee,* 1:64–65, 72–73.

40. Holmes M. Alexander, *Washington and Lee,* 72; Thomas, *Lee,* 49, 51; Dowdey, *Lee,* 43; MacDonald, *Mrs. Lee,* 63, 80, 246.

41. Thomas, *Lee,* 54, 56–60, 63; Dowdey, *Lee,* 47; Robert E. Lee to Charles Carter Lee, May 8, 1830, Robert E. Lee Papers, University of Virginia Library, Charlottesville [hereinafter UVA]; Sanborn, *Portrait,* 76–77; Redway, *Marks of Lee,* 21; Anderson and Anderson, *Generals,* 46; Freeman, *Lee,* 1:104.

Mary and her mother readily agreed to the marriage, but her father hesitated because Lee had no money. Lee left Arlington in October 1830 without a definite answer. Custis had reason to be concerned about Lee's finances. Anne left money and a few slaves to her two daughters, while her three sons divided the proceeds from the sale or lease of her few remaining slaves and assumed the burden of paying taxes on twenty thousand marginal acres in Patrick County. Robert E. Lee received little money but did get ownership of a black woman and her three children, whom he leased to Custis until 1847, when he apparently sold them to his father-in-law. He also assumed responsibility for an elderly tubercular male slave who had belonged to Anne but died shortly after Lee took him to Savannah in 1830.[42]

His future father-in-law need not have worried: Lee was more like frugal Washington than spendthrift Light-Horse Harry. Unlike most of his classmates, he had a positive balance in his account when he left West Point. His proceeds from the sale of some of his mother's slaves and profits from the lease of others were invested in stocks and bonds. By 1846, when he joined the army in Mexico, Lee's portfolio yielded over two thousand dollars annually, much more than his army salary and allowances. Also unlike his father, but much like the popular image of Washington, Lee was scrupulously honest, a trait made obvious when he returned two extra paychecks that the government mistakenly gave him. He continued to invest after the Mexican War, almost doubling his worth by the mid-1850s. During the same period, his salary also nearly doubled, providing a comfortable living for his family.[43]

Lee completed his tutelage in the shadow of Washington by marrying in 1831. Custis gave his permission, and plans were laid for the summer. By that time, Lee had been transferred to Fort Monroe on the coast of Virginia. As arranged, Lee came to Arlington on his wedding day, June 30, and found the big house filled with friends and relatives, including Joseph E. Johnston and Sydney Smith Lee, who was the best man. Extra

42. Robert E. Lee to Charles Carter Lee, Sept. 22, 1830, Jan. 4, 1831, Lee Papers, UVA; Thomas, *Lee,* 56–57, 63, 72, 108; Sanborn, *Portrait,* 26, 67; White, *Southern Confederacy,* 28; Long, *Memoirs of Lee,* 26; Joseph C. Robert, "Lee the Farmer," *Journal of Southern History* 3 (Nov. 1937): 429–30; Norma B. Cathbert, "To Molly: Five Early Letters from Robert E. Lee to His Wife, 1832–1835," *Huntington Library Quarterly* 15 (May 1952): 262.

43. Thomas, *Lee,* 54, 56, 108–9, 159; Anderson and Anderson, *Generals,* 88.

silver and bedding for the guests came from Anna Maria Fitzhugh, wife of William H. Fitzhugh, Mary's uncle and Lee's mother's sponsor, who had died the previous year. More pictures may have been added; a witness recalled that the "Halls and chambers were adorned with portraits of the patriots of the Revolution and of the 'Father of His Country.'" As the couple marched in, Custis' sister Nelly played the harpsichord given to her by Washington while "portraits and relics brought as a heritage from Mount Vernon bore witness from the walls." The ceremony went smoothly, though the minister was soaked by rain and wore clothes borrowed from Custis. Of course, the men emptied the punch bowl that had been given to Washington by William F. Fitzhugh, the bride's late grandfather.[44]

It would be unfair to declare, as some have, that Lee was "perhaps . . . as much enamored of Arlington as he was of Mary," but it is true that with marriage "he came as close as possible to becoming a member of the Washington family." Lee enjoyed his new family circle. After a few weeks at Arlington, the couple toured their relatives' homes with Lee's new mother-in-law. In January 1832, Lee attended the funeral of Custis' older sister at Mount Vernon with other Washington relatives. Although Lee admitted to a friend that his "black face looked longer than usual," he carefully recounted how he stood that day among the Washington kin. He had come full circle, not only embracing the heritage of the Lees, but also becoming a relative of the great Washington. This was exciting for Lee, for whom Washington "was as real as though he had stepped down nightly from the canvas at Arlington."[45] Lincoln's "mystic chords of memory" clearly bound Lee tightly to Virginia's Revolutionary heritage, and to George Washington.

44. *Arlington House*, 19; Sanborn, *Portrait*, 76, 85–86; Thomas, *Lee*, 63–65; MacDonald, *Mrs. Lee*, 32–35 [1st quote]; White, *Southern Confederacy*, 27 [2nd quote].

45. Connelly, *Marble Man*, 171 [1st quote]; De Butts, *Journal of Agnes Lee*, xi [2nd quote]; Thomas, *Lee*, 65; Robert E. Lee to Elizabeth A. [Mackay] Stiles, Jan. 8, 1832 [3rd quote], Mackay-McQueen Family Papers, Colonial Dames Collection, Georgia Historical Society, Savannah; Hume, "Cincinnati," 280 [4th quote].

2

✣ The Old Revolutionary Blood
Coming of Age in the Army

While waiting for an answer to his demand for John Brown's surrender at Harpers Ferry in October 1859, Robert E. Lee heard hostage Lewis W. Washington yell, "Never mind us—fire!" Before ordering an assault, Lee muttered, "The old Revolutionary blood does tell."[1] Lee referred to the fact that Washington was the great-nephew of the first president, but he might as easily have referred to his own "Revolutionary blood." As an army officer, Lee remained fascinated with his Revolutionary heritage and that of his adopted Washington family. He enjoyed his relationship with his wife, children, and in-laws, who were a living branch of the Washington family tree, and he surrounded himself as much as possible with treasured Washington relics. Sadly, however, he had failed to achieve the same level of success in the military as Washington or his father, renowned as Light-Horse Harry. This brought frustration and disappointment as Lee faced middle age.

Lee's interest in his father's lineage revived when he read a work by his half brother Henry Lee IV on Thomas Jefferson. Scorned as Black-Horse Harry and stranded in Algiers when the Senate rejected Andrew Jackson's nomination of him as a consul, Henry Lee IV settled in France and worked as a biographer until his death in 1837. He wrote a study

1. Emory M. Thomas, *Robert E. Lee: A Biography* (New York, 1995), 181.

of Jefferson in response to the publication of some of the latter's papers that contained some negative remarks about Light-Horse Harry, attempting to rehabilitate his father's reputation at the expense of Jefferson's. Robert E. Lee did not share the enthusiasm for the book of his brother Charles Carter Lee, who had the volume reprinted, but the work spurred his interest in his family heritage.[2]

In 1833, a year after the appearance of Henry Lee IV's book, Lee asked a friend to buy for him a few items with the Lee family crest. Unfortunately, he admitted, "all I know concerning it is borne on the impression I gave you." He asked again in 1837 for a ring with the Lee crest upon it. That year, Black-Horse Harry died, and Lee bought his watch as a memento. Perhaps troubled by this tragic event, Lee wrote to his cousin Cassius F. Lee, "I begin in my old age to feel a little curiousity [sic] relative to my forefathers." He requested an accurate seal, as well as a copy of the Lee family tree. Cassius sent a genealogy by William Lee, from which Lee learned much about his family, and a crest, though neither Cassius nor Lee was convinced of its authenticity. Nevertheless, Lee had this seal emblazoned upon silverware and other objects. At the same time, he and his wife hired a painter to preserve their own images for posterity.[3]

Lee was intrigued with his father's relatives, but he played a more active role as a member of Washington's family. During a ride in 1856

2. Ibid., 37, 59, 79, 97–98; Margaret Sanborn, *Robert E. Lee: A Portrait* (Philadelphia, 1966), 71; Clifford Dowdey, *Lee* (Boston, 1965), 48–49; Burton J. Hendrick, *The Lees of Virginia: Biography of a Family* (Boston, 1935), 402–3; Robert W. Winston, *Robert E. Lee: A Biography* (New York, 1941), 43; Douglas S. Freeman, *R. E. Lee: A Biography*, 4 vols. (New York, 1934), 1:116–17; Paul C. Nagel, *The Lees of Virginia: Seven Generations of an American Family* (New York, 1990): 216–29.

3. Robert E. Lee to Andrew Talcott, Dec. 1, 1833 [1st quote], Robert E. Lee Papers, Library of Virginia, Richmond [hereinafter LV]; Lee to Cassius F. Lee, Aug. 20, 1838 [2nd quote], Edmund J. Lee Papers, Jesse Ball Dupont Library, Stratford Hall, Va. [hereinafter SH]; Lee to Charles Carter Lee, Jan. 7, 1839, Robert E. Lee Papers, University of Virginia Library, Charlottesville [hereinafter UVA]; Lee to John Carroll Brent, Apr. 2, 1843, Robert E. Lee Papers, SH; Sanborn, *Portrait*, 113–14, 123; Cassius F. Lee to Lee, Sept. 8, 1838, Lee Family Papers, Virginia Historical Society, Richmond [hereinafter VHS]; Gamaliel Bradford, *Lee the American* (Boston, 1912; rev. ed., Cambridge, Mass., 1929), 3–4; Nancy S. Anderson and Dwight Anderson, *The Generals: Ulysses S. Grant and Robert E. Lee* (New York, 1988), 87; *Arlington House: A Guide to Arlington House, the Robert E. Lee Memorial, Virginia* (Washington, D.C., 1990), 37; Thomas, *Lee*, 92.

with John Bell Hood, who had been a cadet at West Point when Lee was superintendent and now served under him in the 2nd Cavalry, Lee declared, "Never marry unless you can do so into a family which will enable your children to feel proud of both sides of the house."[4] This statement made an impression on Hood, who wrote about it years later, but he probably did not realize how deeply Lee was committed to that maxim. Having been born into the Lee lineage, Lee wanted to be accepted as a member of the Washington family, for himself as well as his children.

After his marriage to Mary Anna Randolph Custis and their honeymoon in 1831, Lee returned with her to Fort Monroe. Mary proved to be an emotional "liability" because she was "spoiled and helpless" when they married and became more so. Following the birth of their second child, a daughter, in July 1835, Mary became quite ill and continued to decline until arthritis made her an invalid. Mary and her husband thus became very different: she required attention, while he remained self-reliant. This may well have had much to do with their long periods apart but does not mean that they did not love each other or that Lee regretted his marriage. He endured Mary's idiosyncracies "in usually good humor," and his chiding of her in frequent letters was gentle.[5]

Despite Mary's poor health, she and Lee had seven children. Like Lee's parents, they named none of their children for Lee ancestors, though several received the names of Washington relatives. Their first son was named in honor of his maternal grandfather: George Washington Custis Lee. Lee proudly wrote to Charles Carter Lee, "I have got me an heir to my Estates! Aye, a Boy! to cherish the memory of his *Father* & 'walk in the light of his renown.'" Mary Custis Lee, who bore her mother's name, was born next, followed by William Henry Fitzhugh Lee, who was named for Lee's mother's sponsor. Another girl, named Anne Carter Lee for Lee's mother, was followed by a third, called Eleanor Agnes Lee for her maternal grandfather's sister. The family was completed with Robert E. Lee, Jr., and Mildred Childe Lee, whose name honored Lee's younger sister. Lee had no apparent animosity toward his

---

4. John Bell Hood, *Advance and Retreat* (New Orleans, 1880), 8.
5. Thomas, *Lee*, 17 [1st and 2nd quotes], 67, 71–72 [3rd quote], 83–84; Charles P. Roland, *Reflections on Lee: A Historian's Assessment* (Mechanicsburg, Pa., 1995), 8–9.

exiled father's lineage and in fact jested with his brother Carter that if Carter did not name a son Henry, he and Mary might do so. Lee simply honored those with whom he had spent more time.[6]

Lee remained devoted to his growing and often absent family. He wrote to Carter from Fort Monroe in December 1833 that Mary and their son Custis were at Arlington, "where they are all as happy to have them as I am sad to lose them." With them gone, he added, "I cannot say that my home has many charms for me now." Later, anticipating a trip to retrieve them, he wrote to his friend Jack Mackay that he "would not be unmarried for all you could offer me." Lee gradually developed a more formal writing style, but his devotion did not dim. From West Point in 1853 he wrote to Mary, "As regards our separation, I pray it may be short, & that neither you nor those in whom I am interested may suffer any loss or inconvenience from my absence, & that it may not be as grievous to any as myself." Returning to Texas in 1860 on the eve of the secession crisis, he confessed, "It was very sad to me to leave you, & my departures grow harder to bear with years."[7]

Lee also remained close to his in-laws, to whom he referred as "Father" and "Mother" in his letters. This relationship developed in part because his own family was dead or scattered. He worked especially hard to develop a relationship with his father-in-law, though his initial attempt to become involved in the family business was not encouraging. When he was sent in 1832 to inspect some Smith's Island estates owned by Custis, he was quite frank about their worthlessness and the experiment was not repeated. On a happier note, Lee discovered that his father-in-law shared his love of cats. Lee's overtures were reciprocated by Custis, who welcomed him at Arlington and gave him a watch that Lee would thereafter always carry.[8]

6. Thomas, *Lee,* 71, 83–84, 86, 97, 102, 103; Lee to Charles Carter Lee, Sept. 28, 1832 [quote], Mar. 18, 1848, Lee Papers, UVA.

7. Lee to Charles Carter Lee, Dec. 6, 1833, Lee Papers, UVA [1st and 2nd quotes]; Robert K. Black, ed. "Robert E. Lee, A Sesquicentennial Tribute: Ten Autograph Letters from Lee to his Closest Friend, John Mackay of Georgia, 1834–1843" (Typescript, n.d. [1950], Rice Institute Library, Houston, Tex.), 2 [3rd quote]; Lee to Mary Custis Lee, July 9, 1853 [4th quote], Mar. 3, 1860 [5th quote], De Butts-Ely Collection, Library of Congress, Washington, D.C. [hereinafter LC]; Paul D. Casdorph, *Lee and Jackson: Confederate Chieftains* (New York, 1992), 48–49.

8. Nagel, *Lees of Virginia,* 203–4, 232–34; Thomas, *Lee,* 76–77; Dowdey, *Lee,* 61; Martin W. Crimmins, ed., "Robert E. Lee in Texas: Letters and Diary," *West Texas Historical Association Yearbook* 8 (1932): 13; James C. Young, *Marse Robert, Knight of the*

The most substantial link between Lee and Custis was their veneration of Washington. Lee shared his father-in-law's outrage when one of
his paintings of Washington was rejected by Congress in early 1836.
Custis sent an agent to retrieve the "unfortunate picture," but added in
a letter to his detractors that he resented the harsh criticism of "hired
scribblers who infest the Capitol." Lee commiserated about the "severe
animadversions" that had been heaped upon Custis' painting, which he
agreed were politically motivated. The painting, which showed Washington in the battle at Princeton, was subsequently destroyed, but
another of him at Monmouth was retrieved safely from the Capitol.[9]

Lee tried to lessen Custis' bitterness over the rejection of his Princeton
painting. While traveling during the summer of 1837, he wrote to his
father-in-law that he was "much pleased" to hear about the "extensive
sale" of Jared Sparks's biography of Washington, the concluding work
in a twelve-volume set by Sparks focusing on the general. Like John
Marshall and Parson Weems, both of whom had previously written
studies of Washington, Sparks was very adulatory and focused primarily
on the Revolution. In fact, he altered documents to improve upon Washington's writing and present him as a perfect "symbol of the American
nation." Lee was pleased to discover expensive "calfskin editions" in
"many places where [he] least expected." He found such copies in the
homes of two "ship carpenters," who displayed them "along side of the
Bible in a glass case," and one of them informed Lee that he had read it
with much pleasure. Lee added that a friend had reported that Sparks's
agent said that thousands of the books had been sold. He concluded, "It
speaks greatly in favor of the People, which I am sure you will give them
credit for, and must tend vastly to their benefit in every respect."[10]

Although Lee did not often write to Custis, he wrote about him in his

Confederacy (New York, 1929; reprint, New York, 1932), 65; Lee to "Father" [George
W. P. Custis], May 22, 1832, Robert E. Lee Papers, William G. Perkins Library, Duke University, Durham, N.C. [hereinafter DU]; Rose M. E. MacDonald, *Mrs. Robert E. Lee* (Boston, 1939), 57; J. William Jones, *Life and Letters of Robert Edward Lee* (New York,
1906), 79, 86.

9. George W. P. Custis to William Noland, Apr. 25, 1836 [quotes], Berkeley Collection, UVA; *Arlington House,* 38; Lee to Charles Carter Lee, May 2, 1836, Lee Papers,
UVA.

10. Lee to Custis, Aug. 25, 1837 [1st, 2nd, and 4th–8th quotes], Lee Papers, UVA;
William A. Bryan, *George Washington in American Literature, 1775–1865* (New York,
1952), 98–100 [3rd quote].

letters and sometimes asked Mary to convey messages. In August 1857 he suggested that she urge her ailing father to take a trip. Among the sites that Lee suggested Custis should visit was the place where Washington took Gen. Edward Braddock after he was wounded, and where Braddock died and was buried. Two months later, Lee received a telegram in Texas telling him of the death of his "kind & dear father-in-law." He wrote in his diary, "The shock was as unexpected as afflicting." He hurried to Arlington to find "all, sad suffering & sick & the chair of him who had always rec'd me with paternal kindness & affection *vacant*." He recalled these sentiments in a letter to Anna Maria Fitzhugh, confessing poignantly, "I miss every moment him that always rec'd me with the kindness & affection of a father, & I grieve to find his chair empty & his place vacant."[11]

Lee was also very fond of his mother-in-law, Mary Fitzhugh Custis, who shared his interest in the Revolutionary generation as well. While Lee lived in Baltimore in 1852, Congress debated whether to buy the draft of Washington's Farewell Address for the Library of Congress. During the discussions, arguments about its authorship resurfaced. Lee, like the majority of Americans, was convinced that Washington alone wrote the speech. When questions about this were raised, Lee wrote to his mother-in-law, asking her to send him a biography of John Jay that she had given him. He wanted to reread Jay's letter about the authorship of the Farewell Address. Alexander Hamilton's son insisted that his father actually wrote the speech, but Lee believed that if this were true, it "would take from this matchless paper its greatest value." He added, however, that he did not "think Washington's fame will ever need defense," and he assured his mother-in-law that "Ages to come will I hope read with admiration & benefit that maxim of his wisdom & rectitude." Ironically, Lee himself would later have cause to reflect uncomfortably on the strong endorsement of the Union contained in Washington's Farewell Address.[12]

11. Francis R. Adams, ed., "An Annotated Edition of the Personal Letters of Robert E. Lee, April 1855–April, 1861" (Ph.D. diss., University of Maryland, 1955), 401, 404; Robert E. Lee Diary [1st–3rd quotes], Lee Family Papers, VHS; Lee to Anna Maria Fitzhugh, Nov. 22, 1857 [4th quote], Lee Papers, DU.

12. Lee to Mary Fitzhugh Custis, Mar. 17, 1852 [quotes], Robert E. Lee Letterbooks, De Butts-Ely Collection, LC; George B. Forgie, *Patricide in the House Divided* (New York, 1979), 25; Thomas, *Lee,* 76–77; Mortimer J. Adler et al., eds., *The Annals of America,* 18 vols. (Chicago, 1968), 3:607–11.

The death of Mary Fitzhugh Custis was devastating to Lee. His wife hurried to Arlington for her mother's funeral in April 1853, and he joined her after he obtained leave from West Point. It was then that Lee, who was a regular churchgoer and had served on the vestry of St. John's Church in New York, was confirmed as an Episcopalian alongside two of his daughters. The ceremony at Christ Church in Alexandria, where Washington was a vestryman, in July 1853 was quite possibly a memorial for his deceased mother-in-law, who was very pious. After returning to West Point, Lee wrote to Mary, "As a son I have always loved her, as a son I deeply mourn her." At about the same time, he wrote to Martha Custis Williams, Mary's cousin and his confidant, that he worried about Custis, whose "affection," he wrote, "I experienced in boyhood, who since has been to me all a father could, & whom I shall never cease fondly to regard & love as such—God knows how I grieve over his affliction!"[13]

In 1853 Lee asked Mary to bring Custis with her when she and the children returned to New York. Lee's in-laws rarely visited his posts, but Custis broke that pattern during the last years of his life. Previously he and his wife stayed with the Lees once at Fort Monroe, and each later made a separate trip to the Lee home in Baltimore. There Lee's father-in-law was lured outside only by an invitation to make a speech about Washington, while his mother-in-law strolled each evening with the family through nearby Mount Vernon Place and admired its monument to Washington. The pair also visited Lee and his wife at Fort Hamilton in the summer of 1845. After that visit, Lee had written to Martha Custis Williams, "It is a sad parting & we have enjoyed their Compy [*sic*] a long time." Custis had come to West Point once before; after his wife's death he returned twice before his health precluded long trips.[14]

13. Sanborn, *Portrait*, 226; *Arlington House*, 19; Thomas, *Lee*, 159–61; Lee to Mary Custis Lee, n.d. [1st quote], De Butts-Ely Collection, LC; Avery Craven, ed., *"To Markie": The Letters of Robert E. Lee to Martha Custis Williams from the Originals in the Huntington Library* (Cambridge, Mass., 1933), 30–31, 39 [2nd and 3rd quotes].

14. Lee to Mary Custis Lee, n.d., De Butts-Ely Collection, LC; Thomas L. Connelly, *The Marble Man: Robert E. Lee and His Image in American Society* (Baton Rouge, 1977), 126; Hendrick, *Lees of Virginia*, 405; Lee to Andrew Talcott, Aug. 2, 1833, Lee to Margaret Elliott, July 12, 1853, Lee Papers, LV; Craven, *"To Markie,"* 16 [quote]; Mary P. Coulling, *Lee Girls* (Winston-Salem, N.C., 1987), 30; Mary Custis Lee De Butts, ed., *Growing Up in the 1850s: The Journal of Agnes Lee* (Chapel Hill, N.C., 1984), 25, 45; Jones, *Life and Letters*, 74–75; Sanborn, *Portrait*, 227.

One reason that Lee's in-laws rarely visited him was that his wife and children often traveled to Arlington. Army life kept Lee from spending as much time as the rest of his family at Arlington, but he readily left them there when duty called him to areas he considered unsuitable. Like Mary and the children, Lee was most happy at Arlington, surrounded by memories of Washington. As he confessed to his mother-in-law in 1839, if he could live where he pleased, he would be at Arlington. He could not, however, because he had chosen the only vocation for him that approximated the careers of his father and Washington. As he explained to his brother Carter shortly before his marriage to Mary, the army provided all he wanted, and he could not imagine leaving it.[15]

Lee's life in the military initially proved to be much less interesting than he expected. Nat Turner's revolt in August 1831 scarcely attracted his attention. He was never involved and wrote disparagingly of the hysteria to his in-laws. The arrival of Black Hawk and the Prophet at Fort Monroe likewise received little notice in letters to friends and family. The death of "the good LaFayette," as Lee referred to him, in the summer of 1834, though, was noteworthy. Lee wrote that "We have been *celebrating* the death of the good LaFayette *all day*." The memorials of Congress for Lafayette pleased Lee as well.[16]

Bored, Lee asked for a transfer and was exiled to a pile of rocks and sand that later supported Fort Wool. He stayed only a few months before being called to Washington to become a clerk and lobbyist. As a young man of distinguished lineage, Lee had great connections, which he enhanced by taking an interest in politics. For example, he did not approve of the opposition of his old sponsor, Andrew Jackson, to nullification, but he happily accepted his invitation to a reception, where he met Martin Van Buren, Daniel Webster, and Washington Irving. Jackson responded by visiting the Lees, playing with young Custis and letting the infant handle a portrait of his beloved late wife, Rachel. Lee met other notables in Washington, but his prolonged exposure to politics

15. Thomas, *Lee,* 71; Lee to Mary Fitzhugh Custis, Nov. 7, 1839, De Butts-Ely Collection, LC; Coulling, *Lee Girls,* 10–50 passim; Lee to Charles Carter Lee, Sept. 30, 1830, Lee Papers, UVA.

16. Robert R. Ellis, "The Lees at Fort Monroe," *Military Engineer* 42 (1950): 1–5; Thomas, *Lee,* 68; Young, *Marse Robert,* 33–34; Lee to Charles Carter Lee, June 30, 1834 [1st quote], Lee Papers, UVA; Lee to Jack Mackay, June 26, 1834 [2nd quote], Gilder Lehrman Collection, Pierpont Morgan Library, New York; Casdorph, *Lee and Jackson,* 38.

soon appalled him. In May 1837, Lee left his family at Arlington for a job in St. Louis: redirecting the flow of the Mississippi River. He asked to be sent west because, he explained to Jack Mackay, "I was cognisant of so much iniquity in more ways than one, that I feared for my morality, at no time *strong,* and had been trying for two years to quit."[17]

Lee quickly discovered that he loved the St. Louis area but hated the heat, miserable quarters, and rough people. He eagerly returned to Arlington for Christmas and then brought his wife and two sons to St. Louis in the spring of 1838. That summer tested the family: they lived in close quarters, the boys irritated an ailing Mary, and Lee struggled with a budget that was a third of what he needed. Nevertheless, he enjoyed having family with him. He confessed to Mackay, "It is a rough country to bring them to I acknowledge, but they smooth it to me most marvellously [*sic*]." Promotion to captain helped, even as it became apparent that his efforts were not much appreciated officially. He often thought fondly of returning to Virginia, but he endured several more hot summers in St. Louis before the money for his project ran out.[18]

Lee's achievements at St. Louis were much less than he had envisioned, but he made the harbor more accessible and carved a channel through one of several rapids upriver. As a reward, he anticipated a return to Virginia but was disappointed. He was sent to inspect forts in North Carolina, an assignment he hated, returning home in January 1841. He was then ordered to New York to renovate four military posts. He stayed for six years, during which time he had other assignments that kept him from Virginia, including a stint on the Board of Visitors for West Point. His family joined him at Fort Hamilton in New York in

17. Lee to Mackay, Jan. 23, 1833, Mackay-McQueen Family Papers, Colonial Dames Collection, Georgia Historical Society, Savannah [hereinafter GHS]; Lee to Charles Carter Lee, Feb. 1, 1833, June 30, 1834, Feb. 24, 1835, Lee Papers, UVA; Lee to Andrew Talcott, Feb. 21, 1833, Lee Papers, LV; Lee to Talcott, Mar. 1, 1833, Robert E. Lee Papers, United States Military Academy Library and Archives, West Point, N.Y. [hereinafter USMA]; Thomas, *Lee,* 69, 75, 78, 81–82, 86, 94–95; Sanborn, *Portrait,* 97, 126; MacDonald, *Mrs. Lee,* 50; Coulling, *Lee Girls,* 3; Black, "Sesquicentennial Tribute," 4; Lee to Mackay, June 27, 1838 [quote], Lee Papers, USMA; George G. Shackelford, "Lieutenant Lee Reports to Captain Talcott on Fort Calhoun's Construction on the Rip Raps," *Virginia Magazine of History and Biography* 60 (July 1952): 482–83; Freeman, *Lee,* 1:157–58.

18. Thomas, *Lee,* 86–99; Stella M. Drumm, "Robert E. Lee and the Improvement of the Mississippi River," *Collections of the Missouri Historical Society* 6 (Feb. 1929): 161; Lee to Mackay, June 27, 1838 [quote], Lee Papers, USMA.

1841, but they spent much time at Arlington or school while he worked.[19]

Lee understandably began to chafe at the frustrations of peacetime military life. He had many opportunities daily to practice the self-restraint and self-sacrifice embodied in the version of Washington's life with which he was familiar, but he received none of the rewards. In a communication to Mackay he railed, "The manner in which the Army is considered and treated by the country and those whose business it is to nourish and take care of it, is enough to disgust every one with the service, and has the effect of driving every good soldier from it, and rendering those who remain discontented, careless and negligent." Years of moving did little to improve Lee's attitude. He wrote to Carter: "I suppose I must continue to work out my youth for little profit & *less* credit, & when old be laid on the shelf."[20]

Much of Lee's frustration lay in his failure to get into combat, which had brought glory to his father and to Washington. He missed the Black Hawk War and the second Seminole War, and he fretted that the war with Mexico, which loomed on the horizon by 1845, would pass him by as well. In response to a circular that asked whether Lee would accept a transfer if Congress created new units, he wrote, "In the event of war with any foreign government I should desire to be brought into active service in the field with as high a rank in the regular army as I could obtain." If that could not be done in the engineers, then he would transfer but would "accept no situation under the rank of field officer." Lee thus made it clear that, if war erupted, he would not spend the duration behind a desk.[21]

War with Mexico initially brought Lee little opportunity to make a name for himself. He was kept at Fort Hamilton until the late summer of 1846, when he was told to join Maj. Gen. John E. Wool in Texas. He complained to Carter that he had "but little hope of accomplishing anything, or having anything to accomplish" with Wool, but he duti-

---

19. Thomas, *Lee,* 101, 103–5; Sanborn, *Portrait,* 137–38; Lee to Mackay, Mar. 16, 1841, Mackay-McQueen Family Papers, Colonial Dames Collection, GHS.

20. Lee to Mackay, June 27, 1838 [1st quote], Lee Papers, USMA; Lee to Charles Carter Lee, Aug. 20, 1843 [2nd quote], Lee Papers, UVA.

21. Lee to Joseph G. Totten, June 17, 1845, Lee Letterbooks, De Butts-Ely Collection, LC; Lee to Mackay, June 21, 1846, Mackay-McQueen Family Papers, Colonial Dames Collection, GHS.

fully made his way to San Antonio. There his happiest moment came when he embellished a Christmas feast with "Revolutionary knives & forks" used by Washington while he was commander of the Continental Army. Lee had used bank checks emblazoned with the image of Washington while stationed at Fort Hamilton, and now he topped himself. He had brought Washington's field kit from Arlington. When Wool's officers pooled "various table equipage" and food for a dinner, Lee "paraded" Washington's flatware, positioning a piece before each guest, including Wool. After they left, Lee scribbled a note to Mary, asking her to tell her father that Washington's utensils "were passed around the table with much veneration & excited universal attention."[22]

After a march of almost a thousand miles, during which he never saw combat, Lee joined Winfield Scott's forces in January 1847. Lee had first met Scott in 1844 when they served together on the Board of Visitors for West Point, and Lee was impressed. The admiration must have been mutual because when General Scott was assigned to land at Vera Cruz and push into Mexico City, he asked for Lee. More important, Lee soon joined Scott's inner circle of advisors and made a name for himself with his scouting and map making in the company of Pierre G. T. Beauregard. All in all, it was a great opportunity to make a name, and Lee wrote excitedly to a friend that he had finally joined a *"Grande Armee."*[23]

Lee's aspirations little prepared him for the emotional reality of combat. During the bombardment of Vera Cruz in March 1847, he supervised the placing of six naval guns and directed their fire. Sydney Smith Lee was among the navy officers serving the battery, and Robert E. Lee later wrote that he could not imagine what he would have done if Smith

22. Lee to Martha C. Williams, Nov. 10, 1845, Gilder Lehrman Collection, Pierpont Morgan Library; Lee to Charles Carter Lee, July 13 [1st quote], Sept. 1, 1846, Lee Papers, UVA; Lee to Mary Custis Lee, Aug. 13, Sept. 4, 9, 13, and 21, Dec. 25 [2nd–5th quotes], 1846, De Butts-Ely Collection, LC; Thomas, *Lee,* 112, 115–18; Sanborn, *Portrait,* 161, 165. Checks imprinted with an image of George Washington and used by Robert E. Lee at Fort Hamilton can be found in collections of his papers at the Chicago Historical Society, Chicago; John Hay Library, Brown University, Providence, R.I.; and Houghton Library, Harvard University, Cambridge.

23. Lee to "My Dear Major" [William G. Williams], Feb. 28, 1847 [quote], Lee-Jackson Collection, Washington and Lee University Library, Lexington, Va. [hereinafter W&L]; Lee to Mackay, June 21, 1846, Mackay-McQueen Family Papers, Colonial Dames Collection, GHS; Thomas, *Lee,* 110–11, 118–19, 129; Dowdey, *Lee,* 80–81.

had fallen. He also wrote that his "heart bled for the inhabitants" as the guns pounded Vera Cruz, adding that "it was terrible to think of the women and children." He showed little concern for himself, however, even when an American, perhaps a deserter, fired at him and Beauregard. After Vera Cruz surrendered, Scott marched inland, and at Cerro Gordo Lee added to his growing reputation. There he found a way around Gen. Antonio Lopez de Santa Anna's flank and led a division to deliver a crushing assault on April 17. Cerro Gordo was Lee's first actual battle, and he wrote to his son Custis that it was a "horrible sight." Lee also had to comfort his friend Joseph E. Johnston, who was wounded and literally collapsed when he learned that his nephew had been killed.[24]

By mid-August 1847 Scott faced Santa Anna again at Mexico City, which could only be reached by narrow raised roads guarded by an army more than twice the size of his own. Again Lee and Beauregard found a path around the Mexican flank, through a lava bed thought to be almost impassible. Lee performed heroically in aligning units for attacks, placing batteries for cover fire, and locating men to provide a diversion for the decisive assault on August 20. Impressed, Scott asked Lee to plan his advance to Churubusco; Lee chose a path that allowed the army again to fall on the flank of Santa Anna's defenders, routing them. The North Americans seized Molino del Rey on September 8 and prepared to assault the fortress of Chapultepec. For this, Lee placed three batteries and worked with Scott on a plan. When the attack went forward, Lee accompanied one of the divisions. In less than two hours, Scott's forces opened two roads into Mexico City. Lee suffered his first wound, and the loss of blood combined with a lack of sleep caused him to faint, but he rode with Scott into the central square of the capital the next day.[25]

By the time they marched into Mexico City, Lee and Scott had become quite fond of each other. The young officer impressed the general, who allegedly told Reverdy Johnson that "his success in Mexico was largely due to the skill, valor and undaunted energy of Robert E.

24. Thomas, *Lee,* 121–23 [1st and 2nd quotes], 125–27; Lee to G. W. Custis Lee, Apr. 25, 1847 [3rd quote], De Butts-Ely Collection, LC; Dowdey, *Lee,* 86; Anderson and Anderson, *Generals,* 107; Casdorph, *Lee and Jackson,* 92.

25. Thomas, *Lee,* 127–36.

Lee." In turn, Lee proved to be as devoted to Scott as Light-Horse Harry had been to Washington. Lee agreed with Scott's estimate of himself that "He is a great man on great occasions." As a leader, Lee wrote, Scott's "judgement is as sound as his heart is bold & daring." Most important, Lee found that Scott was "Careful of his men [and] never exposes them but for a worthy object & then gives them the advantage of every circumstance in his power." Lee and Scott stayed in touch after the war, and Scott visited Lee while he was superintendent at West Point.[26]

Scott considered Lee a protege, and indeed the latter learned much in Mexico. From his reading of Antoine Henri de Jomini and works on Napoleon, Lee understood that a smaller army could defeat a superior opponent through maneuver. He saw this done in Mexico. Scott also realized that a decisive defeat could lead an enemy to negotiate by undermining its will to fight. This approach was reminiscent of Washington's in the Revolution as well as Napoleon's. Also like Washington and Napoleon, Scott checked his ground, spoke with subordinates but made his own decisions, and left execution of his plans to officers in the field. The results were victories with light losses. At the same time, Lee observed that, like Washington and Napoleon, Scott focused on the Mexican armies, forbidding his men to harm civilians. In sum, Lee had seen how a single primary army, if properly led, could win a war against superior numbers.[27]

26. Ibid., 158–59; Earl S. Miers, *Robert E. Lee: A Great Life in Brief* (New York, 1956), 20 [1st quote]; Fitzhugh Lee, *General Lee* (New York, 1894; reprint, Wilmington, N.C., 1989), 42; Lee to Mackay, Oct. 2, 1847 [2nd–4th quotes], Robert E. Lee Papers, United States Army Military History Institute, Carlisle, Penn. [hereinafter USAMHI]; Gary W. Gallagher, ed., "'We Are Our Own Trumpeters': Robert E. Lee Describes Winfield Scott's Campaign to Mexico City," *Virginia Magazine of History and Biography* 95 (July 1987): 373–74; Jones, *Life and Letters*, 56.

27. Thomas, *Lee*, 140, 158–59; Freeman, *Lee*, 1:296, 2:239–40; Russell Weigley, *The American Way of War* (New York, 1973; reprint, Bloomington, Ind., 1977), 72–74; Grady McWhiney and Perry D. Jamieson, *Attack and Die: Civil War Military Tactics and the Southern Heritage* (Tuscaloosa, Ala., 1982), xiii, 28, 31, 40; James W. Pohl, "The Influence of Antoine Henri de Jomini on Winfield Scott's Campaign in the Mexican War," *Southwestern Historical Quarterly* 77 (July 1973): 88–109; Dowdey, *Lee*, 91; Edward Hagerman, *The American Civil War and the Origins of Modern Warfare* (Bloomington, Ind., 1988), xiii; James T. Flexner, *Washington: The Indispensable Man* (New York, 1974), 110, 179; Thomas L. Connelly and Archer Jones, *The Politics of Command: Factions and Ideas in Confederate Strategy* (Baton Rouge, 1983), 7, 16, 34–35.

Despite having done well, Lee was saddened by his experience in Mexico. In the flush of victory he wrote jovially to Mackay, "I think a little lead, properly taken, is good for a man." Noting that many were not as fortunate as he, he added, "I am truly thankful, however, that I escaped all internal doses, & only recd. some external bruises, contusions & cuts." Lee did have to send the bloody sword belt of Maj. William G. Williams, who had been killed, to his daughter Martha Custis Williams. "Markie" and her brother Orton had frequently visited Arlington, and in 1844, when she was eighteen, Markie stayed with the Lees at Fort Hamilton. She and Lee remained close; they wrote often to each other, and she married only after he died.[28]

Lee was also disappointed by his failure to advance beyond the brevet rank of colonel, though he should have remembered that his father and Washington emerged from their first wars with that rank. Lee in fact had risen quite quickly from captain to brevet colonel. Nevertheless, in a letter to Carter he complained that regular army officers were being overlooked for promotion, though Scott had been careful to praise them. A few months later, he thanked his father-in-law for interceding to get "favours" from President James K. Polk. Although Lee enjoyed his brevet, he wrote to Custis, "I cannot consider myself highly complimented" because men who had done less got as much or more.[29]

Lee was especially embittered by the treatment of Scott. Jealousy led to conflict between Scott and two major generals, and Polk relieved Scott from command and ordered him to attend a court of inquiry. All charges were dropped, but Scott's military and political ambitions were seriously threatened. Lee wrote to Carter five days before Scott was removed that he was tired of "croakers" criticizing the general, whose "boldness of heart, self reliance & indomitable courage are glorious." When Lee had to testify about the imbroglio, he wrote again to his brother, saying, "The [country] is always first in my thoughts & efforts, & the feelings & interests of individuals should be sacrificed to its good." He concluded, "But it is difficult to get men to act on this

28. Adams, "Personal Letters," 1, 3, 41; Gallagher, "Trumpeters," 372–73; Dowdey, *Lee,* 94–95; Craven, *"To Markie,"* 20–21; Anderson and Anderson, *Generals,* 90–91, 95–96; Thomas, *Lee,* 106, 149; Connelly, *Marble Man,* 174; Lee to Mackay, Oct. 2, 1847 [quotes], Lee Papers, USAMHI.

29. Lee to Charles Carter Lee, Feb. 13, 1848, Lee Papers, UVA; Lee to Custis, Apr. 8, 1848 [quotes], De Butts-Ely Collection, LC.

principle."[30] Lee found it difficult to understand how a hero could be treated so shabbily, much as his father and even occasionally the great Washington himself had been.

Lee also struggled with reservations about the war itself. He had written to Mary in May 1846, after news arrived of clashes along the Texas frontier, "There ought surely to be no hesitation any longer on our part," but he added, "I fear the country is already disgraced for its puerile conduct." He believed the only reason for the advance into Mexico was to encourage the Mexicans to attack and "thus bring on the war we had not the frankness or the manliness to declare." In sum, he declared, "I wish I was better satisfied as to the justice of our cause." Two years of war made little difference in his opinion. He wrote to Mary in February 1848 that the army had "drubbed [Mexico] handsomely and in a manner no man might be ashamed of," but he admitted that "we bullied her," and "For that I am ashamed."[31]

Lee's discontent with his experience in Mexico led him to consider leaving the army. He proudly joined the Aztec Club of 1847, patterned after the Society of the Cincinnati founded by his father and other Revolutionary veterans, but at the same time wrote to Carter that he might quit the army. He found himself thinking more about family. The army, he readily admitted, "has had my best days & energies," but he knew that "A young family has some claims." Yet Lee did not resign. He did not have the resources to become a planter, nor the inclination for politics. In the army, he had become the "living legacy" of Washington; as a civilian, he would share this distinction with his father-in-law. He therefore remained a soldier and became frustrated as he aged with no chance to enhance his reputation.[32]

30. Lee to Charles Carter Lee, Feb. 13 [1st and 2nd quotes], Mar. 18 [3rd and 4th quotes], 1848, Lee Papers, UVA; Dowdey, *Lee,* 95; Freeman, *Lee,* 1:287–91; Sanborn, *Portrait,* 190, 193.

31. Lee to Mary Custis Lee, May 12, 1846 [1st–4th quotes], De Butts-Ely Collection, LC; Young, *Marse Robert,* 49 [6th and 7th quotes]; Freeman, *Lee,* 1:292 [5th quote]; Thomas, *Lee,* 111–12.

32. Lee to Charles Carter Lee, Mar. 18, 1848 [1st and 2nd quotes], Lee Papers, UVA; Anderson and Anderson, *Generals,* 134–35 [3rd quote]; Richard H. Breithaupt, Jr., *Aztec Club of 1847, Military Society of the Mexican War: Sesquicentennial History, 1847–1997* (Los Angeles, 1998), 4, 7, 953. Interestingly, though Lee joined a military society modeled after the one established by veterans of the Revolution, he never followed Washington's example in becoming a Mason. See William Tate, ed., "A Robert E. Lee Letter on Aban-

Lee returned to Arlington in June 1848 and resumed work. He was appointed to be one of four dozen "managers" for Zachary Taylor's inaugural ball, but he missed the affair because he was on an inspection tour of the southern coastline. In the summer of 1849, he moved to Baltimore to direct work on Fort Carroll, named in honor of the last surviving signer of the Declaration of Independence. His family stayed at Arlington until the town house rented from his Uncle Williams Carter, near Mount Vernon Place with its monument to Washington, was ready. While waiting, Lee received some unusual guests. Gen. Narcisco Lopez approached Jefferson Davis in 1849 with a plan to overthrow the Spanish government of Cuba. Davis sent him to Lee, who met with Lopez but declined his offer of command. Lee was uncomfortable with Lopez, but it is interesting that when revolutionaries approached Davis, he thought of Lee as their kindred spirit.[33]

An appointment to serve as superintendent of West Point in 1852 compelled Lee to relocate his family again. He was on familiar ground, though; he had not only graduated from the academy but had returned in 1843 to design a dormitory and in 1844 to serve on a Board of Visitors chaired by Scott. Moreover, Washington's headquarters still stood on the campus. To enhance his feeling of belonging, Lee decorated his home and office with items from Arlington. He had refused to allow Mary to do this at Fort Monroe, but by the time they settled at Fort Hamilton, shipping relics from Arlington had become customary. Walt Whitman noted at about that time that many homes had portraits of Washington, but Lee did them one better. The focus of Lee's office at West Point was a copy by Ernest Fischer of the Charles Willson Peale painting of Washington as a militia colonel, but a friend wrote that it

---

doning the South After the War," *Georgia Historical Quarterly* 37 (September 1953): 255–56.

    33. Thomas, *Lee,* 142–43, 146, 148; Sanborn, *Portrait,* 200–201; Philip Van Doren Stern, *Robert E. Lee, The Man and the Soldier: A Pictorial Biography* (New York, 1963), 86–87; James M. McPherson, *Battle Cry of Freedom: The Civil War Era* (New York, 1988), 104–7; Anderson and Anderson, *Generals,* 132–33; Coulling, *Lee Girls,* 26, 28; Varina H. Davis, *Jefferson Davis, Ex-President of the Confederate States of America: A Memoir by His Wife,* 2 vols. (New York, 1890), 1:412–13; J. William Jones, *Army of Northern Virginia Memorial Volume* (Richmond, 1880; reprint, Dayton, Ohio, 1976), 15; "Tributes to General Lee," *Southern Magazine* 8 (Jan. 1871): 24.

also held other "pictures and pieces of furniture from Arlington connected in one way or another with Washington."[34]

Many visitors to the Lees' home at West Point were dazzled by the Washington relics that were commonly used. They continued the tradition of having cadets to dinner, but their table was now always set with Washington's silverware. The Lees also began a custom of hosting balls for faculty brides. Large silver wine coolers and a candelabrum, all of which had been Washington's, graced the table each time, as well as a set of silver utensils from Arlington. Some guests may even have been chosen for their Washington connection. Washington Irving visited Arlington in early 1852. He traveled to West Point two years later to watch the graduation exercises, in which Lee's oldest son was first in his class, and to dine with Lee. Certainly the talk must have turned to the first president, as Irving would publish the first of five volumes on Washington one year later. Laudatory of Light-Horse Harry and Washington, Irving's tomes, with their focus on the Revolution, became some of Lee's favorites to read aloud.[35]

Not all of the cadets who dined with the Lees were impressed with the Washington relics. Edward L. Hartz wrote to his father that while dining with the Lees he "had the sacred satisfaction of eating [his] supper with the identical silver & knives and forks that constituted part of Washington's tea service." He also noted that the "center piece, cake & fruit baskets, urns & other articles massive and of solid silver were inherited directly by Col Lee's family from Genl Washington with whom he is connected." Lee succeeded in establishing his connection with his

34. William W. Bailey, "General Robert E. Lee at West Point" (Manuscript, n.d., USMA) [quote]; Holmes M. Alexander, *Washington and Lee: A Study in the Will to Win* (Boston, 1966), 51, 90; Sanborn, *Portrait*, 142; Forgie, *Patricide*, 185; *Arlington House*, 34; Thomas, *Lee*, 159; MacDonald, *Mrs. Lee*, 36, 42, 83; Morris Schaff, *Spirit of Old West Point* (Boston, 1907), illustration facing p. 184.

35. Lee to Jerome N. Bonaparte, May 31, 1854, Lee Papers, LV; Sanborn, *Portrait*, 218, 227–28; De Butts, *Growing Up*, 9; Bryan, *Washington in American Literature*, 104–5; Winston, *Lee*, 384; Anderson and Anderson, *Generals*, 138; Thomas, *Lee*, 159; Robert A. Brock, ed., *Gen. Robert Edward Lee: Soldier, Citizen, and Christian Patriot* (Richmond, 1897), 117–18; Stephen E. Ambrose, *Duty, Honor, Country* (Baltimore, 1966), 166; William D. Hoyt, Jr., ed., "Some Personal Letters of Robert E. Lee, 1850–1858," *Journal of Southern History* 12 (Nov. 1946): 565; Edward H. O'Neill, *A History of American Biography, 1800–1935* (Philadelphia, 1935), 164–66.

hero in Hartz's mind, but not his reverence. Hartz concluded, "I don't think, however, that with all the eclat of this circumstance—my supper tasted any better than it did when eaten with the iron, bone handled, knives off of ordinary tin plates at home, after my return from a hard days work in the machine shop." Lee probably misunderstood this lack of favorable response as a reaction to him. He wrote to his friend Jerome Napoleon Bonaparte, a nephew of the emperor, that some cadets found the "Supt & his dame, dull commodities in the interchange of social pleasures."[36]

The Lees took their Washington relics with them when they left West Point, but a few years later Lee was asked to assist with the transfer to the academy of a more permanent legacy of the first president. In 1854 Lee's father-in-law had presented his Revolutionary flags to President Millard Fillmore, who later turned them over to the War Department. They were in fact the two banners surrendered to Washington by the British and Hessian troops at Yorktown that the Continental Congress had given to the general-in-chief and Custis had purchased after Martha's death. In September 1858 the flags were shipped to West Point, which had a military museum. Lee must have remembered the flags among the treasures of Arlington, but he confessed to Anna Maria Fitzhugh that he knew little about them other than family lore and the facts of their donation.[37]

Lee was a reluctant superintendent, but he worked hard. He would do his best, he wrote to Bonaparte, "But when called upon, shall relinquish that charge with more cheerfulness than I felt reluctance in taking it." Lee was more explicit in a note to Beauregard: "The Superintendent can do nothing right and must father every wrong." However, Lee had accomplishments as superintendent; Secretary of War Jefferson Davis approved Lee's expansion of the curriculum to five years to accommodate classes in languages and military science and his adoption of a tactics manual by William J. Hardee. Adapted from an earlier work by

36. Edward L. Hartz to "Father," Nov. 3, 1854 [1st–3rd quotes], Edward L. Hartz Papers, LC; Hoyt, "Personal Letters," 561–62 [4th quote].

37. Winston, *Lee,* 58; United State Military Academy, Post Orders, USMA, 175–76, 178–79; De Butts, *Growing Up,* 36; Lee to Anna Maria Fitzhugh, Sept. 13, 1858, Lee Papers, DU.

Scott, Hardee's book incorporated more from Napoleon's strategy and addressed the introduction of rifles.[38]

Lee's years at West Point allowed him to renew his study of the Revolution and Napoleon. He wrote to his daughter Agnes in that time period, "Much good can be derived from books." From them, careful readers could get "True & correct ideas, that we can exemplify & practice." For such reasons, he had not liked Henry Lee IV's biography of Napoleon, which he found to be much too distorted in an attempt to draw clear parallels between the emperor and Light-Horse Harry. More to his liking was an 1838 edition of Antoine Henri de Jomini's *Precis de l'Art de la Guerre*. In the campus library he found more books that suited his interests. He supplemented his reading with academic exercises as a member of the Napoleon Club, organized by engineering professor Dennis Hart Mahan. Lee had not studied under Mahan, who had returned to West Point in 1830 and subsequently taught from Jomini's works, emphasizing that Napoleon's tactics were derived from principles employed by Frederick the Great. Lee probably enjoyed the link to Washington's hero. He joined Mahan's Napoleon Club while he was superintendent and presented at least one paper to the club.[39]

Lee observed in a letter to Bonaparte in the fall of 1854 that Davis was very supportive of his alma mater. He should have added that the Secretary of War was also impressed with him, for soon thereafter he became lieutenant colonel of the 2nd United States Cavalry, commanded by Col. Albert Sydney Johnston. Lee left West Point in April and, after a short stay at Arlington, arrived in Louisville to organize his new charges in Johnston's absence. He was again concerned about hav-

38. Thomas, *Lee,* 152, 154, 158; Lee to Bonaparte, Mar. 12, 1853, [1st quote], Lee Papers, LV; "A Robert E. Lee Letter to P. G. T. Beauregard," *Maryland Historical Magazine* 51 (Sept. 1956): 250 [2nd quote]; Ambrose, *Duty, Honor, Country,* 141; McWhiney and Jamieson, *Attack and Die,* 49–53; Anderson and Anderson, *Generals,* 139; Hoyt, "Personal Letters," 561.

39. Jay Luvaas, "Lee and the Operational Art," *Parameters* 22 (Autumn 1992): 13; Edgar E. Hume, "Light-Horse Harry and His Fellow Members of the Cincinnati," *Virginia Magazine of History and Biography* 15 (Apr. 1935): 277; Lee to Agnes Lee, Sept. 5, 1857 [quotes], Mrs. Mason Barret Collection, Howard-Tilton Library, Tulane University, New Orleans [hereinafter TU]; Holmes M. Alexander, *Washington and Lee,* 80; Nagel, *Lees of Virginia,* 220–21, 225; Freeman, *Lee,* 1:353–58; Thomas, *Lee,* 160; Craven, *"To Markie,"* 51; Ambrose, *Duty, Honor, Country,* 100–101, 138–39.

ing to leave his family behind, but he might have been somewhat mollified had he known that William P. Johnston, the colonel's son, would
later write that Lee greatly resembled Washington when he met him at
Louisville.[40]

Personal matters briefly called Lee back east. During the summer of
1855, he and Mary took charge of Arlington because of the poor health
of her father and began an extensive renovation of the home. Much
remodeling was completed after Lee returned west, but he sent clear
orders to his wife, especially about Washington relics. In August 1855,
he asked when the Arlington furnishings would be returned from West
Point and "how the pictures bore the travel & seclusion." He agreed
with her that Custis' "battle pieces" would look good "in a line with
Washington & Col Parke & smaller pictures interspersed among them."
Several images, such as Peale's portrait of Washington, were refurbished
and all were rehung. On Mary's initiative "three venerable presses from
Mt. Vernon filled with old & mouldy books" were also refinished.[41]

Lee may have been so careful about the Washington relics because
the generosity of Mary and her father had greatly reduced the family
collection. While Lee was in Mexico, Mary got a note from Elizabeth
Mackay Stiles, Jack Mackay's sister. Stiles was in Vienna with her husband, who had become the chargé d'affaires, and wanted a "Cincinnati
China" dish to use or give as a gift. Mary found her "stock" was so
reduced that there was not a whole plate remaining. Instead, she forwarded a "small tureen, which you must value very highly because they
are getting very rare & it is almost like parting with one of my family to
send it so far." She asked only that they "present it where . . . it will be
most prized & valued."[42]

40. Lee to Bonaparte, Nov. 4, 1854, Lee Papers, LV; Thomas, *Lee,* 108, 161, 163–64,
171; Lee to Joseph G. Totten, Mar. 15, 1855, United States Military Academy, Superintendents' Letter Books, USMA; Freeman, *Lee,* 1:348–49; Sanborn, *Portrait,* 238–39; Hoyt,
"Personal Letters," 569; William P. Johnston, "Reminiscences of General Robert E. Lee,"
Belford's Monthly 5 (June 1890): 84–85; W. G. Bean, "Lee Talks Frankly of the War and
His Final Months in Lexington," *Washington and Lee Alumni Magazine* 41 (Winter
1966): 2–9.

41. Thomas, *Lee,* 164–65; De Butts, *Growing Up,* 71 [4th quote], 72; Adams, "Personal Letters," 46–48, 50 [1st–3rd quotes]; Lee to Mary Custis Lee, n.d., De Butts-Ely
Collection, LC.

42. Mary Custis Lee to Mrs. William H. [Elizabeth Mackay] Stiles, Nov. 1, 1847,
Mackay-McQueen Family Papers, Colonial Dames Collection, GHS.

Lee arrived at Fort Mason, Texas, where the 2nd Cavalry was assigned, in March 1856. There he found many officers with whom he had previously served. Despite this welcome company, frontier life was harsh, and Lee despised the Comanches with whom he was frequently in close contact. Assignments to military courts were long and tedious, and his single foray against hostile Comanches resulted in no substantive success. In a letter to Mary he wearily referred to Texas as a "desert of dullness."[43]

The death of his father-in-law in October 1857 brought Lee home to Arlington, where he remained on leave until 1859 to serve as executor for his estate. Custis' will specified that Mary would have the use of Arlington during her life, but at her death it would go to her eldest son, whose name should be changed to Washington to perpetuate the line. To Rooney, Custis left White House on the Pamunkey River, where Martha Washington had lived with her first husband, borne four children, and met General Washington. The Lees' youngest son, Robert, got Romancoke, an estate near White House that had also belonged to George and Martha Washington. Custis' will ordered Mary to divide the "family plate" among her children, but all of the "Mount Vernon plate, together with every article I possess relating to Washington, and that came from Mount Vernon," had to stay at Arlington. Like Washington, Custis freed his slaves in his will, though Lee could retain them for five years to produce income for the estate.[44]

Lee did not welcome the role of planter but did well at it. He told Anna Maria Fitzhugh that he "would prefer relinquishing to the boys the property at once, with its responsibilities—They are young & might make something of it." But, he added, "Mary naturally clings to the place of her birth & the graves of her parents, & all have the desire to see the old home resuscitated." When his eldest son Custis heard of the will, he tried to convey his title to his father, but the elder Lee declined

43. Lee to Mrs. William Henry [Elizabeth Mackay] Stiles, May 24, 1856, Lee Papers, SH; Thomas, *Lee,* 165–68; Fitzhugh Lee, *General Lee,* 63–69, 73; Carl C. Rister, *Robert E. Lee in Texas* (Norman, Okla., 1946), 19–95 passim [quote on p. 83].

44. Lee to Anna Maria Fitzhugh, Nov. 22, 1857, Lee Papers, DU; Lee to Lorenzo Thomas, June 16, 1859, Lee Papers, LV; Karl Decker and Angus McSween, *Historic Arlington: A History of the National Cemetery from Its Establishment to the Present Time* (Washington, D.C., 1892), 19; Fitzhugh Lee, *General Lee,* 71 [quotes]; Winston, *Lee,* 38; MacDonald, *Mrs. Lee,* 272.

and went to work. Arlington was in poor shape, so he labored to improve it and settle debts. He wrote to Anna Maria Fitzhugh, "Everything is in ruins and will have to be rebuilt," adding that he felt "more familiar with the military operations of a campaign than the details of a farm." Just like Washington at Mount Vernon, Lee and his sons planted food crops at all three estates, and Lee rented the mill at Arlington to a neighbor. All of the estates prospered, to the delight of Mary.[45]

Part of Lee's unhappiness with being a planter was that he had to participate more directly in the institution of slavery. The Custis estate included 196 slaves, all of whom were to be freed within five years. This was scant comfort to Lee, whose ideas about slavery remained like those of many Virginians of the Revolutionary era. For them, it was a hated institution, and manumission was to be practiced when possible. Light-Horse Harry had denounced slavery as a "dreadful evil which the cruel policy of preceding times had introduced." Richard Henry Lee inherited forty slaves and had only a handful at his death. Washington, who declared that slaves would prove to "be a very troublesome species of property," freed his in his will. In keeping with this custom, Robert E. Lee in a will he wrote before going to Mexico provided for the manumission of the only slaves he owned, a woman and her children inherited from his mother and apparently leased to his father-in-law and later sold to him. Only when his family was with him did he use slaves; several from Arlington worked at Fort Monroe and West Point.[46]

While Lee had qualms about slavery, he was never an ardent abolitionist. His father-in-law joined the American Colonization Society, and Lee helped several ex-slaves to emigrate to Liberia. However, the radi-

45. Thomas, *Lee,* 174–76; Lee to Anna Maria Fitzhugh, Nov. 22, 1857 [quotes], Lee to Custis Lee, Feb. 15, Mar. 17, 1858, Lee Papers, DU; Custis Lee to Mary Custis Lee, n.d., Lee Family Papers, VHS; Flexner, *Washington,* 49–50; Dowdey, *Lee,* 114–15; Lee to Crabb & Brother, Jan. 31, 1859, Robert E. Lee Papers, New York Historical Society, New York; Joseph C. Robert, "Lee the Farmer," *Journal of Southern History* 3 (Nov. 1937): 438–39.

46. Thomas, *Lee,* 113, 174–75; Hendrick, *Lees of Virginia,* 102–3, 141–42; Winston, *Lee,* 45, 53, Sanborn, *Portrait,* 150, 159, 242–43, 254, 260–61, 271; "Will Written on August 31, 1846, and Probated on November 7, 1870," Robert E. Lee Papers, W&L; Coulling, *Lee Girls,* 40; Rister, *Lee in Texas,* 68, 113; Adams, "Personal Letters," 92, 96–97, 331, 335, 337, 588; MacDonald, *Mrs. Lee,* 42; Thomas Boyd, *Light-Horse Harry Lee* (New York, 1931), 207 [1st quote]; Ulrich B. Phillips, ed., *Plantation and Frontier Documents, 1649–1863,* 2 vols. (Cleveland, Ohio, 1909), 2:5 [2nd quote].

cals of the Anti-Slavery Society infuriated Lee, especially when they attacked the Founding Fathers. He wrote in a fury to his mother-in-law that they called "The founders of the Constitution & the fathers of the Revolution *Swindlers,*" and he enclosed an article about the Society for his father-in-law so that he could "see to what extent some men are carried by their evil passions." In 1856 he wrote to Mary, "In this enlightened age, there are few I believe, but what will acknowledge, that slavery as an institution, is a moral & political evil in any country." He believed, though, that "emancipation will sooner result from a mild and melting influence than the storms and contests of fiery controversy." As for radical abolitionists, he warned that the "efforts of certain people of the North, to interfere with & change the domestic institutions of the South" might well lead to "a civil & servile war."[47]

The restlessness of his late father-in-law's slaves further vexed Lee. He wanted to settle debts before freeing them, so those he did not use were leased. Several of the latter came home, complaining about new employers, and in January 1858 two female slaves robbed Arlington and fled with their children to Washington. There they were joined by two leased slaves. Lee recaptured three and sent them to southern Virginia, but two anonymous notes in the New York *Tribune* accused him of worse. They said that he had had the three runaways brutally whipped; Lee himself supposedly beat one woman. Most tellingly, one wrote, "Next to Mount Vernon, we associate the Custis place with the 'Father of this free country.'" The writer then asked, "Shall 'Washington's body guard' be thus tampered with, and never a voice raised for such utter helplessness?" Lee refused to answer the charges, but they were refuted by an anonymous missive that blamed abolitionists for the stories. An abolitionist was later jailed for troubling the Lees, but this provided little solace. To his son Custis, Lee wrote that his father-in-law "left me an unpleasant legacy."[48]

47. *Arlington House,* 24; Freeman, *Lee,* 4:400; Thomas, *Lee,* 110; Lee to Mary Fitzhugh Custis, Apr. 13, 1844 [1st and 2nd quotes], George B. Lee Papers, VHS; Lee to Mary Custis Lee, Dec. 27, 1856 [3rd and 4th quotes], De Butts-Ely Collection, LC; Fitzhugh Lee, *General Lee,* 64; Winston, *Lee,* 70; Judith W. Maguire, *General Robert E. Lee, The Christian Soldier* (Richmond, 1873), 127–28.

48. Thomas, *Lee,* 177–78; Sanborn, *Portrait,* 283; Anderson and Anderson, *Generals,* 181–82; Freeman, *Lee,* 1:390–92 [1st and 2nd quotes]; Adams, "Personal Letters," 457, 472–73, 541–42 [3rd quote], 702, 724, 736; William M. E. Rachal, ed., "'Secession Is

Lee found that being a planter like Washington had some very distasteful aspects, but he got some comfort from inheriting the role of a keeper of the Washington memorabilia, which he shared with Mary. He continued to remodel Arlington, providing display space for relics. Mary took great pride in showing these to all visitors, especially Martha's dresses. As a result of the Lees' enthusiasm, "Even the most sophisticated callers felt the spirit of the father of the country hovering over Arlington." Lee also became involved with the publication of Custis' memoirs and Washington letters, which Mary published in 1859 as *Recollections and Private Memoirs of Washington.* Lee praised the work and pushed for the production of a second, improved edition. He wrote to Mary in 1860 that he had found a speech lauding Washington that should be included. He also had a list of errors to be corrected and asked that a note from John Parke Custis be deleted because it referred to privateers. Nevertheless, he declared the first edition to be wonderful and showed it to anyone who expressed interest.[49]

Lee was at Arlington on the morning of October 17 when a young lieutenant, James Ewell Brown Stuart, brought an order for Lee to take charge of troops sent to cope with an emergency at Harpers Ferry, where an unknown number of men had occupied the federal armory. Stuart was familiar to Lee, having been a cadet at West Point during Lee's superintendency and having dined with the Lees there and at Arlington several times. Lee accepted his offer to serve as an aide and hurried with him to join a company of marines on the railroad west to Harpers Ferry.[50]

Nothing but Revolution': A Letter of R. E. Lee to His Son Rooney," *Virginia Magazine of History and Biography* 69 (Jan. 1961): 4; *Arlington House,* 25; Dowdey, *Lee,* 113–14; Lee to Lorenzo Thomas, June 16, 1859, Lee Papers, LV; Jones, *Life and Letters,* 102; Mary Custis Lee to Mrs. William Henry [Elizabeth Mackay] Stiles, Feb. 9, 1861, Mackay-McQueen Family Papers, Colonial Dames Collection, GHS. At least one author does believe that Lee had the runaway slaves brutally whipped. See Ervin L. Jordan, Jr., *Black Confederates and Afro-Yankees in Civil War Virginia* (Charlottesville, Va., 1995), 162.

49. Anderson and Anderson, *Generals,* 175–76 [quote]; Sally N. Robins, "Mrs. Lee During the War," in Brock, *Gen. Robert Edward Lee,* 330; Lee to Mary Custis Lee, Apr. 4, 1860, De Butts-Ely Collection, LC; Adams, "Personal Letters," 580–81, 602, 632; MacDonald, *Mrs. Lee,* 128–30.

50. Thomas, *Lee,* 179–80; Walter C. Preston, *Lee: West Point and Lexington* (Yellow Springs, Ohio, 1934), 33–34; Lee to Custis Lee, August 17, 1859, Lee Papers, DU; J. E. B. Stuart to "Mama," Jan. 31, 1860, Lee Papers, UVA; Peter W. Hairston, ed., "J. E. B. Stu-

By the time Lee arrived at the armory on the night of October 17, several raiders had already been killed. The rest had moved with their hostages into a firehouse, where they were surrounded by throngs of onlookers. Lee cleared the area, had the marines encircle the building while he posted militia, and sent Stuart to exact an unconditional surrender. Early in the morning, Stuart handed a surrender demand to the group's leader, whom he recognized as John Brown. It was while Brown argued with Stuart that Lewis W. Washington, the great-nephew of George Washington, to the distress of his fellow hostages shouted, "Never mind us, fire!" Stuart, rebuffed by Brown, signaled for marines to storm the firehouse. Washington pointed out Brown, and a marine lieutenant beat the raider unconscious. Two others were captured as well, while two more were killed. All of the hostages were released unharmed.[51]

Lee represented his family well at Harpers Ferry. While the raiders held the firehouse, he stood quietly on a knoll, issuing orders within range of their guns. Reflecting the same studied calm, Lewis Washington refused to emerge after his rescue until he was properly dressed and even then walked out at a casual stroll. In his report Lee dismissed Brown as a "fanatic or madman," and in his diary he referred to Brown and his men as "Banditti" and "Robbers." He returned to Arlington one day after the attack and then went back to Harpers Ferry to command the troops during the trial in November. Stuart wrote to his mother that Lee deserved a "gold medal" for his "*immense* but quiet service," and he claimed that Gov. Henry A. Wise said that "Lee was 'fit for any command on earth.'"[52]

Lee was doubly gratified with the successful termination of the siege at Harpers Ferry. Not only did he rescue a relative, he also recovered a treasured Washington relic. When the raiders kidnapped Washington, they also took, at Brown's order, a sword bequeathed by George Washington to his nephew, Lewis' father, and a pistol given to General Wash-

art's Letters to His Hairston Kin, 1850–1855," *North Carolina Historical Review* 51 (July 1974): 297, 300, 308.

51. Thomas, *Lee*, 180–82 [quote]; Stanley F. Horn, ed., *The Robert E. Lee Reader* (Indianapolis, 1949), 85; Stuart to "Mama," Jan. 31, 1860, Lee Papers, UVA.

52. Sanborn, *Portrait*, 288; Thomas, *Lee*, 183; Horn, *Reader*, 85 [1st quote]; Robert E. Lee Diary [2nd and 3rd quotes], Lee Family Papers, VHS; Stuart to "Mama," Jan. 31, 1860 [4th–6th quotes], Lee Papers, UVA.

ington by Lafayette. While trapped in the firehouse, Brown carried the sword, which many, including Lewis, mistakenly believed had been sent by Frederick the Great to Washington. Lewis' delay in leaving the firehouse may well have been due to a frantic search for the sword, which was found where Brown dropped it. The pistol was returned to the Washington family years later by one of Brown's sons.[53]

Lee found himself much in demand after Harpers Ferry, but he returned to Texas rather than exploiting other opportunities. In January 1860, he went to Richmond to help reorganize the militia. Afterwards, having declined an invitation from Scott to serve as his secretary, Lee took charge of the Department of Texas. Most of his energy was spent chasing Comanches and Juan Cortina, a rustler who had gained hundreds of followers by claiming that he was defending Mexican rights north of the Rio Grande. Cortina made raids along the border with the support of Mexican officials until Lee drove him south. Lee's mood was vile, especially when he chased American filibusterers as well. In late 1860 he quit his departmental command and returned to Fort Mason.[54]

Exiled again on the Texas frontier, Lee reflected unhappily upon his life. He did not mind the work; in fact, he had written earlier to Elizabeth Mackay Stiles, "I like the wilderness, & the vicissitudes of camp life, are no hardship to me." However, he wrote, "I grieve over my separation from my wife & children." He added that she should tell her son not to enlist; unless he became a general, "he [could] never rise to any military eminence." He also wrote to Edward Vernon Childe, the husband of his sister Mildred, "The separation from my dear wife & children is very grievous to me, & I do not know how long I can stand it. I fear it will eventually drive me from the service." Told of his father-in-law's death, Lee wrote Col. Albert Sydney Johnston that he did not know whether to stay in the army or resign. He explained, "My prefer-

53. W. W. Scott, ed., "The John Brown Letters," *Virginia Magazine of History and Biography* 9 (Apr. 1902): 388–90; William E. Brooks, *Lee of Virginia: A Biography* (Garden City, N.Y., 1932), 64; Eugene E. Prussing, *The Estate of George Washington, Deceased* (Boston, 1927), 59–60, 482.

54. Lee Diary, Lee Family Papers, VHS; Adams, "Personal Letters," 534–35; Anderson and Anderson, *Generals,* 180; Thomas, *Lee,* 183–186; Rister, *Lee in Texas,* 96–149 passim; John H. Jenkins, ed., *Lee on the Rio Grande: The Correspondence of Robert E. Lee on the Texas Border, 1860* (Austin, 1988), 1–7, 24; Henry A. White, *Robert E. Lee and the Southern Confederacy, 1807–1870* (New York, 1897), 96–97.

ences which have clung to me from boyhood impel me to adopt the former course, but yet I feel that a man's family has its claims, too." In 1860 he wrote to Anna Maria Fitzhugh, "A divided heart I have too long had, & a divided life too long led." Meeting military and family obligations brought "small progress," he wrote, and "thus I live & am unable to advance either."[55]

Lee had good reason to think that his progress in the army might be at an end by 1860. A lieutenant colonel with a brevet of colonel, Lee hoped for a general's star, but the prospect was unlikely. He wrote to Mary in 1856 that she should not expect him to advance because it was not "right to indulge improper and useless hopes," but later he wrote, "[I]f anything should turn up in the way of promotion, ask your father if suitable & proper to apply in my behalf." When Joseph E. Johnston was promoted by his cousin, Secretary of War John B. Floyd, Lee fumed to his son Custis that although Johnston was a "good soldier & worthy man," Floyd's action had "thrown more discredit than ever on the system of favouritism & making brevets."[56]

Lee also had personal reasons to be unhappy by 1860. His responsibility at Arlington brought frustration that exacerbated the effect of family deaths and Mary's failing health. In 1855 he had written to his brother Carter, "I have grieved over the death of my good old Uncle Fitzhugh, whose kindness to me & us all, & our dear Mother, I shall never forget." His grief was compounded a year later when their sister, Catherine Mildred Lee Childe, died in Paris, where she lived with her husband. Lee declared that "this sudden, harsh & terrible separation has not been the less distressing, because it was distant & unlooked for. It has put an end to all hope of our meeting in this world." Later Lee

---

55. Lee to Mrs. William Henry [Elizabeth Mackay] Stiles, May 24, 1856 [1st–3rd quotes], Lee to Edward Vernon Childe, Nov. 1, 1856 [4th quote], Lee Papers, SH; Lee to Mrs. William Henry [Elizabeth Mackay] Stiles, Aug. 14, 1856, Robert E. Lee Papers, Special Collections, University of Texas at Arlington; Lee to Albert Sydney Johnston, Oct. 25, 1857 [5th quote], Barret Collection, TU; Lee to Anna Maria Fitzhugh, June 6, 1860 [6th–8th quotes], Robert E. Lee Papers, Eleanor S. Brockenbrough Library, Museum of the Confederacy, Richmond; Marilyn M. Sibley, "Robert E. Lee to Albert Sydney Johnston, 1857," *Journal of Southern History* 29 (Feb. 1963): 103–4.

56. Crimmins, "Lee in Texas," 8 [1st quote]; Adams, "Personal Letters," 233 [2nd quote], 612–13 [3rd and 4th quotes]; Dowdey, *Lee,* 122–23; Horn, *Reader,* 88; Jones, *Life and Letters,* 114.

wrote that "every recurrence of the thought" of her death brought "scalding tears & sad reflection." Returning to Arlington to find Mary crippled must have seemed a crowning blow. He lamented to Anna Maria Fitzhugh, "[W]hat am I to do—I fear Mary will never be well enough to accompany me in my wandering life, & it seems to be cruel to leave her."[57]

Throughout his life, Lee had lived in Washington's shadow. As the 1850s ended, Lee's admiration of Washington must have aggravated his own frustration because, unlike his idol, he became older without greatly increasing in prestige. Washington was forty-three years of age when he became general-in-chief. Lee passed his fifty-third birthday with no prospect of doing as well. Historian George B. Forgie would look at Lee's generation and declare that "we can detect among many ambitious men in the post-heroic period a gradual shift from a concern over how posterity would judge them to a concern that posterity might not take the trouble to judge them at all."[58] Lee felt these pangs more deeply than most. He had been raised in an atmosphere saturated with the memory of the Revolution. By 1860, he could believe that he would never equal the achievements of Washington or the Revolutionary Lees, and most of the latter, including his own father, had died relatively young. Time was running out.

In comparison with the achievements of the generation that won the Revolution, Lee's accomplishments did indeed seem pale. When John Livingston invited Lee to be included in his work on notable Americans, Lee declined, explaining, "I fear the little incidents of my life would add nothing to the interest of your work." In a sardonic response to George W. Cullum's inquiries for his register of West Point graduates, Lee wrote that he was inundated with requests from militia to certify their service at Harpers Ferry and had concluded that he would rather be among the Comanche. Lee wrote to Rooney in April to congratulate him on the birth of a son, "this promising scion of my scattered house, who will I hope resuscitate its name and fame." That month he wrote to Mary, "I hope he may . . . do his part to supply the deficiencies of his Grdfather

57. Lee to Charles Carter Lee, May 10, 1855 [1st quote], Lee Papers, UVA; Thomas, *Lee,* 168; Adams, "Personal Letters," 144 [2nd quote], 166 [3rd and 4th quotes]; Lee to Anna Maria Fitzhugh, Nov. 22, 1857 [5th quote], Lee Papers, DU.

58. Forgie, *Patricide,* 69.

[*sic*]." When the baby was named for him, Lee wrote, "I wish I could offer him a more worthy name and a better example," and in January 1861 he wrote that he hoped his grandson would "be a wiser and more useful man than his namesake."[59]

Lee wrote to his son Custis in February 1861 that he was "cheered in [his] downward path by the onward and rising course of [his] dear sons." He had written to a nephew in 1853: "To you life is new & bright. . . . To me, looking at the future from the past, it brings feelings of apprehension and resignation."[60] Not much in the ensuing years had improved his mood. Having failed to reach the heights of Washington's career, Lee resigned himself to watching as his sons made their bid to create a legacy of value. He did not realize that the opportunity was close at hand for him to assume the mantle of revolutionary leadership. Ironically, it would be an attack on the Union created by the great Washington and his contemporaries, including Lee's father, that would allow Lee to become an army commander like his idol.

59. Lee to John Livingston, Oct. 20, 1854 [1st quote], Superintendents' Letter Books, USMA; Lee to George W. Cullum, Dec. 24, 1859, Lee Papers, USMA; Adams, "Personal Letters," 600 [2nd quote], 617, 628 [3rd quote], 734 [4th quote]; Jones, *Life and Letters,* 112–13; Rachal, "Lee to His Son Rooney," 4 [5th quote].

60. Adams, "Personal Letters," 741 [1st quote]; Jones, *Life and Letters,* 160; Lee to Edward Lee Childe, Oct. 31, 1853 [2nd quote], Lee Papers, SH.

3

 Granny Lee

Secession and Obscurity

Lee became a reluctant revolutionary. He revered the Union established by George Washington and his comrades and believed they could not have been so foolish as to provide for secession. To him, any attempt to nullify federal authority was revolution. This he thought any people had a right to do, but such a radical step could not be justified in 1861. After Virginia seceded, though, he accepted the decision of its convention and was hailed as Washington's successor in his home state. It was a decision immortalized by poet William G. Simms, who asked later that year,

> Art Ready for this, dear brother, who still
> Keeps't Washington's bones upon Vernon's hill?[1]

Despite this auspicious welcome, Lee's start as a revolutionary proved disappointing. He lost Arlington and was mocked as Granny Lee, a defeated commander known more for digging than fighting.

   Just as Washington had been reluctant to rebel against the British empire, Lee hesitated to endorse the dissolution of the Union created by

---

1. William G. Simms, "The Soul of the South: An Ode," *Southern Literary Messenger* 36 (Feb.–Mar. 1862): 101. This poem was first published under the pseudonym "Tyrtaeus," with the title, "The Voice of the South," in the Charleston *Mercury*. See William G. Simms, ed., *War Poetry of the South* (New York, 1867), 32.

Washington and the other Founding Fathers. In 1853 he wrote to his nephew Edward Lee Childe that the United States was "where it seems to me the human race is most elevated & ennobled." Later, he praised his nephew's father, Edward Vernon Childe, for opposing sectionalism, declaring, "I know no other country, no other government, than the *United States* & their *Constitution*." Lee welcomed James Buchanan's election as president in 1856 because it demonstrated "that the Union & the Constitution is [*sic*] triumphant." Of Buchanan, Lee wrote to his wife Mary that "I hope he will be able to extinguish fanaticism in North & South, & cultivate love for the Country & Union, & restore harmony between the different sections."[2]

The unrest of Buchanan's administration undermined Lee's faith in sectional compromise, but he still supported the Union. Stationed in Texas, far from Virginia, Lee worried as the crisis worsened. When a Texan asked his advice on a Southern filibuster into Mexico, Lee responded that federal forces along the border would best protect Texans' "rights & peace . . . in conformity to the Constitution & laws of the Country." Lee also praised Gov. Sam Houston for "his position in favor of the Constitution & Union." Ironically, Houston supported the filibusters but would be removed by the Texas secession convention for his Unionism. Observing the Democratic conventions, Lee opined that Stephen A. Douglas should endorse John C. Breckinridge in order to promote unity but added, "Politicians I fear are too selfish to be our martyrs."[3]

Lee was dismayed by the turmoil in the South after the election of Abraham Lincoln. He wrote to his eldest son Custis that "The Southern States seem to be in a convulsion." As for himself, he wrote, "I feel as if I could easily lay down my life" for the "safety" of the country. Continued protests across the South enraged Lee. He exploded in another note

2. Robert E. Lee to Edward Lee Childe, Oct. 31, 1853 [1st quote], Lee to Edward Vernon Childe, Jan. 9, 1857 [2nd quote], Robert E. Lee Papers, Jesse Ball Dupont Library, Stratford Hall, Va. [hereinafter SH]; Lee to Mary Custis Lee, Nov. 19, 1856 [3rd quote], Dec. 13, 1856 [4th quote], De Butts-Ely Collection, Library of Congress, Washington, D.C. [hereinafter LC].

3. Lee to Albert M. Lea, Mar. 1, 1860 [1st and 2nd quotes], Robert E. Lee Papers, Center for American History, University of Texas at Austin [hereinafter CAH]; Carl C. Rister, *Robert E. Lee in Texas* (Norman, Okla., 1946), 102–6; Lee to Earl Van Dorn, July 3, 1860 [3rd quote], De Butts-Ely Collection, LC.

to Custis about "the cotton states as they term themselves. In addition to their selfish & dictatorial bearing, the threats they throw out against the border states as they call them, if they will not join them, argues little for the benefit or peace of Virginia should she determine to coalesce with them." He insisted to Custis and to his cousin Annette Carter that he hoped war could be averted.[4]

While Southern states began adopting secession ordinances, Lee continued to hope they would not destroy "the Constitution & the Union established by our forefathers." On his birthday in 1861, Lee secluded himself and read Edward Everett's biography of Washington, which Mary had sent. Everett was a Massachusetts senator whose speaking tour had raised money to remodel Mount Vernon. Everett stressed Washington's love for the Union in the brief 1860 encyclopedia article that Lee read. Lee wrote to Mary that Washington's "spirit would be grieved, could he see the wreck of his mighty labors." Lee would not "believe, until all the ground for hope [had] gone, that the fruit of [Washington's] noble deeds [would] be destroyed and that his precious advice and virtuous example [would] so soon be forgotten by his countrymen."[5]

Soon after reading Everett's article, Lee responded to a note from Martha Custis Williams, his beloved "Markie." She warned him that his son Custis and her brother Orton planned to resign from the army and accept "captaincys in the Army of the Southern Republic." Lee

4. Francis R. Adams, ed., "An Annotated Edition of the Personal Letters of Robert E. Lee, April 1855–April, 1861" (Ph.D. diss., University of Maryland, 1955), 671; Lee to G. W. Custis Lee, Nov. 24, 1860 [1st–3rd quotes], Dec. 14, 1860 [4th quote], Robert E. Lee Papers, William G. Perkins Library, Duke University, Durham, N.C. [hereinafter DU]; Lee to Annette Carter, Jan. 16, 1861, Lennig Collection, Washington and Lee University Library, Lexington, Va. [hereinafter W&L]; William F. Chaney, *Duty Most Sublime: The Life of Robert E. Lee as Told through the "Carter Letters"* (Baltimore, 1996), xi, 62.

5. Lee to George W. Jones, Mar. 22, 1869 [1st quote], Robert E. Lee Letterbooks, De Butts-Ely Collection, LC; Lee to Mary Custis Lee, Jan. 23, 1861 [2nd and 3rd quotes], De Butts-Ely Collection, LC; Henry A. White, *Robert E. Lee and the Southern Confederacy, 1807–1870* (New York, 1897), 98; Fitzhugh Lee, *General Lee* (New York, 1894; reprint, Wilmington, N.C., 1989), 84; Robert W. Winston, *Robert E. Lee: A Biography* (New York, 1941), 76; George B. Forgie, *Patricide in the House Divided* (New York, 1979), 168–72; William A. Bryan, *George Washington in American Literature, 1775–1865* (New York, 1952), 78–79; Edward H. O'Neill, *A History of American Biography, 1800–1935* (Philadelphia, 1935), 166.

responded plaintively, "I am unable to realize that our people will destroy a government, inaugurated by the blood & wisdom of our patriot fathers." In a colorful aside he added, "I wish for no other flag than the Star-Spangled Banner & no other air than 'Hail Columbia.'"[6]

Lee's opposition to disunion was rooted not only in his reverence for Washington's Union, but also in his belief that the Founding Fathers would not have condoned secession. He wrote to Custis, after hearing of his plan to resign, that Washington and "all the other patriots of the Revolution" had never provided for a right of secession. He expanded upon this idea in a letter to his second son, Rooney. To Lee, it was clear that "The framers of our Constitution never exhausted so much labour, wisdom & forbearance in its formation & surrounded it with so many guards & securities if it was intended to be broken by every member of the Confederacy at will." They had intended for the Union to be "perpetual," so "It is idle to talk of secession."[7]

While Lee believed that the Founding Fathers would never have endorsed secession, he also thought that people had a right to initiate revolution if circumstances were unbearable. This of course was an idea he shared with the leaders of the Revolution and many Southerners. Jefferson Davis himself invoked the memory of the Founding Fathers in his inaugural address as president of the Confederacy. Lee declared to Annette Carter that the South's grievances must be fairly heard, and "then if the rights guaranteed by the Constitution are denied us, & the citizens of one portion of the country are granted privileges not extended to the other, we can with a clear conscience separate." This would truly be "revolution & war at last, and cannot be otherwise, so we might as well look at it in its true character." In his earlier letter to Custis, Lee had also asserted that the Founding Fathers created a government "which can only be dissolved by revolution, or the consent of all the people in convention assembled." That same day he had warned

6. Avery Craven, ed., *"To Markie": The Letters of Robert E. Lee to Martha Custis Williams from the Originals in the Huntington Library* (Cambridge, Mass., 1933) 58–59 [quotes]; Stanley F. Horn, ed., *The Robert E. Lee Reader* (Indianapolis, 1949), 90–91.

7. Adams, "Personal Letters," 721–22 [1st quote]; Lee to William H. F. Lee, Jan. 29, 1861 [2nd–4th quotes], George B. Lee Papers, Virginia Historical Society, Richmond [hereinafter VHS].

Mary that their country could soon be "dragged into the gulf of revolution."[8]

Lee's opposition to secession was thus a stand against a revolution that he believed could not be justified in early 1861. After all, Washington himself in his first inaugural address had declared that Americans had to remember the distinction between "oppression and the necessary exercise of lawful government." Lee explained to Markie: "I believe that the South justly complains of the aggressions of the North & I have believed that the North would cheerfully redress the grievances complained of. I see no cause of disunion, strife & civil war & I pray that it may be averted." He was more specific in a note to his daughter Agnes, endorsing the resolutions of John J. Crittenden as "fair & just," declaring the peace convention at Washington would find a solution, and disparaging the occupation of Federal property by Southern militia as "unnecessary."[9]

Lee was especially concerned that his sons should understand his position. He explained to Rooney, "The South in my opinion has been aggrieved by the acts of the North as you say." However, he could "anticipate no greater calamity for the country than a dissolution of the Union. It would be an assum[p]tion of all the evils we complain of." He hoped "that all constitutional means [would] be exhausted, before there is a resort to force," and added, "Secession is nothing but revolution." To Custis, Lee confessed, "there is a prospect of Virginias seceding as it is termed politely, or revolutionizing." He concluded sadly, "May God rescue us from the folly of our acts, save us from our selfishness, & teach us to love our neighbor as ourself."[10]

8. Lee to Annette Carter, Jan. 16, 1861 [1st and 2nd quotes], Lennig Collection, W&L; Chaney, *Duty Most Sublime*, 62; Adams, "Personal Letters," 721–22 [3rd quote]; Lee to Mary Custis Lee, Jan. 23, 1861 [4th quote], De Butts-Ely Collection, LC; James M. McPherson, *Battle Cry of Freedom: The Civil War Era* (New York, 1988), 240–41; James Oakes, *The Ruling Race: A History of American Slaveholders* (New York, 1982), 239–42; James D. Richardson, comp., *The Messages and Papers of Jefferson Davis and the Confederacy, 1861–1865*, 2 vols. (Washington, D.C.; reprint, New York, 1981), 1:36.

9. Arthur H. Shaffer, *The Politics of History: Writing the History of the American Revolution, 1783–1815* (Chicago, 1975), 27 [1st quote]; Craven, *"To Markie,"* 58–59 [2nd quote]; Horn, *Lee Reader*, 90–91; Lee to Agnes Lee, Jan. 29, 1861 [3rd and 4th quotes], De Butts-Ely Collection, LC.

10. Lee to William H. F. Lee, Jan. 29, 1861 [1st–4th quotes], George B. Lee Papers, VHS; William M. E. Rachal, ed., " 'Secession is Nothing But Revolution': A Letter of R. E. Lee to His Son Rooney," *Virginia Magazine of History and Biography* 69 (Jan. 1961): 5–6; Lee to Custis Lee, Jan. 30, 1861 [5th and 6th quotes], Lee Papers, DU.

Although Lee did not believe that events in 1861 justified revolution, he did make it clear that if the people of Virginia endorsed secession, he would go with them. He discussed leaving the army as early as December 1860, and he repeated this possibility during the ensuing weeks. To Custis he admitted that "a Union that can only be maintained by swords and bayonets, and in which strife and civil war are to take the place of brotherly love and kindness, has no charm for me." If the Union dissolved, he would go home "and save in defence [would] draw [his] sword on no one." He reiterated this to Rooney, adding, "As an American citizen I take great pride in my country, her prosperity & institutions, & would defend any state if her rights were invaded."[11]

Lee left Texas on orders from Gen. Winfield Scott to report to Washington. As he made his way to the coast in February 1861, he was dismayed at preparations he saw for war. He told Capt. George B. Cosby, an associate who became a Confederate brigadier general, that he hoped Virginia would not secede, the Union would be preserved, and war would be avoided. Cosby noted that Lee spoke emotionally, even tearfully. Lee was furious when Texas officials stopped him in San Antonio and demanded that he swear loyalty to the Confederacy, which he did not do. He told a friend there that if Virginia remained in the Union, then he would also. However, he added that "if she secedes (though I do not believe in secession as a constitutional right, nor is there a sufficient cause for revolution), then I will follow my native State with my sword, and, if need be, with my life." In a last communication hastily penned at a stage stop in Sutherland Springs, Lee declared that he was "unable to see a single good that [would] result from" the secession of Texas.[12]

Back at Arlington, Lee struggled to maintain a facade of normalcy. He did not arrive until early March, but he still held a dinner party to commemorate Washington's birthday. Ironically, among the guests were

11. Adams, "Personal Letters," 721–22 [1st and 2nd quotes]; Lee to William H. F. Lee, Jan. 29, 1861 [3rd quote], George B. Lee Papers, VHS; Rachal, "Letter to Rooney," 6; Craven, *"To Markie,"* 58–59; Horn, *Lee Reader,* 90–91; Lee to Custis Lee, Dec. 5, 1860, Lee Papers, DU.

12. Rister, *Lee in Texas,* 160–61; Emory M. Thomas, *Robert E. Lee: A Biography* (New York, 1995), 186–87 [1st quote]; Emory Speer, *Lincoln, Lee, Grant, and Other Biographical Addresses* (New York, 1909), 55; Margaret Sanborn, *Robert E. Lee: A Portrait* (Philadelphia, 1966), 305–6; "Lee's Farewell to Texas, February 9, 1861," *Military History of Texas and the Southwest* 14 (1978): 244–45 [2nd quote]; Charles A. Culberson, comp., *The Greatest Confederate Commander* (Washington, D.C., 1907), 12.

six future generals of the Confederate and Federal armies. He may have been reassured to learn that Lincoln in his inaugural address had reiterated his own dearly held maxim that what was afoot was revolution, and that the situation did not merit such drastic action. Lee was certainly pleased when a Virginia secession convention rejected disunion. His meetings with Scott were also reassuring, as Scott shared his aversion to civil war. Scott's orders to Lee were soothingly mundane: he would serve on a board to revise army regulations. Thus with a clear conscience Lee ignored an offer of a brigadier generalship from Confederate Secretary of War Leroy Pope Walker and accepted a promotion to colonel in the United States Army.[13]

Lee's complacency was shattered when Confederate Brig. Gen. Pierre G. T. Beauregard told his gunners to fire on Fort Sumter at Charleston, South Carolina. The Federal garrison surrendered, and Lincoln called for volunteers to crush the rebellion. The secession convention reassembled in Virginia, and the representatives' intent to leave the Union became clear. Lee went to Washington on April 18 after an invitation came from Francis P. Blair, Sr., through his cousin John F. Lee, a grandson of Richard Henry Lee who was the judge advocate general of the United States Army and brother-in-law to Blair's daughter Elizabeth. When Lee met with Blair, the latter with the endorsement of Lincoln and other prominent officials informally asked Lee to command the main Federal army at Washington.[14]

Confronted with an offer that arguably would make him a peer of Washington in rank, Lee declined. He later wrote to Reverdy Johnson that he had informed Blair "as candidly and courteously as [he] could, that, though opposed to secession and deprecating war, [he] could take

---

13. White, *Southern Confederacy,* 92–93; Thomas, *Lee,* 187; Francis MacDonnell, "The Confederate Spin on Winfield Scott and George Thomas," *Civil War History* 44 (Dec. 1998): 257; *Arlington House: A Guide to Arlington House, the Robert E. Lee Memorial, Virginia* (Washington, D.C., 1990), 37; Lee to Lorenzo Thomas, Mar. 30, 1861, Martin L. Crimmins Papers, CAH; William Allan, "Memoranda of Conversations with General Robert E. Lee," in Gary W. Gallagher, ed., *Lee the Soldier* (Lincoln, Nebr., 1996), 9–10, 12.

14. Thomas, *Lee,* 188; John Bigelow, "Robert E. Lee and Secession: A Study of Loyalty" (Typescript, 1936, John Bigelow Papers, LC), 67; Burton J. Hendrick, *The Lees of Virginia: Biography of a Family* (Boston, 1935), 430–32; J. William Jones, *Personal Reminiscences, Anecdotes, and Letters of Gen. Robert E. Lee* (New York, 1874), 357–58.

no part in an invasion of the Southern States." Blair appealed to Lee "as the representative of the Washington family & c." to accept the commission, but to no avail. Blair then asked if Lee's involvement in slavery prevented him from supporting the Federal government. Lee "indignantly" responded that if he owned every slave, he would free them all to save the Union. This was a well-rehearsed line that Lee had used in other conversations, but it did convey his point. Lee continued to hope that "some way" would be "found to save the country from the calamities of war." Rather than hinder efforts for peace, he would "pass the remainder of [his] life as a private citizen," without his wife's slaves if need be.[15]

After speaking with Blair, Lee visited Scott to tell him about his response to the offer of Federal command. Lee's mentor said that his refusal was the "greatest mistake of [his] life" and urged Lee to decide about resigning from the army, as he had spoken of doing. Lee next met with his elder brother Sydney Smith Lee, who was on assignment with the navy in the national capital. The elder Lee agreed that nothing had to be done until Virginia made a decision. None of them knew that the convention in their home state had decided that day to leave the Union.[16]

Lee endured a restless night at Arlington and then went into Alexandria, where he saw a newspaper in a local drugstore announcing the secession of Virginia. He glumly told the proprietor, "I must say I am one of those dull creatures that cannot see the good of secession." He returned to Arlington, but when it filled with guests that evening, he slipped outside to pace alone. Later, he walked the floor in his room, then wrote a one-line letter of resignation and a longer note of explanation to Scott. In the latter he wrote that he would have resigned earlier "but for the struggle it has cost me to separate myself from a service to which I have devoted all the best years of my life, & all the ability

15. Lee to Reverdy Johnson, Feb. 25, 1868 [1st quote, 4th–6th quotes], Lee Letterbooks, De Butts-Ely Collection, LC; Allan, "Memoranda," 9–10 [2nd quote], 12; Armistead L. Long, *Memoirs of Robert E. Lee* (New York, 1886), 92 [3rd quote]; Jones, *Personal Reminiscences*, 142; Thomas, *Lee*, 188; Bigelow, "Lee and Secession," 70; William E. Brooks, *Lee of Virginia: A Biography* (Garden City, N.Y., 1932), 85; Joseph P. B. Wilmer, *Gen'l. Robert E. Lee: An Address Delivered before the Students of the University of the South, October 15, 1870* (Nashville, 1872), 7.

16. Thomas, *Lee*, 188 [quote]; Bigelow, "Lee and Secession," 73.

I possessed." Markie's brother Orton, who remained on Scott's staff, delivered Lee's notes on April 20.[17]

Having resigned from the army, Lee wrote to several family members to explain himself. To his sister Ann, whose husband and son supported the Union, he declared, "The whole South is in a state of revolution, into which Virginia, after a long struggle, has been drawn." He could still see "no necessity for this state of things and would have forborne and pleaded to the end for redress of grievances, real or supposed," he wrote, "yet in my own person I had to meet the question, whether I should take part against my native state." Regarding his decision, he asserted, "With all my devotion to the Union, and the feeling of loyalty and duty of an American citizen, I have not been able to make up my mind to raise my hand against my relatives, my children, my home." Thus he had resigned, adding, "save in defence of my native state, I hope I may never be called upon to draw my sword." These same lines filled letters to his brother Smith and his cousin Roger Jones, a young lieutenant who had served briefly as a member of the faculty at West Point while Lee was superintendent.[18]

Lee did not offer any advice to family or friends, nor did he resent Virginians who did not follow Washington's example by supporting the new revolution, such as Scott. Scott had been effusive in his praise of Lee as "the greatest living soldier in America" and allegedly had said that if he died, Lee should be given command of the army. This regard was mutual. As late as May 1861, Lee and Scott exchanged messages asking each other to work against war. On July 4 of that same year, a father and his young son gave Lee a Bible. Prompted by his father, the boy declared that Lee would "whip" Scott. Lee corrected the child, insisting that Scott was a "great and good soldier." Perhaps to ease his rebuke, Lee later gave the boy a gift: George W. P. Custis' *Recollections*

17. Clifford Dowdey and Louis H. Manarin, eds., *The Wartime Papers of Robert E. Lee* (Boston, 1961), 8–9; John S. Mosby, *The Memoirs of Colonel John S. Mosby*, ed. Charles W. Russell (Boston, 1917; reprint, Bloomington, Ind., 1959), 379 [1st quote]; Lee to Winfield Scott, Apr. 20, 1861 [2nd quote], De Butts-Ely Collection, LC; Lee to Simon Cameron, Apr. 20, 1861, Crimmins Papers, CAH; Speer, *Biographical Addresses*, 60–61.

18. Lee to Ann K. L. Marshall, Apr. 20, 1861 [quotes], Mrs. Mason Barret Collection, Howard-Tilton Library, Tulane University, New Orleans; Thomas, *Lee*, 188; Dowdey and Manarin, *Wartime Papers*, 10; Lee to Roger Jones, Apr. 20, 1861, Robert E. Lee Papers, United States Military Academy Library and Archives, West Point, N.Y.

and Private Memoirs of General Washington. Four years later, after reading Scott's autobiography, Lee wrote to Mary, "The General, of course, stands out prominently, and does not hide his light under a bushel, but he appears the bold, sagacious, truthful man that he is."[19]

Lee did not wait for official acceptance of his resignation before taking the final steps in becoming a revolutionary. The shadow of Washington and his generation lay heavily upon him as he assumed command of Virginia's new revolutionary army. The Alexandria *Gazette* urged his appointment because his name was known for its "revolutionary and patriotic associations." He went with John Robertson to Richmond on April 22, understanding that he would be presented to the convention as their commander. After they arrived in Richmond, Lee took a walk. His destination was the capitol, where an equestrian statue of Washington stood on the grounds. He went to Gov. John Letcher's office, the same that Light-Horse Harry had occupied, and accepted Letcher's proposal to nominate him. Led to the rotunda to await his presentation to the convention, Lee stood under the gaze of Jean Antoine Houdon's life-size statue of Washington, the only image of him made from life and revered as the best likeness. John Critcher, chosen to lead Lee before the convention, noticed that Lee stared hard at the statue. Just before they went before the delegates, Lee quietly said, "I hope we have seen the last of secession."[20]

While Lee waited, the secession convention quickly agreed to his appointment. Many delegates had been among the legislators who less

19. "Tributes to General Lee," *Southern Magazine* 8 (Jan. 1871): 5, 37; J. William Jones, "The Friendship between Lee and Scott," *Southern Historical Society Papers* 11 (1883): 424–26 [1st quote]; Thomas W. Bullitt, "Lee and Scott," *Southern Historical Society Papers* 11 (1883): 446; Jones, *Personal Reminiscences,* 409–10 [2nd and 3rd quotes]; Dowdey and Manarin, *Wartime Papers,* 918 [4th quote]; Emily V. Mason, *Popular Life of Gen. Robert E. Lee* (Baltimore, 1870), 382; J. William Jones, *Life and Letters of Robert Edward Lee, Soldier and Man* (New York, 1906), 127–29.

20. Speer, *Biographical Addresses,* 60–61; MacDonnell, "Confederate Spin," 257–58; Richmond *Enquirer,* Apr. 25, 1861 [1st quote]; W. W. Scott, "Some Personal Memories of General Robert E. Lee," *William and Mary Quarterly* 6 [2nd Series] (Oct. 1926): 278–82; Gene Smith, *Lee and Grant: A Dual Biography* (Norwalk, Conn., 1984), 99–100; Douglas S. Freeman, *R. E. Lee: A Biography,* 4 vols. (New York, 1934), 1:447–48; Clifford Dowdey, *Lee* (Boston, 1965), 141–42; Thomas, *Lee,* 189; Mosby, *Memoirs,* 379 [2nd quote]; R. Walton Moore, "General Washington and Houdon," *Virginia Magazine of History and Biography* 41 (Jan. 1933): 5–8.

than a month earlier had appropriated one thousand dollars to move Light-Horse Harry's remains from Cumberland Island to the Virginia Military Institute. The war interrupted this effort, but they were happy to accept his son to lead their new revolution. The command was formally tendered to Lee by John Janney, president of the convention. Lee stood as Janney recalled "the statesmen, the soldiers and sages of bygone days, who have borne your name, and whose blood flows in your veins," adding that when it became apparent that Virginia needed a military leader, "all hearts and all eyes . . . turned to the old county of Westmoreland," the birthplace of Washington and Lee. Paraphrasing Light-Horse Harry's eulogy of Washington, Janney said to Lee that he hoped "that it will soon be said of you, that you are 'first in peace,' and when that time comes you will have earned the still prouder distinction of being 'first in the hearts of your countrymen.' "[21]

In a response that editor Edward A. Pollard recalled as being "Washington-like in its modesty," Lee accepted command of Virginia's new revolutionary army. A single sentence comprised his brief acceptance: "Trusting to Almighty God, an approving conscience & the aid of my fellow-citizens, I will devote myself to the service & defence of my native State, in whose behalf alone would I have ever drawn my sword." He had used the phrase about his sword many times, and Janney's welcome revealed one possible source for it. Janney recounted that when Washington wrote his will, he gave swords to five of his nephews, with the charge "that they should never be drawn from their scabbards except in self-defence, or in defence of the rights and principles of their country." Lee thus accepted "Washington's mantle" with words associated with him, but certainly some who were present also knew that such words were included in the oath sworn by cadets at West Point and by any person who received an army commission.[22]

Virginia's secession and subsequent call to service were not wel-

21. Thomas, *Lee*, 193; Dowdey and Manarin, *Wartime Papers*, 5 [quotes]; Freeman, *Lee*, 1:466–67; Fitzhugh Lee, *General Lee*, 91; William P. Snow, *Lee and His Generals: Their Lives and Campaigns* (New York, 1867; reprint, New York, 1982), 43; William Couper, "War and Work," *Proceedings of the Rockbridge Historical Society* 1 (1939–41): 32; "Robert E. Lee: Virginia Chooses Her Leader," *Virginia Magazine of History and Biography* 30 (Apr. 1922): 108–10.

22. Edward A. Pollard, *The Early Life, Campaigns, and Public Services of Robert E. Lee* (New York, 1871), 55 [1st quote]; Thomas, *Lee*, 193; Dowdey and Manarin, *Wartime Papers*, 5 [3rd quote], 11 [2nd quote]; Freeman, *Lee*, 1:467–68; White, *Southern Confed-*

comed by Lee, but he could not refuse. When Virginia declared her independence from the British empire, Washington accepted the role of revolutionary leader. When Virginia again engaged in a revolution less than a century later, what alternative did a man raised in his shadow have? And who was more qualified to be the new Washington? For Lee, the answers clearly provided a mandate. Concerning his military oath, Lee well knew that Washington had also violated his pledge as a militia officer. He wrote to Beauregard in 1865, "I need not tell you, that true patriotism requires of men sometimes, to act exactly contrary at one period, to that which it does at another; & that the motive which impels them, viz. the desire to do right, is precisely the same." Washington "at one time . . . fought against the French, under Braddock, in the service of the King of Great Britain; at another he fought with the French at Yorktown, under the orders of the Continental Congress of America, against him."[23] Washington had made his decision, and Lee, like his father, followed his idol's example.

Mary fully endorsed Lee's decision, but not all members of his family followed Washington as he did. Those closest to him did join the Confederate cause, but some Lees did not. His brother Smith resigned from the United States Navy and joined the Confederate naval forces, and their eldest brother Charles Carter Lee served in a militia detachment. Robert E. Lee's two eldest sons, Custis and Rooney, became major generals, as did Smith's son Fitzhugh. Robert E. Lee, Jr., joined the Rockford Artillery and later his brother Rooney's staff. Lee tried to convince his namesake to stay in college and not enlist, but when the boy insisted, he accompanied him to get his equipment. Meanwhile, cousin Samuel P. Lee, a grandson of Richard Henry Lee, became a Federal rear admiral, and his brother John F. Lee remained judge advocate general of the Federal army until his removal.[24]

Installed as commander, Lee outlined a strategy that recalled the Revo-

---

eracy, 103; Snow, *Lee and His Generals,* 44; Fitzhugh Lee, *General Lee,* 91–92; Eugene E. Prussing, *The Estate of George Washington, Deceased* (Boston, 1927), 59–60; "Virginia Chooses Her Leader," 110; Joseph L. Harsh, *Confederate Tide Rising: Robert E. Lee and the Making of Southern Strategy, 1861–1862* (Kent, Ohio, 1998), 73 [4th quote].

23. Lee to Pierre G. T. Beauregard, Oct. 3, 1865, Lee Letterbooks, De Butts-Ely Collection, LC [quotes]; Jones, *Life and Letters,* 390.

24. Mary Custis Lee to Ralph R. Gurley, n.d. [1861], Robert E. Lee Papers, University of Virginia Library, Charlottesville [hereinafter UVA]; Thomas, *Lee,* 250; Jennings C. Wise, *Robert E. Lee: Unionist* (Harrisburg, Pa., 1927), 8–9; Hendrick, *Lees of Virginia,*

lution. He received a letter through his cousin Cassius F. Lee, a Unionist with whom he had spoken before going to Richmond. Cassius enclosed an emotional inquiry from James May, who asked that if Virginia had given "us our original independence through her Washington," as well as "our National Constitution through Jefferson, Madison & others," could "she not now, while we are threatened with the immeasurable evils of civil war, give us through Col. Lee, peace?" Lee responded that "no earthly act would give me so much pleasure, as to restore peace to my country. But I fear it is now out of the power of man, & in God alone must be our trust." About strategy, Lee added, "I think our policy should be purely on the defensive. To resist aggression & allow time to allay the passions & allow reason to resume her sway."[25] Confronted like Washington by a superior foe, Lee would focus on outlasting the enemy's will to win and hope for a plea for negotiations.

As he organized Virginia's defenses, Lee kept the example of the Revolution in mind. He clearly understood that the nation would "have to pass through a terrible ordeal before peace is again established." But, as he explained to John Imboden, "I believe we can succeed in establishing our independence, if the people can be made to comprehend at the outset that they must endure a longer war and far greater privations than our forefathers did in the Revolution of 1776." Interestingly, Virginians drilled at Camp Lee, named for Light-Horse Harry, and Lee adopted the appearance of Washington. Like his idol, Lee wore the uniform of a colonel throughout the war. In another "manifestation of his ambition and self-perception," Lee also cultivated a reserved facade worthy of the aloof Washington. Mary Chesnut wrote after her first view of Lee, "He looks so cold and quiet and grand."[26]

430–32; Thomas, *Lee*, 217; Jones, *Personal Reminiscences*, 357–58, 397; Jones, *Life and Letters*, 229; Fitzhugh Lee, *General Lee*, 132; Lee to Mary Custis Lee, Mar. 15, 1862, De Butts-Ely Collection, LC; Edmund J. Lee, *Lee of Virginia, 1642–1892* (Philadelphia, 1895; reprint, Baltimore, 1983), 396, 399.

25. Cassius F. Lee to Lee, Apr. 23, 1861 [1st–3rd quotes], Lee to Cassius F. Lee, Apr. 25, 1861 [4th and 5th quotes], Edmund J. Lee Papers, SH; "The Spirit of 1861: Correspondence of General R. E. Lee," *Southern Historical Society Papers* 6 (1878): 91–94; Harsh, *Confederate Tide Rising*, 187; Bigelow, "Lee and Secession," 88; Edmund J. Lee, *Lee of Virginia*, 416–20.

26. Lee to Hugh M. Mercer, May 3, 1861, William K. Bixby Papers, Washington University, St. Louis, Mo. [1st quote]; Gamaliel Bradford, *Lee the American* (Boston, 1912; rev. ed., Cambridge, Mass., 1929), 87; John D. Imboden, "Reminiscences of Lee and Jack-

While preparing for war, Lee also labored to protect his family's Washington relics. Days after accepting his Virginia commission, he wrote to Mary that she should prepare to move to a safer place than Arlington. He specifically told her that the "Mt. Vernon plate & pictures ought to be secured." He repeated his admonition on April 30, adding "The war may last 10 years." He suggested that some objects should be stored at Ravensworth, the residence of Anna Maria Fitzhugh. Because it lay deeper in Virginia, Lee thought that Ravensworth would be safer.[27]

Mary refused at first to leave Arlington but began sending its relics to more secure hiding places. On May 5, she wrote to her daughter Mildred that the "silver & valuables" had been sent to Richmond, while other items had been shipped to Ravensworth. The "valuables" included chests of Washington's papers. Mary removed paintings from frames and rolled them for transport to Ravensworth. Washington's bed, along with carpets and drapes, including a set that belonged to Martha Washington, went into the attic at Arlington. Books were locked in closets. What remained of Martha's dishes and Cincinnati china as well as Washington's punch bowl and other relics were put in the cellar or buried.[28]

Lee received the chests at Richmond and had to decide where to put

---

son," *Galaxy* 12 (Nov. 1871): 628 [2nd quote]; Louis H. Manarin, "Lee in Command: Strategical and Tactical Policies . . . ," (Ph.D. diss., Duke University, 1965), 16–18, 57; Couper, "War and Work," 27; George W. P. Custis, *Recollections and Private Memoirs of Washington,* ed. Mary C. Lee (Washington, D.C., 1859), 5; Edward D. C. Campbell, Jr., "The Fabric of Command: R. E. Lee, Confederate Insignia, and the Perception of Rank," *Virginia Magazine of History and Biography* 98 (Apr. 1990): 261–90 [3rd quote]; C. Vann Woodward, ed., *Mary Chesnut's Civil War* (New Haven, Conn., 1981), 116 [4th quote]. Herman Hattaway speculates that Lee's adoption of the same insignia as Washington was "*perhaps,* an act of *extreme* egotism" (Hattaway's italics) as he sought to identify with his idol. See *Shades of Blue and Gray: An Introductory Military History of the Civil War* (Columbia, Mo., 1997), 59–60.

27. Dowdey and Manarin, *Wartime Papers,* 13 [1st quote], 15 [2nd quote], 18; Adams, "Personal Letters," 65.

28. Fitzhugh Lee, *General Lee,* 94; Mary Custis Lee to Mildred Childe Lee, May 5, 1861 [1st quote], De Butts-Ely Collection, LC; Nancy S. Anderson and Dwight Anderson, *The Generals: Ulysses S. Grant and Robert E. Lee* (New York, 1988), 244–45; Mary P. Coulling, *Lee Girls* (Winston-Salem, N.C., 1987), 86–87; Mary Custis Lee to Lee, May 9, 1861, Lee Family Papers, VHS; Rose M. E. MacDonald, *Mrs. Robert E. Lee* (Boston, 1939), 150; Eleanor L. Templeman, "Cincinnati Export Porcelain: The Washington and Lee Services," *Art and Antiques* 5 (Jan. 1982): 76.

them. They would not be safe in the Confederate capital, so he sent most of the trove to the Virginia Military Institute in Lexington, where they were hidden and later buried, under the direction of Commandant Francis H. Smith, as Lee carefully explained to Mary in case she had to retrieve them without him. He kept only his personal papers and a single Washington relic: a sword once owned by General Washington. The provenance of this weapon is uncertain; Washington allegedly gave the one he carried in the Revolution to Nathaniel Greene, and he left others to his nephews in his will. However, Lee "showed with great pride" a "plain and dull" sword to a young lady after the Civil War. He told her that it had been presented to Washington during or after the Revolution, that George W. P. Custis had donated it to the Patent Office, that the government had presented it to him after the Mexican War, and that he had kept it with him during the Civil War.[29]

Mary complied with Lee's wishes concerning the Washington relics, but she stubbornly stayed at Arlington. She was finally convinced by Orton Williams, who served as a liaison with Scott, that the Federals would occupy Arlington, and so she left. She and her daughters stayed with family for the rest of the summer. Mary intended to return, but the house was occupied by Federals about ten days after she departed. Lee sympathized with her, but he also wrote that she should understand that it would not be "prudent or right" to go back "while the United States troops occupy that country." In spite of his warning, Mary applied for permission to visit the estate and was refused. In a fury, she wrote to the commander at Arlington, informing him that she had been "*incredulous*" when told by "an anxious friend" to hide her treasures and now was outraged to learn that she had lost some of those and her home as well. She asked that the slaves be allowed to continue "their usual occupations unmolested," and for him "to permit my maid Marcellina to send me some small articles that I did not bring away." Trying to protect what was not secured, she added there was "nothing at Arlington in any

29. Lee to Mary Custis Lee, May 8 and 11, 1861, De Butts-Ely Collection, LC; Lee to Francis H. Smith, July 4, 1864, Mary Custis Lee to Francis H. Smith, Mar. 30, [1865], Sara Henderson Smith Papers, VHS; Couper, "War and Work," 34, 36, 39–40; Dowdey and Manarin, *Wartime Papers,* 769; Custis, *Recollections,* 13; Long, *Memoirs of Lee,* 469 [quotes]; Prussing, *Estate of Washington,* 481–83; Custis, *Recollections,* 159–60.

way connected with the public or domestic life of the father of his country."[30]

Maj. Gen. Irvin McDowell had established his headquarters at Arlington, and he answered Mary in a note that was—no doubt infuriatingly—addressed from her own house. He assured her that her slaves were being allowed their freedom and that the home was well kept. The officer in charge of the house had been given careful orders, and McDowell assured Mary, "When you desire to return, every facility will be given you for so doing." He also pointed out that Scott had ordered that if the Lee family still occupied Arlington, a guard was to be posted and no soldier was to enter the home. In keeping with that directive, McDowell had at first refused to enter the house. When he was compelled by duties to do so, he kept the cellar and attic sealed, perhaps concerned that Mary was not being entirely truthful concerning the items she left behind in her haste.[31]

Despite McDowell's efforts to guard the Washington relics and the valiant attempts of Lee's relatives to rescue them, many items were stolen by Federals. Mary never returned to Arlington during the war, but Britannia Kennon, Markie's aunt who had been a bridesmaid at the Lees' wedding, rescued carpets and drapes and took them to her Georgetown home for safekeeping. Markie herself retrieved Custis' painting of Washington at Monmouth, which had hung in the nation's Capitol, and stored it at the house she shared with her aunt. Meanwhile, the Washington punch bowl, some of Martha Washington's china, and other items were sold openly by Federal soldiers and freedmen. Caleb Lyon sent some Cincinnati dishes to the Patent Office for safekeeping, but

30. Mary Custis Lee to Lee, May 12, 1861, Lee Family Papers, VHS; Coulling, *Lee Girls,* 86, 89, 92–93; MacDonald, *Mrs. Lee,* 148–49; Mary Custis Lee to Ralph P. Gurley, n.d. [1861], Lee Papers, UVA; Fitzhugh Lee, *General Lee,* 99; White, *Southern Confederacy,* 108; Lee to Mary Custis Lee, May 25, 1861 [1st and 2nd quotes], De Butts-Ely Collection, LC; Mary Custis Lee to —— Sanford, May 30, 1861 [3rd–6th quotes], Enoch A. Chase Papers, VHS; Thomas, *Lee,* 195–96; Snow, *Lee and His Generals,* 39 [7th quote]; Winston, *Lee,* 112.

31. Irvin McDowell to Mary Custis Lee, May 30, 1861, Chase Papers, VHS; Snow, *Lee and His Generals,* 40; *The War of the Rebellion: A Compilation of the Official Records of the Union and Confederate Armies,* 130 vols. (Washington, D.C., 1880–1902), ser. I, vol. 2:655 [hereinafter *OR*].

kept others. The only known painting of Lee's mother, which may have hung at Arlington, was found years later in Italy, and another relative's portrait that belonged to the Lees was found in the cellar at Mount Vernon at about the same time.[32]

McDowell was distressed by the looting and decided to have the remaining Washington relics taken to the Patent Office. An expert, perhaps Lyon, was brought to the house and allowed to identify objects. He found some of Martha Washington's china, as well as the Cincinnati dishes. Two vases and the foyer lamp from Mount Vernon were also located, along with Martha's tea table and her husband's bookcase. Most of these treasures arrived at the Patent Office and were later sent to the national museum, whence they were returned to the family by order of President William F. McKinley in 1901. When Markie visited Arlington in the summer of 1862 to retrieve what remained of the home's contents, she found very little of value. She wrote to Mary that it was a "sad, sad visit," as she found much evidence of deterioration. Lincoln's secretary, John Nicolay, and a reporter had visited Arlington in May 1861 and found the place full of furniture and pictures; when Nicolay returned in 1864, he discovered the home was empty.[33]

The occasion for Nicolay's return to Arlington was the establishment of a national cemetery on the grounds on June 15, 1864. In January of that year, the residence had been sold at auction to the Federal government for nonpayment of taxes. A relative of the Lees tried to pay the taxes, but the effort was refused by Federal authorities. By 1864 the Lees would have been appalled at the condition of their home. Fortifications had been built near the house, which was used as a hospital, and the

32. Edward Lee Childe, *The Life and Campaigns of General Lee,* trans. George Litte (London, 1875), 33, 165; Karl Decker and Angus McSween, *Historic Arlington: A History of the National Cemetery from Its Establishment to the Present Time* (Washington, D.C., 1892), 43, 60; Coulling, *Lee Girls,* 172; Thomas L. Connelly, *The Marble Man: Robert E. Lee and His Image in American Society* (Baton Rouge, 1977), 125; *Arlington House,* 38; Templeman, "Cincinnati Export Porcelain," 76–77; Francis A. MacNutt, "A Lee Miscellany: Portrait of Mrs. Anne Hill (Carter) Lee," *Virginia Magazine of History and Biography* 33 (Jan. 1925): 371; Charleston *Mercury,* June 9, 1863.

33. Snow, *Lee and His Generals,* 40; Coulling, *Lee Girls,* 95; Freeman, *Lee,* 1:105; MacDonald, *Mrs. Lee,* 31, 211; Jones, *Life and Letters,* 87–88; Templeman, "Cincinnati Export Porcelain," 77; Margaret Sanborn, *Robert E. Lee: The Complete Man* (Philadelphia, 1967), 83 [quote]; New York *Herald,* May 29, 1861; Philip Van Doren Stern, *Robert E. Lee, the Man and the Soldier: A Pictorial Biography* (New York, 1963), 185.

woods popularly known as "Washington's Forest" on Four Mile Run, which had been bequeathed to Lee's father-in-law by the first president, had been leveled. There was also a freedmen's village on the grounds that remained through the end of the century. The War Department began burying its dead there, and the site became a national cemetery with 5,291 graves around the home by 1865. The Lees' shrine to Washington had become a charnel house.[34]

Lee certainly was not aware of the future of Arlington in 1861, but the loss of it and the danger posed to the Washington relics pained him. He wrote to Mary on May 11, 1861, "It is sad to think of the devastation, if not ruin, [war] may bring upon a spot so endeared to us." McDowell's actions offered some hope, but by late June Lee admitted to Mary, "There is no saying when you can return to your home, or what may be its condition when you do return." He tried to inject Revolutionary levity into the situation, writing to his daughter Mildred that her cat, left behind, "no doubt lords it in a high manner over the British at Arlington." Nevertheless, the sad reality was, as he repeated to his wife in October 1861, "There is no prospect of your returning to Arlington."[35]

The loss of Arlington embittered Lee. On Christmas Day, 1861, he wrote to Mary that if Arlington was not yet destroyed, "it is vain to think of it being in a habitable condition." He continued, "I fear . . . books, furniture, & the relics of Mount Vernon will be gone. It is better to make up our minds to a general loss." He assured her that their memories of the place "will remain to us as long as life will last," but urged her to accept that the home was gone forever. In a burst of defiance he concluded, "They cannot take away the remembrances of the spot, &

34. Decker and McSween, *Historic Arlington*, 61–67, 69, 76, 79, 82; MacDonald, *Mrs. Lee,* 173; White, *Southern Confederacy,* 443; *Arlington House,* 7, 31; Prussing, *Estate of Washington,* 226–30; Felix James, "The Establishment of Freedman's Village in Arlington, Virginia," *Negro History Bulletin* 33 (Mar. 1970): 90–93; Joseph P. Reidy, "'Coming From the Shadows of the Past': The Transition from Slavery to Freedom at Freedmen's Village, 1863–1900," *Virginia Magazine of History and Biography* 95 (Oct. 1987): 409–27; Ervin L. Jordan, Jr., *Black Confederates and Afro-Yankees in Civil War Virginia* (Charlottesville, Va., 1995), 86–87.

35. Lee to Mary Custis Lee, May 11 [1st quote], June 11, 24 [2nd quote], Oct. 7 [4th quote], 1861, Lee to "My Precious Life" [Mildred Childe Lee], June 29, 1861 [3rd quote], De Butts-Ely Collection, LC; Dowdey and Manarin, *Wartime Papers,* 55.

the memories of those that to us render it sacred." That same day he sent an angrier note to a daughter, asserting that "Your old home, if not destroyed by our enemies, has been so desecrated that I cannot bear to think of it." He added, "I should have preferred it to have been wiped from the earth, its beautiful hill sunk, and its sacred trees buried, rather than to have been degraded by the presence of those who revel in the ill that they do for their own selfish purposes."[36]

Lee tried to maintain his Washingtonian facade regarding Arlington, but the mask occasionally slipped. He wrote to his eldest son Custis in January 1862 that "Every thing at Arlington will I fear be lost," but he added that "if honour & independence is left us I will be content." On Christmas Day in 1863 Lee spoke with Fitzgerald Ross, an English military observer, about the dislocation of Virginians by the Federals. When Ross mentioned the loss of Arlington, Lee brushed the remark aside, saying, "That I can easily understand, and for that I don't care; but I do feel sorry for the poor creatures I see here starved and driven from their homes for no reason whatever." His Christmas 1862 letter to Mary, though, echoed the bitter emotions of a year earlier. British general Garnet J. Wolseley noted that "tears filled his eyes" when Lee talked about the loss of Arlington and the "reckless plunder" of the Washington relics.[37]

While her husband seethed, Mary settled at another home with strong Washington ties: White House. Left to her son Rooney by her father, the estate on the Peninsula southeast of Richmond had belonged to Martha Washington. Mary explained to a friend, "My grandmother was living there when she first met Genl Washington at the house of a neighbor & they were married at the old English church of St Peters quite near, but only remain[ed] a short time at the White House as Genl Washington soon removed to Mount Vernon which had recently been

36. Lee to Mary Custis Lee, Dec. 25, 1861 [1st–4th quotes], De Butts-Ely Collection, LC; Dowdey and Manarin, *Wartime Papers*, 96; Jones, *Personal Reminiscences*, 385–86; Mason, *Popular Life*, 90–91; Jones, *Life and Letters*, 156 [5th and 6th quotes]; Edmund J. Lee, *Lee of Virginia*, 438.

37. Lee to Custis Lee, Jan. 19, 1862 [1st and 2nd quotes], Lee Papers, DU; Fitzgerald Ross, *A Visit to the Cities and Camps of the Confederate States* (London, 1865), 169 [3rd quote]; Dowdey and Manarin, *Wartime Papers,* 381; Garnet J. Wolseley, "General Lee," in Gallagher, *Lee the Soldier,* 98–99 [4th and 5th quotes]; Charleston *Mercury,* June 9, 1863.

left him by his brother." Mary's reference to Martha, her great-grand-mother, as "grandmother" and her omission of the fact that the original house had burned indicate a strong identification of herself and the home with the Washingtons, which her husband shared. Before March 1860, when she visited Rooney, she had not seen the house in thirty-five years, but Lee inspected it in April 1861 and suggested that she settle there. Mary arrived in the fall of 1861 and remained with Rooney's wife and children and several Lee daughters.[38]

Having lost Arlington, Lee briefly contemplated acquiring Stratford, another home that had strong Revolutionary associations for him. Learning that two daughters, Anne and Agnes, had visited his birth-place, Lee wrote to them in November 1861 that "It is endeared to me by recollections & it has always been a great desire of my life to be able to purchase it." He readily admitted that "Now that we have no other home, & the one we so loved has been so foully polluted, the desire is stronger with me than ever." In his Christmas letter to Mary that year, he wrote again that he wanted to buy Stratford, the only place available "that would inspire me with feelings of pleasure & local love." Mary clearly did not share her husband's interest in Stratford, which faded as his war-related concerns increased.[39]

While enduring the loss of Arlington, Lee also confronted disappoint-ment as the Confederacy proved slow to appoint him to combat com-mand. Initially, he focused on preparing Virginia's army, insisting to President Jefferson Davis that such a task was "satisfactory." By the end of May 1861, Lee had 40,000 men in the field. Some welcomed the opportunity to fight under a new Washington. James P. Smith remem-bered that Jack Thornton, a delegate to the secession convention, made a speech in which he said that Westmoreland County had provided Washington to lead Virginia in its "first revolution" and now sent Lee

---

38. Horn, *Reader,* 207–8; Mary Custis Lee to ———, Dec. 22, 1869 [quote], Gratz Collection, Historical Society of Pennsylvania, Philadelphia; Snow, *Lee and His Generals,* 53; Dowdey, *Lee,* 176; MacDonald, *Mrs. Lee,* 159; Mary Custis Lee to E. G. W. Butler, Mar. 1860, Lee Papers, DU; Robert E. Lee, Jr., *Recollections and Letters of General Robert E. Lee* (New York, 1904), 35; Allan, "Memoranda," 10; Lee to Agnes Lee, Apr. 14, 1860, Robert E. Lee Papers, Special Collections, Lehigh University, Bethlehem, Pa.

39. Dowdey and Manarin, *Wartime Papers,* 88–89 [1st and 2nd quotes], 96; Lee to Anne Carter Lee and Agnes Lee, Nov. 22, 1861, Lee to Mary Custis Lee, Dec. 25, 1861 [3rd quote], De Butts-Ely Collection, LC.

to command in a "second revolution." Smith recalled, "It thrilled me to think that Virginia had found another Washington." Lee included a real Washington on his staff: John A. Washington, his cousin who lived at Mount Vernon. The grandnephew of Lee's idol and executor of his estate, as well as a great-grandson of Richard Henry Lee, Washington was the focus of rumors in the North that he had moved his great-uncle's body from Mount Vernon to a place safe from Yankee intruders.[40]

The admission of Virginia to the Confederacy, ratified by the voters of that state on May 23, compelled Lee to transfer his troops and himself to the authority of the new government. This came as no surprise; on the day he got his Virginia commission, he had met with Vice President Alexander Stephens and assured him that he would cooperate fully. Lee may have thought of Stephens as a soul mate; the diminutive statesman had made a speech in Richmond that same day asserting that the North had pushed the South into "revolution." Stephens had also expressed the hope that "the principles that Washington fought for" would be restored and asked Virginians to fight to protect the "tomb of Washington" from "desecration." Lee had been appointed a brigadier general of the Confederacy on May 14 and two days later received the rank of general from the Confederate Congress. His relationship with Davis suffered a setback when Lee, rather than go himself, sent his old friend Joseph E. Johnston to report on Virginia to the president. Davis recovered from the slight, however, and the two soon developed a "solid, professional working relationship."[41]

40. Dowdey and Manarin, *Wartime Papers,* 21 [1st quote]; Thomas, *Lee,* 194–95; Lee to Edward Waln, Feb. 21, 1870, Lee Letterbooks, De Butts-Ely Collection, LC; Robert E. Lee, Jr., *Recollections,* 40; Hendrick, *Lees of Virginia,* 365, 431; Walter H. Taylor, *Four Years with General Lee* (New York, 1877; reprint, New York, 1962), vi–vii, 200; Sallie W. S. Hoover, "Col. John Augustine Washington, C.S.A.," *Confederate Veteran* 34 (Mar. 1926): 96; New York *Herald,* May 15, 1861; James P. Smith, "With Stonewall Jackson in the Army of Northern Virginia," *Southern Historical Society Papers* 43 (1920): 4–5 [2nd–4th quotes]; Frank Moore, ed., *The Rebellion Record: A Diary of American Events,* 12 vols. (New York, 1861–1868; reprint, New York, 1977), 1: "Poetry and Incidents," 127–28.

41. Jones, *Personal Reminiscences,* 167; Freeman, *Lee,* 1:501, 559; Dowdey and Manarin, *Wartime Papers,* 44; Thomas, *Lee,* 198; Moore, *Rebellion Record,* 1: "Documents," 134–35 [1st–4th quotes]; Joseph T. Glatthaar, *Partners in Command: The Relationships Between Leaders in the Civil War* (New York, 1993), 227 [5th quote]; Steven

Lee was apparently unclear about his status as his troops entered Confederate service. He certainly was not being hailed as a second Washington by the national administration. Davis did not discuss his commission, believing that Lee would assume the rank conferred on him by the Confederate Congress. Lee apparently was unaware of the commission, however, and the day after he transferred his units, he declared to Mary that he would "like to retire to private life, so that I could be with you & the children, but if I can be of service to the state or her cause, I must continue." He even prepared to disband his staff and join Rooney's cavalry company as a private before notice of his appointment arrived. He appeared content to become Davis' advisor. When Mary prodded him to ask for the rank of "commander in chief of the Southern army," he explained that he had "never heard" of such a position, nor did he have "any expectation or wish for it." In fact, Washington had held such a title, but the Confederate system bestowed that power upon Davis as president. Lee and Mary had to be content with less for the time being.[42]

The uncertainty of Lee's status was due at least in part to the fact that he remained unknown to many in the summer of 1861. Furthermore, his focus on defense and rejection of schemes such as a march on Baltimore led to rumors that he was not committed to the cause. His insistence that the war would be long and costly was not what many people wanted to hear, and some suggested that he should be replaced. The person on whom Lee could rely was Davis, who readily accepted his advice. Lee toured the lines at Manassas, saw the importance of the place, and advised sending Beauregard there as commander. Davis agreed and then supported Lee when he rejected Beauregard's proposal to advance on Washington. When McDowell marched south from Arlington in July 1861, he encountered Confederates at Manassas in positions devised by Lee and supported by the arrival of reinforcements led by Johnston that

---

E. Woodworth, *Davis and Lee at War* (Lawrence, Kans., 1994), 153; Joseph L. Harsh, *Confederate Tide Rising: Robert E. Lee and the Making of Southern Strategy, 1861–1862* (Kent, Ohio, 1998), 51; Jefferson Davis, *Robert E. Lee,* ed. Harold B. Simpson (Hillsboro, Tex., 1966), 6.

42. Lee to Mary Custis Lee, June 9, 1861 [1st quote], De Butts-Ely Collection, LC; Jones, *Personal Reminiscences,* 168; Jones, *Life and Letters,* 164; Fitzhugh Lee, *General Lee,* 108 [2nd–4th quotes]; Freeman, *Lee,* 1:559; Thomas, *Lee,* 204.

Lee had recommended. Lee stayed in Richmond during the battle, which aggravated him, but the victory pleased him.[43]

Seven days after the battle at Manassas, Lee got his field command. On July 28, he traveled to western Virginia to inspect the defenses there as a consultant. His retinue included four others: two slaves, his distant cousin Walter H. Taylor, serving as an aide, and John A. Washington. The latter two shared Lee's tent. Lee happily wrote to Mary in early August, asking her to tell Washington's daughter "that her father is sitting on his blanket sewing the strap on his haversack. I think she ought to be here to do it." It was a bright moment in an otherwise dismal scene. Taylor later remembered that he never was more disheartened than when they met the shivering troops during a cold rain at Valley Mountain. The poorly equipped and disorganized Confederates had already been beaten at Rich Mountain, and Federals were poised to move into the Shenandoah Valley. Lee also found that many of the men were seriously ill. The rain would not stop, increasing the misery, and Lee worried that the populace was decidedly pro-Union, offering little aid and keeping the enemy informed.[44]

Lee's authority to deal with the situation in western Virginia was not clear. He was sent there only after Johnston refused the assignment, and his orders did not specify whether he was to command or to advise. Moreover, he had to work with men who believed they had more authority than he and who hated each other. Brig. Gen. William W. Loring had outranked Lee in the antebellum army and did not respond well to direct orders from the newcomer. Complicating matters were Henry A. Wise, governor of Virginia during the John Brown affair, and John B. Floyd, also a former Virginia governor as well as James Buchanan's

---

43. Woodworth, *Davis and Lee,* 20; Thomas, *Lee,* 197; Anderson and Anderson, *Generals,* 240; Manarin, "Lee in Command," 60; Lee to Philip St. George Cooke, May 15, 1861, Philip St. George Cooke Papers, UVA; Fitzhugh Lee, *General Lee,* 108, 112; Charles P. Roland, *Reflections on Lee: A Historian's Assessment* (Mechanicsburg, Pa., 1995), 30; Lee to Mary Custis Lee, July 27, 1861, De Butts-Ely Collection, LC.

44. Robert E. Lee, Jr., *Recollections,* 40, 50; Dowdey, *Lee,* 169; Jones, *Life and Letters,* 150; Fitzhugh Lee, *General Lee,* 117–18, 124; MacDonald, *Mrs. Lee,* 158; Adams, "Personal Letters," 588; Winston, *Lee,* 124; Lee to Mary Custis Lee, Aug. 4, Dec. 22, 1861, De Butts-Ely Collection, LC; Dowdey and Manarin, *Wartime Papers,* 62, 64 [quote], 70; Walter H. Taylor, *Four Years,* 17; Thomas, *Lee,* 199, 201–2.

secretary of war. As brigadier generals, they feuded constantly with each other and with Loring, making Lee's task even more difficult.[45]

Lee recalled in a letter to Mary that the last time he was in western Virginia was when he went to St. Louis in 1840. He wryly noted that if anyone had told him what his mission would be the next time he came there, "I should have supposed him insane." Despite the unexpected circumstances in which he found himself there again in the late summer of 1861, he took charge and began developing as a leader. His style blended elements of Washington and Napoleon as shaped by his experience with Scott. Rather than issue definite orders, he offered suggestions and left the details to his subordinates. As he explained to Justus Schiebert, a Prussian visitor, "I plan and work with all my might to bring the troops to the right place at the right time; with that I have done my duty. As soon as I order the troops forward into battle, I lay the fate of my army in the hands of God." He desired harmony and, ironically, avoided confrontation himself while he prepared his men for an offensive. Soon after his arrival, he told the Richmond authorities that he was preparing a "successful blow" and wrote to Custis that he was "anxious to begin a battle."[46]

Lee's opponent in western Virginia was Brig. Gen. William S. Rosecrans. The two strong points of Rosecrans' line were Cheat Mountain and Gauley Bridge. At the former site, Brig. Gen. Henry R. Jackson faced Federal Brig. Gen. John J. Reynolds. Lee saw that a secondary road could be used to bypass Cheat Mountain and cut the Baltimore and Ohio Railroad, thereby isolating Reynolds. This would force the Federals to abandon their push on Staunton, terminus of the Central Railroad in the Shenandoah Valley, and might compel a withdrawal. Jackson liked this plan, but his superior, Loring, asked for more time to prepare, negating Lee's request for speed. Lee found a solution when a scout discovered a trail by which the Confederates could surprise the Federal flank. It was an opportunity reminiscent of Scott's maneuvers in Mex-

45. Lee to Jerome N. Bonaparte, Apr. 11, 1853, Robert E. Lee Papers, Library of Virginia, Richmond; Dowdey, *Lee,* 166–67; Woodworth, *Davis and Lee,* 45, 61.

46. Fitzhugh Lee, *General Lee,* 117 [1st quote]; Thomas, *Lee,* 204, 246; Freeman, *Lee,* 2:239–40, 347–48; Justus Schiebert, *Seven Months in the Rebel States* (Tuscaloosa, Ala., 1958), 120 [2nd quote]; Manarin, "Lee in Command," 126 [3rd quote], 134; Jones, *Life and Letters,* 146–47 [4th quote].

ico, in which Lee played a key role, and it also combined Washingtonian audacity with a Napoleonic envelopment. Lee's attacking columns, though, developed problems. Green troops refused to cross creeks that appeared too deep, got their weapons and themselves soaked in a rainstorm, and fired guns while cleaning them, warning the Federals. The attack stalled after some Confederates would not advance because they thought their enemy was too numerous.[47]

The bitterness of his failure at Cheat Mountain was augmented for Lee by the death of his staff officer and cousin John A. Washington. The latter and Rooney, a cavalry officer in Loring's command, rode forward on September 13 to scout Federal positions. Lee himself occasionally scouted positions with Taylor and Washington, but Washington was always eager to go on scout, and so for the first time Lee let him do so without going along. Tragically, the two rode into Union pickets. Washington was shot and killed. Rooney's horse was hit three times, but he grabbed his fallen cousin's sword and horse and rode to safety. Lee received the body under a flag of truce and sent it home for burial. Washington's death upset Lee because he was a trusted officer on whom the Federals found a "sketch of the whole campaign" intended by Lee, forcing him to abandon his plans for another attempt at Cheat Mountain, but more important, Washington was a relative who was the last of his name to live at Mount Vernon, providing Lee with a direct link to the legacy of the Revolution while he lived.[48]

Lee wrote often about Washington during the ensuing weeks. To Edward C. Turner, a cousin, Lee confessed that "His death is a grievous affliction to me. . . . The country has met with a great loss in his death." He added bitterly, "Our enemy's [sic] have stamped their attack upon our rights with additional infamy by killing the lineal descendant and representative of him who under the guidance of Almighty God established them & by his virtue rendered our Republic immortal." To Mary,

47. Thomas, *Lee,* 201, 203, 206–7; Dowdey and Manarin, *Wartime Papers,* 63–64; Dowdey, *Lee,* 166.

48. Tim McKinney, *Robert E. Lee and the Thirty-Fifth Star* (Charleston, W.Va., 1993), 74–77; Reid Mitchell, *Civil War Soldiers* (New York, 1988), 1–2; Thomas, *Lee,* 207; Walter H. Taylor, *Four Years,* 22, 29; Long, *Memoirs of Lee,* 121; Susan P. Lee to Edwin G. Lee, Sept. 22, 1861 [quote], William N. Pendleton Papers, Southern Historical Collection, University of North Carolina, Chapel Hill; Lee to Edward C. Turner, Sept. 14, 1861, Beverly D. Tucker Papers, UVA; Dowdey and Manarin, *Wartime Papers,* 74.

Lee declared that Washington's death was a "heavy loss that grieves me deeply." He explained, "Since I had been thrown in such intimate relations with him, I had learned to appreciate him very highly." Lee also mentioned Washington in official reports. To Samuel Cooper, he wrote that his defeat was "much enhanced by the death of Lt. Col. J. A. Washington, the representative of the immortal Washington & the last proprietor of Mt. Vernon." He told Governor Letcher that "Our greatest loss [at Cheat Mountain] is the death of my dear friend, Colonel Washington."[49]

Lee accomplished little more in western Virginia before he returned to Richmond. He did grow a beard, which added to the solemn dignity of his appearance, and acquired a gray horse that he renamed Traveller, perhaps because his idol had a favorite mount by the same name. Such cosmetic changes did not impress his many critics, who were more interested in victory. This he had not achieved, and so he was derided as "Granny Lee." Davis once more proved to be Lee's most reliable ally. He dismissed the criticism and sent Lee to command the Department of South Carolina, Georgia, and Florida. There was concern about a Union attack there, and Lee was to strengthen the defenses. It was an interesting post for Lee; Light-Horse Harry had campaigned in the Carolinas during the Revolution, and the younger Lee had served at Savannah. Lee arrived in Charleston on November 7. Hurrying to Coosawhatchie, he learned that the Federals had occupied Port Royal, and there were few men and resources to defend the rest of the coast. To Lee, it appeared to be yet "Another forlorn hope expedition. Worse than western Virginia."[50]

The editor of the Charleston *Mercury* had derided Lee as the "Great

49. Fitzhugh Lee, *General Lee,* 122; Lee to Turner, Sept. 14, 1861 [1st and 2nd quotes], Tucker Papers, UVA; Dowdey and Manarin, *Wartime Papers,* 74–75 [3rd, 4th, and 6th quotes], 78; Mary Custis Lee to Anne Carter Lee, Oct. 21, 1860, Mary Custis Lee to Mildred Childe Lee, Sept. 21–22, 1861, Lee Family Papers, VHS; Lee to Samuel Cooper, Sept. 16, 1861 [5th quote], Robert E. Lee Papers, VHS.

50. Thomas, *Lee,* 208–11; Sanborn, *Complete Man,* 36; Winston, *Lee,* 143; McPherson, *Battle Cry,* 302–3; John C. Fitzpatrick, ed., *The Writings of George Washington,* 39 vols. (Washington, D.C., 1931–1944), 32:436, 36:151; Russell Weigley, *The American Way of War* (New York, 1973; reprint, Bloomington, Ind., 1977), 100; Lee to Charles Carter Lee, May 26, 1831, Lee Papers, UVA; Dowdey and Manarin, *Wartime Papers,* 86 [quote].

Entrencher," and Lee did little to improve his reputation. He had brought Taylor with him as the core of a new staff that included another Washington. Capt. Thornton A. Washington, a West Point graduate and acquaintance from Texas, became Lee's adjutant. With them, Lee focused on a mobile defense along an inland line to neutralize the Union advantage in ships and men. The number of Confederates in the department swelled from twelve thousand to twenty-five thousand, and they labored to obstruct rivers and construct new defenses. Lee was criticized for abandoning some sea islands and tiny ports, but he ignored the critics while hurrying everywhere, supervising the digging and other work astride Traveller.[51]

The Federals did not expand their toehold on the Carolina coast before Lee left for Richmond in March 1862, but his brief exile from Virginia proved eventful. His dinner on December 11 in Charleston was disturbed by a fire that destroyed many blocks. He fumed when the Federals sank twenty stone-filled ships in the main channel at Charleston on December 20, the anniversary of South Carolina's secession. He explained to Secretary of War Judah P. Benjamin that "This achievement, so unworthy any nation, is the abortive expression of the malice & revenge of a people which they wish to perpetuate by rendering more memorable a day hateful in their calendar." The fact that these obstructions, and others sunk a month later, had almost no effect provided some solace. He later realized that such actions indicated that the enemy did not have any intention of taking the city, which allowed him to focus his attention on Savannah.[52]

Lee's assignment to the southern coast did allow him to make a reconciliation of sorts with his father. Lee had not visited his father's grave on Cumberland Island while he was in Savannah in the 1830s, nor had he done so since. In January 1862, though, he stopped at Light-Horse Harry's grave on his return from an inspection trip. He found the site much as his son Custis, who had visited in 1855, had described it, with a "plain marble slab" purchased by Henry Lee IV still in place. Accord-

---

51. J. Cutler Andrews, *The South Reports the Civil War* (Princeton, 1970), 118 [quote]; Walter H. Taylor, *Four Years,* 201; *OR,* I, 6:312; Adams, "Personal Letters," 424, 426; Thomas, *Lee,* 213; Manarin, "Lee in Command," 178, 181.

52. Thomas, *Lee,* 214; Dowdey and Manarin, *Wartime Papers,* 92–93 [quote], 107; *OR,* I, 6:42–43; Lee to Mary Custis Lee, Dec. 22, 1861, De Butts-Ely Collection, LC.

ing to Capt. Armistead L. Long, a member of Lee's staff who accompanied him, the general lingered alone for a "few moments of silence." Perhaps it was a gesture of atonement for taking part in the destruction of the Union that the elder Lee had helped to create. Or maybe it was a quiet acknowledgment that Lee and his father now had something in common. Both were revolutionaries, risking grave consequences on behalf of their fellow Virginians and a new nation.[53]

It was a gloomy spring for the Confederacy, but Lee remained staunch in his support. He admonished Mary in February 1862 that "The news from Kentucky and Tennessee is not favourable, but we must make up our minds to meet with reverses and overcome them." A few weeks later he added that more setbacks would require "renewed energies & redoubled strength on our part, & I hope will produce it." A similar tone pervaded a letter to Custis; Federal victories could "have the effect of arousing them & imparting an earnestness & boldness" to his troops, and thus "be beneficial." His daughters Mildred and Anne received almost identical advice from their father; he wrote to Mildred that "reverses were necessary to make us brace ourselves for the work before us. We were getting careless & confident & required correction."[54]

As the end of Lee's first year as a Confederate approached, he had little to show for his decision to emulate Washington as a revolutionary. He had lost Arlington, along with many of its Washington relics, and had failed in his only assignment to combat command. His efforts in

53. Thomas, *Lee,* 36; Hendrick, *Lees of Virginia,* 397; Adams, "Personal Letters," 41, 44–45; Dowdey and Manarin, *Wartime Papers,* 103–4 [1st quote]; Long, *Memoirs of Lee,* 22–23 [2nd quote]; Lee to Custis Lee, Jan. 19, 1862, Lee Papers, DU. Whether Lee visited his father's grave during the 1830s is debated. See John M. Dederer, "Robert E. Lee's First Visit to His Father's Grave: Reevaluating Well-Known Historical Documents," *Virginia Magazine of History and Biography* 102 (Jan. 1994): 73–88; J. Anderson Thomson, Jr., and Carlos M. Santos, "The Mystery in the Coffin: Another View of Lee's Visit to His Father's Grave," *Virginia Magazine of History and Biography* 103 (Jan. 1995): 75–94; and John M. Dederer, "In Search of the Unknown Soldier: A Critique of the Mystery in the Coffin," *Virginia Magazine of History and Biography* 103 (Jan. 1995): 95–116.

54. Robert E. Lee, Jr., *Recollections,* 64 [1st quote]; Dowdey and Manarin, *Wartime Papers,* 118 [2nd quote], 121–22; Lee to Custis Lee, Feb. 23, 1862 [3rd and 4th quotes], Robert E. Lee Papers, Eleanor S. Brockenbrough Library, Museum of the Confederacy, Richmond; Lee to [Mildred Childe Lee], n.d. [5th quote], William G. McCabe Papers, UVA.

western Virginia had also led to the death of the last Washington to live at Mount Vernon. Lee tried to make light of his losses, writing jovially to his daughter Anne that if her sister Mildred were truly concerned about her cat that she had left at Arlington, he would "get Genl Johnston to send in a flag of truce and make inquiries."[55] Yet his losses and failures still weighed heavily upon him, especially as the Confederacy's fortunes ebbed in early 1862. It was with a heavy heart, and little promise of a better future, that Lee received orders from Davis to return to Richmond in March 1862.

55. Dowdey and Manarin, *Wartime Papers,* 122.

4

Audacity Personified
Northern Virginia in 1862

Hard pressed at Richmond in June 1862, many Confederates wondered if their new commander, Robert E. Lee, could save their capital. Maj. E. Porter Alexander discussed this with Capt. Joseph C. Ives, who had served on Lee's staff in South Carolina. Ives assured Alexander that Lee was "audacity personified." Lee proved this when he made himself the focus of the Confederate war effort, as he believed George Washington was for the Revolution, and aggressively pursued decisive victories to force the North to negotiate. He thus transformed his image from "Evacuating Lee," as editor Edward A. Pollard had called him, into a "grandson of Washington," as Peter W. Alexander, the "Prince" of Confederate reporters, hailed him by 1863. Many agreed with John B. Jones, who wrote that Lee showed "genius" as well as "audacity," but the general was disappointed. The North refused to negotiate, and so victory equivalent to that of Washington's triumph eluded him.[1]

1. Emory M. Thomas, *Robert E. Lee: A Biography* (New York, 1995), 226; E. Porter Alexander, "Lee at Appomattox: Personal Recollections of the Break-Up of the Confederacy," *Century* 63 (Mar. 1902): 921 [1st quote]; E. Porter Alexander, *Fighting for the Confederacy: The Personal Recollections of General Edward Porter Alexander,* ed. Gary W. Gallagher (Chapel Hill, N.C., 1989), 91; E. Porter Alexander, *Military Memoirs of a Confederate* (New York, 1907; reprint, Dayton, Ohio, 1977), 110–11; Clifford Dowdey, *Lee* (Boston, 1965), 175; Charleston *Mercury,* Apr. 25, 1862 [2nd quote]; J. Cutler Andrews,

Lee was called to Richmond from South Carolina by Jefferson Davis in March 1862. The president had grown weary of trying to corral his recalcitrant generals and had asked Congress to create the position of general-in-chief. He intended to appoint Lee, with whom he was on good terms and who seemed to share his ideas. Congress complied, but the bill was amended and Davis vetoed it. After Lee came to Virginia, Davis appointed him to supervise all armies "under the direction of the president." With this vague authority, Lee had to work with Davis to coordinate a host of units. As Charles Marshall, who joined Lee's staff, noted, Lee had to mediate between Davis, the cabinet, Congress, and generals as little more than a de facto "assistant Secretary of War."[2]

Lee was not happy with his new assignment, but he prepared to do his best. He reorganized his staff, creating a core of three that would stay with him for the duration of the war. The veteran Walter H. Taylor remained, and he was joined by Charles S. Venable and Marshall, a descendant of John Marshall, who wrote Lee's reports and orders. At Davis' urging, one of Marshall's first tasks was to produce a conscription plan that provided for a "total mobilization" similar to that enacted during the French Revolution. Like the levies of Napoleon, all men between the ages of eighteen and forty-five, with few exceptions, would be eligible. Lee was unhappy when Marshall's plan was amended by Congress. It reduced the upper age to 35, added exemptions, and provided for the election of regimental officers by enlisted personnel. The legislators would eventually expand the age limits and reduce exceptions

---

The South Reports the Civil War (Princeton, 1970), 50 [4th quote], 194 [3rd quote]; James M. McPherson, *Battle Cry of Freedom: The Civil War Era* (New York, 1988), 462; John B. Jones, *A Rebel War Clerk's Diary,* ed. Howard Swiggett, 2 vols. (New York, 1935), 1:138 [5th and 6th quotes]; Robert Stiles, *Four Years under Marse Robert* (New York, 1903), 108.

2. Thomas, *Lee,* 216; McPherson, *Battle Cry,* 366; Steven E. Woodworth, *Davis and Lee at War* (Lawrence, Kans., 1994), 102–3 [1st quote]; *The War of the Rebellion: A Compilation of the Official Records of the Union and Confederate Armies,* 130 vols. (Washington, D.C., 1880–1902), ser. I, vol. 5:1099 [hereinafter *OR*]; Joseph T. Glatthaar, *Partners in Command: The Relationships Between Leaders in the Civil War* (New York, 1993), 113; Charles Marshall, *An Aide-de-Camp of Lee, Being the Papers of Colonel Charles Marshall, Sometime Aide-de-Camp, Military Secretary, and Assistant Adjutant General on the Staff of Robert E. Lee,* ed. Frederick Maurice (Boston, 1927), 6 [2nd quote].

later in the war, but for two crucial years military manpower for the Confederacy was much less than Lee wanted.[3]

Left with less force than he considered optimal, Lee did his utmost to mold an effective primary army. To Maj. Gen. John C. Pemberton in South Carolina, Lee wrote that he needed to transfer some of his men to Virginia and would get no muskets for any left behind. Instead, he offered pikes for those in coastal batteries so their guns could be given to men in field units. Such orders alarmed those who suspected that Lee would abandon other regions in order to defend Virginia, but he had no such intention. For example, he reacted quickly to news from North Carolina, sending troops from Norfolk and Richmond to defend the railroads after the Confederate defeat at New Bern. Likewise, Lee found muskets for Pemberton and told him, "Let it be distinctly understood by everybody that Charleston and Savannah are to be defended to the last extremity." Lee would create a primary army to win the war, as he believed Washington had done, but the peripheries would be defended, just as Washington had sent troops, some led by Lee's own father, to fight in the south.[4]

One obstacle to the immediate fulfillment of Lee's plans was the fact that the principal Confederate army, that which defended Richmond, was not under his direct control until May 1862. Lee had to work within his limited authority to do what he could. By mid-April it was obvious that Union Maj. Gen. George B. McClellan was shifting his base of operations to the Peninsula southeast of Richmond, so Davis held a

3. Marshall, *Aide,* xiii–xv, 8, 30–33, 179, 181; Clifford Dowdey and Louis H. Manarin, eds., *The Wartime Papers of Robert E. Lee* (Boston, 1961), 127–28, 180; Robert E. Lee to Charles Carter Lee, Mar. 14, 1862, Robert E. Lee Papers, Eleanor S. Brockenbrough Library, Museum of the Confederacy, Richmond; Louis H. Manarin, "Lee in Command: Strategical and Tactical Policies . . ." (Ph.D. diss., Duke University, 1965), 257; Charles B. Flood, *Lee: The Last Years* (Boston, 1981), 11; Fitzhugh Lee, *General Lee* (New York, 1894; reprint, Wilmington, N.C., 1989), 10; Thomas, *Lee,* 219; Douglas S. Freeman, *R. E. Lee: A Biography,* 4 vols. (New York, 1934), 2:25, 28–29; Charles P. Roland, *Reflections on Lee: A Historian's Assessment* (Mechanicsburg, Pa., 1995), 36–37 [quote].

4. Lee to John C. Pemberton, Apr. 20 and 29, May 29 [quote], 1862, Robert E. Lee Papers, Library of Virginia, Richmond [hereinafter LV]; Lee to Francis W. Pickens, May 29, 1862, Gilder Lehrman Collection, Pierpont Morgan Library, New York; Russell Weigley, *The American Way of War* (New York, 1973; reprint, Bloomington, Ind., 1977), 103–4.

council. Gen. Joseph E. Johnston, the commander of the forces in the field, insisted the Peninsula was not a good place for a battle. He wanted to retire to Richmond. There he would fight McClellan far from his supply base with more new troops from the Carolinas and Georgia. However, Lee opposed withdrawing troops from Charleston and Savannah, and he believed that the Peninsula offered good opportunities for an effective blow. Davis agreed with Lee, and Johnston was told to stand fast.[5]

Lee had moved some of Johnston's men to the Peninsula before Johnston was ordered to hold that front. The conference with Davis allowed him to complete the transfer, leaving only a small Confederate force between Washington and Richmond. This set the stage for Lee's most audacious operation in the spring of 1862. Lee learned that Maj. Gen. Irvin McDowell was advancing toward Fredericksburg in support of McClellan. The best solution, Lee decided, was to create a diversion by striking a blow elsewhere, so he turned to Maj. Gen. Thomas J. Jackson, who had earned the nickname "Stonewall" for his success at First Manassas. Jackson had earlier advocated a diversion in the Shenandoah Valley; now he was reinforced with the division of Maj. Gen. Richard S. Ewell, whom Lee urged to "strike a successful blow at the enemy." The result was what Lee wanted: Jackson repeatedly beat the Federals in his front in May and early June 1862, forcing McDowell to abandon his efforts to support McClellan's operations on the Peninsula.[6]

While Jackson's efforts pleased Lee, Johnston's actions as the commander of his primary army alarmed him. To the surprise of Davis and Lee, Johnston ordered Norfolk to be abandoned, then Yorktown. Bloody fighting followed on May 5 at Williamsburg, where Confederate

5. Thomas, *Lee,* 220–22; Fitzhugh Lee, *General Lee,* 138, 139; Woodworth, *Davis and Lee,* 112–17; Glatthaar, *Partners,* 119; Joseph L. Harsh, *Confederate Tide Rising: Robert E. Lee and the Making of Southern Strategy, 1861–1862* (Kent, Ohio, 1998), 37; Armistead L. Long, *Memoirs of Robert E. Lee* (New York, 1886), 152–53.

6. Freeman, *Lee,* 2:17, 19, 31; Dowdey, *Lee,* 190–96; Harsh, *Confederate Tide Rising,* 41; Thomas, *Lee,* 224; Glatthaar, *Partners,* 22–25; Woodworth, *Davis and Lee,* 122; McPherson, *Battle Cry,* 455–57; Manarin, "Lee in Command," 217–22; Paul D. Casdorph, *Lee and Jackson: Confederate Chieftains* (New York, 1992), 95–96, 108–9, 114–15; John F. C. Fuller, *Grant and Lee: A Study in Personality and Generalship* (Stevenage, U.K., 1933), 152–154; Lee to Richard S. Ewell, Apr. 17, 1862 [quote], Polk-Brown-Ewell Family Papers, Southern Historical Collection, University of North Carolina, Chapel Hill.

wounded were left by retreating comrades. Lee tried in vain to have the ironclad *Virginia*, left homeless by the abandonment of Norfolk, make a sortie in the York River, but the crew burned her without a fight on May 11. The Norfolk garrison and the crew of the *Virginia* settled at Drewry's Bluff, placing guns and sinking obstructions to block a probe by the *Monitor* and other gunboats in a three-hour clash on May 15.[7]

As Johnston withdrew up the Peninsula, he complained that his authority was being usurped by Lee, who in fact did appear to be trying to assume command of his army. The result was not what Johnston intended: Davis became convinced that Johnston was the problem and Lee was the solution. Lee busily shuttled between the two, diplomatically trying to ease tensions but also giving an increasing amount of welcome advice to the president. Davis and Lee together visited with Johnston near Richmond on May 12. Concerned, Davis then told Lee to meet with his cabinet on May 14. Asked by Davis about the proper line of defense if Richmond were abandoned, Lee emotionally responded that the city should not be lost. Davis agreed to remain, relieved that Lee understood Richmond's importance to him and to the cause.[8]

Tragedy for Johnston allowed Lee to assume direct command of what he considered the primary army. Davis met Johnston again on May 18 and was surprised to find his camp in the suburbs of Richmond itself. Distressed, the president asked Lee to urge Johnston once more to attack McClellan at the Chickahominy River. Johnston agreed to hit the Federals as soon as they were divided by the river. McClellan obliged by posting two of his corps on the west bank and leaving the balance of his army on the eastern shore. When heavy rain created a torrent between the two parts of the Union army, Johnston hurled most of his troops at the two isolated corps at Seven Pines on May 31. Lack of coordination in the Confederate attacks and a bold river crossing by Union reinforcements deprived the Confederates of a decisive victory, and Johnston was struck in the ribs by a shell fragment and shot in the shoulder. Lee and

7. Fitzhugh Lee, *General Lee,* 139; Woodworth, *Davis and Lee,* 119; Thomas, *Lee,* 222–23; Dowdey, *Lee,* 199.

8. Thomas, *Lee,* 223; Dowdey, *Lee,* 201–2; Woodworth, *Davis and Lee,* 128; Harsh, *Confederate Tide Rising,* 52; Stanley F. Horn, ed., *The Robert E. Lee Reader* (Indianapolis, 1949), 151; John H. Reagan, *Memoirs* (Austin, 1968), 139.

Davis met Johnston on the battlefield and consoled him and then rode back to Richmond together. They said little, but Davis told Lee that Johnston's army was now his.[9]

Lee did not have Washington's rank of commander-in-chief, but he continued to assume that his new command was the principal army of the Confederacy. This army would win the decisive victory, or victories, that would force the North to sue for peace. Lee thus prepared carefully, trying to inspire his men while they slowly dug trenches to blunt any thrust by McClellan toward Richmond. In advice reminiscent of that given by Washington to Light-Horse Harry after he zealously executed a deserter, Lee told Long that a "volunteer army is more easily disciplined by encouraging a patriotic spirit than by a strict enforcement of the Articles of War." In that vein, he asked his troops in an order announcing his assumption of command to "maintain the ancient fame of the Army of Northern Virginia." The Department of Northern Virginia had in fact existed only since the fall, and Lee had begun referring to the units he now led as the Army of Northern Virginia only in March.[10] Investing the title with a hallowed past, however, might stir patriotic pride. The past was important to Lee, and he would use it to lead.

Command of the South's primary army was to have been Lee's only until Johnston recovered, but success made the reassignment permanent. Almost from the first moment that he took charge, Lee prepared to seize the initiative by striking a blow. Davis came to Lee's camp on June 3 and found him consulting with some of his generals. The latter were "despondent," but both Lee and Davis scolded them for insisting on a retreat. The pair then went for a ride, during which Lee proposed an attack that would leave only a thin line of Confederate troops entrenched between McClellan and Richmond. Davis had reservations, but Lee argued that such a risk was necessary and that he would hit the

9. Woodworth, *Davis and Lee*, 133, 135, 136; Manarin, "Lee in Command," 249–50; Varina H. Davis, *Jefferson Davis, Ex-President of the Confederate States of America: A Memoir by His Wife*, 2 vols. (New York, 1890), 276, 277; Thomas, *Lee*, 225; Dowdey, *Lee*, 209–13; Jefferson Davis, *The Rise and Fall of the Confederate Government*, 2 vols. (New York, 1881), 2:130.

10. Long, *Memoirs of Lee*, 166 [1st quote]; Dowdey and Manarin, *Wartime Papers*, 134, 138, 182; *OR*, I, 11:569 [2nd quote]; Lee to Joseph E. Johnston, May 16, 1862, Gilder Lehrman Collection, Pierpont Morgan Library; Freeman, *Lee*, 2:77–78.

Federals before they reached the capital. Perhaps pleased that Lee shared his own commitment to seizing the initiative, the president agreed.[11]

Lee set his men to digging trenches. As Mary Chesnut wrote in her diary, "Lee is king of spades. They are all once more digging for dear life." Laboring with shovels and picks, however, Lee's Confederates felt anything but inspired. Lee responded to Davis, who had made his own anxious inquiries, that he was well aware of the complaints, but the digging had worked for McClellan on the Peninsula and for the Romans before him. Davis may well have appreciated Lee's reference to the Romans; it was taken from S. F. Guy de Vernon's *Treatise on the Science of War and Fortification,* used in West Point engineering courses when Davis and Lee were cadets.[12] As he assumed the role of Washington, Lee had not forgotten his study of other masters.

Lee assembled a tremendous number of troops as he prepared to attack. In the same letter in which he defended his trenches to Davis, he asked for reinforcements. Lee understood that Davis needed to be reassured that more units could make a difference. He wrote that "It will require 100,000 men to resist the regular siege of Richmond," and he assured Davis that he would conduct a less costly campaign of maneuver. The president ignored those who criticized Lee and brought more troops from Georgia and the Carolinas to Richmond. Davis even suggested that Lee should bring Jackson from the Valley to join his army. In his order commanding Jackson to come to Richmond, Lee added, "[S]hould an opportunity occur for striking the enemy a successful blow, do not let it escape you." That day, Jackson defeated the Federals at Cross Keys, and the next day he did the same at Port Republic. Lee ordered several of his brigades to join Jackson, expecting to exploit the

11. Davis, *Memoir,* 2:307–9; Davis, *Rise and Fall,* 2:130–32; Jefferson Davis, *Robert E. Lee,* ed. Harold B. Simpson (Hillsboro, Tex., 1966), 8–9; Harsh, *Confederate Tide Rising,* 18, 21; Woodworth, *Davis and Lee,* 150–51, 153–54; William Allan, "Memoranda of Conversations with General Robert E. Lee," in Gary W. Gallagher, ed., *Lee the Soldier* (Lincoln, Nebr., 1996), 15; William Allan, *Army of Northern Virginia in 1862* (Boston, 1892), 58 [quote].

12. Woodworth, *Davis and Lee,* 387 [quote]; Thomas, *Lee,* 225; Lee to Jefferson Davis, June 5, 1862, Robert E. Lee Papers, United States Military Academy Library and Archives, West Point, N.Y. [hereinafter USMA]; Dowdey and Manarin, *Wartime Papers,* 184; Edward Hagerman, *The American Civil War and the Origins of Modern Warfare* (Bloomington, Ind., 1988), 6.

blow already struck, but Jackson reminded Lee that concentrating at Richmond was best. Lee agreed and Jackson, after shuffling his units to confuse the Federals, arrived at Lee's headquarters on June 23.[13]

Jackson was escorted into Lee's tent by his brother-in-law, Maj. Gen. Daniel H. Hill. Maj. Gens. Ambrose P. Hill and James Longstreet completed the group. Lee told them that Brig Gen. James E. B. Stuart and his troopers had ridden completely around McClellan with the loss of one man, destroying a wagon train and taking 165 prisoners. More important, Stuart reported that the Union right flank was exposed. Lee explained that he wanted to attack this flank and then left his generals to settle details. This had become Lee's style of command; once the field was chosen and the tactic was selected, Lee left dispositions to his subordinates. He had read that this was how both Washington and Napoleon had operated, and he had seen it done effectively by Winfield Scott in Mexico. He had enjoyed little success in western Virginia with this approach but decided he could trust his new officers. After the four commanders talked, Lee returned and issued his official orders incorporating their decisions.[14]

The plan that Lee developed in the meeting on June 23 was to hold McClellan's left front, south of the Chickahominy, with two divisions. Jackson would move around McClellan's right flank, north of the river, with his men. As soon as Jackson engaged on June 26, Ambrose P. Hill was to attack the front of the Federal army north of the Chickahominy. As the Union lines fell back, Daniel H. Hill and Longstreet would cross the river and assail the units on McClellan's right that were not trapped within the pocket created by Jackson and Ambrose P. Hill.[15]

13. Lee to Davis, June 5, 1862 [1st quote], Lee Papers, USMA; Dowdey and Manarin, *Wartime Papers,* 184 [2nd quote]; Woodworth, *Davis and Lee,* 154, 156; Allan, "Memoranda," 15; Davis, *Memoir,* 2:307–9; Davis, *Lee,* 8–9; Davis, *Rise and Fall,* 2:130–32; Harsh, *Confederate Tide Rising,* 54, 83–84; McPherson, *Battle Cry,* 458–60; Allan, *Army of Northern Virginia,* 60; Thomas, *Lee,* 232; Freeman, *Lee,* 2:94–104; Thomas L. Connelly and Archer Jones, *The Politics of Command: Factions and Ideas in Confederate Strategy* (Baton Rouge, 1983), 32; George T. Denison, Jr., "A Visit to General Robert E. Lee," *Canadian Monthly* 1 (Mar. 1872): 233–35.

14. Thomas, *Lee,* 232–33; Freeman, *Lee,* 2:107; Lee to Davis, June 7, 1862, Lee Papers, LV; Lynda L. Crist, Mary S. Dix, and Kenneth H. Williams, *The Papers of Jefferson Davis: Volume 8, 1862* (Baton Rouge, 1995), 229–30; James Longstreet, *From Manassas to Appomattox* (Philadelphia, 1896), 121.

15. Thomas, *Lee,* 231, 233–34.

Lee's plan was almost spoiled before he began and then proved to be too complex for his new command to execute. The Federals suddenly attacked south of the Chickahominy, where Lee's line was thin, on June 25. When McClellan did not press this advantage, Lee saw a chance to seize the initiative and subsequently fumed as his opportunity went awry. Jackson did not attack until late on June 26. Frustrated, Ambrose P. Hill ordered his men forward without Jackson's supporting assault. As Hill pushed past the bridge at Mechanicsville, Daniel H. Hill and Longstreet crossed and joined him. The Federals fell back as expected until resistance stiffened at Beaver Dam Creek, where they made a stand supported by artillery. The Union forces might have been overwhelmed if Jackson had been at their rear, but he halted three miles away to rest. Nightfall ended the fighting.[16]

Lee was bitterly disappointed with his first fight as an army commander at Mechanicsville, but he managed to retain the initiative. His orders had not been executed, and only a fourth of his men had gotten into action. Those that did fight suffered 10 percent losses, four times the number of casualties absorbed by McClellan. He vented his anger on Davis, who remained at a prudent distance for most of the remainder of the week's battles, and was curt with Jackson when the latter approached late in the day. During the night, he moved Longstreet forward to support Ambrose P. Hill, while Daniel H. Hill joined Jackson on the Union right. The following morning, McClellan withdrew rather than let Jackson flank him. Lee thus converted his failure into a Union retreat, but his focus on a decisive victory pushed him to try for more. Ambrose P. Hill, supported by Longstreet, attacked the center of the new Federal line at Gaines's Mill, while Daniel H. Hill and Jackson pressed the Union flank. As darkness fell, all of the Confederates made a concerted rush. Spearheaded by Brig. Gen. John Bell Hood's Texans, the Southerners broke through and the Federals ran, giving Lee his first clear triumph.[17]

Lee's casualties at Gaines's Mill on June 27 totaled 8,751, more than five times the number he had lost the day before and many more than his

16. Thomas, *Lee*, 233–36; Dowdey and Manarin, *Wartime Papers*, 199; Allan, "Memoranda," 16; Woodworth, *Davis and Lee*, 163.

17. Thomas, *Lee*, 236–38; Freeman, *Lee*, 2:135; Woodworth, *Davis and Lee*, 164, 166; McPherson, *Battle Cry*, 466–67.

enemy's loss of 6,837. However, though his losses were heavy and he had not destroyed even a substantial portion of McClellan's army, Lee was pleased. His first win as commander of an army was quite exciting, perhaps especially so since he had demonstrated courage that made him a worthy heir of Washington. While moving forward, a South Carolina regiment came under fire and wavered. Lee rode into the rain of bullets to rally them, despite the pleas of his staff that he move out of range.[18]

The morning after Gaines's Mill, the Federals retired south. Lee sent troops to cut the railroad and isolate McClellan from his supply base, but the Confederates found the Union depot in ashes, and Lee realized that McClellan intended to retreat to the James River. Hoping to destroy at least part of the Union army before they reached their new base, Lee sent two divisions to press the Federal rear while Longstreet and Ambrose P. Hill marched to hit McClellan in White Oak Swamp. Daniel H. Hill and Jackson swung north. The Confederate pursuers did not move quickly, so it was not until June 29 that a division caught the Federals at Savage Station. No other Confederate units supported them, so the Union rearguard, despite heavy casualties, repulsed the attackers while their comrades pushed through the swamp. Lee bitterly realized that his enemy might escape without a decisive defeat.[19]

Determined to strike a blow before McClellan reached the James, Lee ordered an attack at White Oak Swamp on June 30. He talked personally with each of his subordinates, pressing upon them the urgency of the day. In spite of his efforts, again his attacks were uncoordinated and the Federals escaped Lee's noose. Under the supervision of Lee and briefly Davis, Longstreet and Ambrose P. Hill attacked in the center. Jackson and others, however, once more failed to make flanking attacks that would have enveloped McClellan's army. The losses were about equal on both sides, but this provided scant consolation. In a display of the temper that a staff member would recall as one of his more Washingtonian features, Lee barked to Brig. Gen. Jubal A. Early that McClellan would "get away because I cannot have my orders carried out!"[20]

18. Dowdey and Manarin, *Wartime Papers,* 216; Thomas, *Lee,* 238; Freeman, *Lee,* 2:144.

19. Thomas, *Lee,* 239–240; Dowdey, *Lee,* 255; Dowdey and Manarin, *Wartime Papers,* 205.

20. Thomas, *Lee,* 241; Dowdey, *Lee,* 264–65; Allan, *Army of Northern Virginia,* 112, 119; Woodworth, *Davis and Lee,* 168; J. William Jones, *Life and Letters of Robert Edward Lee, Soldier and Man* (New York, 1906), 181–82; Horn, *Reader,* 352 [quote].

Lee's focus on a decisive victory led to a tragic error. McClellan out-raced the pursuing Confederates and occupied Malvern Hill. Ironically, the site had once been owned by Charles Hill Carter, who had left it in a trust for his daughter Anne so that her wayward husband, Light-Horse Harry, could not have it. But Lee was more concerned with it now as the last place to strike at McClellan before he reached the protection of his gunboats. The Federal positions were strong, but Lee had seen a sim-ilar situation at Chapultepec, Mexico, where an American assault had succeeded. On the advice of Longstreet, another officer who had partici-pated in that effort, Lee massed his artillery to disrupt the Union center and allow an infantry assault to punch through. It was a classic Napole-onic tactic, but the result, according to Daniel H. Hill, "was not war—it was murder." The Confederate guns proved ineffective or were sup-pressed by Federal fire, while Lee's infantry attacked piecemeal and was cut down. Lee again lost more than McClellan, suffering fifty-three hun-dred casualties, while inflicting only thirty-two hundred on the enemy.[21]

Longstreet consoled Lee by assuring him that "you hurt them about as much as they hurt you." To this, Lee allegedly retorted that he was "glad we punished them well, at any rate." In truth, Lee was miserable, especially when McClellan withdrew safely to his gunboats. This pre-cluded any reasonable possibility of a continued pursuit, but Lee inspected the new Union positions just in case there was any opportu-nity. He observed the litter left behind by retreating Federals and under-stood that they were, as Maj. Gen. Joseph Hooker confessed after the war, a "whipped army," but he had to tell Davis that "there is no way to attack to advantage." The president deferred to Lee's judgment.[22]

Lee was "deeply, bitterly disappointed" with his Peninsula campaign.

21. Hagerman, *Origins,* 15; Nancy S. Anderson and Dwight Anderson, *The Generals: Ulysses S. Grant and Robert E. Lee* (New York, 1988), 16; Lee to Mrs. Thomas J. Jackson, Jan. 25, 1866, Robert E. Lee Letterbooks, De Butts-Ely Collection, Library of Congress, Washington, D.C. [hereinafter LC]; Thomas, *Lee,* 242; Hagerman, *Origins,* 15; James Longstreet, *Manassas to Appomattox,* 143–45; Freeman, *Lee,* 2:211; E. Porter Alexander, *Memoirs,* 160–62; Daniel H. Hill, "McClellan's Change of Base and Malvern Hill," in Robert U. Johnson and Clarence C. Buel, eds., *Battles and Leaders of the Civil War,* 4 vols. (New York, 1956), 2:390–94 [quote].

22. Freeman, *Lee,* 2:223 [1st and 2nd quotes], 227–28; Henry A. White, *Robert E. Lee and the Southern Confederacy, 1807–1870* (New York, 1897), 167 [3rd quote]; Lee to Davis, July 4, 1863, Lee Papers, LV [4th quote]; Crist, Dix, and Williams, *Papers of Jefferson Davis: Vol. 8,* 276.

As commander of the Confederacy's principal army, he had driven McClellan back, and Federal operations on the North Carolina coast stalled while troops were transferred to Virginia, but he failed to win a decisive victory and force the North to negotiate. He had also lost more men than McClellan, further increasing the disparity in their armies. This lent a hollow ring to his reassurance to Mary that "Our enemy has met with a heavy loss from which he must take some time to recover." In mid-August, Lee reported to Davis that McClellan had abandoned the Peninsula. Lee noted that this made him "greatly mortified." He agreed that the "abandonment" of McClellan's effort to take Richmond was a "great relief," but he "ought not to have got off so easily."[23]

Lee did not produce a report on the Peninsula Campaign until March 1863, which gave him time to reflect on his first battles as an army commander. He declared again that the "Federal Army should have been destroyed," but circumstances, especially the "want of correct and timely information," dictated otherwise. It was clear that he had been undone by bad maps, an inexperienced staff, and a cavalry reconnaissance force that was often poorly managed. In addition, he had relied too much on subordinates to undertake complex maneuvers. Lee assumed most of the blame, but others did not agree with his self-criticism. The Confederacy was impressed with its new commander. The Richmond *Whig,* which had criticized Lee for digging while Jackson fought in the Valley, compared Lee to Washington in July 1862, declaring that Lee's "modesty is only equalled by his merits." Jackson himself wrote at the same time, "I am willing to follow him blindfolded."[24]

The burning of White House by McClellan's Federals added to Lee's frustration. Mary had settled during the fall of 1861 at White House, where her grandmother Martha had lived while being courted by Wash-

---

23. E. Porter Alexander, *Fighting for the Confederacy,* 96; Woodworth, *Davis and Lee,* 173; Dowdey and Manarin, *Wartime Papers,* 230 [1st and 2nd quotes]; Lee to Davis, Aug. 17, 1862 [3rd–6th quotes], Jefferson Davis Collection, Howard-Tilton Library, Tulane University, New Orleans; Crist, Dix, and Williams, *Papers of Jefferson Davis: Vol. 8,* 344–45.

24. Dowdey and Manarin, *Wartime Papers,* 219, 221 [1st and 2nd quote]; Fitzhugh Lee, *General Lee,* 164; Richmond *Dispatch,* July 9, 1862; Richmond *Whig,* June 12, July 14 [3rd quote], 1862; Freeman, 2:232–41, 261 [4th quote]; Stephen W. Sears, ed., *The Civil War: The Best of American Heritage* (Boston, 1991), 47; Edward Lee Childe, *The Life and Campaigns of General Lee,* trans. George Litte (London, 1875), 218.

ington. Lee wrote to her in April 1862 that Union troops might occupy the property and that she should "get out of the way." He did not think she would be harmed, but her capture would be "annoying and embarrassing," and some might "delight in persecuting [her]." He repeated his warning in a second letter, and Mary left after posting a note on the door asking "Northern soldiers who profess to reverence Washington" to "forbear to desecrate the home of his first married life, the property of his wife, now owned by her descendants." She signed her note as the "Grand-daughter of Mrs. Washington." After leaving White House, Mary stayed too long at the home of Edmund Ruffin, and she and two daughters were captured.[25]

McClellan gallantly provided for the safe return of Lee's captive wife and daughters, but he could not save White House. He ordered White House, because of its connection to Washington, to remain untouched, but complaints reached Congress. Abraham Lincoln, in response to a congressional resolution of protest, told Edwin Stanton to use the home as a hospital. Hearing that Federals were living at White House, Mary wrote to their commander, Brig. Gen. Fitz-John Porter, that "all the plate & other valuables have long since been removed to Richmond & are now beyond the reach of Northern marauders who may wish for their possession." By mid-July she learned the fate of the home: a "deserter from a New York regiment" had torched it when the supply depot burned.[26]

Other fine estates were damaged as well during McClellan's advance,

25. Lee to Mary Custis Lee, Apr. 4 [1st–3rd quotes], 22, 1862, De Butts-Ely Collection, LC; William P. Snow, *Lee and His Generals: Their Lives and Campaigns* (New York, 1867; reprint, New York, 1982), 53 [4th–6th quotes]; Thomas, *Lee*, 230; Anderson and Anderson, *Generals*, 308; Frank Moore, ed., *The Rebellion Record: A Diary of American Events*, 12 vols. (New York, 1861–1868; reprint, New York, 1977), 6: "Poetry and Incidents," 5.

26. Dowdey, *Lee*, 205, 214; Horn, *Reader*, 205–6; Burke Davis, *Gray Fox: Robert E. Lee and the Civil War* (New York, 1956), 108 [1st quote]; Thomas L. Connelly, *The Marble Man: Robert E. Lee and His Image in American Society* (Baton Rouge, 1977), 34; Mary Custis Lee to Anne Carter Lee, July 17, 1862, Lee Family Papers, Virginia Historical Society, Richmond [hereinafter VHS]; U.S. House, *Occupation of the "White House" in Virginia*, 37th Cong., 2nd sess., 1862, H. Exec. Doc. 145, serial 1138, 3–7; U.S. House, *White House on Pamunkey River*, 37th Cong., 2nd sess., 1862, H. Exec. Doc. 135, serial 1138, 1; Gene Smith, *Lee and Grant: A Dual Biography* (Norwalk, Conn., 1984), 133 [2nd quote]; Margaret Sanborn, *Robert E. Lee: The Complete Man* (Philadelphia, 1967), 62.

but the loss of White House dominated references to such events. Stuart in his report noted the "deceitfulness of the enemy's pretended reverence for everything associated with the name of Washington—for the dwelling house [which Stuart wrote was a "former plantation residence of General George Washington"] was burned to the ground, not a vestige left except what told of desolation and vandalism." The commander of the 4th Virginia Cavalry derided the Federals who burned White House as "a foe respecting nothing, sparing nothing." Mary wrote to a friend that she had left furniture behind, "not supposing such an act of vandalism could be committed on a place sacred as having been the early home of Washington in wedded life with my Grandmother." She complained that Federal troops robbed the house and even took the slaves, who, ironically, "by [her] father's will [would] have been free [that] winter." Mary visited the ruins in November, and Lee commiserated that the sight "must have brought sad thoughts."[27]

After the Seven Days' Battles, Lee tended to his family and his army. Mary settled in Richmond, despite Lee's urging that she find a more secure place, and eventually lived at the Mess, a town home used by Lee and other officers, including his son Custis. There Lee could visit her. The first time was in July 1862, when they were joined by their youngest son, Robert. Just one day after Gaines's Mill, Lee had found his namesake asleep under a caisson. He was probably more pleased to see him at the Mess in Richmond. Lee also settled matters within his army. Many were sent away, but the two Hills retained their divisions, while Jackson and Longstreet were given command of the two wings, later renamed corps, of the army. Henceforth Lee would issue commands to his wing or corps commanders and trust them to make dispositions. The only exception to this Napoleonic pattern was not assigning cavalry to each wing or corps; instead, Lee kept his mounted brigades united as a division under the leadership of Stuart.[28]

27. *OR,* I, 11, pt. 2:529 [1st quote]; Davis, *Rise and Fall,* 2:150 [2nd quote]; Mary Custis Lee to Elizabeth A. [Mackay] Stiles, July 5, 1862 [3rd and 4th quotes], De Butts-Ely Collection, LC; Anderson and Anderson, *Generals,* 314; Dowdey, *Lee,* 274; Mary P. Coulling, *Lee Girls* (Winston-Salem, N.C., 1987), 106 [5th quote]; Jones, *Life and Letters,* 62.

28. Thomas, *Lee,* 231, 246–47; Harsh, *Confederate Tide Rising,* 100–102, 105–6; Lee to Mary Custis Lee, Sept. 29, 1862, De Butts-Ely Collection, LC; Horn, *Reader,* 207–8; Sally N. Robins, "Mrs. Lee During the War," in Robert A. Brock, ed., *Gen. Robert*

Federal authorities in Washington rightly judged that they could expect little from McClellan. Rather than continue to send reinforcements to him, they gathered the Union forces in northern Virginia and assigned Maj. Gen. John Pope to command them. Pope aggravated Lee with his bragging and hostile orders. He decreed that men disloyal to the Union should be banished or held as hostages for the return of Federals taken by Confederates. Furthermore, if Union troops were ambushed, homes would be "razed to the ground." At Davis' request, Lee protested against these and other excesses, warning that if such policies were not dropped, retaliations would escalate "until the voice of an outraged humanity shall compel a respect for the recognized usages of war." Maj. Gen. Henry W. Halleck responded that such threats were insulting, but the Federals did repudiate Pope's words.[29]

Lee's protest against Pope's declarations and other Federal actions against noncombatants reflected his understanding that Washington had avoided war on civilians. He may not have known that one of Washington's orders to spare civilians had been prompted by the excesses of Light-Horse Harry, and he was upset to learn that his nephew was with Pope. Lee's sister Ann had married Louis Marshall. Their son had graduated from West Point and remained an officer like Lee, who visited often before the war. Lee wrote to his daughter Mildred that he could forgive her cousin for staying with the Union, but not for serving under "such a miscreant as Pope." When another nephew, Johnny Lee, spoke to Marshall and reported that he looked "wretchedly," Lee wrote to Mary, "I am sorry he is in such bad company, but I suppose he could not help it." He had earlier asked her, perhaps playfully, to tell their youngest son, who was still in Richmond, to capture his cousin. Instead, Rooney almost nabbed Marshall when Stuart hit

---

Edward Lee: Soldier, Citizen, and Christian Patriot (Richmond, 1897), 331; Robert E. Lee, Jr., *Recollections and Letters of General Robert E. Lee* (New York, 1904), 73–74; Manarin, "Lee in Command," 280, 313; Jay Luvaas, "Lee and the Operational Art," *Parameters* 22 (Autumn 1992): 8.

29. Earl S. Miers, *Robert E. Lee: A Great Life in Brief* (New York, 1956), 91–92 [1st quote]; Thomas, *Lee*, 249; Fitzhugh Lee, *General Lee*, 174–75; Horn, *Reader*, 213; Davis, *Memoir*, 2:355–60; Charleston *Mercury*, Dec. 27, 1862; John E. Cooke, *A Life of Gen. Robert E. Lee* (New York, 1883), 106 [2nd quote].

Pope's camp in August. Lee wrote to Rooney's wife that his nephew "escaped at the first onset, leaving his toddy untouched."[30]

Aside from his disgust with Pope's punitive orders, Lee was uneasy with Pope's having fifty-five thousand men along the Rappahannock River while McClellan remained on the Peninsula with ninety thousand. Lee sparred with McClellan's troops and sent Jackson north from Richmond with two divisions in July. When Jackson reported that these were not enough, Lee ordered Ambrose P. Hill to join Jackson in front of Pope. He was determined that Pope must "be suppressed" before he cut a vital railroad or provoked severe retaliations. Reinforced by Hill, Jackson hit Pope at Cedar Mountain on August 9. Lee congratulated Jackson for his victory but added that he hoped this was "but the precursor of others over our foe in that quarter which will entirely break up and scatter his army." More important, the fight pushed Federal authorities to have McClellan return to the vicinity of Washington. His troops began to embark in mid-August, by which time Lee divined his intention and sent Longstreet and Stuart to join Jackson for another attack. Lee intended to have Jackson swing around Pope's flank to cut his rail line while Longstreet provided a diversion. Unfortunately for Lee, Stuart's adjutant general was captured with Lee's plan. Thus warned, Pope retired north of the Rappahannock.[31]

Lee had forced Pope to withdraw, but he wanted more. Stuart repaid

---

30. Thomas, *Lee,* 249; Dowdey and Manarin, *Wartime Papers,* 240; Lee to Mildred Childe Lee, July 28, 1862 [1st and 2nd quotes], Lee to Mary Custis Lee, July 28, 1862 [3rd quote], De Butts-Ely Collection, LC; Lee to G. W. Custis Lee, Jan. 17, 1858, Robert E. Lee Papers, William G. Perkins Library, Duke University, Durham, N.C. [hereinafter DU]; Dowdey, *Lee,* 284–86; Fitzhugh Lee, *General Lee,* 182; Jones, *Life and Letters,* 190, 198; Moore, *Rebellion Record,* 9: "Documents," 245–47; Robert W. Winston, *Robert E. Lee: A Biography* (New York, 1941), 56; J. William Jones, *Personal Reminiscences, Anecdotes, and Letters of Gen. Robert E. Lee* (New York, 1874), 392 [4th quote]; Noel B. Gerson, *Light-Horse Harry Lee* (Garden City, N.Y., 1966), 49; Hagerman, *Origins,* xiii; Connelly and Jones, *Politics of Command,* 7; Charles Royster, *Light-Horse Harry Lee and the Legacy of the American Revolution* (New York, 1982), 36–38.

31. Thomas, *Lee,* 249, 251; Lee to Davis, July 26, 1862, Lee Papers, USMA; Dowdey and Manarin, *Wartime Papers,* 225, 239 [1st quote], 251 [2nd quote], 271; Dowdey, *Lee,* 283; Crist, Dix, and Williams, *Papers of Jefferson Davis: Vol. 8,* 302–3; Woodworth, *Davis and Lee,* 176; Harsh, *Confederate Tide Rising,* 114; White, *Southern Confederacy,* 174–76; Allan, *Army of Northern Virginia,* 183, 190; Frederick Maurice, *Robert E. Lee, the Soldier* (Boston, 1925), 129–30.

the insult of losing his adjutant general with a raid in which he got Pope's baggage and personal papers, among which were communications indicating that McClellan would reinforce Pope. Lee decided to attack before McClellan arrived. On August 25, he sent Jackson with two divisions around Pope's flank. Jackson's troops seized Pope's supply depot at Manassas Junction, ate all they could, carried away some provisions, and burned the rest. They repulsed a weak Union attack and then, as the main Federal army approached, settled into a line anchored in an unfinished railroad cut. Pope scoured the area until late on the afternoon of August 28, when Jackson had his concealed units fire on Federals crossing their front. For the rest of that day and all of the next, Jackson's outnumbered Confederates held their posts against uncoordinated Union attacks. Meanwhile, Lee and Longstreet arrived on Pope's left flank without being detected. On August 30, Longstreet attacked while Jackson pressed the Federal front. Surprised and flanked, Pope retired with heavy losses, protected from a total disaster only by the stubborn stand of a few Union regiments.[32]

Second Manassas was a great victory for Lee, but it was not decisive, as Pope escaped in good order. Lee pursued, but the Federals repulsed all efforts to inflict more losses as they fell back toward Washington. Lee did lose an old friend, Union Maj. Gen. Philip Kearny, who rode into the Confederate lines during a clash in a rainstorm at Ox Hill. Lee had Kearny's body returned to the Union army and then spent his own money to recover his sword, saddle, and horse at his widow's request. Lee's staff worried that he might be next since he continued to work near the front. Union cavalry harassed Longstreet's troops before Second Manassas and almost captured Lee. Only quick action by his staff, who formed a screen in front of Lee, saved their commander. After Lee arrived on Jackson's right, he went forward alone to take a look. Later he "quietly remarked" that a "sharpshooter came near killing me just now," and they saw a mark on his cheek where a bullet had grazed him. The only serious injury Lee suffered during the war was while chasing Pope. On August 31, he was holding the reins of his horse when the animal panicked and pulled him down. Lee's weight landed on his hands.

32. Allan, *Army of Northern Virginia*, 197–98, 200, 260–61, 25; James Longstreet, *Manassas to Appomattox*, 162; Woodworth, *Davis and Lee*, 179–81; Maurice, *Lee, the Soldier*, 132–33; Fitzhugh Lee, *General Lee*, 186–88; Freeman, *Lee*, 2:332–35.

Perry, a slave from Arlington, had to dress and feed Lee, and he could not ride for weeks.[33]

Pope's retreat, combined with McClellan's withdrawal, gave Lee the opportunity for a campaign he had long considered. The idea that his army had to win the war was never far from his mind. In a line that military historian Russell Weigley opined "George Washington might have written," Lee wrote to Davis on August 30, hours before Longstreet flanked Pope, that "My desire has been to avoid a general engagement, being the weaker force, and by maneuvering[,] to relieve the portion of the country referred to." He had won a great triumph; now he would provide relief, as he added in his message to the president, to "other portions of the country" by a maneuver that would compel "the enemy to collect his strength here." Upon the advice of some of his closest associates, and in keeping with his assumption that he, like Washington, commanded the primary army of his cause, Lee proposed to invade the North. In 1861 he had dissuaded an eager Jackson from such a bold move, but the time had come, as he had told Davis earlier, to "change the character of the war."[34]

Johnston had abandoned plans to invade the North in April 1862 as did Jackson in June of that year, the latter insisting that such an invasion would be of little value unless the ground could be held. Lee disagreed; he believed that a raid would help his cause by forcing the North to

---

33. Thomas, *Lee*, 251–55; Harsh, *Confederate Tide Rising*, 163–64, 205–7; Walter H. Taylor, *General Lee: His Campaigns in Virginia, 1861–1865* (Norfolk, Va., 1906), 115–16; Lee to Mrs. Philip Kearny, Sept. 28 and Oct. 4, 1862, Philip Kearny Papers, New Jersey Historical Society, Newark, N.J.; Long, *Memoirs of Lee*, 192–93, 542–43; Lee to "Miss Mason," Aug. 31, 1840, Lee Letterbooks, De Butts-Ely Collection, LC; Francis R. Adams, ed., "An Annotated Edition of the Personal Letters of Robert E. Lee, April 1855– April, 1861" (Ph.D. diss., University of Maryland, 1955), 648, 651; Dowdey, *Lee*, 288–89; E. Porter Alexander, *Memoirs*, 196; Charles S. Venable, "Personal Reminiscences of the Confederate War," n.d., McDowell-Miller-Warner Family Papers, University of Virginia Library, Charlottesville, 55–56 [quotes], 59; Robert E. Lee, Jr., *Recollections*, 78–79; Lee to Anne Carter Lee and Agnes Lee, n.d., De Butts-Ely Collection, LC.

34. Weigley, *American Way of War*, 108 [1st quote]; Harsh, *Confederate Tide Rising*, 159–60, 163; Lee to Davis, Aug. 30, 1862 [2nd and 3rd quotes], Lee Papers, LV; Lee to Thomas J. Jackson, May 10, 1861, Montrose J. Moses Papers, DU; Crist, Dix, and Williams, *Papers of Jefferson Davis: Vol. 8*, 225–26 [4th and 5th quotes]; Glatthaar, *Partners*, 11–12; Joseph E. Johnston to Lee, Apr. 30, 1862, Civil War Miscellany, Western Reserve Historical Society, Cleveland, Ohio.

focus on his army. If he won a decisive victory in the North, the effect would be significant, whether he could remain on the field or not. Lee had also embraced a suggestion from Johnston and proposed to Davis in July that the success won by Col. John Hunt Morgan in Kentucky should be exploited with an infantry invasion of that state. He retained this idea in the plan for a dual raid he revealed to Davis on September 3, 1862. Lee admitted that his men were "not properly equipped," but he insisted that his army "cannot afford to be idle." Because "new levies" for the "two grand armies of the United States" had not begun, "The present seems to be the most propitious time, since the commencement of the war, for the Confederate Army to invade Maryland." At the same time, Lee hoped that Gen. Braxton Bragg's army could march into Kentucky to support his raid.[35]

Lee started his army across the Potomac River into Maryland on September 3 without waiting for Davis to answer his letter. The general clearly hoped to win a decisive victory and thereby force negotiations. As biographer Emory M. Thomas has written, Lee at this time "seemed to fancy himself as some combination of George Washington and Prince Metternich," with the opportunity to shape both military and political events simultaneously. He was well aware that elections would soon be held in the North, and that a Confederate victory might lead to an electoral mandate for a negotiated settlement. If he could decisively defeat a Union army, then the Davis administration might successfully sue for peace and Southern independence. An uprising by the people of Maryland in support of Lee, which he hoped would occur, could enhance the impact of his raid.[36]

Lee's first week in Maryland passed without incident, encouraging him to think in even grander terms. In the mold of Washington, Lee forbade his soldiers to loot and issued strict orders not to disturb civilians. He wanted to compel the North to negotiate, but he could not condone

35. Harsh, *Confederate Tide Rising*, 36, 77–79; Thomas, *Lee*, 228, 247, 255–56; Dowdey and Manarin, *Wartime Papers*, 184, 193, 238, 293 [quotes]; Lee to Davis, July 26, 1862, Lee Papers, USMA; Crist, Dix, and Williams, *Papers of Jefferson Davis: Vol. 8*, 303; Johnston to Lee, Apr. 30, 1862, Civil War Miscellany, Western Reserve Historical Society.

36. Long, *Memoirs of Lee*, 205; Woodworth, *Davis and Lee*, 185; Thomas, *Lee*, 256–57, 289 [quote]; Hagerman, *Origins*, 115; Glatthaar, *Partners*, 41; Allan, *Army of Northern Virginia*, 331; Dowdey, *Lee*, 297.

attacks on nonmilitary personnel. Such attacks might have occurred during the Revolution, but Lee did not believe they had helped Washington win. For the most part, Lee's men behaved well. Quiet success led Lee to consider marching into Pennsylvania, and he asked Davis to open negotiations for Southern independence. Lee declared that this would be well timed because his army was poised to strike a blow. Furthermore, it "would show conclusively to the world that our sole object is the establishment of our independence, and the attainment of an honourable peace." If Lincoln rejected Davis' overture, it would show the world that the blame for the war lay with the North, not the South. Last but not least, it would help define the issue for Northern voters. On the same day, in response to a suggestion from Davis, Lee issued a call to the "People of Maryland" to "return to [their] natural position" by embracing the Confederacy "freely and without restraint."[37]

Davis proposed that he join Lee in Maryland, but Lee sent Walter H. Taylor to dissuade the president. As for Lee's suggestion that negotiations be initiated for independence, Davis decided to wait and see if Lee could win a decisive victory in Maryland. Both proved to be prudent. As early as September 7, Lee admitted that he did "not anticipate any general rising of the people in our behalf" in Maryland, though he insisted that recruits would yet join him. He desperately needed them; his own men were weary, hungry, and often barefoot. Straggling reduced his effective strength by as much as half. While Lee argued that his army was the "best in the world," he admitted that some "individuals" had to be weeded out. As he wrote in a letter to Davis, "It is true that the army has had hard work to perform, long and laborious marches, and large odds to encounter in every conflict, but not greater than were endured by our revolutionary fathers, or than what any army must encounter to be victorious."[38]

37. Lee to Davis, Sept. 4, 8, 1862, Lee Papers, LV; Dowdey, *Lee,* 298; Horn, *Reader,* 238–39 [quotes], 241; Connelly and Jones, *Politics of Command,* 5; Roland, *Assessment,* 45–46; Childe, *Campaigns,* 141; John G. Walker, "Jackson's Capture of Harper's Ferry," in Johnson and Buel, *Battles and Leaders,* 2:604–5; Richard R. Duncan, "Marylanders and the Invasion of 1862," *Civil War History* 11 (Dec. 1965): 372–75, 377; Dowdey and Manarin, *Wartime Papers,* 301; White, *Southern Confederacy,* 200; Davis, *Rise and Fall,* 2:333; Thomas, *Lee,* 257; OR, I, 19:598–99.

38. Thomas, *Lee,* 257; Fitzhugh Lee, *General Lee,* 198; Taylor, *Four Years,* 66; Walter H. Taylor to ———, Sept. 16, 1862, Walter H. Taylor Papers, LV; Woodworth, *Davis and*

Those that did remain in the ranks had to be fed, for which Lee depended upon a long supply line back to Virginia. Though the main Federal army under McClellan stood before him in eastern Maryland, Lee was discomfited by the Union garrison at Harpers Ferry to his rear. He had expected that Federal troops would evacuate the town as his much larger force threatened to isolate them, but they had not budged. To Lee, this was an opportunity: he could secure his supply line and capture twelve thousand Federals with minimal effort. Jackson invested Harpers Ferry, and the garrison surrendered on September 15. It was a small victory, but Lee hoped that it would have an effect on Northern voters.[39]

Lee expected that McClellan would move slowly toward the Confederate units posted in the mountains between his troops and Lee's scattered army, allowing the latter to invade Pennsylvania. There he could concentrate and strike a blow with the expectation of winning a decisive victory. Lee was thus quite surprised when McClellan moved more quickly than expected. Lee did not know it, but a copy of his orders with the disposition of his forces had fallen into Union hands. Its authenticity had been confirmed, and McClellan began to press the Confederates guarding the passes at South Mountain. Confronted with overwhelming force, Lee's troops made a stand on September 14 and won time for the capture of Harpers Ferry and a concentration of his army. Lee assembled his units, minus those at Harpers Ferry, near Sharpsburg.[40]

Sharpsburg lay near the Potomac River, so many assumed that Lee would cross into Virginia. To fight a superior foe with his back to a river seemed impractical, if not suicidal, but that is what Lee decided to do. In truth, he had to fight at Sharpsburg because to retreat into Virginia

---

Lee, 188; Crist, Dix, and Williams, *Papers of Jefferson Davis: Vol. 8,* 379–80 [1st quote], 387–88; Lee to Davis, Sept. 7, 1862 [2nd and 3rd quotes], Lee Papers, DU; Lee to Davis, Sept. 7, 9, and 21 [4th quote], 1862, Lee Papers, LV; E. Porter Alexander, *Memoirs,* 244; James Longstreet, *Manassas to Appomattox,* 222.

39. E. Porter Alexander, *Fighting for the Confederacy,* 140; Manarin, "Lee in Command," 362; Allan, "Memoranda," 7; Freeman, *Lee,* 2:360.

40. Allan, "Memoranda," 8, 13; Walker, "Jackson's Capture," 605–6; Freeman, *Lee,* 2:360, 362; Fitzhugh Lee, *General Lee,* 203; D. Scott Hartwig, "Robert E. Lee and the Maryland Campaign," in Gallagher, *Lee the Soldier,* 342; James D. McCabe, *Life and Campaigns of General Robert E. Lee* (Atlanta, 1866), 253; Allan, *Army of Northern Virginia,* 345–46.

without a battle would belie his effort in Maryland and reduce his impact on Northern morale less than two months before the elections. Securing negotiations for independence would be almost impossible if the primary Southern army withdrew without a fight. Lee's position behind Antietam Creek was good, he had little respect for McClellan, and Jackson's absent troops might yet come. If Lee won a decisive victory by repulsing the Federals and then delivered a counterblow like that against Pope, then his raid might yet prove successful.[41]

Lee did not have much of an army to challenge McClellan when the Federals attacked on September 17, but the Union leader, as Lee expected, fumbled every opportunity to annihilate his foe. McClellan's assaults were uncoordinated and ineffective. Lee once again had to intervene personally to bolster his thin line, leaving his ambulance to be led on Traveller to the front by an orderly. Among the units he rallied was the Rockbridge Artillery, in which his youngest son served. When the artillerymen, who had lost three of their four guns, asked if they truly had to reenter the battle, Lee replied with a smile that they "must do what [they could] to help drive these people back." Ambrose P. Hill arrived with his tired division from Harpers Ferry in time to secure a bloody stalemate for Lee, who lost a fourth of his thirty-nine thousand troops killed, wounded, or captured. McClellan had 71,500 men, but he lost 12,410 and failed to exploit breaks in the Confederate line because he would not use most of his reserve, concerned that their loss would allow Lee to extend his campaign in Maryland.[42]

Lee repulsed every attack but never got what he wanted: a chance to deliver a counterblow and secure a decisive victory. When a lull occurred in the afternoon, he asked Jackson about the possibility of a flank march around the Union right, but Jackson replied that it would be too dangerous. When Lee spoke with his officers that night, each said the same thing: they had suffered heavy casualties and should retreat. Lee disagreed and ordered them to be ready to hold their positions in the morning. He declared that many stragglers would rejoin the army

41. Hartwig, "Maryland Campaign," 349; E. Porter Alexander, *Memoirs,* 225; Manarin, "Lee in Command," 373; Woodworth, *Davis and Lee,* 191; Freeman, *Lee,* 2:381; Thomas, *Lee,* 258–60; Fitzhugh Lee, *General Lee,* 205.

42. Thomas, *Lee,* 261–63; Allan, *Army of Northern Virginia,* 434; White, *Southern Confederacy,* 218, 226; Fitzhugh Lee, *General Lee,* 210; Robert E. Lee, Jr., *Recollections,* 76–78 [quote].

that night, and thousands did. He again asked Jackson about a flank attack on September 18, but Jackson, after a scout, convinced him that it should not be attempted. Told that McClellan had received reinforcements, Lee began withdrawing on the night of September 18. He had made sure of one point, though: the Federals had not driven him from the field, so he had not been defeated. Lee was among the last to cross the Potomac, and Union troops who pursued too closely suffered heavily in a fight with his rearguard.[43]

Lee did not accomplish what he had hoped in Maryland, and his hollow triumph at Antietam underscored that fact. Davis did not demand peace negotiations because Lee did not secure a decisive victory. There was no rush by Marylanders to join Lee, and no significant amount of Federal troops had to be transferred from other theaters to cope with his raid. Despite Lee's insistence to his daughter that "we repulsed all their attacks, held our ground, and retired when it suited our convenience," McClellan remained in Maryland while Lee retired southward. Lee could truthfully insist that he and his troops "did not consider [themselves] beaten," but they had achieved little to convince Northerners to accept Southern independence. Supporters of Lee then and later pointed out that his losses were less than half of those suffered by the Federals in Maryland; in fact, Lee's men killed, wounded, or captured the equivalent of 50 percent of their own number.[44] The effect of such losses on the Union army was substantial, but it did not have the impact of a decisive victory.

Keeping in mind the impending elections in the North, Lee struggled to find a way to strike another blow against Northern morale. He wrote to Davis within a few days of his return to Virginia that he intended to recross into Maryland, but straggling and the protests of subordinates convinced him that it would be impossible. Still seeking a thunderbolt to hurl, he discussed a march into Pennsylvania with Confederate infantry

43. White, *Southern Confederacy,* 224–25; Horn, *Reader,* 252, 254; Freeman, *Lee,* 2:403–4; Woodworth, *Davis and Lee,* 193–94; E. Porter Alexander, *Memoirs,* 269; Glatthaar, *Partners,* 86; Taylor, *Four Years,* 74; James Longstreet, *Manassas to Appomattox,* 256–57.

44. Woodworth, *Davis and Lee,* 194; Emily V. Mason, *Popular Life of Gen. Robert E. Lee* (Baltimore, 1870), 147–48 [quotes]; Freeman, *Lee,* 4:408; Sears, *Best of American Heritage,* 49; Fitzhugh Lee, *General Lee,* 215; Archer Jones, "Military Means, Political Ends," in Gabor S. Boritt, *Why the Confederacy Lost* (New York, 1992), 61.

posted in the Shenandoah Valley. He finally had to settle for a cavalry raid. Stuart rode into Maryland and Pennsylvania during October 1862. His losses were slight, and he succeeded in disrupting the Federal supply lines in another circuit of McClellan's army.[45] But the escapade did little to offset the withdrawal of Bragg's troops from Kentucky, which ended all hope of securing anything substantial from the late summer raids into the North.

Ironically, while Lee tried to offset failure in Maryland by striking another blow, Lincoln took advantage of his withdrawal to secure a vital diplomatic victory by issuing the Emancipation Proclamation. Lee futilely hoped that the proclamation, along with Lincoln's invocation of martial law, would turn the North against him. He ignored the diplomatic importance of the proclamation, primarily because he believed from the first that the North would have the support of world leaders who opposed slavery. Like Washington, he refused to depend on the possibility of foreign aid, insisting that Southerners would have to "win [their] independence alone." As he wrote to Davis, all "efforts & energies should be devoted" to defeating the enemy, not futilely chasing foreign support.[46] Foreign assistance, though, had proven decisive for George Washington, and Lincoln's proclamation ensured that Lee would not get it.

Just as Lee dismissed the impact of Lincoln's Emancipation Proclamation on his military efforts, he also ignored its effect on his personal life. He proceeded with the settlement of his father-in-law's will in late 1862 as if the proclamation did not exist. George W. P. Custis had bequeathed freedom to his slaves but also stipulated that they could be held for five years after his death to generate income to settle the debts of his estate. The war made it impossible for the Lees to earn any significant amount, while a Virginia court insisted that the deadline must be respected. Lee signed the necessary documents on December 29, 1862. Of course, the Arlington slaves and most from White House were

45. Thomas, *Lee,* 264–265; Taylor to ———, Sept. 28, 1862, Taylor Papers, LV; *OR,* I, 19, pt. 1:143; Lee to Davis, Sept. 25, 1862, Lee Papers, LV; Allan, *Army of Northern Virginia,* 451; Woodworth, *Davis and Lee,* 194–95; Fitzhugh Lee, *General Lee,* 219.

46. Crist, Dix, and Williams, *Papers of Jefferson Davis: Vol. 8,* 422; John D. Imboden, "Reminiscences of Lee and Jackson," *Galaxy* 12 (Nov. 1871): 628; Dowdey and Manarin, *Wartime Papers,* 96 [1st quote], 98, 816; Lee to Custis Lee, Dec. 29, 1861, Lee to Davis, July 6, 1864 [2nd quote], Lee Papers, DU; Weigley, *American Way of War,* 5.

gone, but Lee found work for a few that remained and paid them. Perry stayed with Lee and received wages. Lee noted that he was "slow & inefficient & moves much like his father Lawrence, whom he resembles very much," but he would stay with Lee "until he or I can do better."[47]

McClellan also proved slow and inefficient in the fall of 1862. He did not pursue Lee, who used the time to resupply his battered army. The resulting improvement in morale brought an increase in numbers, but Lee also became involved in debates over money and military organization. When the Confederate Congress discussed whether to make its treasury notes legal tender, Lee wrote to Davis that no less a personage than Washington had recommended to the Continental Congress that it do so and it had complied. There was no clear solution to this problem, but Lee had better luck with reorganizing his army. The wings led by Longstreet and Jackson became corps under legislation approved by Congress for appointing "Commanders of Corps d'Armee." Both men became lieutenant generals. Lee also convinced Davis not to send men from his army to North Carolina, where renewed Union activity raised concerns. When McClellan finally crossed into Virginia in late October, Lee was able to put Longstreet's corps of forty thousand in his front and leave Jackson's corps of about the same number on his flank in the Valley.[48]

Lee welcomed his dilatory opponent's decision to advance, but Lincoln soon became exasperated with McClellan's refusal to engage Lee and replaced him with Maj. Gen. Ambrose E. Burnside. Burnside, to Lee's relief, proved as predictable as McClellan and moved directly upon Richmond by way of Fredericksburg. When the Federals had to wait for pontoons to cross the Rappahannock, Lee prepared a strong

47. Lee to Custis Lee, Jan. 19, 1862, Lee Papers, DU; Lee to William H. F. Lee, Feb. 16, 1862, George B. Lee Papers, VHS; Thomas, *Lee*, 273–74; Jones, *Life and Letters*, 286–87; Dowdey and Manarin, *Wartime Papers*, 354 [1st quote]; Winston, *Lee*, 124; Thomas N. Page, *Robert E. Lee, Man and Soldier* (New York, 1911), 620 [2nd quote]; Dowdey, *Lee*, 333; Long, *Memoirs of Lee*, 240–41; Taylor, *General Lee*, 221; Fitzhugh Lee, *General Lee*, 232; Robert E. Lee, Jr., *Recollections*, 85, 132; Ervin L. Jordan, Jr., *Black Confederates and Afro-Yankees in Civil War Virginia* (Charlottesville, Va., 1995), 258.

48. Dowdey and Manarin, *Wartime Papers*, 325; Crist, Dix, and Williams, *Papers of Jefferson Davis: Vol. 8*, 408 [quote], 421; Thomas, *Lee*, 265, 267; McCabe, *Life and Campaigns*, 281; Jones, *Diary*, 1:174; Woodworth, *Davis and Lee*, 206–7.

line on the heights beyond the town despite his reluctance to make it a battleground. On Charles Street stood the home purchased by Washington for his mother in 1772. Nearby was Kenmore, the house of Washington's sister and her husband. Just across the river was Ferry Farm, boyhood home of Washington. Burnside settled at Chatham, the estate of William F. Fitzhugh. After the war Lee told a woman how he had strained during the battle to see Chatham, the place where he had courted Mary and Washington had wooed Martha. The Confederates were ordered not to shell any of these sites, but Union threats forced an evacuation of the town in a freezing rain. The sight of refugees struggling in the mud and ice angered Lee. Residents returned when it appeared safe, and some were trapped when the Federals did shell the town in December. Lee gave money to a relief fund for the victims.[49]

Burnside's bombardment of Fredericksburg was prompted by his decision to attack Lee. Lee was confident and wrote to Davis that his united army was "never in better health or better condition for battle than now." When Union bridge builders began their labors, murderously accurate gunfire by Mississippi troops along the Fredericksburg waterfront slowed their efforts until Burnside brushed the Confederates back by shelling and occupying the town. The Federals were across the river by December 12 and attacked Lee the next day. They briefly secured a foothold on Lee's right flank, but those that charged the heights on the left were butchered. It was here that Lee stood, apparently calm even when a shell fell nearby and later one of his cannons exploded. More impressed with the carnage before him, Lee muttered, "It is well this is so terrible! We should grow too fond of it!" A jubilant Longstreet assured Lee that his men, if given enough ammunition, could kill every Federal before them. Burnside suffered 12,653 casualties, Lee less than half that.[50]

Several of Lee's subordinates were puzzled when he did not order a

49. Lee to Custis Lee, Nov. 10, 1862, Lee Papers, DU; Thomas, *Lee,* 268–69; Winston, *Lee,* 26; Horn, *Reader,* 39; Robert E. Lee, Jr., *Recollections,* 57; Dowdey and Manarin, *Wartime Papers,* 327, 343; Freeman, *Lee,* 2:434–35; Cooke, *Life of Lee,* 177; McCabe, *Life and Campaigns,* 310–12; Van Dyk MacBride, "The Autographed Field Letters of General Robert E. Lee," in *The Stamp Specialist India Book* (New York, 1946), 13; Douglas S. Freeman, "Lee and the Ladies, Part II," *Scribner's,* 78 (Nov. 1925): 471.

50. Dowdey and Manarin, *Wartime Papers,* 353 [1st quote]; Thomas, *Lee,* 271–72; Cooke, *Life of Lee,* 184 [2nd quote]; James Longstreet, *Manassas to Appomattox,* 312.

counterblow. The repulse of the Federals was spectacular but hardly a decisive victory, as Lee himself admitted to Mary. Lee in fact could not believe that such clumsy assaults were the main Union effort. He thought that Burnside would attack again. Information provided by prisoners reinforced this assumption. He explained to Mary, "I was holding back all day and husbanding our strength and ammunition for the great struggle, for which I thought I was preparing." Lee also later told some associates that to advance under the Union artillery would have been as disastrous for him as Burnside's attack was for the Federals. Lee had to be content with repulsing a foe who had intended to attack again but was persuaded not to do so by his own officers.[51]

Having missed a chance for a counterblow at Fredericksburg, Lee asked the Richmond authorities to support a winter campaign against Burnside. He was told that a rise in the price of gold in the North coupled with Burnside's defeat was expected to force the Federals to sue for peace in a few months. His request for support for an offensive was declined. Frustrated, Lee exploded in a letter to Secretary of War James A. Seddon that his army could not secure a "successful and speedy termination" of the war if it was not properly supported. Lee still believed his army had to win the war, and he had grown tired of wasting the lives of his men in less-than-decisive victories. While he fumed, Burnside tried his own winter campaign, became mired in mud and ice, and quit, providing yet another reason for Lincoln to replace him with Maj. Gen. Joseph Hooker in late January 1863.[52]

Lee and his army endured a miserable winter from January through April 1863. It was not only cold but wet, and short rations increased the misery of his "poor bushmen," as Lee called his troops in a letter to Mary. Lee's memories of Revolutionary heroes revived when an "ardent" young French officer arrived. Lee wrote, "at last, a Lafayette comes," but he glumly added that either the "appearance of things" or the icy weather "will cool him," for he had no blankets. As for Hooker,

51. Dowdey and Manarin, *Wartime Papers,* 365 [quote]; Robert E. Lee, Jr., *Recollections,* 89; James Longstreet, *Manassas to Appomattox,* 316; John Bell Hood, *Advance and Retreat* (New Orleans, 1880), 50; Allan, "Memoranda," 13; Jones, *Personal Reminiscences,* 267; Childe, *Campaigns,* 183; Long, *Memoirs of Lee,* 559–60; Woodworth, *Davis and Lee,* 211–12.

52. James Longstreet, *Manassas to Appomattox,* 317; Dowdey and Manarin, *Wartime Papers,* 289 [quote]; Thomas, *Lee,* 276–77; Woodworth, *Davis and Lee,* 214–15.

Lee observed that the Union commander seemed "obliged to do something" but clearly could not decide on a course of action. Instead, as Lee wrote to his daughter Agnes, "He is playing the Chinese game. Trying what frightening will do. He runs out his guns, starts his wagons & troops up & down the river, and creates an excitement generally. Our men look on in wonder, give a cheer, & all again subsides 'in status quo ante bellum.'" Serious chest pain in March 1863, the first sign of heart disease, did little to improve Lee's mood.[53]

As the first anniversary of Lee's return to Richmond passed, he had little to comfort him. Through audacity, he had made his army the focus of his cause and had become an inspiring leader, just as Washington had been. Confederate newsmen praised Lee and compared him favorably to his Revolutionary predecessor. Peter W. Alexander described Lee in the *Southern Literary Messenger* of January 1863 as having, like Washington, "those qualities which are indispensable in the great leader and champion upon whom the country rests its hope of present success and future independence." Many others believed the same. Mary Jones, a Georgia woman who had raised funds for remodeling Mount Vernon before the war, wrote in December 1862, "I feel thankful that in this great struggle the head of our army is a noble son of Virginia, and worthy of the intimate relation in which he stands connected with our immortal Washington." Such words brought little cheer to Lee because he had not yet realized Washington's great triumph: forcing his foe to sue for peace.[54]

Lee's disappointment was compounded by grief. His youngest daughter, Anne Carter Lee, died in October 1862 at the same North Carolina resort where her nephew, Rooney's son, had died earlier in the year. Lee confessed sadly to Mary, "To know that I shall never see her again on earth, that her place in our circle, which I always hoped one day to rejoin is forever vacant, is agonizing in the extreme." To Mary, his eldest daughter, Lee wrote, "In the hours of night, when there is

53. Dowdey and Manarin, 411; James C. Young, *Marse Robert, Knight of the Confederacy* (New York, 1929; reprint, New York, 1932), 214 [1st–6th quotes]; Lee to Agnes Lee, Feb. 6, 1863 [7th quote], De Butts-Ely Collection, LC; Thomas, *Lee,* 278–79.

54. Andrews, *South Reports the War,* 50, 194; Peter W. Alexander, "Confederate Chieftains," *Southern Literary Messenger* 35 (Jan. 1863): 35 [1st quote]; Robert M. Myers, *Children of Pride* (New Haven, Conn., 1972), 400, 496–97, 511, 1001 [2nd quote].

nothing to lighten the full weight of my grief, I feel as if I should be over-whelmed." He had anticipated spending time with Anne if he survived the war, "But year after year my hopes go out, and I must be resigned." Rooney's infant daughter died while Lee was at Fredericksburg, adding to his sorrow.[55] Stoically, he refused to let emotions interfere with duties. As spring approached, he remained sure that a decisive victory by his army would win independence.

55. Thomas, *Lee,* 266; Coulling, *Lee Girls,* 104, 110; Lee to Mary Custis Lee, Oct. 26, 1862 [1st quote], De Butts-Ely Collection, LC; Jones, *Life and Letters,* 198–99, 200 [2nd and 3rd quotes]; Freeman, *Lee,* 2:421; Mason, *Popular Life of Lee,* 157; Jones, *Personal Reminiscences,* 395; William F. Chaney, *Duty Most Sublime: The Life of Robert E. Lee as Told through the "Carter Letters"* (Baltimore, 1996), 109–11, 170–71; Philip Van Doren Stern, *Robert E. Lee, the Man and the Soldier: A Pictorial Biography* (New York, 1963), 163.

Stratford Hall, where Robert E. Lee believed he was born in the same room as two Lees who signed the Declaration of Independence. *Courtesy National Archives*

Light-Horse Harry Lee, as Robert E. Lee preferred to remember him.
Courtesy National Archives

Anne Carter Lee, wearing the portrait pin given to her by George Washington when she married Light-Horse Harry. *Courtesy Special Collections, Leyburn Library, Washington and Lee University*

Chatham, where allegedly both George Washington and Robert E. Lee proposed to their wives. *Courtesy National Archives*

Robert E. Lee, painted by William E. West in 1838. Lee added this portrait of himself to the Washington family gallery at Arlington. *Courtesy Library of Congress*

Mary Custis Lee, painted by William E. West in 1838 to accompany the portrait of her husband. *Courtesy Library of Congress*

Robert E. Lee in 1863, wearing the three stars of a colonel.
Courtesy Library of Congress

Federal soldiers at Arlington in June 1864, about the time that the grounds became a national cemetery. *Courtesy National Archives*

Federal soldiers among the ruins of White House, where George Washington courted Martha, and where Mary Custis Lee sought refuge during the Civil War. *Courtesy Library of Congress*

A postwar image of Robert E. Lee on Traveller, who bore the name of one of Washington's favorite mounts. *Courtesy Library of Congress*

Robert E. Lee (right) in 1870 with Joseph E. Johnston, his
roommate at West Point whose father served under
Light-Horse Harry Lee. *Courtesy Library of Congress*

Equestrian statue of George Washington in Richmond. *Courtesy National Archives*

George Washington iconography at the tomb of Robert E. Lee in the chapel of Washington and Lee University. *Courtesy Library of Congress*

Unveiling of equestrian statue of Robert E. Lee in Richmond, 1890. *Courtesy United States Army Military History Institute*

Statues of George Washington and Robert E. Lee in the national Capitol, donated by Virginia in 1908. *Courtesy Library of Congress*

5

A Very Bold Game

Showdown at Gettysburg

Robert E. Lee raided Pennsylvania during the summer of 1863 in search of a "showdown, a battle of annihilation that would end the war in a single afternoon." He still believed that he would win or lose Southern independence, just as the fate of the colonies had rested with George Washington and his army. Lee knew that the Confederacy was hard pressed elsewhere, but he insisted that a decisive victory by his army in the North, where there was a growing peace movement, would make other events matter little. He realized that "he was playing a very bold game," as he told William Allan after the war, but he was certain that "it was the only *possible* one." He understood the zeal among Southerners that pushed William G. Simms to write,

> Now burns thy soul, Virginia's son!
> Strike then for wife, babe, gray-haired sire,
> Strike for the grave of Washington!

The war had reached a critical juncture, and it was not only the South that believed that. Abraham Lincoln allegedly prayed for a Federal victory as Lee marched North, knowing his administration could not absorb the demoralization of another defeat.[1]

---

1. Emory M. Thomas, *Robert E. Lee: A Biography* (New York, 1995), 288–89 [1st quote]; William Allan, "Memoranda of Conversations with General Robert E. Lee," in

Unfortunately for Lee, it was during this second year of his tenure as commander of the Army of Northern Virginia that serious flaws in his Washingtonian strategy became evident. He greatly underestimated the resiliency of the Federal armies, which did not have the same logistical problems as the British troops that fought Washington. Union forces were more quickly supplied, more numerous, and more easily reinforced. Federal leaders did not have to concentrate their efforts in a single theater; they could and did attack in several at once. Lee erred in thinking that he could win the war with one hard blow in the North. It could be argued that even if he had won at Gettysburg, the North still might not have negotiated for peace as he wished.

Lee was very eager for the spring campaign to begin in 1863, but Hooker tried hard not to lose the initiative. Lee complained to Mary in February and again in April about Hooker's inactivity, and he told Davis, "I think it all important that we should assume the aggressive by the first of May," when not only Hooker's army but other Federal forces would be reduced by the expiration of enlistments. Hooker then moved first, sending five corps around the Confederate flank, far up the Rappahannock River, while he menaced Lee at Fredericksburg with two corps. Hooker expected to hit Lee's left and rear with an overwhelming force, but Lee saw the Federal effort as a chance to mimic Napoleon by striking the divided halves of his enemy from a central position. Lee did not have Lt. Gen. James Longstreet and two of his divisions, having sent them on a fruitless campaign in southeastern Virginia, but Hooker was without cavalry, having sent most of his troopers on a long raid. The Federals would be blind, while Confederate moves would be shielded by woods and Maj. Gen. J. E. B. Stuart's riders.[2]

Awakened on May 1 and informed that Hooker's infantry had

Lee the Soldier, ed. Gary W. Gallagher (Lincoln, Nebr., 1996), 17 [2nd and 3rd quotes]; Henry A. White, *Robert E. Lee and the Southern Confederacy, 1807–1870* (New York, 1897), 287; William G. Simms, ed., *War Poetry of the South* (New York, 1867), 55 [4th quote].

2. Robert E. Lee to Mary Custis Lee, Feb. 23, 1862, De Butts-Ely Collection, Library of Congress, Washington, D.C. [hereinafter LC]; Clifford Dowdey and Louis H. Manarin, eds., *The Wartime Papers of Robert E. Lee* (Boston, 1961), 428–29; Lee to Jefferson Davis, Apr. 16, 1863 [quote], Robert E. Lee Papers, William G. Perkins Library, Duke University, Durham, N.C. [hereinafter DU]; John F. C. Fuller, *Grant and Lee: A Study in Personality and Generalship* (Stevenage, U.K., 1933) 188–89; Clifford Dowdey, *Lee* (Boston, 1965), 344; Steven E. Woodworth, *Davis and Lee at War* (Lawrence, Kans., 1994), 218–19.

crossed the Rappahannock, Lee confidently jested, "Say to General Jackson that he knows just as well what to do with the enemy as I do." Maj. Gen. Richard H. Anderson's division was ordered to confront the Federals near Chancellorsville while Lee remained with the troops led by Maj. Gen. Jubal A. Early on the heights west of Fredericksburg. When it became clear that the main Union effort would be on Anderson's front, Lee talked with Lt. Gen. Thomas J. "Stonewall" Jackson. The latter pressed for an attack on Early's front, but Lee said that the Federals facing Anderson offered a better opportunity, so they rode to Chancellorsville.[3]

While Jackson and Lee talked, Anderson's men attacked at Chancellorsville. Hooker reacted by withdrawing into the woods and entrenching. When Lee arrived, he also had his troops dig fieldworks, a lesson learned at West Point and revived by the carnage endured in 1862. He wanted to separate Hooker's left flank from the river, but a personal reconnaissance revealed no weak point to attack. Lee spoke to Jackson that night while staff officers checked the ground. Their opinion that a frontal assault would be unwise, coupled with a report by Brig. Gen. Fitzhugh Lee that Hooker's right remained unsecured, led Lee to propose that troops be sent around the Union right. Jackson readily agreed. Lee asked how many men Jackson needed and was "floored" to hear that he wanted his entire corps, leaving only two divisions in Hooker's front. After a pause, Lee agreed.[4]

3. John E. Cooke, *A Life of Gen. Robert E. Lee* (New York, 1883), 258 [quote]; Robert K. Krick, "Lee at Chancellorsville," in Gallagher, *Lee the Soldier*, 361–63; Armistead L. Long, *Memoirs of Robert E. Lee* (New York, 1886), 251–52.

4. Thomas, *Lee*, 280–82; Krick, "Lee at Chancellorsville," 364–67; Dowdey, *Lee*, 346–47; Long, *Memoirs of Lee*, 252, 254; Charles Marshall, *An Aide-de-Camp of Lee* . . . , ed. Frederick Maurice (Boston, 1927), 166–67; Douglas S. Freeman, *R. E. Lee: A Biography*, 4 vols. (New York, 1934), 2:523 [quote]; Philip Van Doren Stern, *Robert E. Lee, the Man and the Soldier: A Pictorial Biography* (New York, 1963), 170–71; D. Scott Hartwig, "Robert E. Lee and the Maryland Campaign," in Gallagher, *Lee the Soldier*, 350; Edward Hagerman, *The American Civil War and the Origins of Modern Warfare* (Bloomington, Ind., 1988), 122–25; Edward Hagerman, "The Tactical Thought of Robert E. Lee and the Origins of Trench Warfare in the American Civil War, 1861–1862," *Historian* 38 (Nov. 1975): 23–24; Edward Hagerman, "From Jomini to Dennis Hart Mahan: The Evolution of Trench Warfare and the American Civil War," *Civil War History* 13 (Sept. 1967): 200, 202–4; Jay Luvaas, "Lee and the Operational Art," *Parameters* 22 (Autumn 1992): 7; Louis H. Manarin, "Lee in Command: Strategical and Tactical Policies . . ." (Ph.D. diss., Duke University, 1965), 281; Grady McWhiney and Perry D.

The initiative at Chancellorsville thus shifted to Lee, who sent Jackson with twenty-six thousand troops around Hooker's flank on May 2. This left Lee with 17,000 men in front of Hooker, who had 73,000, and Early with 10,000 at Fredericksburg facing 23,000 Federals. By late on May 2 Jackson had six brigades in line to attack the Federals, most of whom remained unaware of the danger. When the Confederates charged out of the woods, many Union troops fled. Hooker's flank "rolled in a sheet of flame upon his center" until darkness halted the fighting.[5]

Lee's bold maneuver reaped great benefits, but at a heavy cost. Jackson fell after dark, mortally wounded by his own men. Command of his corps passed to Stuart, who on May 3 drove the Federals back and established a link with Lee. For a moment at Chancellorsville, when Lee rode into the yard of the ruined house whence Hooker, stunned by a shell, had been evacuated, he allowed himself to believe that this might be the decisive victory he had sought. Encircled by cheering soldiers in the burning woods, Lee relished the thought. Charles Marshall, recalling the look on Lee's face, wrote, "I thought that it must have been from some such scene that men in ancient days ascended to the dignity of gods." The notion passed quickly, however, swept aside by the cries of wounded men and a reminder that Jackson was injured.[6]

Lee's triumph was also spoiled by reports that Early had abandoned his lines at Fredericksburg. Lee had sent a staff officer to tell Early that if the Federals in his front pressed hard, he could fall back. Unfortunately, the officer delivered the message as an order for a withdrawal, and Early obeyed. He left one brigade to face the Federals, who overran them on May 3. Lee ordered Maj. Gen. Lafayette McLaws to support Early with his division, and McLaws arrived in time to bolster a stand at Salem Church. The next morning, May 4, Lee sent Anderson's divi-

---

Jamieson, *Attack and Die: Civil War Military Tactics and the Southern Heritage* (Tuscaloosa, Ala., 1982), 75, 102.

5. Dowdey, *Lee*, 350; Long, *Memoirs of Lee*, 255; Thomas, *Lee*, 283–84; Fitzhugh Lee, *General Lee* (New York, 1894; reprint, Wilmington, N.C., 1989), 250 [quote].

6. Thomas, *Lee*, 284–85; White, *Southern Confederacy*, 273; Marshall, *Aide*, 173 [quote]; J. William Jones, *Personal Reminiscences, Anecdotes, and Letters of Gen. Robert E. Lee* (New York, 1874), 150–51; J. William Jones, *Life and Letters of Robert Edward Lee, Soldier and Man* (New York, 1906), 239; "Tributes to General Lee," *Southern Magazine* 8 (Jan. 1871): 29.

sion to join McLaws' and Early's troops in an attack. McLaws fumbled his preparations, so it was late before the assault began. The Federals retired safely across the Rappahannock that night.[7]

Chancellorsville became Lee's finest victory on May 6, when Hooker withdrew the rest of his army north of the Rappahannock. With a force inferior to that of his enemy, who almost enveloped him, Lee had seized the initiative and beaten the separated parts of the stymied Army of the Potomac. He was not pleased, though. He had not eliminated a sizable portion of Hooker's forces, nor was his victory decisive. Hooker had withdrawn in relatively good order and stood between Lee and the Federal capital. Lee's anger had surfaced on May 4, when Col. E. Porter Alexander found him "feeling . . . real wicked" about McLaws' failure to attack. Lee hurried McLaws' and Anderson's divisions to Chancellorsville on May 5 and prepared to assail Hooker's entrenched Federals, but they fled before the blow could be delivered. To Brig. Gen. W. Dorsey Pender, Lee fumed, "That is the way you young men always do. . . . I tell you what to do, but you don't do it!"[8]

Chancellorsville was not a decisive victory, but Hooker's defeat permitted Lee to press for what he had been planning for months: another invasion of the North to secure such a triumph. Observing that the Federal Congress had authorized vast amounts of money and men, Lee had written to Custis that the only thing that could stop them from waging the "most desolating war that was ever practised" was a revolt in the North, which would come only after "systematic success" by the South. For Lee, this had to be done by his army. When Lee complained to Secretary of War James A. Seddon in January 1863 about wasting men in hollow victories, he was already considering a march north. He ordered a map of a route up the Shenandoah Valley to Pennsylvania and began lobbying for support. He wrote to Mary in April, "If [we are] successful this year, next fall there will be a great change in public opinion at the

7. Krick, "Lee at Chancellorsville," 369, 372–73; Jubal A. Early, *War Memoirs,* ed. Frank E. Vandiver (Philadelphia, 1912; reprint, Bloomington, Ind., 1960), 200–201, 203–10, 217–18, 227; Robert Stiles, *Four Years under Marse Robert* (New York, 1903), 176–78.

8. Thomas, *Lee,* 284–85; E. Porter Alexander, *Fighting for the Confederacy: The Personal Recollections of General Edward Porter Alexander,* ed. Gary W. Gallagher (Chapel Hill, N.C., 1989), 213 [1st quote], 214; Krick, "Lee at Chancellorsville," 373–74; Burke Davis, *Gray Fox: Robert E. Lee and the Civil War* (New York, 1956), 203 [2nd quote].

North. The Republicans will be destroyed & I think the friends of peace will become so strong as that the next administration will go in on that basis."⁹

The primary concern of Seddon and Jefferson Davis with Lee's plan was that much of the material he wanted might better be used elsewhere. Lee was well aware of the situation in other theaters but believed that a decisive victory by his army would offset any losses in other areas. While chastising Seddon in January 1863, Lee also agreed that "Wilmington . . . should be held to the last extremity." As early as April 1862, Lee had observed, "If [the] Mississippi Valley is lost [the] Atlantic states will be ruined," and a year later he insisted, "I consider it of vital importance that we maintain our possession of the Mississippi River." Lee's solution for these problems was clear. To Maj. Gen. Gustavus W. Smith, who was concerned with Federal activity in North Carolina, Lee explained in January 1863 that "Partial encroachments of the enemy we must expect, but they can always be recovered, and any defeat of their large army will reinstate everything." Three months later, Lee declared to Davis that the best way to relieve the Carolinas and Mississippi was for him to mount an offensive. His plan, as he explained to Seddon, was to invade the North.¹⁰

Soon after Hooker slipped to safety across the Rappahannock, Lee renewed his efforts to wring approval from Davis and Seddon. He reiterated that a march north would force the Federals to move troops to his front from other theaters. Seddon had continued to press for transferring units from Virginia to the west, though, and found a new ally in Longstreet, who agreed that he should be sent with two divisions to join Gen. Braxton Bragg in Tennessee. Concerned, Lee met with Davis and

9. Lee to G. W. Custis Lee, Feb. 28, 1863, Lee Papers, DU [1st and 2nd quotes]; Lee to Mary Custis Lee, Apr. 19, 1863, De Butts-Ely Collection, LC [3rd quote]; Dowdey and Manarin, *Wartime Papers*, 411, 438; Manarin, "Lee in Command," 418; Woodworth, *Davis and Lee*, 214–15, 220–21; Luvaas, "Operational Art," 3; Thomas, *Lee*, 276–77.

10. Douglas S. Freeman, ed., *Lee's Dispatches: Unpublished Letters of General Robert E. Lee, C. S. A., to Jefferson Davis and the War Department of the Confederate States of America, 1862–65* (New York, 1915), 69 [1st quote]; Archer Jones, "The Gettysburg Decision," *Virginia Magazine of History and Biography* 68 (July 1960): 332–35, 340; Dowdey and Manarin, *Wartime Papers*, 145 [2nd quote], 384 [4th quote], 433 [3rd quote], 435; Fuller, *Grant and Lee*, 103, Freeman, *Lee*, 2:504; Lee to Davis, Apr. 16, 1863, Lee Papers, DU.

his cabinet in mid-May to argue strongly in favor of his own proposal. The president had already decided that Lee was right, and most of his cabinet agreed.[11]

Lee had confidence that his army would win in the North. He told a visiting cousin in May 1863 that he wished he "could get at those people over there," indicating Hooker's nearby camp. At about the same time, Lee responded warmly to William C. Rives: "I heartily unite in your commendation of this army. . . . There never were such men in any army before, & there never can be better in any army again." Washington himself never offered greater praise for his Continentals or expected so much from them. Lee really had no choice about the latter. Unlike the previous summer, he would not be marching north in tandem with Confederate advances in other theaters. In 1863, Lee would be the sole focus of Confederate offensive efforts.[12]

Despite Lee's confidence, he worried about his commanders. He grieved over the loss of Jackson, whose left arm had to be amputated. There was hope that he would rally, but pneumonia claimed his life on May 10. Lee thus lost an officer on whom he relied greatly, and he feared that he could never replace him. On the same day that he wrote to Rives, Lee also corresponded with Maj. Gen. John Bell Hood and declared, "I agree with you in believing that our army would be invincible if it could be properly organized and officered." He added, "But there is the difficulty—proper commanders. Where can they be obtained?" The answer for Lee lay in reorganizing his army from two corps into three, led by Longstreet and two new lieutenant generals, Ambrose P. Hill and Richard S. Ewell.[13]

In preparation for his march north, Lee also did his best to have

11. Manarin, "Lee in Command," 444; Freeman, *Lee,* 2:503, 3:15, 18–19; Jones, "Gettysburg Decision," 333–34, 337–41; Woodworth, *Davis and Lee,* 228–31; James M. McPherson, *Battle Cry of Freedom: The Civil War Era* (New York, 1988), 646–47; James Longstreet, *From Manassas to Appomattox* (Philadelphia, 1896), 331.

12. Davis, *Gray Fox,* 207 [1st quote]; Lee to William C. Rives, May 21, 1863 [2nd quote], Jefferson Davis Collection, Howard-Tilton Library, Tulane University, New Orleans [hereinafter TU].

13. Dowdey and Manarin, *Wartime Papers,* 452–53, 488–89, 490 [quotes]; Thomas, *Lee,* 286, 289–90; Lee to Davis, May 20, 1863, Lee Papers, DU; John Bell Hood, *Advance and Retreat* (New Orleans, 1880), 53; Walter H. Taylor, *Four Years with General Lee* (New York, 1877; reprint, New York, 1962), 86.

troops sent to him from areas farther south. Because Davis still did not fully accept Lee's concept of his operation—the president persisted in regarding the effort as a disruptive raid rather than an all-out push to win the war—not all of the units Lee requested joined him. A few brigades arrived, but many of them were green, while veteran units remained on detached service. Lee suggested that some of the veterans stationed at Charleston should be sent to Mississippi, while much of the remainder could be brought to northern Virginia under the command of Gen. Pierre G. T. Beauregard to support the march north by making a feint at Washington.[14]

During the first week of June 1863, Lee started his infantry northward, pausing only to review Stuart's troopers near Brandy Station. Lee wrote to Mary that their sons Rooney and Robert E. Lee, Jr., looked "well and flourishing" as they rode with the general's nephew, Fitzhugh Lee. Lee almost lost his sons when Stuart was surprised the day after the review by Federal cavalry and infantry. Hard pressed, Stuart won a narrow victory, but Lee reported to Mary that he had seen their son Rooney carried from the field as a casualty. He was taken to Hickory Hill, the home of his wife's brother, Brig. Gen. Williams Carter Wickham, and their grandfather, Williams Carter, Lee's maternal uncle. The family gathered to nurse Rooney, but they could not protect him from Federal cavalry. On June 26, the Federals stormed the house, beat Carter, and captured Rooney. His brother Robert escaped while Rooney's wife Charlotte packed her husband's clothes. It was the last time she saw Rooney; she died in December 1863 while he was in prison. Riding north, Lee could not take the time to cope with his son's capture. It was not until July 26 that he sent a note to Charlotte consoling her about the taking of her husband and the beating of his "dear Uncle Williams."[15]

14. Woodworth, *Davis and Lee,* 235–36, 240–41; Lee to Davis, May 28, June 7, 1863, Robert E. Lee Papers, Library of Virginia, Richmond [hereinafter LV].

15. Thomas, *Lee,* 266, 290–91, 305; Dowdey and Manarin, *Wartime Papers,* 477; Lee to Mary Custis Lee, June 9 [1st quote], 11, 1863, De Butts-Ely Collection, LC; Fitzhugh Lee, *General Lee,* 263; Robert E. Lee, Jr., *Recollections and Letters of General Robert E. Lee* (New York, 1904), 81, 98–99, 101, 114; Paul D. Casdorph, *Lee and Jackson: Confederate Chieftains* (New York, 1992), 374–75; Emily V. Mason, *Popular Life of Gen. Robert E. Lee* (Baltimore, 1870), 170; Jones, *Life and Letters,* 228–29, 278; Robert W. Winston, *Robert E. Lee: A Biography* (New York, 1941), 240; William P. Johnston, "Memoranda of Conversations with General R. E. Lee," in Gallagher, *Lee the Soldier,* 33; Mary P. Coulling, *Lee Girls* (Winston-Salem, N.C., 1987), 126–27; William F. Chaney, *Duty Most Sub-*

Lee's concern for Rooney may well have been compounded by the June 1863 execution of Orton Williams, the younger brother of Lee's confidant, Markie Williams. Orton had been a playmate and later a suitor of Agnes Lee before the war began and served as a liaison between her father and Winfield Scott before leaving the army in the summer of 1861. Lee had arranged for his appointment as a staff officer with the Army of Tennessee, but he also served as an aide for Lee at Fredericksburg while on leave. The war had brought violent changes in Orton, though, and his visit with Agnes at Hickory Hill during Christmas 1862 upset her. Returning west, Orton volunteered for a mysterious mission and was captured on June 9 while disguised as a Union officer. Six hours after his arrest, he was hanged. Lee wrote to Markie three years later that when he thought of Orton, "my blood boils at the thought of the atrocious outrage, against every manly & christian sentiment which the Great God alone is able to forgive."[16]

Lee's family concerns were great, but he remained focused on his duties as commander of the South's principal army. He had written to Davis in late May that an apparent advance by Hooker might force him to withdraw, but the Federal leader's retirement toward Washington allowed Lee to initiate his march north. Ewell defeated the Federals at Winchester on June 15, 1863. He crossed the Potomac River two days later, and Lee followed with Hill and Longstreet. Despite this windfall, Lee still worried. Because "uncertainty" about Hooker had caused delay, Lee wrote, "it may be now too late to accomplish all that was desired." He also did not have all the troops he wanted. He lectured Davis by mail, "It seems to me that we cannot afford to keep our troops

lime: The Life of Robert E. Lee as Told through the "Carter Letters" (Baltimore, 1996), 12; Francis R. Adams, ed., "An Annotated Edition of the Personal Letters of Robert E. Lee, April 1855–April, 1861" (Ph.D. diss., University of Maryland, 1955), 82; Nancy S. Anderson and Dwight Anderson, *The Generals: Ulysses S. Grant and Robert E. Lee* (New York, 1988), 177; Rose M. E. MacDonald, *Mrs. Robert E. Lee* (Boston, 1939), 167; Jones, *Personal Reminiscences,* 400 [2nd quote]; Margaret Sanborn, *Robert E. Lee: The Complete Man* (Philadelphia, 1967), 137; Anne Wickham to Charles Carter Lee, n.d. [1863], Ethel Armes Papers, LC.

16. Anderson and Anderson, *Generals,* 90–91; Coulling, *Lee Girls,* 66, 90, 114, 122–25; Dowdey, *Lee,* 400; Avery Craven, ed., *"To Markie": The Letters of Robert E. Lee to Martha Custis Williams from the Originals in the Huntington Library* (Cambridge, Mass., 1933), 71–72 [quote]; Marshall W. Fishwick, *Lee after the War* (New York, 1963), 92–93; Charles B. Flood, *Lee: The Last Years* (Boston, 1981), 73–75.

awaiting possible movements of the enemy, but that our true policy is, as far as we can, so to employ our own forces as to give occupation to his at points of our own selection."[17]

Lee had selected his point: Pennsylvania. By going there, he would force Hooker out of Virginia, draw Union reinforcements from other theaters, and strike a decisive blow. Lee knew the resources of the Confederacy were failing, so his third objective remained the most important. He expected a "great battle" in Pennsylvania, as he informed Maj. Gen. Isaac Trimble. With such a battle, Lee wrote, "if God gives us the victory, the war will be over and we shall achieve the recognition of our independence." Lee encouraged Davis to support any peace movement in the North, even one that sought to restore the Union. He wrote that when a Confederate victory strengthened antiwar sentiment in the North, Davis could reveal his true conditions because "the desire of our people for a distinct and independent national existence will prove as steadfast under the influence of peaceful measures as it has shown itself in the midst of war." The time had come again, as it had in September 1862, to push for independence, but now Lee, with a larger and better-equipped army, would lend weight to Southern demands by winning a decisive victory. Even after he retreated from Pennsylvania, he contended that a victory there would have won Southern independence.[18]

Lee emphasized his primary objective in a letter to Davis in late June. As part of his commitment to "an all-out end-the-war gamble," Lee asked him again to transfer more troops to northern Virginia, where they would work under the command of Beauregard in support of Lee's operation. This would leave the defenses of Charleston and Richmond virtually denuded, but Lee was playing to win. He believed that reinforcing Beauregard would push the Federals to assign troops to protect Washington, reduce the numbers he would confront in Pennsylvania, and "greatly increase the probability" of decisive victory. He also

17. Lee to Davis, May 30, June 15 [1st and 2nd quotes], 25 [3rd quote], 1863, Davis Collection, TU.

18. Dowdey and Manarin, *Wartime Papers*, 509, 569–70; Marshall, *Aide*, 189; Long, *Memoirs of Lee*, 268–69; McPherson, *Battle Cry*, 660; Freeman, *Lee*, 3:59 [1st and 2nd quotes]; Woodworth, *Davis and Lee*, 242, 245; Allan, "Memoranda," 14; Jones, *Life and Letters*, 237; *The War of the Rebellion: A Compilation of the Official Records of the Union and Confederate Armies*, 130 vols. (Washington, D.C., 1880–1902), ser. I, vol. 27, pt. 3:881–82 [3rd quote; hereinafter *OR*].

argued that the concentration of Federals in the east might allow Confederates to march into Kentucky. Lee repeated his plea several times, insisting Beauregard's force would be useful even if it was only an "effigy" of an army, but Davis never agreed.[19]

Lee entered Pennsylvania in June 1863, almost ten months after he had first planned to do so. Like Washington, Lee again ordered his men "to abstain, with most scrupulous care, from unnecessary or wanton injury to private property." This was a reminder of his order in early June against theft or vandalism, issued on the same day that Lee had regaled his staff with a discussion of how British prisoners during the Revolution had built a large house that stood near his camp. He repeated in his second missive that "we make war only upon armed men" and that "no greater disgrace" could befall his army than to commit "barbarous outrages" like "the enemy in our own country." However, as hungry or angry Confederates ignored his orders, Lee proved no more able to control his men than George Washington had been; among those who had disappointed Washington in this regard was Lee's own father.[20]

Lee continued to fret about Hooker as he marched north. The Union commander might not cooperate by leaving Virginia; in fact, he might attack Richmond. Hooker had obliged Lee by withdrawing into a position near Washington, but apart from that little was known about his movements. Ordinarily Lee would have relied upon Stuart for information, but the cavalry leader was more focused upon vindication for Brandy Station. Given vague orders by Lee, Stuart interpreted these directions freely and again rode around the Army of the Potomac. He did not rejoin Lee until after the Army of Northern Virginia engaged the Federals at Gettysburg.[21]

19. Lee to Davis, June 25, 1863, Davis Collection, TU; Woodworth, *Davis and Lee,* 239 [1st quote]; Thomas, *Lee,* 292; Dowdey and Manarin, *Wartime Papers,* 527–28 [2nd quote], 530–33, 543–44; Freeman, *Lee,* 3:50 [3rd quote]; OR, I, 27, 3:924–25, 930–32; I, 27, 1:76–77.

20. Cooke, *Life of Lee,* 291 [1st quote]; Walter H. Taylor, *General Lee: His Campaigns in Virginia, 1861–1865* (Norfolk, Va., 1906), 185–86; OR, I, 27:912–13, 942–43 [2nd–5th quotes]; Marshall, *Aide,* 198–99; McPherson, *Battle Cry,* 649; Frank Moore, ed., *The Rebellion Record: A Diary of American Events,* 12 vols. (New York, 1861–1868; reprint, New York, 1977), 7: "Documents," 325.

21. Fuller, *Grant and Lee,* 168–69; Thomas, *Lee,* 292, 293, 298; James Longstreet, *Manassas to Appomattox,* 373.

Lee did not learn until the night of June 28, from a spy, that Maj. Gen. George G. Meade had replaced Hooker in command and led the Army of the Potomac north. Hooker's blunders had finally convinced Lincoln to remove him. Lee knew Meade; his father had served in the militia led by Light-Horse Harry during the Whiskey Rebellion, and the two sons had been in the engineers during the Mexican War. Lee respected Meade, who, he said, would make no mistakes and would take full advantage of any the Confederates made. For that reason, and because he himself had no effective cavalry, Lee ordered his army to concentrate at Cashtown. This would put the Confederates east of the mountains, between Meade and their own supply line to Virginia, and in a good position, Lee hoped, to choose the place for a fight.[22]

On June 30, a Confederate brigade commanded by Brig. Gen. James J. Pettigrew was marching toward Gettysburg, where there were shoes and other supplies, when it encountered Union cavalry. The next day, the Southerners pushed aside the blue-clad troopers but slammed into Union infantry. By the time Lee arrived, four of his divisions were engaged with two Federal infantry corps on the west side of Gettysburg. As he watched, Ewell arrived on the north side, driving Union troops through the town and onto the heights to the south. Lee told Ewell to storm the hills if he thought they could be taken, but unlike his predecessor Jackson, Ewell was not so daring. He believed that his troops were tired and disorganized, and Federals were reported to be on his flank. Those in his front appeared to be strong and held good ground. Even a visit by Lee did not stir Ewell, though he did assure Lee that if an assault were made on the far end of the Union line the next day, he would take the hills in his front as a diversion.[23]

Lee did not think Gettysburg was a good spot to fight, but he decided that it offered the best opportunity he would get. His army had not yet concentrated, and without cavalry he could not be sure if his supply line was secure or where the main enemy army was located. Once the battle began and Ewell assured him that he could take the hills south of the

22. Marshall, *Aide,* 217–19, 221, 223; Thomas, *Lee,* 293; Fitzhugh Lee, *General Lee,* 269; White, *Southern Confederacy,* 289; Freeman, *Lee,* 3:62–64.

23. Thomas, *Lee,* 294–95; Walter H. Taylor, *General Lee,* 190; James Longstreet, *Manassas to Appomattox,* 358–59; Walter H. Taylor, *Four Years,* 95; Fitzhugh Lee, *General Lee,* 271–72, 276–77; Marshall, *Aide,* 232–33; Dowdey, *Lee,* 369–72; Alan T. Nolan, "General Lee," in Gallagher, *Lee the Soldier,* 491–93.

town, Lee decided that Gettysburg was the place to attack. He returned from his visit to Ewell and told Longstreet and Hill that he wanted to assault the Union left the following day "as early as practicable." He expected that by that time most of his army would be present.[24]

Longstreet disagreed with Lee about attacking. Before the Confederates left Virginia, Longstreet and other officers had spoken with Lee and thought he intended to lure the Federals into an assault as he had done at Second Manassas and at Fredericksburg. Longstreet believed that Chancellorsville was not a great victory because it had cost the Army of Northern Virginia too much: Lee had lost 22 percent of his troops, while Hooker lost only about 15 percent. The balance when the Confederates stood on the defensive had been much more favorable. Longstreet reminded Lee of this as they talked on July 1, adding that Napoleon had pointedly advised one of his marshals to force the foe to attack. Longstreet declared that this could be done by slipping between Meade and Washington.[25]

Lee may have assured Longstreet and others that he would not attack, but neither Washington nor Napoleon had won decisively by standing on the defensive. Moreover, while other Union commanders had advanced into disaster, Lee did not think that Meade would be as inept. Finally, Lee refused to lose the initiative to Meade, as Hooker had lost it to Lee. The first day of battle at Gettysburg had ended well for the Confederates, despite Ewell's balking, and Lee believed that his troops would succeed when they attacked on July 2. As far as he could tell, only part of the Federal army was in his front, and thus he had a chance to defeat Meade before all of his army could be on the field. Longstreet insisted that if the Federals were present the next day, Meade would have all of his army at hand, but Lee ignored him. When Long-

24. White, *Southern Confederacy,* 292–98; Long, *Memoirs of Lee,* 277; Marshall, *Aide,* 232–34 [quote]; Fitzhugh Lee, *General Lee,* 276–77; Dowdey, *Lee,* 371–72; Fuller, *Grant and Lee,* 197; William P. Snow, *Lee and His Generals: Their Lives and Campaigns* (New York, 1867; reprint, New York, 1982), 101; John J. Bowen, *The Strategy of Robert E. Lee* (New York, 1914), 150.

25. Helen D. Longstreet, *Lee and Longstreet at High Tide* (Gainesville, Ga., 1904), 49; James Longstreet, *Manassas to Appomattox,* 329–31; Dowdey and Manarin, *Wartime Papers,* 426; James Longstreet, "Lee in Pennsylvania," in Gallagher, *Lee the Soldier,* 383–84, 388–89; McPherson, *Battle Cry,* 645; Marshall, *Aide,* 232–33; Fitzhugh Lee, *General Lee,* 276–77; Francis Lawley, "General Lee," in Gallagher, *Lee the Soldier,* 92.

street argued that they should maneuver rather than fight, Lee replied that that would be impossible without Stuart.[26] At last, Lee thought that at Gettysburg the conditions appeared right for the decisive victory that would secure Southern independence.

Lee met with Longstreet and two of his division commanders, Hood and McLaws, before dawn on July 2 to discuss the impending action. Longstreet renewed his objections to an attack, but Lee was adamant. Longstreet would assail the Union left while Ewell attacked the hills in his front on the right. Lee believed that after the Federals on the field were swept from their positions, Meade could be defeated in detail. Leaving Longstreet, a visibly excited Lee hurried to talk with Ewell again to make certain that he would attack the hills as he had promised.[27]

When Lee returned from Ewell's camp at about ten in the morning on July 2, he was annoyed to find Longstreet where he had left him on Seminary Ridge. The march to the far left end of the Union line would take much time, and Longstreet had not yet begun. Lee had not told Longstreet precisely when to attack, adhering to his usual policy of allowing his subordinates to make their own arrangements within the scope of his defined tactic, but he had assumed that his corps commander understood that his assault had to come before more Federals arrived. Lee urged Longstreet to move immediately, only to hear another version of what the latter had told Hood: he preferred to wait until all of his troops were on the field before committing any of his units. Earlier he had been waiting for Maj. Gen. George E. Pickett's division; now he said he wanted all of Brig. Gen. Evander M. Law's troops at hand. Lee waited with Longstreet until Law tardily arrived in the early afternoon; only then did Longstreet's divisions march, far behind schedule.[28]

26. Helen D. Longstreet, *High Tide,* 38; James Longstreet, *Manassas to Appomattox,* 358–59; Long, *Memoirs of Lee,* 278; Fitzgerald Ross, *A Visit to the Cities and Camps of the Confederate States* (London, 1865), 76.

27. Arthur J. L. Fremantle, *Three Months in the Southern States, April–June, 1863* (London, 1863), 257; James Longstreet, *Manassas to Appomattox,* 362–63; Hood, *Advance and Retreat,* 57; Marshall, *Aide,* 232–33; Fitzhugh Lee, *General Lee,* 276–77; James Longstreet, "Lee in Pennsylvania," 388–89; Thomas, *Lee,* 297–98; Freeman, *Lee,* 3:90–91.

28. James Longstreet, "Lee in Pennsylvania," 388–89; Dowdey, *Lee,* 375–76; Jones, *Life and Letters,* 257; Thomas, *Lee,* 297–98; Long, *Memoirs of Lee,* 281–82; E. Porter Alexander, *Fighting for the Confederacy,* 237; Hood, *Advance and Retreat,* 57.

Longstreet hit the Union left at four in the afternoon, long after more Federals arrived and extended their flank to the hills known as the Round Tops. After Longstreet's departure, Lee left him to his own devices and either stood with Hill, awaiting the sound of Longstreet's attack, or sat by himself on a stump. This was his usual mode of command, and it again proved unfortunate. Without knowing that the Federals had extended their lines, Lee had insisted that Longstreet put his divisions across Emmitsburg Road for an advance toward the end of Cemetery Ridge. This would have flanked the Union line as he understood it to be, but by the late afternoon it exposed the charging Confederates to flanking fire from the Round Tops. Hood saw this and, with the support of McLaws, asked Longstreet to change his dispositions, but Longstreet insisted that the charge should be made as Lee had ordered.[29]

Hood's and McLaws' troops failed miserably. Longstreet later wrote that his men "broke every line they encountered" as they advanced but were repulsed due to heavy casualties and a lack of support. Lee would have agreed with this evaluation. Some attackers reached the top of Cemetery Ridge, where Lee saw their flags, but they were thrown back by Federal reinforcements. As Longstreet withdrew, Ewell's units reached the top of Cemetery Hill and established a position on the slopes of Culp's Hill, but their supports also failed. In a few hours they were driven from Cemetery Hill, and a second effort on the morning of July 3 accomplished nothing.[30]

Lee was disappointed that Longstreet's attack had not broken the Union line, but he was encouraged by the sight of Confederate flags on Cemetery Ridge before they were swept away. He thought that the reinforcements that met Longstreet and Ewell came from the Federal center, which must have been weakened. Perhaps an assault on this point, preceded by an artillery bombardment and properly supported, would break the Union line. Antoine Henri de Jomini himself had stressed that an attack should hit the enemy where it was weak, even if at the center. Lee had seen such an effort succeed at Chapultepec, where several young

29. White, *Southern Confederacy,* 297–305; Fremantle, *Three Months,* 260; Manarin, "Lee in Command," 481–82; Hood, *Advance and Retreat,* 58–59; Dowdey, *Lee,* 377–78; Freeman, *Lee,* 3:97–99.

30. James Longstreet, "Lee in Pennsylvania," 393 [quote]; Thomas, *Lee,* 297–98; E. Porter Alexander, *Memoirs,* 386–87; Dowdey, *Lee,* 379–81, 385–86; White, *Southern Confederacy,* 307; Marshall, *Aide,* 235–36.

lieutenants, including Longstreet, won glory. Lee would now ask him to repeat his triumph on another field.[31]

Lee was correct that the Union lines had been hard pressed on July 2, but they were far from breaking. Meade had seriously considered a withdrawal on the night of July 2, but the capture of dispatches that told of Davis' refusal to put Beauregard in northern Virginia to threaten Washington convinced him to stay. Meade's officers concurred. Longstreet suspected that the Federal lines were stronger than Lee knew, and on the morning of July 3 he again argued in favor of slipping between Meade and Washington. Lee brushed aside this counsel. He had considered hitting both Union flanks again, but Meade's repulse of Ewell from the hills on his right precluded another flank attack. Now Lee focused on an assault on the center of Cemetery Ridge, to be led by Pickett's division of Longstreet's corps. A Chapultepec veteran, Pickett was eager, his men were fresh, and he understood that they would be accompanied by two divisions of Hill's corps, which had rested on July 2. Longstreet reluctantly acquiesced.[32]

The assault on July 3 that became known as Pickett's Charge made a grand spectacle, but it failed. Col. E. Porter Alexander directed the Confederate guns, about half of Lee's total of 159, in a bombardment, but it had little effect. Given the authority to say whether the assault should proceed, Alexander noted that Union counterbattery fire seemed to be slackening. But the decreasing Federal fire was a deception employed by Meade's chief of artillery, Brig. Gen. Henry J. Hunt. Longstreet received Alexander's report and nodded his assent for Pickett to advance, then joined Alexander, who confessed that he had no ammunition left to support Pickett's attack. Longstreet responded that Lee wanted it, so he had no choice. Again no one told Lee, who watched as almost fifteen thousand men assailed Cemetery Ridge. Brig. Gen. Lewis A. Armistead, who as a lieutenant had charged at Chapultepec, led about five hundred men

31. Dowdey and Manarin, *Wartime Papers,* 479; Thomas, *Lee,* 299–300; James Longstreet, "Lee in Pennsylvania," 397; Thomas L. Connelly and Archer Jones, *The Politics of Command: Factions and Ideas in Confederate Strategy* (Baton Rouge, 1983), 11, 16; Dowdey, *Lee,* 93; White, *Southern Confederacy,* 44; Margaret Sanborn, *Robert E. Lee: A Portrait* (Philadelphia, 1966), 187.

32. White, *Southern Confederacy,* 310; Thomas, *Lee,* 299–300; James Longstreet, "Lee in Pennsylvania," 397; Dowdey, *Lee,* 383; Fitzhugh Lee, *General Lee,* 297–98; Frederick T. Hill, *On the Trail of Grant and Lee* (New York, 1911), 188.

to the stone wall at the base of Cemetery Ridge and fell mortally wounded. A shattered remnant of Pickett's three brigades, as well as six of Hill's brigades, trickled back through the storm of gunfire.[33]

Lee may or may not have realized that his bombardment had not disrupted the Union center, but he certainly noticed that a key element was missing. He had agreed with Longstreet that the Confederates who reached Cemetery Ridge on July 2 had failed because they were not properly supported. During his conversation with Longstreet and others on July 3, Lee thought that the importance of support had been addressed. Most of his staff agreed later that Lee verbally told Longstreet to arrange for three brigades to exploit any breach. Tragically, however, Lee did not issue a written order specifying the source of these brigades. Even his staff later debated whether they were to be from Hood and McLaws or from one of Hill's divisions. Having left the decision to Longstreet, Lee watched angrily as no one supported Armistead's forlorn assault. Two brigades from Hill's corps advanced a half hour after Pickett had failed, in what Alexander described as an "absurd and tragic" effort that won nothing.[34]

As the survivors of Pickett's Charge made their way back, Lee rallied them in a scene that reminded some of Washington at Monmouth. With Longstreet's assistance, he positioned them for the counterstroke he expected from Meade. None came because the Federal army had suffered more than 26 percent casualties among the 88,289 men engaged. While this paled in comparison with Lee's loss of over 37 percent of about 75,000 troops engaged, Meade was not inclined to continue the slaughter if Lee would withdraw. Contrary to his tactic at Antietam, Lee quickly prepared to do just that, working long after nightfall to begin his

33. Fitzhugh Lee, *General Lee*, 290–91; Dowdey, *Lee*, 93, 95, 388; E. Porter Alexander, "Letter on Causes of Lee's Defeat at Gettysburg," in Gallagher, *Lee the Soldier*, 443–44; Thomas, *Lee*, 299–300; James Longstreet, "Lee in Pennsylvania," 397; Dowdey and Manarin, *Wartime Papers*, 480; Freeman, *Lee*, 3:109–10, 115–21.

34. Long, *Memoirs of Lee*, 288; Walter H. Taylor, *General Lee*, 293, 294; Dowdey and Manarin, *Wartime Papers*, 480; Walter H. Taylor, *Four Years*, 104, 107–8; Stanley F. Horn, ed., *The Robert E. Lee Reader* (Indianapolis, 1949), 322–23; Jones, *Life and Letters*, 265–67; Dowdey, *Lee*, 386; Fitzhugh Lee, *General Lee*, 287–89, 291–92; E. Porter Alexander, *Military Memoirs of a Confederate* (New York, 1907; reprint, Dayton, Ohio, 1977), 425 [quote]; White, *Southern Confederacy*, 311, 318; E. Porter Alexander, *Fighting for the Confederacy*, 280–83.

retreat into Virginia. Only once did anyone see his reserve break. About midnight, Lee rode into Brig. Gen. John D. Imboden's camp. The latter, who had just arrived that day with his men, listened as Lee spoke angrily about the attack and the failure to send any support, which he declared he had been told would be provided. Lee asserted that if Pickett had been supported, he could have broken the Federal line. Lee concluded, "Too bad! *Too bad!!* OH! TOO BAD!!!"[35]

The issue of support for Pickett's Charge became one of the main points of discussion about Gettysburg among Confederates, in part because it allowed them to blame Longstreet for the defeat. Regardless of whether Lee asked for more brigades, the fact remains that he attacked the center of a well-placed enemy line. He thus violated a "fundamental principle" of Jomini's discussion of Napoleon's strategy. Even if such an assault were successful, it would be too costly. Why did Lee do it? He wanted the decisive victory that would win the war. As he told Fitzgerald Ross, an Austrian officer who had joined him as an observer during the retreat in July 1863, he attacked believing that Meade had only part of his army on the field and "that a successful battle would cut the knot so easily and satisfactorily that he had determined to risk it." Washington had his decisive victory at Yorktown; Lee would have his at Gettysburg, or so he thought. Long after, he insisted that if he had won there, the South would be independent. Many Southerners, including Davis, agreed.[36]

Lee's retreat became a ten-day nightmare, but he maintained a stoic facade throughout the ordeal. At Hagerstown his army was trapped by a swollen Potomac River, but Lee joked with Imboden, laughing and asking, "Does it ever quit raining about here? If so, I should like to see a clear day." To Davis he initially wrote, "It is believed that the enemy has suffered severely in these operations, but our own loss has not been light." He provided more details to the president three days later, refer-

35. Thomas, *Lee,* 300–301; Sanborn, *Complete Man,* 130–31; John D. Imboden, "Lee at Gettysburg," *Galaxy* 11 (Apr. 1871): 508–9 [quote]; Fitzhugh Lee, *General Lee,* 300; Dowdey, *Lee,* 390; Horn, *Reader,* 324–25.

36. James Longstreet, "Lee in Pennsylvania," 399–401, 503; White, *Southern Confederacy,* 311; Gamaliel Bradford, *Lee the American* (Boston, 1912; rev. ed., Cambridge, Mass., 1929) 181 [1st quote]; Thomas, *Lee,* 302; Horn, *Reader,* 331 [2nd quote]; Jefferson Davis, *The Rise and Fall of the Confederate Government,* 2 vols. (New York, 1881), 2:447.

ring to the "unsuccessful issue of our final attack on the enemy." Finally, on July 8 he wrote that his army was "reduced in numbers," but "its condition" was "good, and its confidence unimpaired." He expected Meade to attack, but Meade's officers urged caution and Lee crossed safely to Virginia.[37]

Criticism of Lee emerged after Gettysburg, but Davis stood firmly behind his general. Shortly after returning to Virginia, Lee spoke with a staff officer sent by the president to interview him. Lee emphasized that popular opinion was of no value because neither the people nor the press ever understood the importance of a battle. For example, they were ecstatic with Fredericksburg and Chancellorsville, while he had been disappointed because the enemy escaped. Furthermore, Lee declared, "we did whip them at Gettysburg, and it will be seen for the next six months that that *army* will be as quiet as a sucking dove." When critics remained vocal, Lee wrote to Davis that his army could not be blamed for failing to do what he expected, saying, "I am alone to blame, in perhaps expecting too much of its prowess & valour." Lee later offered to resign, but Davis refused to accept the offer.[38]

Clerk John B. Jones noticed that when Davis and Lee rode together in September 1863, there were none of the usual cheers. Lee had revealed serious flaws in his Gettysburg campaign. The latitude he allowed subordinates led to the absence of Stuart and permitted Ewell and Longstreet to exercise damaging discretion. His focus on decisive victory led to excessive casualties. Perhaps the most serious flaw was in his strategic vision. As John F. C. Fuller wrote later, the invasion "began as a political move and it ended in a political fiasco." Accepting Lee's claim that he could win, Davis demanded that the Lincoln administra-

---

37. Imboden, "Lee at Gettysburg," 513 [1st quote]; Thomas, *Lee,* 305; Lee to Davis, July 4 [2nd quote], 7 [3rd quote], 8 [4th–6th quotes], 1863, Davis Collection, TU; Lee to Richard S. Ewell, July 11, 1863, Robert E. Lee Papers, United States Army Military History Institute, Carlisle, Pa.; Hill, *Trail,* 196–97.

38. Edward A. Pollard, *The Lost Cause: A New Southern History of the War of the Confederates* (New York, 1867), 404–5; "Leading Confederates on the Battle of Gettysburg," *Southern Historical Society Papers* 4 (1877): 153–55 [1st quote]; Dowdey and Manarin, *Wartime Papers,* 565 [2nd quote], 589–90, 593; Thomas, *Lee,* 306–8; Lee to Davis, July 31, 1863, Lee Papers, LV; Freeman, *Lee's Dispatches,* 110; White, *Southern Confederacy,* 325; Woodworth, *Davis and Lee,* 249; J. Cutler Andrews, *The South Reports the Civil War* (Princeton, 1970), 318.

tion discuss independence with a Confederate delegation. Lee's defeat allowed Lincoln to reject this demand, and the fall of Vicksburg at the same time enhanced the crushing disappointment of Lee's failure. Lee feebly expressed "regret" for the loss of the last Confederate bastion on the Mississippi River, but this was scant comfort.[39] Lee was mistaken that the Federals would have to concentrate on a single theater each season and that his army alone could compel them to negotiate. Even if Lee had won, the loss of Vicksburg would have allowed Lincoln to spurn Davis.

Lee never admitted that his campaign was a failure, though he did regret the cost of what he insisted was a partial success. To Mary on July 12 he confessed that "our success at Gettysburg was not so great as reported." Three days later he wrote to her that his return to Virginia was "sooner than [he] had originally contemplated," but he had done what he intended: to draw the Federal army north of the Potomac River. Nearly two weeks of reflection and criticism led him to write to his wife that "The army . . . has accomplished all that could have been reasonably expected. It ought not to have been expected to have performed impossibilities or to have fulfilled the anticipations of the thoughtless & unreasonable." To Margaret Stuart that same day, and to others later, he identified the source of the expectations as himself but added that his army "responded to the call nobly and cheerfully, and tho it did not win a victory, it conquered a success." His third letter that day, however, was a sad note of consolation to Charlotte, the wife of his captive son Rooney. To her, Lee admitted that "the loss of our gallant officers and men throughout the army causes me to weep tears of blood, and to wish I could never hear the sound of a gun again."[40]

---

39. John B. Jones, *A Rebel War Clerk's Diary,* ed. Howard Swiggett, 2 vols. (New York, 1935), 2:32; James Longstreet, *Manassas to Appomattox,* 358; Allan, "Memoranda," 14; Nolan, "General Lee," 485–90; Gary W. Gallagher, " 'If the Enemy Is There, We Must Attack Him': R. E. Lee and the Second Day at Gettysburg," in Gallagher, *Lee the Soldier,* 511; Long, *Memoirs of Lee,* 295; Marshall, *Aide,* xvii–xviii; Fuller, *Grant and Lee,* 201 [1st quote]; Dunbar Rowland, ed., *Jefferson Davis, Constitutionalist: His Letters, Papers, and Speeches,* 10 vols. (Jackson, Miss., 1923), 5:567 [2nd quote].

40. Fitzhugh Lee, *General Lee,* 306 [1st quote]; Dowdey and Manarin, *Wartime Papers,* 551 [2nd quote], 560 [3rd quote]; Lee to Margaret Stuart, July 26, 1863 [4th quote], William G. McCabe Papers, University of Virginia Library, Charlottesville [hereinafter UVA]; Lee to S. Bassett [Gibbs?] French, July 31, 1863, Robert E. Lee Papers, Archives and Library Division, Mississippi Department of Archives and History, Jackson; Jones, *Personal Reminiscences,* 400 [5th quote].

Despite his melancholy confession to Charlotte, Lee did not consider Gettysburg to be an omen of defeat. Longstreet later asserted that Lee "at Gettysburg looked something like Napoleon at Waterloo," but Lee never made such a connection. It remained to him a lost opportunity of some importance but hardly a catastrophic event. He declared in a letter to Davis on July 31, 1863, that his army "achieved under the guidance of the Most High a general success, though it did not win a victory." Five years later, in a conversation with William Allan, Lee insisted again that he "inflicted more damage than he received, and broke up the Federal summer campaign" in 1863. Col. John H. Mosby, who spoke with Lee two months after the battle, recalled that he "did not seem in the least depressed, and was as buoyant and aggressive as ever." In the spring of 1864 Lee told Maj. Gen. Henry Heth, who had been wounded at Gettysburg, that if he could find the troops and supplies to repeat the effort, he would do so.[41]

As he refitted his battered army, Lee did realize that his losses meant that he would have to shift his strategic focus. Since the beginning of the war, he had stressed the importance of decisive victories over military endurance as the key to forcing the North to negotiate. Henceforth, he had to accept that his capacity to attack had been greatly reduced, if not eliminated. That did not mean he would lose the war; rather, he would focus on keeping his army active in the field as long as he could. He would fight, but he would not again attempt extended raids into the North. He hoped that either Northern voters would tire of Lincoln's aggression, as months passed and losses increased, and elect someone more amenable to accepting Southern independence, or Lincoln himself would realize the futility of his efforts and ask for negotiations. Either way, Lee still believed the primary focus of the war would remain his army, just as Washington and the Continentals had been the focus of the Revolutionary War. As he wrote to Margaret Stuart, "We must now prepare for harder blows, harder work."[42]

41. James Longstreet, *Manassas to Appomattox*, 405 [1st quote]; Lee to Davis, July 31, 1863, Lee Papers, LV; Freeman, *Lee's Dispatches*, 110 [2nd quote]; John S. Mosby, *The Memoirs of Colonel John S. Mosby*, ed. Charles W. Russell (Boston, 1917; reprint, Bloomington, Ind., 1959), 374 [3rd quote]; "Leading Confederates on Gettysburg," 153; Allan, "Memoranda," 14 [4th quote]; Thomas, *Lee*, 315.

42. Woodworth, *Davis and Lee*, 250–51; Thomas, *Lee*, 306; Freeman, *Lee*, 3:162, 164–65; Lee to Margaret Stuart, July 26, 1863 [quote], McCabe Papers, UVA.

One of the greatest threats to the efficacy of Lee's army, as it had been to Washington's, was desertion, which increased rapidly after Gettysburg. Lee initially asked for an amnesty proclamation from Davis. Amnesty did not entice many to return, however, and so Lee asked for harsher measures, including "rigid enforcement of the death penalty in future in cases of conviction." This demand provided a sharp contrast to the approach preferred by Davis, who was more inclined to leniency. Despite his ferocious stance, Lee himself suspended the death penalty in a number of cases when he thought clemency might be effective. Neither mercy nor swift executions, however, made much difference in the steady increase of desertion from Lee's army through 1864 and into 1865.[43]

Lee also struggled with his superiors to keep his army together. On August 31, 1863, he urged Longstreet to prepare for a new offensive, adding, "I can see nothing better to be done than to endeavour to bring General Meade out & use one effort to crush his army while in its present condition." Soon after, Bragg's abandonment of east Tennessee led Davis to ask Lee if he would go west and assume command of Bragg's army for a single campaign. When Lee insisted that this was a bad idea, the president asked that Longstreet and his corps be sent to Bragg. Lee did not like this either, but he agreed when Davis insisted. After Lee held a grand review on September 9, Longstreet's troops boarded trains for the long journey west.[44]

Two of Longstreet's brigades went to hard-pressed Charleston and Pickett's division stayed in Richmond, but Longstreet with McLaws' and Hood's divisions helped win a victory for Bragg on Chickamauga Creek during the third week of September 1863. Lee congratulated Longstreet but added, "Finish the work before you, my dear General, and return to me. I want you badly, and you cannot get back too soon." Lee's hopes faded as Bragg besieged Chattanooga. Maj. Gen. William S. Rosecrans, who had lost at Chickamauga, was replaced with Maj. Gen. George H. Thomas, who took orders from a new theater commander, Maj. Gen.

43. Thomas, *Lee,* 308–9; Freeman, *Lee's Dispatches,* 122–24 [quote], 149–50, 154–58; Woodworth, *Davis and Lee,* 252–53, 303–4; Long, *Memoirs of Lee,* 629–30.

44. Lee to James Longstreet, Aug. 31, 1863 [quote], John Fairfax Papers, Virginia Historical Society, Richmond [hereinafter VHS]; Woodworth, *Davis and Lee,* 255–56; Snow, *Lee and His Generals,* 111; James Longstreet, *Manassas to Appomattox,* 409, 437.

Ulysses S. Grant. Bragg sent Longstreet away in a futile attempt to take Knoxville and then was himself defeated and driven into Georgia.[45]

The turmoil in the west did provide Lee with a chance for a fall offensive. After Longstreet departed, Lee settled into a defensive position and then learned that Meade had sent two corps to Tennessee. Although suffering from chest pain that often forced him to ride in a wagon rather than on horseback, Lee sent Hill's and Ewell's corps around Meade's right flank. When the Federals withdrew to stay between the Confederates and Washington, Lee pursued until Hill's leading division was mauled near Bristoe Station, losing 1,361 men in a pointless assault.[46]

When Lee decided to withdraw to the south, Meade followed and struck a heavy blow. Five days after Bristoe Station, Lee wrote to Mary that if his men were properly clothed, he would move north of the Potomac, but they were not, and he "could not bear to expose them to certain suffering on an uncertain issue." Lacking shoes, coats, and blankets, the South's primary army had to be taken below the Rappahannock by its commander, who left a small force on the northern bank to guard the crossings. Ten days later, Lee and Early both hurried to Rappahannock Bridge in response to reports of Union activity. Under Lee's direction, reinforcements were sent, but after nightfall Lee decided there would be no great effort and so he retired. Soon afterward, the bridgehead was overrun, with a loss of 2,023 Confederates.[47]

The loss of so many troops troubled Lee, but he wrote to Mary that he thought that Meade would attack his main position on the Rapidan River. There the Confederates, who had learned to "work now like beavers," had prepared formidable works. Meade would not assault Lee's trenches, though, so the latter tried once more to seize the initiative by attacking. When the Confederates advanced, they discovered that Meade had withdrawn. The Southern pursuit netted hundreds of prisoners but did not win a decisive victory. The Mine Run campaign ended in December 1863 with Meade secure in northern Virginia, much to Lee's chagrin.

---

45. Thomas, *Lee,* 309; Woodworth, *Davis and Lee,* 255–56; White, *Southern Confederacy,* 326 [quote].

46. Thomas, *Lee,* 310–12; Freeman, *Lee,* 3:181–83; White, *Southern Confederacy,* 325; Cooke, *Life of Lee,* 355.

47. Thomas, *Lee,* 310–12; Freeman, *Lee,* 3:181–83; White, *Southern Confederacy,* 327, 328; Fitzhugh Lee, *General Lee,* 317 [quote]; Early, *War Memoirs,* 309–15.

Not even the defeat of the Union cavalry in what became known as the "Buckland Races" could ease Lee's disappointment.[48]

Lee's frustrations during the fall of 1863 prompted him again to consider resigning. After Mine Run, Lee said bitterly, "I am too old to command this army," adding, "we should never have permitted those people to get away." Poor health and frustration must have made retirement very alluring, but Lee stayed with his troops. That winter became known as the Valley Forge of the Confederacy as a lack of food, clothing, and shelter made Lee's camp miserable. The general was further disheartened by the death of his beloved daughter-in-law, Charlotte. Depressed over the deaths of her children and distraught over the capture of her husband, Charlotte had declined rapidly. Lee could easily recall the day that Charlotte had married Rooney in the same room at Shirley where Anne Hill Carter became Light-Horse Harry's bride. He wrote to Mary on December 27, 1863, "I grieve for our lost darling as a father can only grieve for a daughter."[49]

Mindful of Lee's mood and the condition of his army, the Confederate Congress approved a joint resolution of gratitude. Fond of thinking of themselves as the "heirs of 1776, a latter-day Continental Congress under a flag of thirteen stars," the members were pleased that Adj. Gen. Samuel Cooper included their words in a general order on January 16, 1864, that asked, "Let all press forward in the road to independence, and for the security of the rights sealed to us in the blood of the first revolution." Lee issued a similar order: "SOLDIERS! You tread with no unequal step the road by which your fathers marched through suffering, privation and blood to independence. Continue to emulate in the future, as you have in the past, their valour in arms, their patient endurance of hardships, their high resolve to be free, which no trial could shake, no bribe seduce, no danger appall, and be assured that the just God who crowned their efforts with success will, in His own good time, send down His blessing upon yours." Although Lee slipped in his paternal reference (most of his men were grandsons of the Revolutionary genera-

48. Thomas, *Lee,* 310–12; Freeman, *Lee,* 3:181–83; Dowdey and Manarin, *Wartime Papers,* 622; Walter H. Taylor, *Four Years,* 120–22 [quote].

49. Cooke, *Life of Lee,* 359, 367, 369–70; Thomas, *Lee,* 171, 179, 312, 314; Freeman, *Lee,* 3:202 [1st and 2nd quotes]; Dowdey and Manarin, *Wartime Papers,* 625, 631, 645 [3rd quote]; White, *Southern Confederacy,* 333, 347; Coulling, *Lee Girls,* 69, 132; Jones, *Life and Letters,* 297–98.

tion and not sons like him), his troops understood. Col. Clement A. Evans noted in his diary that month that "Lee is regarded by his army as nearest approaching the character of the great & good Washington than any man living."[50]

Official declarations linking Lee and his army to Washington and the Continentals mirrored public sentiment. A young man who saw Lee in Maryland in 1862 and again in 1863 noted, "I could not help but think of Washington as I looked at that calm, sad face." After popular Southern reporter Peter W. Alexander compared Lee to Washington in the *Southern Literary Messenger,* reprints of his article appeared throughout the South. Editor Edward A. Pollard hailed Lee as a "modern copy of Washington." Infuriated with a Northern cartoon of Lee on his knees asking for pardon, a Georgia woman asserted that he was a "star of light before which even Washington's glory pales." Other Northern publications were more laudatory. The *American Phrenological Journal* condemned Lee for defending slavery but then added, "We are charitable enough to attribute to him no wrong motive, for we remember that George Washington was no less a rebel than is General Lee." Across the Atlantic Ocean, the *Illustrated London News* compared Lee and Washington in a front-page article.[51]

Lee provided confidence to Confederates who accepted him as their Washington, for that commander had won despite many losses. Unlike Washington and his Continentals, however, Lee and his army would win no miraculous victory. All supplies remained scarce due to the blockade

---

50. Flood, *Last Years,* 38 [1st quote]; *OR,* I, 29:910–11 [2nd quote]; Dowdey and Manarin, *Wartime Papers,* 659; Marshall, *Aide,* xxiii–xxiv; General Order Book, 37th North Carolina Infantry, 1864 [3rd quote], Army of the Confederate States of America Collection, DU; Mason, *Popular Life,* 226–27; Robert G. Stephens, Jr., comp., *Intrepid Warrior: Clement Anselm Evans, Confederate General from Georgia* (Dayton, Ohio, 1992), 342 [4th quote]; James D. McCabe, *Life and Campaigns of General Robert E. Lee* (Atlanta, 1866), 434.

51. Davis, *Gray Fox,* 216 [1st quote]; Gary W. Gallagher, "Another Look at the Generalship of Robert E. Lee," in Gallagher, *Lee the Soldier,* 281; Andrews, *South Reports the Civil War,* 194; Peter W. Alexander, "Confederate Chieftains," *Southern Literary Messenger* 35 (Jan. 1863): 34–38; New York *Herald,* Jan. 30, 1865 [2nd quote]; Eliza F. Andrews, *The War-Time Journal of a Georgia Girl, 1864–1865,* ed. Spencer B. King (New York, 1908), 371 [3rd quote]; Thomas, *Lee,* 275; "Robert E. Lee: Portrait, Chronology, and Biography," *American Phrenological Journal* 40 (Sept. 1864): 88 [4th quote]; Snow, *Lee and His Generals,* 167–68; *Illustrated London News,* June 4, 1864.

and the deterioration of the South's railroads, and Lee found it difficult to replenish his depleted ranks. In February 1864, he proposed to Davis that hospitals be combed for men able to return to duty. The Confederate Congress expanded the ages for draftees and reduced the exemptions to the draft, but such changes only partly offset the losses. As spring approached in 1864, Lee had 64,000 men, far less than the 119,000 with Meade, and Lee had hardly half of the division and brigade commanders he had had a year earlier.[52]

Lee remained concerned about the west, but he continued to insist that his army be fed first. He communicated often with Davis about concentrating a larger force in Grant's front, noting that if Federal advances in the west were not halted, then the defense of points on the Atlantic coast were irrelevant. Davis asked Lee again to accept temporary command in the west, but he avoided the assignment and, as spring approached in 1864, began to ask for the diversion of reinforcements from the west to him. Longstreet had grand plans for a mounted raid into Kentucky, but Lee convinced Davis to return his corps commander and his troops to northern Virginia. Lee agreed with Longstreet that reclaiming the west was important, but not more so than sustaining his army, which would win the war. Longstreet's divisions cheered loudly as Lee reviewed them once more in April 1864.[53]

Lee's demands for reinforcements and Longstreet's return reflected the result of months of guesswork over the intentions of the new Federal general-in-chief, Grant. No matter what Lee decided was the dilemma presented by Grant, the solution always seemed to be the same: Lee's army would strike the first blow. He wrote to Davis, "If we could take the initiative and fall upon them unexpectedly, we might derange their plans and embarrass them the whole summer," thus prolonging the war to a breaking point. Later, while agreeing with the president about the importance of Tennessee, Lee added that his army had to be properly

52. Freeman, *Lee*, 3:245–55; Dowdey and Manarin, *Wartime Papers*, 648, 672; Thomas, *Lee*, 318, 320–21.

53. Freeman, *Lee*, 3:206–8; Thomas, *Lee*, 313; Woodworth, *Davis and Lee*, 262–63; Hood, *Advance and Retreat*, 89–94; Lee to Braxton Bragg, Apr. 7, 1864, Gratz Collection, Historical Society of Pennsylvania, Philadelphia; Dowdey and Manarin, *Wartime Papers*, 667, 674–75; Lee to Longstreet, Mar. 8 and 16, 1864, Fairfax Papers, VHS; Thomas, *Lee*, 321–22; Long, *Memoirs of Lee*, 637, 647; E. Porter Alexander, *Memoirs*, 493; Lee to Davis, Apr. 2, 1864, Lee Papers, DU; *OR*, I, 32, 2:667.

supplied "to take the initiative before our enemies are prepared to open the campaign." Lee firmly believed that his army would strike the primary blow in 1864, and in late April he again repeated his demand for proper support.[54]

Having decided that the "approaching storm" would "burst" in Virginia, Lee retrieved his troops from North Carolina. Davis had tried to persuade Lee to take charge there, but again the latter evaded the request. In accordance with an alternative proposed by Lee, Pickett had gone with his division and others in January 1864 to recapture ports occupied by the Federals, but he failed to do so, in part because two ironclads intended for his support were not completed. One of these, the *Albemarle,* later participated in a successful attack on Plymouth by Robert Hoke, who thus won a promotion to major general. Lee was pleased with Hoke, but he asked him to suspend his plans for the recapture of New Bern and return to Virginia. As Lee explained to Davis, a "crowning victory" on the Rappahannock would be more important because it would force the enemy to abandon his plans elsewhere. When Hoke protested, Lee wrote to Davis, "I fully appreciate the advantages of capturing New Berne, but . . . Success in resisting the chief armies of the enemy will enable us more easily to secure the country now occupied by him."[55]

Having gambled and lost at Gettysburg, Lee hoped to win the war by retaining the initiative and extending the conflict until Northern morale broke. His army had been reduced greatly, but it could endure another campaign, and perhaps more. Washington had endured many trials before his last victory, and Lee had not been shaken in his belief that his army would win independence for the Confederacy, just as Washington's beleaguered Continentals had for the colonies. Lee constantly searched for an opportunity to strike a blow, even in winter. Early in 1864, he rode along the Rapidan with Early and others. Spotting a Union camp across the river, Lee asked why they had not been driven

54. Bowen, *Strategy of Lee,* 230–31 [1st quote]; Long, *Memoirs of Lee,* 641, 647; Lee to Davis, Feb. 13, 1864 [2nd quote], Lee Papers, LV; Freeman, *Lee's Dispatches,* 144.

55. Lee to Bragg, Apr. 7, 1864 [1st and 2nd quotes], Gratz Collection, Historical Society of Pennsylvania; Woodworth, *Davis and Lee,* 265; Lee to Davis, Jan. 2, 1864, Lee Papers, DU; Dowdey and Manarin, *Wartime Papers,* 699–700 [3rd quote]; Freeman, *Lee,* 3:265; Lee to Davis, May 4, 1864 [4th quote], Lee Papers, LV; Long, *Memoirs of Lee,* 636, 639–40.

away. When Early asked how his troops could get at them, Lee gruffly answered that they could ford the river. Early then asked what would be done with his "pneumonia patients," to which Lee did not answer.[56] The return of warm weather would remove such concerns, and Lee would be looking for every chance to extend the war and force the North to negotiate.

56. Stiles, *Marse Robert*, 232.

6

Children of the Revolution
Fighting for Time, 1864–1865

As the campaign season began in 1864, Lee remained confident that he could sustain the war until the North grew weary, just as George Washington had done against the British. Appointed general-in-chief of all Confederate armies in February 1865, he assured his troops that "with the liberty transmitted by their forefathers they [had] inherited the spirit to defend it." They must "oppose constancy to adversity, fortitude to suffering, and courage to danger, with the firm assurance that He who gave freedom to our fathers will bless the efforts of their children to preserve it."[1] Lee's foe, however, was not a British public uncertain about a long war to hold distant colonies. Furthermore, the Confederacy's commitment to defending its capital prevented Lee from maneuvering

---

1. Armistead L. Long, *Memoirs of Robert E. Lee* (New York, 1886), 680 [1st quote]; Fitzhugh Lee, *General Lee* (New York, 1894; reprint, Wilmington, N.C., 1989), 368 [2nd quote]; Gamaliel Bradford, *Lee the American* (Boston, 1912; rev. ed., Cambridge, Mass., 1929), 39; *The War of the Rebellion: A Compilation of the Official Records of the Union and Confederate Armies*, 130 vols., (Washington, D.C., 1880–1902), ser. I, vol. 46, pt. 2:1230 [hereinafter *OR*]; Nancy S. Anderson and Dwight Anderson, *The Generals: Ulysses S. Grant and Robert E. Lee* (New York, 1988), 513; John S. Wise, *End of an Era,* ed. Custis C. Davis (New York, 1965), 12; Jubal A. Early, "The Campaigns of Gen. Robert E. Lee," in Gary W. Gallagher, ed., *Lee the Soldier* (Lincoln, Nebr., 1996), 57; Alan T. Nolan, "General Lee," in Gallagher, *Lee the Soldier,* 264; J. William Jones, *Life and Letters of Robert Edward Lee, Soldier and Man* (New York, 1906), 353.

as Washington had done. Northerners committed to the Union inflicted upon an immobilized Lee a fate Washington did not suffer: unconditional surrender and the defeat of his cause.

Lee believed he could thwart whatever Ulysses S. Grant, the new general-in-chief of the Federals, had planned. Grant indeed did worry, and wrote later that if Lee had fought into 1866, the North would have sued for peace. The Union commander did not intend to allow this outcome, and during May 1864 he accompanied the Army of the Potomac as it again marched south into Virginia. Lee let them advance so he could meet his more numerous foe in the thick underbrush of the Wilderness, where he had defeated Maj. Gen. Joseph Hooker a year earlier. The brush would make it difficult for Grant to deploy his artillery, impractical for him to use his cavalry, and hard for his scouts to know Lee's numbers. It would be an infantry fight, and Lee had great faith in his.[2]

Lee struck on the morning of May 5. His II and III Corps, commanded by lieutenant generals Richard S. Ewell and Ambrose P. Hill respectively, assailed the Federals in a confused fight that ended at nightfall. Lee assumed that Lt. Gen. James Longstreet would arrive with his I Corps in time for a morning push around the Union left flank, but the Federals charged Hill's scattered units at dawn on May 6. Longstreet's vanguard arrived before Hill's corps broke, and the battle degenerated into a "wild, weird struggle." At Lee's order, Longstreet prepared an attack, but he fell shot through the neck before he began. Wounded by his own men, Longstreet would not return until October.[3]

Lee took charge of the right after Longstreet fell, but he had to delay his assault until he could get his units organized. By late afternoon, his

2. Robert E. Lee to G. W. Custis Lee, Mar. 29, 1864, Hunter H. McGuire Papers, University of Virginia Library, Charlottesville [hereinafter UVA]; *OR*, IV, 2:447–48; Walter H. Taylor, *Four Years with General Lee* (New York, 1877; reprint, New York, 1962), 207; James D. Richardson, comp., *The Messages and Papers of Jefferson Davis and the Confederacy, 1861–1865*, 2 vols. (Washington, D.C., 1896–1899; reprint, New York, 1981), 1:243–51; Walter H. Taylor to Bettie Saunders, Apr. 3, 1864, Walter H. Taylor Papers, Library of Virginia [hereinafter LV]; John B. Gordon, *Reminiscences of the Civil War* (New York, 1903), 268; John J. Bowen, *The Strategy of Robert E. Lee* (New York, 1914), 231; Robert W. Winston, *Robert E. Lee: A Biography* (New York, 1941), 312; Long, *Memoirs of Lee*, 327; Anderson and Anderson, *Generals*, 448; Henry A. White, *Robert E. Lee and the Southern Confederacy, 1807–1870* (New York, 1897), 352.

3. Fitzhugh Lee, *General Lee*, 330 [quote]; Emory M. Thomas, *Robert E. Lee: A Biography* (New York, 1995), 323–25, 346.

chance for a decisive blow passed because the Federals dug fieldworks. To ease the pressure on his right, Lee rode to the left, spoke with Ewell and two of his division commanders, major generals Jubal A. Early and John B. Gordon, and told the latter to make an attack. Gordon pushed the Federals back but accomplished little more before night ended the fight. Lee had not driven his opponents from the field in the Battle of the Wilderness, as it became known, but he believed that he had struck an effective blow, inflicting casualties at a ratio in excess of two to one, and that Grant would retreat.[4]

Grant was impressed with the fury of the Confederates, but Lee's men were more impressed, or horrified, with their leader's attempt to join in the charge of Longstreet's troops on May 6. When the Federals struck Hill's corps, Lee watched anxiously for Longstreet and rode to meet his men as they arrived. The first were Texans, who refused to go forward until Lee went to the rear. Some wondered if Lee revealed a death wish that day, but he did only what many leaders, including Washington, had done: use his person to shift the balance in favor of his own troops. Lee knew, like others, that at times his presence was needed to avert disaster. On May 6, his army, with its ranks and officer cadre worn thin, was wavering. Lee had written to Custis, "If victorious, we have everything to hope for in the future. If defeated, nothing will be left for us to live for." With that in mind, he rode into battle and would do so again. The message was not lost. Mary Bayard Clark, a North Carolina poet whose husband was wounded in the Wilderness, wrote within a year:

> There he stood, the grand old hero, great Virginia's god-like son,
> Second unto none in glory, equal of her Washington.

Her poem expressed the admiration of many in the Confederacy.[5]

Lee watched his opponent closely after the Wilderness fight. When he

---

4. E. Porter Alexander, *Military Memoirs of a Confederate* (New York, 1907; reprint, Dayton, Ohio, 1977), 506–8; Long, *Memoirs of Lee*, 332.

5. J. William Jones, "General Lee to the Rear," *Southern Historical Society Papers* 8 (1880): 33–34; Walter H. Taylor, *Four Years*, 207; Emily V. Mason, *Popular Life of Gen. Robert E. Lee* (Baltimore, 1870), 245–46; Charles B. Flood, *Lee: The Last Years* (Boston, 1981), 55; Earl S. Miers, *Robert E. Lee: A Great Life in Brief* (New York, 1956), 168–69 [1st quote]; George W. P. Custis, *Recollections and Private Memoirs of George Washing-*

learned that Grant was not retiring but advancing toward Richmond, he quickly sent troops to the junction at Spotsylvania and outraced the Federals by a narrow margin. There seven and a half miles of fieldworks were dug under Lee's direction. Grant probed Lee's left on May 9, following with an assault on May 10 that breached the Mule Shoe, a bulge in the center of Lee's line. The position was held with a desperate counterattack, but Lee erred the next day. A quiet day convinced him that Grant would slip south again. Lee withdrew his artillery from the Mule Shoe and prepared to pursue. At dawn on May 12 a tremendous column of Federals overran the salient. When Lee flung several brigades into the fight, it became a bloody brawl while another trench was dug across the base of the bulge. After dark, the Confederates withdrew into their new line. They left many behind, including five generals killed or mortally wounded.[6]

Lee rode to the front twice at Spotsylvania. On May 10, he tried to lead Early's division into the Mule Shoe until he was dissuaded by Gordon. Two days later, Gordon asked him not to take forward a Mississippi brigade before Walter H. Taylor of Lee's staff intervened and led the advance. In both instances, Gordon noted that Lee rode quietly, with his head uncovered, to the front. He intended to add the force of his presence, not to sacrifice himself. The gesture worked each time, but the danger prompted chastisement. Charles S. Venable told Davis that when Lee rode forward, a "round shot" passed under Traveller, Taylor's horse was killed, and staff member Charles Marshall was wounded. The president sent a reproach, and Postmaster General John H. Reagan met with Lee to discuss his recklessness. Lee's answer to Reagan was similar to

ton, ed. Mary C. Lee (Washington, D.C., 1859), 190–91, 201, 222, 242; James T. Flexner, *Washington: The Indispensable Man* (New York, 1974), 84, 97, 106; Thomas, *Lee,* 332–33; Gary W. Gallagher, "The Army of Northern Virginia in May 1864: A Crisis of High Command," *Civil War History* 36 (June 1990), 110–16; Emily V. Mason, ed., *The Southern Poems of the War,* 3rd ed. (Baltimore, 1869), 386 [2nd quote]; Edwin A. Anderson et al., eds., *Library of Southern Literature,* 17 vols. (New Orleans, 1907–1923), 2:934.

6. John F. C. Fuller, *Grant and Lee: A Study in Personality and Generalship* (Stevenage, U.K., 1933), 216; Thomas, *Lee,* 326–29; Douglas S. Freeman, *R. E. Lee: A Biography,* 4 vols. (New York, 1934), 3:326; James M. McPherson, *Battle Cry of Freedom: The Civil War Era* (New York, 1988), 729–31; Clifford Dowdey and Louis H. Manarin, eds., *The Wartime Papers of Robert E. Lee* (Boston, 1961), 727.

what he said when confronted in the Mule Shoe: he wished someone would tell him where his "proper place" was, because "I am always told I should not be where I am."[7]

While hordes of infantry grappled at Spotsylvania, Maj. Gen. J. E. B. Stuart fell mortally wounded at Yellow Tavern on May 11. Lee was with his officers when he learned of Stuart's death. He told them the news and then, struggling to keep his composure, retreated to his tent, saying that he could not think of Stuart without weeping. He had little time to mourn. Grant tried to move past his right flank on May 13, but Lee later extended his lines and repulsed an attack. More Federals later assailed the new works below the Mule Shoe, but again the Confederates turned them back. Grant marched south again on May 20, and Lee chose a position on the North Anna River that would divide the Union army if it attacked. Reinforced, he eagerly expected to strike a blow at a part of Grant's host, but ptomaine confined him to his cot. Grant again slipped south, avoiding an assault on an isolated portion of his army.[8]

A month of combat had drained Lee's army and eliminated a third of his generals, but he would not surrender the initiative. Not only was Longstreet gone, replaced temporarily with Maj. Gen. Richard H. Anderson, but Ewell had suffered a breakdown and been succeeded by Early. Nevertheless, Lee wrote to Davis on May 18, "I shall continue to strike [Grant] whenever opportunity presents itself," and subordinates recalled that he seemed more eager to strike a blow than ever before. While he lay in his sickbed on the North Anna, he kept saying that Grant had to be attacked, and he told an associate that if he got just one more chance at Grant, he would beat him. He knew that the campaign had

7. Jones, "Lee to the Rear," 33–34; Mason, *Popular Life of Lee,* 245–46; Gordon, *Reminiscences,* 278–82, 431; Walter H. Taylor, *Four Years,* 207; Jefferson Davis, *The Rise and Fall of the Confederate Government,* 2 vols. (New York, 1881), 2:521 [1st quote]; Long, *Memoirs of Lee,* 387 [2nd and 3rd quotes]; J. William Jones, *Personal Reminiscences, Anecdotes, and Letters of Gen. Robert E. Lee* (New York, 1874), 317–18; William P. Snow, *Lee and His Generals: Their Lives and Campaigns* (New York, 1867; reprint, New York, 1982), 127; Steven E. Woodworth, *Davis and Lee at War* (Lawrence, Kans., 1994), 292; Freeman, *Lee,* 3:320, 389–90; Fitzhugh Lee, *General Lee,* 260.

8. Thomas, *Lee,* 327–30; Robert E. Lee, Jr., *Recollections and Letters of General Robert E. Lee* (New York, 1904), 125; Gordon, *Reminiscences,* 273; John E. Cooke, *A Life of Gen. Robert E. Lee* (New York, 1883), 403; Dowdey and Manarin, *Wartime Papers,* 731; Clifford Dowdey, *Lee* (Boston, 1965), 455–56; Winston, *Lee,* 303; Freeman, *Lee,* 3:356, 361.

become vital for Abraham Lincoln's reelection. If Grant lost, so might Lincoln, and Southern independence could be at hand.[9]

Lee's determination to carry the war effort led to a clash with an old friend, Gen. Pierre G. T. Beauregard. The latter had come to Virginia with his Carolina troops to bolster the defenses of Richmond and Petersburg, which were threatened by a Union force commanded by Maj. Gen. Benjamin F. Butler. Beauregard arrived in Petersburg about May 10 and bottled up Butler in Bermuda Hundred. Having done this, he tried to make himself the primary focus of the campaign. He asked Davis to have Lee withdraw to Richmond and send some of his troops south for an attack on Butler. Once that was done, Beauregard would join Lee for an assault on Grant. Lee's response was to ask the president to order Beauregard to bring his units north of Richmond. Lee repeated his demand later and met with Beauregard, but he and most of his troops remained at Petersburg. Only a few joined Lee north of the capital.[10]

Lee tried to strike a blow on June 1 at Cold Harbor, but his attack on an exposed Union corps was bungled by green troops from South Carolina. He retired into trenches to await a counterblow from Grant but told Early to watch for an opportunity to assault the Union right. Early did so with little gain on June 2. As Lee expected, Grant decided that a hard blow upon his depleted foe's works would produce a rupture. The result was murder: when the Federals charged on June 3, almost seven thousand were killed. Orders from Grant to renew the attack were ignored by his subordinates. Sullenly, he refused to ask for a truce to retrieve his wounded, which was customary for a defeated

---

9. George A. Bruce, "Lee and the Strategy of the Civil War," in Gallagher, *Lee the Soldier,* 113–15, 117–18; William Allan, "Memoranda of Conversations with General Robert E. Lee," in Gallagher, *Lee the Soldier,* 11; Douglas S. Freeman, ed., *Lee's Dispatches: Unpublished Letters of General Robert E. Lee, C. S. A., to Jefferson Davis and the War Department of the Confederate States of America . . .* (New York, 1915), 183–84 [quote]; Lee to Mary Custis Lee, May 23, 1864, De Butts-Ely Collection, Library of Congress, Washington, D.C. [hereinafter LC]; Dowdey and Manarin, *Wartime Papers,* 748; Fitzhugh Lee, General Lee, 339; Freeman, *Lee,* 3:359; E. Porter Alexander, *Fighting for the Confederacy: The Personal Recollections of General Edward Porter Alexander,* ed. Gary W. Gallagher (Chapel Hill, N.C., 1989), 397; Cooke, *Life of Lee,* 404; E. Porter Alexander, *Memoirs,* 534.

10. Woodworth, *Davis and Lee,* 270, 272–74, 277–91; White, *Southern Confederacy,* 383–84; Dowdey and Manarin, *Wartime Papers,* 747, 750, 756–57; Freeman, *Dispatches,* 195, 199, 203, 205, 208–9.

commander. He had done the same at Spotsylvania on May 10; now his wounded lay for three days before he sent a white flag. While he waited, Lee fumed to Davis that he was looking for a chance to "strike" at Grant, but the Union commander's careful dispositions made that impossible.[11]

After Cold Harbor, Lee became increasingly concerned with Grant's resiliency. Taylor had written of Grant on May 23, "He certainly holds on longer than any of [his predecessors]." Lee shared Taylor's alarm. In early June he wrote to Ambrose P. Hill that Grant must be kept from choosing the places for battles because "If he is allowed to continue that course we shall at last be obliged to take refuge behind the works of Richmond and stand a siege, which would be but a work of time." Weeks later, after his army had been forced into the trenches, Lee asked in a letter to Custis, "Where are we to get sufficient troops to oppose Grant? . . . His talent & strategy consists in accumulating overwhelming numbers." Looking afield, the elder Lee speculated that if reports were true that the Union forces in the Trans-Mississippi had been reduced, then Confederates there could come east. He still believed a supreme effort, focused on his army, could succeed.[12]

Grant's steady pressure forced Lee to accept a siege in defense of his capital. Federals defeated Lee's cavalry in the Shenandoah Valley during the first week of June, Union troopers tried to cut the Virginia Central Railroad, and Beauregard kept sounding the alarm about Butler in Bermuda Hundred. Early went to the Valley with his II Corps; Maj. Gen. Wade Hampton, Stuart's successor, beat the Union cavalry at Trevilian Station; and Lee sent a division to Beauregard, leaving Lee with only 28,000 troops at Cold Harbor. When Grant slipped south of the James River toward Petersburg, Beauregard blunted his initial thrusts, but on June 18 Lee had to fall back into prepared entrenchments shielding both that city and Richmond. He announced his decision with a simple declaration to Davis: "I go to Petersburg." The quiet tone of that announce-

11. Freeman, *Lee,* 3:377–85; Thomas, *Lee,* 330–31, 334–35; White, *Southern Confederacy,* 386–87; Freeman, *Dispatches,* 219–20 [quote]; Woodworth, *Davis and Lee,* 293–294; E. Porter Alexander, *Fighting for the Confederacy,* 371, 374; Dowdey, *Lee,* 470.

12. Walter H. Taylor, *Four Years,* 133 [1st quote]; Dowdey and Manarin, *Wartime Papers,* 759–60 [2nd quote]; Lee to Custis Lee, July 24, 1864 [3rd quote], Robert E. Lee Papers, William G. Perkins Library, Duke University, Durham, N.C. [hereinafter DU].

ment belied its disastrous portents: Lee was besieged by an army many times larger than his own.[13]

Why did Lee accept a siege when the outcome seemed obvious? Washington, and later Napoleon, focused on armies, not cities. Lee realized the danger of a siege; he told Early that Grant had to be beaten before he reached the James River. Lee added, "If he gets there, it will become a siege, and then it will be a mere question of time." He was forced into the trenches when reports arrived about Beauregard's dire circumstances at Petersburg. He could have abandoned the Confederate capital, as Davis discussed in 1862. The war had progressed, though, and the importance of Richmond had grown. It was one of the few remaining industrial centers for the Confederacy, and it had become a symbol. The fate of Lee's army, the capital city, and the nation had become intertwined for the South and for Davis, who now refused to leave. Lee remained subordinate to civilian authority, like Washington, and thus he had to defend Richmond. As he angrily told Venable, to lose the city without a fight would make him a traitor.[14]

Pinned in the trenches, Lee relied upon Early in the Valley to strike a blow against Northern morale. The decision to detach Early was Lee's twist upon an order from Davis to provide relief for the Valley. Lee explained his gamble to Davis, writing that to keep Early at Richmond "would make us more secure here, but success in the Valley would relieve the difficulties that at present press heavily upon us." Lee had more in mind than saving the Valley. He had urged Maj. Gen. John C. Breckinridge in May, before he was called to Richmond, to invade Maryland if possible. In June he again raised the subject, suggesting that Early could free Confederates held at Point Lookout to bolster his forces.[15]

13. Thomas, *Lee*, 335–38; Dowdey and Manarin, *Wartime Papers*, 792 [quote]; Dowdey, *Lee*, 474–75, 483–85; McPherson, *Battle Cry*, 737–43.

14. Thomas, *Lee*, 339–40; Early, "Campaigns of Lee," 65 [quote]; E. Porter Alexander, *Fighting for the Confederacy*, 430–31; Walter H. Taylor, *Four Years*, 145–46; Freeman, *Lee*, 3:496; Joseph L. Harsh, *Confederate Tide Rising: Robert E. Lee and the Making of Southern Strategy, 1861–1862* (Kent, Ohio, 1998), 65.

15. Woodworth, *Davis and Lee*, 267, 295, 332; Lee to Jefferson Davis, June 15, 1864 [quote], Robert E. Lee Papers, Virginia Historical Society, Richmond [hereinafter VHS]; Lee to James A. Seddon, June 6, 1864, Robert E. Lee Papers, Chicago Historical Society, Chicago; Dowdey and Manarin, *Wartime Papers*, 711, 716, 732, 807, 811; Freeman, *Dispatches*, 269–71.

Early did raid Maryland, but his efforts were no more successful than the plan for a jailbreak at Point Lookout, which had to be canceled. Grant sent reinforcements to face Early. The latter probed the defenses of Washington before he retreated to the Valley, but by August he was outnumbered by a margin of three to one. He accepted combat at Winchester on September 19 and almost defeated Union Maj. Gen. Philip H. Sheridan but fell back to Fisher's Hill and was beaten on September 22. Lee sent his own reinforcements with a request that Early strike a blow. He did so at Cedar Creek on October 19. His men drove the enemy for most of the morning, but Sheridan led a counterattack that routed the Confederates. Early had inflicted more losses on his enemy than the number of men in his army, but his "command was wrecked." Most of the remnant returned to Petersburg; the rest stayed in the Valley with Early and were overwhelmed in 1865.[16]

Lee was bitterly disappointed with Early's Valley campaign, which heightened his concern over events elsewhere. Informed that Davis wanted to replace Gen. Joseph E. Johnston with Lt. Gen. John Bell Hood at Atlanta, Lee responded that such a change in an army as hardpressed as Johnston's was unwise. Furthermore, Hood was a "bold fighter," but Lee noted that he was "doubtful as to other qualities necessary." In a letter written that same night, Lee reluctantly agreed, and Davis did appoint Hood, who bled his army white before evacuating Atlanta. Lee tried to make light of the defeat to Mary, but the subsequent destruction of Hood's army deepened his belief that any hope for victory rested upon him.[17]

Lee looked for more chances to strike a blow. He reported to Davis on June 21 that "The enemy has a strong position, & is able to deal us more injury than from any other point he has ever taken. Still we must try & defeat them." The following day, Brig. Gen. William Mahone attacked two Union corps moving toward the Weldon Railroad south of Petersburg. Mahone took more than sixteen hundred prisoners and checked the Federal advance. This encouraged Lee to order an attack

16. Dowdey and Manarin, *Wartime Papers,* 798–800 [quote], 802, Lee to Davis, Aug. 4, 1864, Robert E. Lee Papers, LV; Lee to Jubal A. Early, Sept. 25, 1864, Robert E. Lee Papers, Eleanor S. Brockenbrough Library, Museum of the Confederacy, Richmond [hereinafter MOC]; Thomas, *Lee,* 344; Dowdey, *Lee,* 524; McPherson, *Battle Cry,* 777–80.

17. Freeman, *Dispatches,* 282–83 [quotes]; Dowdey and Manarin, *Wartime Papers,* 800, 821, 851; Thomas, *Lee,* 343.

near Petersburg on June 24, but that failed. Meanwhile, Union cavalry farther south cut the Weldon line before being routed by Confederate troopers with Mahone's infantry. Lee planned the effort and found some solace in its success.[18]

Another month of probing by Grant ended with a bang on July 30. Before dawn, the Federals detonated four tons of gunpowder packed in a tunnel underneath Lee's works. Stunned Confederates responded slowly to the threat, but fortunately for them the Federals crowded into the break and were easily overwhelmed by reinforcements. Many Federal casualties were blacks, who charged with cries of no quarter. That was what they got from Lee's men, many of whom had not previously fought black troops. Even blacks who surrendered were killed. Lee watched from a house about five hundred yards from the Crater, as the hole became known, and did not intervene, though he had done so earlier to save black prisoners. In all, Grant lost forty-four hundred men, while Lee's losses were fifteen hundred.[19]

Military and family troubles pressed upon Lee as the summer continued. Federal guns often pummeled his lines, but he took the time to write to Mary about the death of his uncle, Williams Carter. In a remark recalling the capture of his son Rooney, he added that Carter was now beyond the "indignities" of poverty and Federal occupation, the latter of which he described as "revolting to my feelings." Even more bothersome were incessant attacks. During August, Grant pushed hard north of the James River, then hurled a strong force at the Weldon Railroad near the Globe Tavern. Hill grabbed twenty-seven hundred prisoners, but the Union troops destroyed a section of rails. Five miles south, at Ream's Station, blue-clad cavalry dismantled more tracks. The Confederates again grabbed thousands of prisoners, but a vital rail link had been lost.[20]

18. Freeman, *Dispatches*, 255 [quote]; Freeman, *Lee*, 3:453–56; Thomas, *Lee*, 319, 339.

19. White, *Southern Confederacy*, 401; Thomas, *Lee*, 341–42; Fitzhugh Lee, *General Lee*, 360; E. Porter Alexander, *Memoirs*, 563–65; Ervin L. Jordan, Jr., *Black Confederates and Afro-Yankees in Civil War Virginia* (Charlottesville, Va., 1995), 280.

20. Lee to Charles Carter Lee, Aug. 12, 1864 [quotes], Robert E. Lee Papers, Washington and Lee University Library, Lexington, Va. [hereinafter W&L]; Walter H. Taylor, *General Lee*, 254; Dowdey and Manarin, *Wartime Papers*, 798, 829; White, *Southern Confederacy*, 403–5; Thomas, *Lee*, 344–45.

Grant's superior numbers allowed him to strike at will. He personally directed the capture of Fort Harrison on September 29. Lee urged his men forward three times, again riding to the front, but he failed to retake the position, a key point in his defense. Angry at his defeat, Lee futilely tried twice more to regain the post. Shifting south, Grant flung parts of three Federal corps across Hatcher's Run on October 27. Their goal was the Southside Railroad, but they were stopped by Hampton's cavalry and Hill's infantry. The sector remained quiet until February 1865, when Grant again ordered an advance that resulted in little gain.[21]

The confinement of Lee's men to the trenches strained their government's ability to support them. Hampton captured twenty-five hundred Union cattle in September 1864, but this brought only temporary relief for just one of many problems. Many civilians, including Lee's wife and daughters, redoubled their efforts to sew clothing for his army. A Richmond woman noted that Mary and the Lee daughters spent much time sewing for soldiers, just as Martha Washington had during the Revolution. In January 1865, Lee proposed laws to prevent the sale of cotton, tobacco, and naval stores to Federals. Lee's proposal included the confiscation of material in areas exposed to raids or close to Federal lines, which could then be used to barter for supplies. Lee also asked for a program to encourage home manufacturing but Davis balked, still believing the war could be won without resorting to such extreme measures.[22]

Supply shortages distressed Lee, but his casualties appalled him. During the first months of the 1864 campaign, his losses had been heavy, but Federal casualties were more than twice as high. In the trenches losses became more equal, and Grant could replace his more easily. Lee wrote to Davis in September, "Our ranks are constantly diminishing by battle and disease, and few recruits are received. The consequences are inevitable." That November, Lee repeated, "Unless we can obtain a reasonable approximation to [Grant's] force, I fear a great calamity will befall us." In a review of the situation in early December, Lee concluded, "All we want to resist them is men." Desertion made the problem worse;

21. Thomas, *Lee,* 345–46, 348; Freeman, *Lee,* 3:501–4, 507–10; Dowdey, *Lee,* 505–7.
22. Thomas, *Lee,* 342, 344–45, 347; Anderson and Anderson, *Generals,* 387; Freeman, *Dispatches,* 318–22, 328–29.

by March 1865, Taylor guessed that one hundred men left each day. After he became general-in-chief in February, Lee with Davis' approval declared amnesty once more to entice deserters to return, but it proved fruitless.[23]

Lee's efforts were undermined by the loss not only of men but of experienced officers. He wrote to his daughter Agnes in November 1864, "Every day is marked with sorrow & every field has its grief, the death of some brave man!" When Grant attacked in February 1865, Maj. Gen. John Pegram was killed just eighteen days after getting married on Lee's birthday. Lee had reviewed Pegram's division on February 2. At that time, Lee knew about the death of a mutual acquaintance, but he could not tell Pegram's wife, who watched the review with him. Now Pegram was gone, and Lee mourned for him and his widow. Two months later, Lee wept after Hill was shot and killed when he and Sgt. G. W. Tucker accidentally encountered Federal skirmishers.[24]

One potential source of replacements for Lee's depleted army was paroled prisoners of war, but Grant suspended most exchanges despite protests from Lee. This led to great overcrowding and many deaths in prisons both north and south. Lee was concerned about the horrifying conditions for Federals held in Confederate prisons, but as he explained to Davis, "Their sufferings are the result of our necessities, not of our policy." Called to testify before the Joint Committee on Reconstruction after the war, Lee pointed out that he had little authority over prisoners of war once they were transferred away from his army. His own soldiers in northern camps were of more interest, and he pressed for their release. Grant relented early in 1865. Lee and Davis spoke to paroled prisoners in February 1865, urging them to return to the ranks, but few did. Earlier the same men had heckled the president. They did not mock Lee, but neither did they obey him.[25]

23. Thomas, *Lee,* 345, 347; Dowdey and Manarin, *Wartime Papers,* 848 [1st quote]; Freeman, *Dispatches,* 305 [2nd quote], 331; Jones, *Life and Letters,* 344 [3rd quote]; John B. Jones, *A Rebel War Clerk's Diary,* ed. Howard Swiggett, 2 vols. (New York, 1935), 2:420; Lee to Davis, Feb. 9, 1865, Lee Papers, W&L; Walter H. Taylor, *Four Years,* 187.

24. Dowdey and Manarin, *Wartime Papers,* 802, 870 [quote]; Dowdey, *Lee,* 541; Thomas, *Lee,* 348, 355, 366; Lee to Mary Custis Lee, n.d., De Butts-Ely Collection, LC.

25. Varina H. Davis, *Jefferson Davis, Ex-President of the Confederate States of America: A Memoir by His Wife,* 2 vols. (New York, 1890), 2:574 [quote]; U.S. House, *Report of the Joint Committee on Reconstruction, Part II,* 39th Cong., 1st Sess., 1865, H. Rpt. 30, serial 1273, 129; Jones, *Diary,* 2:435.

Lee's efforts to free his men from Federal prisons led to a clash over black prisoners. In response to Lee's request for an exchange, Grant in October 1864 asked if blacks would be swapped "the same as white soldiers." Lee answered that his proposal included troops of any color, but not "negroes belonging to our citizens." Grant in turn protested against the mistreatment of former slaves taken prisoner, which he said compelled him to continue his suspension of exchanges. Matters came to a head when Butler began using captured white militia to work on his Dutch Gap Canal in response to reports that black prisoners were used as slaves. Lee wrote that only blacks who were identified as slaves were returned to owners; the remainder were treated as prisoners. This, he asserted, "was the practice of the American states during their struggle for independence." Secretary of War James A. Seddon provided the historical reference for Lee and told him that if Grant's response was not acceptable, he should meet with his officers "as was done by General Washington on a somewhat analogous occasion." Grant told Butler to stop using prisoners, but exchanges resumed only after the Confederates agreed to swap blacks as well as whites.[26]

Lee did not believe that blacks should not be soldiers. In fact, despite opposition within his own army he pressed for the recruitment of blacks as part of an expansion of the Confederate draft. He broached the subject with Davis on September 2, 1864, proposing that soldiers detailed as teamsters, cooks, laborers, and such could be replaced with blacks. He wrote that "It seems to me that we must choose between employing negroes ourselves, and having them employed against us." He linked his proposal to a request for a thorough review of exemptions, prosecution of the draft, and mobilization of reserves. Lee concluded that "hardship to individuals must be disregarded in view of the calamity that would follow to the whole people if our armies should meet with disaster." Lee himself began drafting black laborers, organizing them into battalions.[27]

26. Davis, *Rise and Fall*, 2:599–600 [1st and 2nd quotes]; Ulysses S. Grant to Lee, Oct. 3 and 20, 1864, Mar. 14, 1865, Ulysses S. Grant Papers, LC; Lee to Grant, Oct. 19, 1864 [3rd quote], Robert E. Lee Papers, United States Military Academy Library and Archives, West Point, N.Y. [hereinafter USMA]; *OR*, II, 7, 990–93 [4th quote]; McPherson, *Battle Cry*, 799–800; James D. McCabe, *Life and Campaigns of General Robert E. Lee* (Atlanta, 1866), 535–36; E. Porter Alexander, *Fighting for the Confederacy*, 487–89.

27. Freeman, *Dispatches*, 296–98; Woodworth, *Davis and Lee*, 302; Lee to Davis, Sept. 2, 1864 [quotes], Lee Papers, LV; Dowdey and Manarin, *Wartime Papers*, 848; Lee to Braxton Bragg, Sept. 26, 1864, Robert E. Lee Papers, Lincoln Museum, Fort Wayne,

Lee certainly knew that Washington commanded black soldiers. When Andrew Hunter, a Virginia senator, asked for Lee's opinion, pointedly reminding him that Washington "did not hesitate to give his advice on all great subjects," Lee endorsed the enlistment of blacks. Lee emphasized his support for slavery, but national survival was more important. He even urged paying bounties to black recruits, who should be freed, and added that "gradual and general emancipation" would aid the South by relieving them of the burden of watching blacks, who might even prove supportive. In conversations with others, Lee declared that he had understood the necessity for recruiting blacks since early in the war.[28]

Lee continued to press for black soldiers as the campaign season approached. His letter to Congressman Ethelbert Barksdale of Mississippi, who had introduced a bill for black recruitment, repeated the arguments presented to Hunter but added that blacks "furnish a more promising material than many armies of which we read in history." He again emphasized that any who enlisted had to be freed. Several Richmond newspapers reprinted this letter; the Richmond *Dispatch* praised it as more evidence of leadership not "seen on this continent since the days of George Washington." At their request, Lee spoke to Virginia legislators on the need for black troops. The Confederate Congress approved Barksdale's proposal for recruiting blacks but refused to allow emancipation, despite his invoking Washington as an example of one who had supported the arming of freed slaves. The Virginia legislature adopted a similar bill. Angry, Lee insisted that black soldiers had to be given freedom, and Davis subsequently decreed that all black soldiers would be emancipated.[29]

Ind.; Jordan, *Black Confederates,* 62–66; J. Tracy Power, *Lee's Miserables: Life in the Army of Northern Virginia from the Wilderness to Appomattox* (Chapel Hill, N.C., 1998), 248–55.

28. Thomas, *Lee,* 347; *OR,* IV, 3:1007–8 [1st quote], 1012–13; Lee to Andrew Hunter, Jan. 11, 1865 [2nd quote], MOC; William P. Johnston, "Memoranda of Conversations with General R. E. Lee," in Gallagher, *Lee the Soldier,* 30; Garnet J. Wolseley, "General Lee," in Gallagher, *Lee the Soldier,* 101; Robert F. Durden, *The Gray and the Black: The Confederate Debate on Emancipation* (Baton Rouge, 1972), 207–8, 246–47; Jordan, *Black Confederates,* 238–39, 241, 243.

29. Edward A. Pollard, *The Early Life, Campaigns, and Public Services of Robert E. Lee* (New York, 1871), 146–47 [1st quote]; Richmond *Dispatch,* Feb. 24, 27 [2nd quote], 1865; John H. Reagan, *Memoirs* (Austin, 1968), 148; Emory M. Thomas, *The Confederate Nation, 1861–1865* (New York, 1979), 295–96; Jones, *Diary,* 2:432–33; McCabe, *Life*

Lee was disappointed in the law for the enlistment of blacks and dismayed at its slow implementation. In late March he asked Davis to press the Virginia government for black recruits, and he prodded Ewell, now in command of the Richmond garrison, to enlist blacks as soon as possible. When Marshall wrote again to Ewell on the subject, Ewell, perhaps angry, explained that the primary focus of recruitment ought to be the thousands of blacks roaming the streets of the capital alongside similar numbers of parolees and "vagabond white men." Late on April 2, as his lines crumbled before a Union onslaught, Lee was still begging Davis to expedite the recruitment of blacks.[30]

Pressure made Lee quite testy. Taylor recalled finding a cozy room in a house for Lee, who angrily refused the quarters, prompting Taylor to write, "he is never so uncomfortable as when comfortable." Venable later remarked, "No man could see the flush come over that grand forehead and the temple veins swell on occasions of great trial of patience and doubt that Lee had the high strong temper of a Washington, and habitually under the same control." Venable wrote to his wife at Christmas in 1864 that he hesitated to ask for a leave, remarking, "if you had the pleasure of Gen. Lee's acquaintance you would debate with yourself about asking him for anything." A meeting with Congress in March 1865 pushed Lee to explode to Custis, "they do not seem to be able to do anything except to eat peanuts and chew tobacco, while my army is starving." It was not his first dispute with Congress, but their defeatism angered him. Nevertheless, like Washington he would not defy them, and he rebuffed Speaker Pro Tem Robert M. T. Hunter, who asked him to help seek terms with the Federals.[31]

---

of Lee, 574–75; White, *Southern Confederacy,* 416–17; Robert Stiles, *Four Years under Marse Robert* (New York, 1903), 20; Thomas, *Lee,* 349; Lee to Davis, Mar. 10, 1865, Lee Papers, DU; Freeman, *Dispatches,* 373; Durden, *Gray and Black,* 205–7, 209–10, 246–50; Jordan, *Black Confederates,* 245–47, 249–50.

30. Charles Marshall to Richard S. Ewell, Mar. 27, 30, 1865, George W. Campbell Papers, LC; Ewell to Marshall, Mar. 30, 1865 [quote], Polk-Brown-Ewell Family Papers, Southern Historical Collection, University of North Carolina, Chapel Hill; Davis, *Rise and Fall,* 2:660; Lee to Davis, Mar. 24, 1865, Samuel Richey Collection, Walter Havinghurst Special Collections Library, Miami University, Oxford, Ohio; Dowdey and Manarin, *Wartime Papers,* 776, 927.

31. Thomas, *Lee,* 348, 350–52, 354; Walter H. Taylor, *Four Years,* 141 [1st quote]; Stanley F. Horn, ed., *The Robert E. Lee Reader* (Indianapolis, 1949), 352 [2nd quote]; "Memoir of Mary Cantey (McDowell) Venable" (Typescript, n.d., McDowell-Miller-War-

Despite Lee's concern, he was resolved that he could sustain the Confederate resistance until independence was won. Reporting Lincoln's reelection to Mary, he explained, "we must therefore make up our minds for another four years of war." The failure of negotiators to reach an agreement at Hampton Roads in February 1865 left Lee with no alternative, and his resolve was shared by many others. Longstreet declared to Lee on New Year's Day in 1865, "I believe that we are better able to cope with [Grant] now than we have ever been." He added in another note, "When the time comes I think that we shall make as good a fight as the same number of men ever did." Many Confederate regiments adopted defiant resolutions, some of which focused on the Revolution. The 45th North Carolina Infantry, for example, declared the "good, great and noble Washington" was "equalled by none save our own beloved Lee." The Richmond *Dispatch* went even further, opining that the Revolution was "child's play compared to this struggle" but Lee, whose "military ability" was superior to Washington's, was more than equal to the task.[32]

Because many other Confederates shared Lee's confidence, public demand led to his reluctant acceptance of an appointment as general-in-chief. The Confederate Congress and Virginia legislature adopted resolutions asking for Lee's appointment, but Lee told the president that he did not want the job. Davis was hard pressed to sustain his administration, though, and wanted to share responsibility. On February 9, Lee accepted a rank similar to that bestowed upon Washington. In his first weeks as general-in-chief, he reminded his troops that they were the "children" of the patriots who had fought and won, and he assured them that they also would win. The Richmond *Dispatch* crowed, "Providence raises up the man for the time, and a man for this occasion, we

---

ner Family Papers, UVA), 47 [3rd quote]; George T. Lee, "Reminiscences of General Robert E. Lee, 1865–1868," *South Atlantic Quarterly* 26 (July 1927): 236–37 [4th quote]; Noah A. Trudeau, " 'A Mere Question of Time': Robert E. Lee from the Wilderness to Appomattox Court House," in Gallagher, *Lee the Soldier*, 547.

32. Thomas, *Lee*, 346, 348; Lee to Mary Custis Lee, Nov. 12, 1864 [1st quote], Lee Family Papers, VHS; Longstreet to Lee, Jan. 1 [2nd quote], Feb. 1 [3rd quote], 1865, James Longstreet Letterbook, Center for American History, University of Texas at Austin; McPherson, *Battle Cry*, 822–24; Power, *Lee's Miserables*, 245–49; Richmond *Examiner*, Feb. 25, 1865 [4th quote]; Richmond *Dispatch*, Feb. 3, 1865 [5th and 6th quotes].

believe, has been raised up in Robert E. Lee, the Washington of the second American Revolution."[33]

Lee's promotion provided him with authority over the west. In March he advised Lt. Gen. Richard Taylor to concentrate his troops and attack in Mississippi and Alabama. The situation in the Carolinas was even graver. While Hood's army self-destructed in Tennessee, Maj. Gen. William T. Sherman burned his way through Georgia and then did more damage in the Carolinas. Lee could not send more troops and suggested an evacuation of Charleston. Its garrison joined with the remnants of Hood's army (which had come east at Lee's suggestion) and local forces to confront Sherman. Davis had little faith in Johnston, but Lee, with the support of many Confederate congressmen, selected him to lead this force. As Lee told Davis, Johnston would make "every effort . . . to defeat Sherman wherever he can be struck to most advantage."[34]

Lee's primary focus remained his own army, with which he planned to resume a war of maneuver. He assured Mary in February 1865 that he would "endeavour to do [his] duty & fight to the last," but he also inquired about her plans if he abandoned the capital "to prevent being surrounded." The next day, Washington's birthday, he told Secretary of War James A. Seddon that preparations would be made for an evacuation. At about the same time, he reviewed his options with Maj. Gen. John B. Gordon, commander of the II Corps. Lee said there were three choices: seek terms, retreat and join Johnston, or fight. Lee discarded the first with little comment. In truth, with the permission of Davis he had already asked Grant for a meeting, then dropped the idea when the Federal commander responded that Lincoln insisted upon Lee's surrender. A retreat to ally with Johnston appeared impossible because Davis

33. Woodworth, *Davis and Lee,* 309–11; McPherson, *Battle Cry,* 821; Lee to Davis, Jan. 19, 1865, Lee Papers, LV; Dowdey and Manarin, *Wartime Papers,* 884; Long, *Memoirs of Lee,* 680; Fitzhugh Lee, *General Lee,* 368; Bradford, *Lee the American,* 39; *OR,* I, 46:1230 [1st quote]; James F. Johnson and Hugh W. Sheffey to Davis, Jan. 17, 1865, Gilder Lehrman Collection, Pierpont Morgan Library, New York; Richmond *Dispatch,* Feb. 7, 1865 [2nd quote].

34. Dowdey and Manarin, *Wartime Papers,* 885–86; Thomas, *Lee,* 348; Lee to Davis, Jan. 11, 1865, Lee to Richard Taylor, Mar. 15, 1865, Gilder Lehrman Collection, Pierpont Morgan Library; Woodworth, *Davis and Lee,* 310, 313–14; Alexander H. Stephens et al. to Lee, Feb. 4, 1865, Robert M. T. Hunter to Lee, Feb. 10, 1865, Lee to Stephens et al., Feb. 13, 1865, Louis T. Wigfall Papers, LC; Freeman, *Dispatches,* 313, 315; Lee to Davis, Feb. 4, 1865 [quote], Lee Papers, DU.

would not allow it, the army was depleted, and Grant was near and strong. Lee met with Davis on March 4 and, according to Gordon, afterward said that the president would not allow an evacuation. That left one choice, Lee told Gordon, and that was to fight.[35]

Lee asked Gordon to conduct an assault with the intent of making Grant contract his enveloping lines, but he did not tell him that he still intended to evacuate the capital. He had told Gordon that Davis refused to abandon Richmond, but that was not how the president remembered their conversation. Davis recalled that Lee said that the capital would have to be evacuated, but that he had to wait until the roads were dry and his animals were healthier. Lee assured the president that the loss of the city's factories would be at least partially offset by firms elsewhere and that he would join Johnston. Gordon chose Fort Stedman for a sortie, and Lee told Davis. It was either then or at the earlier conference that Lee told the president, "in language similar to that employed by Washington during the Revolution," that if he retreated to the mountains, he could fight twenty years. This echoed Washington's claim that if he were driven from the coast "he would take refuge in West Augusta, and thereby prolong the war interminably." It was not the first time Lee had said this; in June 1862 he told a friend that if defeated he would retreat to the mountains and fight "for years to come."[36]

Gordon attacked at Fort Stedman believing that he was aiding in a consolidation of Lee's position, not an evacuation. He was apparently unaware that Lee had written to Breckinridge, "If the army can be maintained in an efficient condition, I do not regard the abandonment of our present position as necessarily fatal to our success." Lee was guardedly optimistic: "While the military situation is not favorable, it is not worse than the superior numbers and resources of the enemy justified us in

35. Dowdey and Manarin, *Wartime Papers*, 907, 911; Lee to Mary Custis Lee, Feb. 21, 1865 [quotes], Lee Papers, USMA; Jones, *Life and Letters*, 347–48; Gordon, *Reminiscences*, 389–94; Robert E. Lee, Jr., *Recollections*, 146; James Longstreet, *From Manassas to Appomattox* (Philadelphia, 1896), 583–87; Woodworth, *Davis and Lee*, 314–15; Thomas, *Lee*, 348; Thomas N. Page, *Robert E. Lee, Man and Soldier* (New York, 1911), 615.

36. Davis, *Rise and Fall*, 2:648–51, 656–57 [1st quote]; "Tributes to General Lee," *Southern Magazine* 8 (Jan. 1871): 25; Jones, *Life and Letters*, 347; Cooke, *Life of Lee*, 409 [2nd quote]; Woodworth, *Davis and Lee*, 315; Jones, *Personal Reminiscences*, 294–95 [3rd quote]; Thomas, *Lee*, 348; George T. Lee, "Reminiscences," 236–37.

expecting from the beginning, & indeed, the legitimate military consequences of that superiority have been postponed longer than we had reason to anticipate." The repulse of Gordon's attack on March 25 with the loss of four thousand Confederates was a tremendous blow. Grant's lines continued to press south and west around Lee's works, and each push further reduced Lee's chances to maneuver effectively.[37]

Lee's plans for returning to the field in good order were abruptly canceled when Grant launched an offensive. On March 29, he ordered two infantry corps, masked by cavalry, around Lee's right flank. Maj. Gen. George E. Pickett's infantry with Maj. Gen. Fitzhugh Lee's cavalry repulsed the Federals, but on April 1, while both generals feasted at a shad bake, their commands were overrun at Five Forks. That day, Lee telegraphed Davis that Richmond had to be evacuated. On April 2, with Grant breaking through at several points, Lee donned a full uniform and buckled on a dress sword. He explained that if he had to surrender, "he would do so in full harness." He took charge of a battery posted in front of his headquarters and did not leave until the house was ablaze. He then informed Breckinridge that he was abandoning his lines. Apologetically, Lee also wrote to Davis that he had "hoped that the enemy might expose himself in some way that we might take advantage of, and cripple him." That night he posted himself at a fork in the road that led away from Petersburg and watched as fewer than 30,000 men stumbled past.[38]

Lee's plan, as he had described it in a letter to Longstreet on Washington's birthday in 1865, was to march to Burkeville, where the Danville and Southside railroads intersected, and follow the former to North Carolina for a junction with Johnston. Along the way, Lee added, "We might also seize the opportunity of striking at Grant, should he pursue

---

37. Lee to John C. Breckinridge, Mar. 9, 1865 [quotes], Burton N. Harrison Papers, LC; Dowdey and Manarin, *Wartime Papers,* 913, 917; Gordon, *Reminiscences,* 403; Thomas, *Lee,* 349.

38. Lee to Davis, Mar. 29, 1865, Lee Papers, LV; Freeman, *Dispatches,* 347–48, 358–59; Thomas, *Lee,* 349, 354–55; Davis, *Rise and Fall,* 2:656; Dowdey and Manarin, *Wartime Papers,* 927; Horn, *Reader,* 417 [1st quote]; Lee to Davis, Apr. 2, 1865 [2nd quote], Robert E. Lee Letterbooks, De Butts-Ely Collection, LC; Anderson and Anderson, *Generals,* 521–22, 526; James Longstreet, *Manassas to Appomattox,* 605; Freeman, *Lee,* 4:45, 50–51.

us rapidly, or at Sherman before they could unite." This was a desperate gamble, but Lee believed that he had no choice. The key to prolonging the war for Lee remained his army. He had made this clear in a letter to Davis in March, when he wrote, "The greatest calamity that can befall us is the destruction of our armies. If they can be maintained we may yet recover from our reverses but if lost we have no resource." He had stumbled, but he might recover as Washington had.[39]

Lee's morale remained good until he came to Amelia Court House. There he had ordered supplies to be stockpiled, but he found nothing. That day, April 4, he issued a proclamation to the local citizens, appealing to their "generosity & charity to supply as far as each is able the wants of the brave soldiers who have battled for your liberty for four years." Pursuing Federals gained ground while Lee's forage parties worked. His associates noted that Lee was visibly shaken to realize that "all was over." Asked later why he did not tell his army about his realization, Lee replied that "they had to find out for themselves." Be that as it may, his authority was still subordinate to that of Davis, who expected him to fight. And there was still the possibility that prolonging the war might bring better surrender terms.[40]

Lee's army was failing, but on April 5 those that remained in the ranks plodded west. Mud and exhausted animals hindered their march, but they reached Burkeville. There Lee learned that Union cavalry blocked the road south. He decided to attack, but a report from his son Rooney that there were also two corps of Union infantry convinced him to move west to Farmville, where he understood there were rations. His weary men marched all night, and gaps gradually appeared between units. Some were overwhelmed at Sayler's Creek on April 6. Many officers, including Custis Lee, were lost as emaciated units surrendered. Lee, watching from a hillside, was horrified, muttering, "My God! Has the

39. Lee to Longstreet, Feb. 22, 1865 [1st quote], Lee Papers, LV; Robert E. Lee, "A Letter from Petersburg," *Civil War History* 3 (Dec. 1957): 376 [2nd quote]; Thomas, *Lee,* 357; Dowdey and Manarin, *Wartime Papers,* 908.

40. Thomas, *Lee,* 356–57; Cooke, *Life of Lee,* 451–52; Dowdey, *Lee,* 545–49; "To the Citizens of Amelia County," Apr. 4, 1865 [1st quote], Lee Papers, LV; Edward Lee Childe, *The Life and Campaigns of General Lee,* trans. George Litte (London, 1875), 311 [2nd quote]; Flood, *Last Years,* 56 [3rd quote]; Freeman, *Lee,* 4:59, 66–67.

army been dissolved?" Lee soon recovered and, flag in hand, helped place nearby troops into line to rally the mob fleeing toward them.[41]

Downstream from the clash witnessed by Lee, Gordon lost many wagons and almost his corps in another furious fight on Sayler's Creek. In all, Lee lost about eight thousand troops, most of them taken prisoner, on April 6, reducing his effectives to twelve thousand infantry and three thousand cavalry. Custis Lee was reported among the slain; his father did not learn until the next day that he was only captured. The remainder of Lee's men escaped to Farmville, but there were no rations, and a bridge over the Appomattox River there did not burn in time. Hungry Confederates had to fight to stay ahead of eager pursuers. On the night of April 7, Lee received a request for surrender from Grant. He followed the advice of Longstreet, who said simply, "Not yet."[42]

Longstreet may not have been ready to give up, but the harsh truth was becoming apparent. Lee spoke briefly to Lt. John S. Wise, Henry A. Wise's son, on April 6, saying that more defeats like Sayler's Creek would ruin the Confederacy. Over a makeshift breakfast the next morning, the elder Wise talked with Lee. In less somber times Lee had rebuked Wise for profanity. Wise had retorted, "General Lee, you certainly play the part of Washington to perfection, and your whole life is a constant reproach to me." Perhaps pleased with the connection, Lee had agreed that he would pray for the army while Wise could do the "cussin' for one small brigade." Now Wise addressed a darker aspect of Lee's mimicry of Washington. He told Lee that the Confederacy had ceased to exist a year ago. He insisted that only the loyalty of the men to Lee kept the army together, and to continue would be murder. Lee did not agree to surrender, but when his nephew George T. Lee arrived in camp, the general gently told him that he should not have come because "You can't do any good here."[43]

41. Jones, *Personal Reminiscences,* 296; Winston, *Lee,* 335; Thomas, *Lee,* 358–59; William Mahone, "Memoirs" (Typescript, n.d., United States Army Military History Institute, Carlisle, Pa.), 7–8 [quote]; E. Porter Alexander, *Fighting for the Confederacy,* 521.

42. Dowdey and Manarin, *Wartime Papers,* 931; Thomas, *Lee,* 359; Flood, *Last Years,* 6; Winston, *Lee,* 337; James Longstreet, *Manassas to Appomattox,* 619 [quote].

43. Wise, *End of an Era,* 429, 433–35; Bradford, *Lee the American,* 207 [1st and 2nd quotes]; George T. Lee, "Reminiscences," 238 [3rd quote]; Charles F. Adams, "Lee at Appomattox," in Charles F. Adams, ed., *Lee at Appomattox and Other Papers,* 2nd ed. (Boston, 1903), 8; Charles F. Adams, "The Confederacy and the Transvaal," *American Antiquarian Society Proceedings* 14 (Oct. 1901): 434–35; Winston, *Lee,* 336.

On the same night that Lee refused a surrender request from Grant, Brig. Gen. William N. Pendleton, an Episcopal priest and Lee's chief of artillery, urged him to quit. For a subordinate to advise surrender was a violation of protocol, but Pendleton did not speak just for himself. He was sent by officers who believed the end had come. Their first discussion had been on April 6, when Gordon declared that "further bloodshed" would be "murder almost." The next day, after the fighting at Farmville, others joined them, and Pendleton became a spokesman. Approached by Pendleton as he lay resting, Lee curtly refused to consider a surrender. In fact, Lee said that he had "resolved to die first; and that, if it comes to that, we shall force through or all fall in our places." Lee did talk with Pendleton, insisting that the key to victory was Southern resolve but admitting that foreign aid would become "necessary" in a protracted struggle.[44]

Lee kept his troops moving to Appomattox Court House. He hoped that supplies might be there, but instead on April 8 he found Federals in his front and on both flanks. When a second surrender request arrived from Grant, Lee declined but offered to meet with him as general-in-chief of all Confederate forces to discuss a settlement of the war. Having written that, Lee held a council of war with Longstreet, Gordon, and his nephew Fitzhugh Lee. They only had about ten thousand men, but they agreed to attack in the morning to break through the Federal lines. When Gordon asked where he should stop, Lee smiled and said Tennessee, two hundred miles southwest. The goal, he told them, was to fight until Lincoln offered decent terms.[45]

Lee stood on a hill behind Gordon's infantry, which advanced at daylight with Fitzhugh Lee's cavalry. Venable reported three hours later that Gordon could do no more unless Lee would unleash Longstreet, uncovering the rear. Lee spoke with Longstreet, who asked whether sacrificing the army would aid elsewhere. When Lee said no, Longstreet told him,

---

44. Campbell Brown, "Diary" [1st and 2nd quotes], Campbell Papers, LC; Mahone, "Memoirs," 11; Adams, "Lee at Appomattox," 10; James Longstreet, *Manassas to Appomattox*, 620; Charles Marshall, *An Aide-de-Camp of Lee . . .* , ed. Frederick Maurice (Boston, 1927), 254–55; William Preston, "Personal Recollections of General Lee," *Southern Magazine* 15 (1874): 633 [3rd and 4th quotes]; Fitzhugh Lee, *General Lee*, 392; Long, *Memoirs of Lee,* 416–17; Freeman, *Lee,* 4:109–10; Jones, *Personal Reminiscences,* 297.

45. Thomas, *Lee,* 360–61; Gordon, *Reminiscences,* 434–36; Cooke, *Life of Lee,* 459; Dowdey and Manarin, *Wartime Papers,* 932.

"your situation speaks for itself." Lee replied sadly, "Then there is nothing left me but to go and see General Grant, and I would rather die a thousand deaths." Lee, Marshall, and Sgt. G. W. Tucker, the orderly who was with Hill when he fell, rode to the Union skirmish line. Marshall was delegated to arrange a meeting, but Grant refused to discuss the surrender of all Confederate forces. He would talk about Lee's army only. Lee agreed.[46] With no order from Davis, Lee in fact could not discuss the disposition of all Confederates, but he had to prevent the sacrifice of those directly under his command.

By deciding to speak with Grant about a surrender, Lee put aside any considerations of a guerrilla campaign. He had earlier heard such a proposal from Davis and opposed it. While he waited for the result of Gordon's charge, he talked with Brig. Gen. E. Porter Alexander. The latter said that the army should disperse and conduct a guerrilla campaign, but Lee disagreed. He declared that they were Christian people who did not have a right to inflict chaos on the South. Guerrilla war would bring greater ruin and might increase Northern animosity. Neither was what Lee wanted. Lee, raised to revere Washington and his Continentals and educated at West Point, could not endorse a guerrilla war.[47]

Lee understood that because he had become the focus of the war, his surrender would destroy the Confederacy. Someone did ask, "What will history say of the surrender of the army in the field?" Lee replied that he knew "hard things" would be said, but surrender was proper and he would "take all the responsibility." It was a lesson he had learned early and imparted to his children. When Custis was accused of having liquor in his room at West Point in 1851, Lee had written to his son, "I hold to the belief that you must act right whatever the consequences." Lee knew that he might face terrible penalties, but as he told Taylor, he was responsible for his men. Allegedly he told another officer that he had considered how easy it would be to end his dilemma by riding to the front, but it was his duty and that of his men to live and protect the women and children of the South. He also told Gordon that he wished

46. Thomas, *Lee,* 361–62; James Longstreet, *Manassas to Appomattox,* 625 [1st quote]; Jones, *Personal Reminiscences,* 143 [2nd quote]; Mahone, "Memoirs," 15–16; Adams, "Transvaal," 445.

47. Thomas, *Lee,* 362–63; Adams, "Lee at Appomattox," 12, 21–22, 25; E. Porter Alexander, *Memoirs,* 604–5; Adams, "Transvaal," 445; Gary W. Gallagher, *The Confederate War* (Cambridge, Mass., 1997), 123–52.

he were dead, but then recovered and declared that they both "must live for our afflicted country."[48]

Having agreed to meet with Grant, Lee struggled to keep the opposing troops from killing more of each other. His message to Grant included a request for a truce, but no reply came at first. Federals began advancing and gunfire erupted, but Lee remained in the open and sent another truce demand. When no answer came, Lee moved within his lines, but finally a cessation of hostilities was ordered by Maj. Gen. George G. Meade. At the same time, Lee hurried to tell Fitzhugh Lee, who was riding in with two hundred prisoners, "to be a good boy and not fight any more." This must have been hard because days earlier Lee had told his nephew there would be no surrender, adding, "I will get you out of this."[49]

Washington had provided a model for Lee in many stages of his life, but at Appomattox the Confederate commander stepped beyond his idol's shadow. Lee represented his adopted family well in assuming responsibility and making hard decisions. He also probably did remember that his father had scorned Lord Charles Cornwallis for sending subordinates to negotiate with Washington, so apparently he never really considered avoiding the humiliation of a formal capitulation. After Grant consented to talk, Lee rode to meet him, accompanied by Marshall and Tucker. As the trio departed, Longstreet growled that if Grant did not offer "liberal terms," he should return and the army would "fight it out."[50]

The surrender itself proved anticlimactic. Lee arrived first at Wilmer

48. Gallagher, *Confederate War*, 59, 95–96; Robert E. Lee, Jr., *Recollections*, 151–52; White, *Southern Confederacy*, 423; Jones, *Personal Reminiscences*, 143–44 [1st–3rd and 5th quotes]; Lee to Custis Lee, June 22, 1851 [4th quote], Lee Papers, USMA; Judith W. Maguire, *General Robert E. Lee, the Christian Soldier* (Richmond, 1873), 157–58; Mason, *Popular Life of Lee*, 314.

49. Thomas, *Lee*, 363–64; E. Porter Alexander, "Lee at Appomattox: Personal Recollections of the Break-Up of the Confederacy," *Century* 63 (Mar. 1902): 927; Marshall, *Aide*, 262–66 [1st quote]; Dowdey, *Lee*, 566, 574–76; Flood, *Last Years*, 12; Long, *Memoirs of Lee*, 415 [2nd quote]; Freeman, *Lee*, 4:81.

50. Marshall, *Aide*, 257–58, 268–69; Walter H. Taylor, *Four Years*, 152–53; Edgar E. Hume, "Light-Horse Harry and His Fellow Members of the Cincinnati," *Virginia Magazine of History and Biography* 15 (Apr. 1935): 275; Adams, "Lee at Appomattox," 28 [quotes]; Adams, "Transvaal," 450; E. Porter Alexander, *Memoirs*, 609; James Longstreet, *Manassas to Appomattox*, 628.

McLean's house, wearing a full dress uniform and a magnificent sword. Close associates might have noted that this weapon had been given to him during the war and was not the sword of Washington that remained in his baggage. Grant arrived thirty minutes later, dressed shabbily. He explained that he thought Lee would appreciate his coming at once rather than detouring for clean clothes. Lee agreed, apparently not remembering that once he had ordered Grant to change out of a dirty uniform before he could speak with Winfield Scott. The Union commander reminisced with Lee about the Mexican War, then scribbled generous terms that pleased Lee. After the proper signatures, Lee arranged for rations for his men, spoke briefly with several officers, paused to regain his composure, and rode away on Traveller.[51]

Lee's last day as the Confederacy's principal commander was very emotional. Confederates crowded around as he rode away from the McLean house, crying and wanting to shake his hand or touch him. He could not speak and finally retired silently to compose himself again in the apple orchard where he had waited for Grant. After about an hour, Lee made his way to his tent through crowds of Confederates whose sad attempts to cheer dissolved into sobs. Late that day, he had Marshall compose General Orders Number 9, a farewell to his army. He praised them for "unsurpassed courage and fortitude" and eased the pain of defeat by asserting that they had "been compelled to yield to overwhelming numbers and resources." He reassured them that his surrender was not due to any "distrust" of them but to avoid a "useless sacrifice." The words were Marshall's, but as usual Lee closely edited the draft, deleting what he thought was not appropriate.[52] There was no reference to the Revolutionary tradition that he had failed.

Grant met with Lee on April 10 to ask him to speak with Lincoln about terms for all Confederates, but Lee declined. He agreed that more bloody campaigns should be avoided but insisted that he could not override Davis' authority. All he could do, he told Grant, was to use his influence to pacify people and urge them to support the Union. With

51. Thomas, *Lee,* 394–95; Marshall, *Aide,* 274; Winston, *Lee,* 340–41; Flood, *Last Years,* 9–10, 12.

52. Walter H. Taylor, *Four Years,* 153; Flood, *Last Years,* 16–17; Freeman, *Lee,* 4:144–47; Dowdey, *Lee,* 581–82; Dowdey and Manarin, *Wartime Papers,* 934–35 [quotes].

that in mind, Lee wrote to Davis that continued resistance by his troops would have led only to useless sacrifices. After his army stacked their guns and flags, Lee wrote again to Davis, asserting that guerrilla warfare would not win independence because the "moral condition" of the South had declined. He left the decision to Davis but added, "To save useless effusion of blood, I would recommend measures be taken for suspension of hostilities and the restoration of peace."[53]

Davis and many others initially refused to accept that Lee's surrender brought the end of the Confederacy. Davis had issued a defiant proclamation on April 5, declaring the loss of Richmond was only the start of a "new phase of the struggle." The debacle at Appomattox did not dissuade him. Later in April, he insisted "that the cause was not lost any more than hope of American liberty was gone amidst the sorest trials and most disheartening reverses of the Revolutionary struggle." British journalists agreed that the war did not end with Lee. Instead, they expected guerrilla warfare. Lee's refusal to participate made such a shift difficult, if not impossible. Without their Washington, Southerners realized their revolution was over. Johnston and others followed Lee's example by surrendering their armies.[54]

On April 12, as his troops stacked their weapons and the flags they did not destroy or hide, Lee departed for the Mess, where Mary waited. Three of his staff, Taylor, Venable, and Marshall, rode with him. Another, Maj. Giles B. Cooke, had been wounded and traveled with them in an ambulance. Union cavalry escorted the group until Lee asked to continue with his entourage alone. Venable departed, but Rooney took his place on April 15 as his father left his bivouac in the yard of Charles Carter Lee, whose cabin was too crowded for General Lee. Lee hardly looked like a hero as he rode into the ruins of Richmond. Henry Chapin, a Union soldier, witnessed Lee's arrival and wrote to his father that he "looked sad and downcast he had his hat pulled down over his eyes as though he was ashamed to be seen by the people." Lee need not

53. Marshall, *Aide*, 275; Anderson and Anderson, *Generals*, 557; Stern, *Lee*, 217; Flood, *Last Years*, 21–22; Thomas, *Lee*, 367–68; Lee to Davis, Apr. 12, 20 [quotes], 1865, Lee Letterbooks, De Butts-Ely Collection, LC; Dowdey and Manarin, *Wartime Papers*, 939.

54. Adams, "Transvaal," 431–32, 438–39; Adams, "Lee at Appomattox," 3 [1st quote], 13–14; Bowen, *Strategy of Lee*, 254 [2nd quote]; Lee to Davis, Mar. 14, 1865, Jefferson Davis Papers, Robert W. Woodruff Library, Emory University, Atlanta, Ga.

have worried; Chapin noted that the people of Richmond had "the utmost confidence in him both soldiers and citizens." Lee tipped his hat to a few who greeted him as he made his way to the Mess, where he found a huge crowd. Bowing silently to them, he went inside without further demonstration.[55]

Despite Lee's bitter words during the last few months, the war had come to an end that he had not expected at the outset. He had tried to lead as Washington had done, and he had failed. As a British observer wrote later, "The vision of becoming the new Washington of a new Republic—had he ever entertained it—had faded away, with all its natural ambition." Lee quietly assumed responsibility for the defeat, and it was a heavy burden. When Meade called on him at Appomattox, Lee had asked him jovially why his beard had gotten so gray. Meade responded gallantly that Lee was responsible for most of it.[56] It was a generous remark, but praise could not alleviate the pain of defeat. If "frustrated" was an apt description of Lee before the Civil War, when his life seemed to be ending without a chance to match the achievements of Washington, then no word could describe his mood in April 1865.

55. Flood, *Last Years,* 28–30, 36, 40; Thomas, *Lee,* 344, 346, 348, 368–69; Henry Chapin to Father, Apr. 26, 1865 [quotes], Henry Chapin Papers, UVA; Freeman, *Lee,* 4:162–64.

56. C. C. Chessney, "Cooke's Life of General Robert E. Lee," *Edinburgh Review* 137 (Jan.–Apr. 1873): 388 [quote]; Flood, *Last Years,* 23.

7

Washington without His Reward

After the Civil War

After the Civil War Robert E. Lee continued to emulate and even enhance the legacy of George Washington. Lee failed to obtain a pardon or reclaim Arlington, but he promoted unity and reconciliation. Lee became the president of a college that bore Washington's name, though he chose not to follow his mentor into politics. Lee also recovered Washington relics taken from Arlington, edited a second edition of his father's memoirs, and helped his wife Mary with a second version of her father's work. Benjamin H. Hill later said that Lee was "Caesar, without his ambition; Frederick, without his tyranny; Napoleon, without his selfishness; and Washington, without his reward." If this last circumstance bothered Lee, he never said so. Instead, he wrote, "We failed but in the good Providence of God apparent failure often proves a blessing."[1]

Lee kept his promise to Ulysses S. Grant, and undertook the role of a statesman like Washington, by providing an example of cooperation. Unlike many ex-Confederates, he never seriously considered leaving the

---

1. Douglas S. Freeman, *R. E. Lee: A Biography,* 4 vols. (New York, 1934), 4:202; Benjamin H. Hill, "Address . . . before the Georgia Branch of the Southern Historical Society at Atlanta, February 18th, 1874," *Southern Historical Society Papers* 14 (1886): 495 [1st quote]; Robert E. Lee to George W. Jones, Mar. 22, 1869 [2nd quote], Robert E. Lee Letterbooks, De Butts-Ely Collection, Library of Congress, Washington, D.C. [hereinafter LC].

United States. He declined an offer from Martha Custis "Markie" Williams to escort him to Europe, writing that "there is much to detain me here, & at present at least it is my duty to remain." When E. Porter Alexander visited him, Lee said that he "did not at all sympathise" with Alexander's plan to flee to Brazil. Learning that many of his former troops talked about emigrating, he wrote to his old adjutant, Walter H. Taylor, "Virginia wants all their aid, all their support and the presence of all her sons to sustain and recuperate her." Similar notions appeared in letters to others. To Josiah Tattnall, Lee added, "All should unite in honest efforts to obliterate the effects of the war and to restore the blessings of peace."[2]

Lee urged those who did leave to reconsider. Matthew F. Maury served with Maximilian in Mexico before returning to the Virginia Military Institute. Lee wrote to him, "The thought of abandoning the country & all that may be left in it, is abhorrent to my feelings; & I prefer to struggle for its restoration, & share its fate, than to give up all as lost." Pierre G. T. Beauregard received a similar letter and subsequently declined offers of command in Egypt and Romania, but Jubal A. Early went abroad for years. The latter got a note at Nassau in which Lee chided, "I think the South requires the presence of all her sons now more than at any period of her history and I determined at the outset of her difficulties to share the fate of my people."[3]

2. Emory W. Thomas, *Robert E. Lee: A Biography* (New York, 1995), 372 [1st quote]; E. Porter Alexander, *Fighting for the Confederacy: The Personal Recollections of General Edward Porter Alexander,* ed. Gary W. Gallagher (Chapel Hill, N.C., 1989), 547 [2nd quote]; Walter H. Taylor, *Four Years with General Lee* (New York, 1877; reprint, New York, 1962), 155; New York *Herald,* Apr. 29, 1865; Lee to Walter H. Taylor, June 17, 1865 [3rd quote], Robert E. Lee Papers, Eleanor S. Brockenbrough Library, Museum of the Confederacy, Richmond [hereinafter MOC]; Robert E. Lee, Jr., *Recollections and Letters of General Robert E. Lee* (New York, 1904), 163; Lee to Philip Slaughter, Aug. 31, 1865, Robert E. Lee Papers, University of Virginia Library, Charlottesville; Lee to John Letcher, Aug. 28, 1865, Lee to Josiah Tatnall, Sept. 7, 1865 [4th quote], Lee Letterbooks, De Butts-Ely Collection, LC; J. William Jones, *Life and Letters of Robert Edward Lee, Soldier and Man* (New York, 1906), 386–88.

3. Lee to Matthew F. Maury, Sept. 8, 1865 [1st quote], Lee-Jackson Collection, Washington and Lee University Library, Lexington, Va. [hereinafter W&L]; William Tate, ed., "A Robert E. Lee Letter on Abandoning the South after the War," *Georgia Historical Quarterly* 37 (Sept. 1953): 255–56; Jones, *Life and Letters,* 389–90; Joseph H. Crute, ed., *The Derwent Letters* (Powhatan, Va., 1985), 21; Lee to Pierre G. T. Beauregard, Oct. 3,

Lee also led the way in applying for a pardon. In his letter to Beauregard, Lee explained that he had watched as his surrender led to a "revolution in the opinions & feelings of the people" that made reunification "inevitable." Because of this, he wrote, "it became in my opinion, the duty of every Citizen, the Contest being virtually ended, to cease opposition, & place himself in a position to serve the country." He did not mention that he had been indicted for treason. He refused to evade the proceedings, tearfully declining the offer of Confederate veterans to hide him in the mountains, but he did protest to Grant that he thought the paroles signed at Appomattox protected him from legal vengeance. At the same time, Lee applied to Andrew Johnson for pardon under his proclamation of May 1865. By this, Lee told his eldest son, G. W. Custis Lee, he "set an example."[4]

Lee may have inspired others, but he never got his pardon. Grant spoke with Johnson and threatened to resign if the paroles signed by Lee were not honored. Johnson agreed, but an obstacle to Lee's pardon was his failure to include a loyalty oath with his application. George G. Meade urged Lee to sign an oath, and he did so in the fall of 1865. Like his letter, it brought no response. Lee thought that he was ignored, but in fact his oath was given by Secretary of State William H. Seward to a friend as a souvenir. Without it, Lee's application was useless. Lee was included in Johnson's general amnesty on Christmas Day, 1868, and his indictment was dropped soon afterward, partly because Federal District Judge John C. Underwood found that most Virginia jurors considered Lee to be Washington's equal. Lee's political rights were not restored until long after his death, but he urged others to apply, and many succeeded.[5]

1865, Lee Letterbooks, De Butts-Ely Collection, LC; Lee to Jubal A. Early, Nov. 22, 1865 [2nd quote], Jubal A. Early Papers, LC.

4. Lee to Beauregard, Oct. 3, 1865 [1st–3rd quotes], Lee Letterbooks, De Butts-Ely Collection, LC; Jones, *Life and Letters,* 390; Taylor, *Four Years,* 155; Lee to Taylor, June 17, 1865, Lee Papers, MOC; J. William Jones, *Personal Reminiscences, Anecdotes, and Letters of Gen. Robert E. Lee* (New York, 1874), 320; Thomas, *Lee,* 370; Robert E. Lee, Jr., *Recollections,* 165; G. W. Custis Lee to Charles S. Venable, n.d. [4th quote], Charles S. Venable Papers, Center for American History, University of Texas at Austin.

5. Thomas, *Lee,* 371, 380–81, 390; Ulysses S. Grant to Lee, June 20, 1865, Ulysses S. Grant Papers, LC; Jones, *Life and Letters,* 385–86; Charles B. Flood, *Lee: The Last Years* (Boston, 1981), 53–54, 99–100; Rose M. E. MacDonald, *Mrs. Robert E. Lee* (Boston, 1939), 120–21, 123–28; Gary W. Gallagher, *The Confederate War* (Cambridge, Mass.,

Lee was not greatly concerned about his pardon. He wrote to Early, "The accusations against myself I have not thought proper to notice, or even to correct misrepresentations of my words and acts." Lee added, "We shall have to be patient, and suffer for awhile at least, and all controversy I think, will only serve to prolong angry and bitter feeling, and postpone the period when reason and charity may resume their sway." More practically, he and Custis got statements from Grant declaring that they were exempt from arrest as long as they abided by their paroles. Lee did break his silence about legal matters once, when Sen. Simon Cameron accused him of deceitfully accepting command of Federal forces in 1861 and then deserting. Lee wrote an explanation to Sen. Reverdy Johnson of Maryland, who had offered to defend him in court, and the issue was dropped.[6]

Lee did fret about Davis. Hearing that all charges had been dismissed against his former commander in May 1867, he wrote to a mutual associate, "I have not words to tell the load that it has lifted from my heart, or to express my gratitude to the Giver of all good for this manifestation of his kindness." Lee's relief proved premature. In November 1867, he returned to Petersburg for the first time since the war to attend the wedding of his second son, William H. F. "Rooney" Lee. He also testified for Davis. Prosecutors wanted to assign responsibility for the war to Davis and convict him of treason. Davis in turn wanted the Supreme Court to rule on secession. Lee declared that he acted on his own and not solely at the behest of Davis. Lee was not asked to return, and the trial was dropped by the prosecutors.[7]

1997), 166; Freeman, *Lee,* 4:202, 249. It is interesting that a congressman in 1975 took the opportunity, while his comrades debated Lee's disfranchisement, to link the Confederate's cause with Washington. He demanded that Washington be promoted so that no one would ever outrank him again. See Francis MacDonnell, "Reconstruction in the Wake of Vietnam: The Pardoning of Robert E. Lee and Jefferson Davis," *Civil War History* 40 (June 1994): 119–33.

6. Lee to Early, Mar. 15, 1866 [quotes], Early Papers, LC; Grant to Lee, July 26, 1866, Grant to Custis Lee, July 26, 1866, Grant Papers, LC; Lee to Reverdy Johnson, Feb. 25, 1868, Lee Letterbooks, De Butts-Ely Collection, LC; Flood, *Last Years,* 178–79; Crute, *Derwent Letters,* 15.

7. Lee to James Chesnut, May 17, 1867 [quote], Robert E. Lee Papers, W&L; Robert E. Lee, Jr., *Recollections,* 268; Lee to Jefferson Davis, June 1, 1867, Robert E. Lee Letterbooks, Lee Family Papers, Virginia Historical Society, Richmond [hereinafter VHS]; Flood, *Last Years,* 170–73; Thomas, *Lee,* 386–87.

Lee did struggle to regain Arlington. Its loss infuriated Mary, who complained angrily to an old friend, "My own beautiful home which should have been sacred even from the enemy for its hallowed associations, has been occupied & pillaged for the last 4 years or rather more than 5 years." Lee shared her outrage at the desecration of Arlington, explaining to Sydney Smith Lee, "I should particularly like to terminate the burial of the dead, which can only be done by its restoration to the family." Mary resented that the "graves of those who aided to bring all this ruin on the children and the country" filled the grounds. She wrote, "They are, even planted up to the very door without any regard to common decency." The Lees' anger had no effect. On June 30, 1866, the number of Federals interred there was 9,795; by the time Lee died in 1870, there were 15,932 graves.[8]

Lee's failure to receive a pardon hindered his efforts to recover Arlington, but he persisted. He harbored no illusions about its condition; he wrote to Mary in the fall of 1865 that reports indicated it was "unservicable" as a "future resident [*sic*], even if it can be recovered." Sen. Reverdy Johnson proved to be a faithful ally. Lee wrote to him in July 1866, "I had hoped when passion had subsided, & reason resumed her sway, that the people of the country would prefer, from former associations, seeing Arlington in possession of Mr. Custis' descendants than appropriated to its present use. But that day seems to me now as distant as at the beginning. I may never see it."[9]

Lee did contact several attorneys in northern Virginia. The most industrious was Francis L. Smith, who had to be the bearer of bad news many times. The first was when he told General Lee that Mary, in order to recover the property, would have to take the test oath declaring that she had never supported the Confederacy. Lee had already made clear his opposition to the oath in his note to Reverdy Johnson, and of course

8. Mary Custis Lee to ———, May 9, 1866 [1st quote], Dec. 22, 1869, Gratz Collection, Historical Society of Pennsylvania, Philadelphia; Lee to Sydney Smith Lee, Jan. 4, 1866 [2nd quote], Robert Carter Lee Papers, VHS; Thomas L. Connelly, *The Marble Man: Robert E. Lee and His Image in American Society* (Baton Rouge, 1977), 34 [3rd and 4th quotes]; Karl Decker and Angus McSween, *Historic Arlington: A History of the National Cemetery from Its Establishment to the Present Time* (Washington, D.C., 1892), 71–75.

9. Robert E. Lee, Jr., *Recollections*, 192; Lee to Mary Custis Lee, Oct. 9, 1865 [1st and 2nd quotes], De Butts-Ely Collection, LC; Lee to Reverdy Johnson, Jan. 27, July 7 [3rd quote], 1866, Reverdy Johnson Papers, LC.

it was impossible for Mary to say that she did not support him. Encouraged by reports that the government was considering the restoration of property held or sold for taxes, Lee contacted Smith again in the fall of 1867. He asked Smith to press for the return of Arlington and Smith's Island, which like the estate had been sold for taxes in 1864. Smith petitioned for Smith's Island and was rejected. Undaunted, the Lees appealed to a federal circuit court, which in 1868 awarded the property to them. It was a victory for the family, but it was far less a triumph than the recovery of Arlington.[10]

During the last year of his life, Lee heard of a Supreme Court decision that encouraged him to try for Arlington again. He wrote once more to Smith, who sent a petition to Mary for her signature. Mary's application was given to Cassius F. Lee, her husband's cousin and an attorney in Alexandria. Despite this discreet use of another channel, the attempt failed. Lee never returned to Arlington; the closest he came was looking at it from a railroad car as he traveled to Washington to speak before the Joint Committee on Reconstruction. Mary was slightly more bold. In 1870, she had a driver take her to the house and bring her a cup of water from the spring. Custis finally received title to Arlington from the Supreme Court in 1882, though he sold it back to the government. Stripped of its Washington treasures, the place had little value to him or the other Lee children.[11]

While Lee wrestled with legal issues, he also had to provide for his family. In April 1865 at the Mess, the Lees' rented townhouse in Rich-

10. Lee to William H. Hope, Apr. 5, 1866, Lee to Francis L. Smith, Apr. 5, 1866, Nov. 11, 14, 1867, Lee to John A. Simkins, Jan. 10, 1867, Lee to Hamilton L. Neale, Dec. 24, 1867, May 11, Dec. 10, 1868, Lee Letterbooks, De Butts-Ely Collection, LC; Lee to Hope, Apr. 24, 1866, Lee Letterbooks, Lee Family Papers, VHS; Lee to Reverdy Johnson, Jan. 27, 1866, Reverdy Johnson Papers, LC; Lee to Miers W. Fisher, Dec. 24, 1867, Robert E. Lee Papers, Library of Virginia, Richmond [hereinafter LV]; Thomas, *Lee*, 390; Freeman, *Lee*, 207, 388–89; Clifford Dowdey, *Lee* (Boston, 1965), 706.

11. Lee to Mary Custis Lee, Oct. 9, 1865, Apr. 11 and 18, 1870, De Butts-Ely Collection, LC; Robert E. Lee, Jr., *Recollections*, 396, 414; Avery Craven, ed. *"To Markie": The Letters of Robert E. Lee to Martha Custis Williams from the Originals in the Huntington Library* (Cambridge, Mass., 1933), 69; Robert W. Winston, *Robert E. Lee: A Biography* (New York, 1941), 410; Connelly, *Marble Man*, 35; Armistead L. Long, *Memoirs of Robert E. Lee* (New York, 1886), 33; MacDonald, *Mrs. Lee*, 295–96; Decker and McSween, *Historic Arlington*, 83; Henry A. White, *Robert E. Lee and the Southern Confederacy, 1807–1870* (New York, 1897), 443; Dowdey, *Lee*, 625.

mond, Lee found Mary with two of their daughters, Mildred and Agnes, as well as Custis. Their eldest sister, Mary, was absent but safe. Rooney came with his father, while the third son, Robert E. Lee, Jr., arrived two weeks later. Lee's namesake had been wounded at Petersburg, and Rooney and Custis had been prisoners, but like their surviving sisters they were healthy. Only their mother's health had declined, as she was racked with arthritis. Lee soon decided that he had to leave Richmond, where the many visitors made him uncomfortable. He wanted a more secluded place.[12]

Lee's burden was greatly reduced in June when two of his sons settled at White House, Martha Washington's home that had been burned by a Union soldier. Rooney had lived there before the war; now his younger brother helped him rebuild. Robert later moved to the Romancoke estate left to him by his maternal grandfather, where his shanty remained a family disgrace for years, but in preparation for his wedding Rooney constructed a new home at White House. In the last year of his life, Lee wrote that "it did me good to go to the White House, and *see the mules walking round, and the corn growing.*" He may also have been pleased to find family treasures from other estates preserved at Romancoke, including a small table on which Washington had served breakfast to Martha after their wedding night.[13]

Lee had a plan for moving his dependents out of Richmond. He wrote to former staff member Armistead L. Long that he was "looking for some little quiet house in the woods where I can procure shelter, my daily bread . . . & wish to get Mrs. Lee out of the city as far as practicable." He repeated this notion to Rooney a few months later. By then, Lee was house-hunting. He visited his cousin Thomas H. Carter, but Elizabeth Randolph Cocke offered a house on her farm between Rich-

---

12. Thomas, *Lee,* 344, 369; New York *Herald,* Apr. 29, 1865; Paul D. Casdorph, *Lee and Jackson: Confederate Chieftains* (New York, 1992), 248; Freeman, *Lee,* 3:492; Flood, *Last Years,* 41, 44, 47.

13. Thomas, *Lee,* 371, 378; Winston, *Lee,* 80; White, *Southern Confederacy,* 428; Craven, *"To Markie,"* 77, 81–82; Flood, *Last Years,* 59; Mary P. Coulling, *Lee Girls* (Winston-Salem, N.C., 1987), 152; Edward Lee Childe, *The Life and Campaigns of General Lee,* trans. George Litte (London, 1875), 23–24 [quote]; Lee to Simkins, Jan. 10, 1867, Lee Letterbooks, De Butts-Ely Collection, LC; Lee to Fitzhugh Lee, Sept. 1, 1865, Lee Papers, W&L; Frederick S. Daniel, "A Visit to a Colonial Estate," *Harper's New Monthly Magazine* 76 (Mar. 1988): 518, 520.

mond and Charlottesville. Mary's arthritis made water travel impera-
tive, so she went with Lee, Mildred, and Agnes by canalboat to their
new home, Derwent, where Custis met them.[14]

Lee eventually found a position that allowed him to enhance the legacy of Washington. His daughter, Mary, told a friend that he wanted
to work, not just be a figurehead. Her remark reached the trustees of
Washington College, who boldly decided to ask Lee to be their new
president. Located in Lexington, the school had fallen on hard times.
The previous president was a Unionist and had left during the war. The
school had also been looted in June 1864 by Maj. Gen. David Hunter's
Federals, who also burned Virginia Military Institute. Union troops still
occupied the campus when the trustees wrote to Lee. The board asked
for restitution, but thirty years would pass before Congress paid. Ironically, Hunter had written to Lee, asking him to agree that his actions
against the two schools during the war had been justified, but he was
coldly rebuffed; now Lee was asked to do more for the college.[15]

John W. Brockenbrough, rector of Washington College, went to Derwent to convey the trustees' offer to Lee. He stressed two topics: service
to Virginia and its youth. William N. Pendleton, Lee's former chief of
artillery and now pastor of Grace Episcopal Church in Lexington, sent
a note with Brockenbrough. Lee had avoided academic assignments as
superintendent at West Point and refused postbellum offers from the
University of Virginia and the University of the South, but Washington
College intrigued him. Brockenbrough emphasized the college's ties to
George Washington and its endowments from the Society of the Cincinnati and John Robinson, a veteran of the Revolution. By agreeing, he
said, Lee "could thus revive and perpetuate the work Washington had

14. Lee to Armistead L. Long, May 24, 1865 [quote], Lee Papers, W&L; Crute, *Derwent Letters,* 13–14, 17, 20–21; Thomas, *Lee,* 371, 373; Dowdey, *Lee,* 646; Robert E.
Lee, Jr., *Recollections,* 166; Lee to William D. Cabell, May 24, 1865, Lee Papers, LV; Winston, *Lee,* 347; Coulling, *Lee Girls,* 153.

15. Franklin L. Riley, ed., *General Robert E. Lee after Appomattox* (New York,
1922), 1–2, 75–76, 95; Coulling, *Lee Girls,* 156–57; Ollinger Crenshaw, *General Lee's
College: The Rise and Growth of Washington and Lee University* (New York, 1969), 39,
137–39, 145; *The War of the Rebellion: A Compilation of the Official Records of the
Union and Confederate Armies,* 130 vols. (Washington, D.C., 1880–1902), Series I, Vol-
ume 37, part 1:640; Flood, *Last Years,* 79, 91, 115; Jubal A. Early, *War Memoirs,* ed.
Frank E. Vandiver (Philadelphia, 1912; reprint, Bloomington, Ind., 1960), 380; Crute,
Derwent Letters, 17–18.

done." This notion proved "very potent with General Lee." Brockenbrough left Derwent, however, with no firm answer; Lee would think
about it.[16]

Lee was not allowed to consider Washington College's offer in soli-
tude. Former Gov. John W. Letcher, an alumnus, wrote to him before
the board offered the position. After interviewing Lee, Brockenbrough
sent a letter repeating his appeal. Two weeks later, Lee wrote to the
board that he did not have the "ability" or the "strength" to teach, but
he would accept a position that required no "more than the general
administration & supervision of the Institution." He was also concerned about his lack of a pardon, which could bring "hostility" or
"injury" to the college. If they thought otherwise, he would be glad to
take the job.[17]

The trustees hastened to assure Lee that an acceptance would help,
not hinder, their school, and they agreed that he would be an adminis-
trator, not a teacher. Thus mollified, Lee accepted the presidency. He
had written to Letcher and Pendleton during August that "If I believed
I could be of advantage to the youth of the country, I should not hesitate." The board made it clear, and he was as good as his word. As his
wife Mary explained to a friend, Lee was not "very fond of teaching,
but [was] willing to do anything that [would] give him an honourable
support." In his brief speech on the day he was inaugurated, Lee
declared, "I shall devote my life now to training young men to do their
duty in life." He regarded this effort as a national, not a Southern, cause,
as he explained in letters to Custis and Beauregard.[18]

Lee's new job was especially dear because of its association with
Washington. As Mary wrote to a relative in May 1866, "The Genl

16. Jones, *Life and Letters*, 407 [quotes]; Thomas, *Lee*, 374–75; Winston, *Lee*, 356;
Lee to William M. Green, Sept. 20, 1868, Robert E. Lee Papers, University of the South
Archives, Sewanee, Tenn.

17. Crenshaw, *Lee's College*, 146–47; John W. Brockenbrough to Lee, Aug. 10, 1865,
Lee Papers, LV; Allen W. Moger, ed., "Letters to General Lee after the War," *Virginia Magazine of History and Biography* 64 (Jan. 1956): 45; Lee to "Trustees of Washington College," Aug. 24, 1865 [quotes], Lee Papers, W&L.

18. Thomas, *Lee*, 375; Riley, *Lee after Appomattox*, 9–10; Lee to Letcher, Aug. 28,
1865 [1st quote], Lee to Brockenbrough, Sept. 6, 1865, Lee to Beauregard, Oct. 3, 1865,
Lee Letterbooks, De Butts-Ely Collection, LC; Crute, *Derwent Letters*, 29–30, 36–37 [2nd
quote]; White, *Southern Confederacy*, 437–38 [3rd quote]; Jones, *Life and Letters*, 390.

[desires] his kind regards to you & family & hopes George Washington & Robert Lee may some day do good service to their country." A
friend later wrote that Washington's link to the school "is believed to
have had no small influence on the mind of General Lee, in disposing
him to accept its presidency, and in prompting him to the measures
which he inaugurated for its further endowment and usefulness." William Allan interviewed Lee several times after the war and asserted in
an 1870 eulogy that "the controlling motive with [Lee] in selecting this
particular place as the scene of his labors was the fact that here they
would constitute a tribute to the memory of Washington."[19]

Lee's commitment to Washington College was actually based on mistaken notions about his mentor's involvement with the school. Lee
believed that Washington had participated in its founding. He wrote
that a donation by George Peabody to the college would, even if the gift
never generated funds, "mark his approval of a college founded by
Washington." Lee also thought at least half of the college's endowment
had been provided by Washington. In fact, Washington had not been
involved in the school's founding, and his donation was only one hundred shares of stock in a canal-building company. Washington decided
in 1796 to give these to a school. Light-Horse Harry allegedly suggested
the academies in Staunton or Lexington, and Washington selected Liberty Hall in the latter, which was then renamed Washington Academy.
Lee was at least partly correct, however; this stock was one of the few
assets of any value held by the college in 1865.[20]

Another portion of the endowment was an indirect result of Washington's donation, though it was again less than Lee thought it was. Lee
wrote to an associate that the half of the endowment not donated by
Washington had been provided by John Robinson and the Society of the
Cincinnati of Virginia. The society had been founded as a fraternity for
officers who had served the patriot cause, including Washington and
Light-Horse Harry Lee. When the Virginia chapter disbanded, the survi-

19. Freeman, *Lee,* 4:217; Mary Custis Lee to Mrs. Richard B. Lee, May 10, 1866 [1st
quote], Ethel Armes Papers, LC; Jones, *Personal Reminiscences,* 81 [2nd quote], 470 [3rd
quote].
20. Lee to William W. Corcoran, Oct. 2, 1869 [quote], William W. Corcoran Papers,
LC; Flood, *Last Years,* 79, 164; Lee to Townsend Wade, Jan. 15, 1866, Lee Letterbooks,
De Butts-Ely Collection, LC; Crenshaw, *Lee's College,* 26–29; Eugene E. Prussing, *The
Estate of George Washington, Deceased* (Boston, 1927), 173–84.

vors gave their funds to the school that bore Washington's name. Legal wrangles delayed the gift, but the college received about twenty-five thousand dollars. In the meantime, Robinson, a Lexington resident who had fought under Washington, bequeathed seventy-five thousand dollars in 1826.[21]

Regardless of Lee's incomplete knowledge of the contribution of the Society of the Cincinnati to the endowment, he welcomed an opportunity to expand upon its legacy. In 1864, Davis had sent him a proposal for the revival of the society. Lee had refused to support this, recalling that many still held some animosity to its memory. Now he could do better. Society funds had been used to establish a joint professorship with the Virginia Military Institute and a commencement tradition of a Cincinnati oration by a student. The faculty position was lost in 1865, but the student speech was continued by Lee. It remained part of a celebration that began with Washington's birthday each year and included debates by the Washington Literary Society. Lee regularly enjoyed these.[22]

Lee had other family ties to the college. Henry Lee IV had attended the school. Another president, Louis Marshall, was the father-in-law of Lee's sister Ann. Lee revered their relative John Marshall and as president accepted an oil painting of him from another family member as payment of his fees. As a bonus, the painting was by William J. Hubard, whose copy of the statue of Washington in the Virginia capitol had been dedicated on the Virginia Military Institute campus in a ceremony attended by Lee in 1866; Custis had begun teaching there in 1865. Lee hung the Marshall portrait in the college library for all to "enjoy the privilege of beholding the likeness of the friend of Washington."[23]

21. Lee to Wade, Jan. 15, 1866, Lee Letterbooks, De Butts-Ely Collection, LC; Crenshaw, *Lee's College*, 31–32; Edgar E. Hume, "Light-Horse Harry and His Fellow Members of the Cincinnati," *Virginia Magazine of History and Biography* 15 (Apr. 1935): 275, 277–78; James T. Flexner, *Washington: The Indispensable Man* (New York, 1974), 201; Emily V. Mason, *Popular Life of Gen. Robert E. Lee* (Baltimore, 1870), 354.

22. Clifford Dowdey and Louis H. Manarin, eds., *The Wartime Papers of Robert E. Lee* (Boston, 1961), 704; Crenshaw, *Lee's College*, 33, 60–61, 93, 109–10; Lee to Mildred Childe Lee, Feb. 23, 1867, De Butts-Ely Collection, LC; Robert E. Lee, Jr., *Recollections*, 256; Craven, *"To Markie,"* 84.

23. Lee to Francis H. Smith, Aug. 17, 1866, Robert E. Lee Papers, Virginia Military Institute Archives, Lexington, Va.; Ethel Armes, *Stratford Hall: The Great House of the Lees* (Richmond, 1936), 315; Winston, *Lee*, 373; Marshall W. Fishwick, *Lee after the War*

Lexington was also the repository of some of the Washington mementoes. When Mary had sent the Washington papers and silver to Lee at Richmond in May 1861, he forwarded them to the Virginia Military Institute for safekeeping. Hunter's raid alarmed the Lees, but General Lee had written to his wife that to remove the treasure would be too dangerous, adding, "It must bide its fate." The institute's superintendent, Francis H. Smith, arranged for an ordnance sergeant, John Hampsey, to bury the boxes. Lee thanked Smith "for the care of the relics [he] so kindly undertook to guard" and also expressed gratitude to "Mrs. S. and the trusty friend who acted in the matter." Near the war's end, Mary again thanked Smith "for [his] care of [their] silver & papers."[24]

Soon after the Lees settled in Lexington, their youngest son went with Hampsey to unearth the Washington relics. Lee gave him an autographed picture of himself as a token of appreciation. On the back of the image, Mary scribbled her thanks to Hampsey for "preserving by his faithfulness for me the most valuable property saved from Arlington." The silver was cleaned, but many of the documents had been ruined. Mary recalled in a letter to a friend "that our Washington [papers] were destroyed by the damp during the long time they were underground. I almost wept as I had to commit to the flames papers that had been cherished for nearly a century, those that remained were defaced & stained." Lee shared her grief at the loss. They saved only a few items, some of which were later donated to the college.[25]

(New York, 1963), 57–58; Mason, *Popular Life,* 352; Flood, *Last Years,* 92; Thomas, *Lee,* 377; Allen W. Moger, "The Value of a Portrait," *Civil War History* 3 (Dec. 1957): 435–36 [quote], 437; William Couper, "War and Work," *Proceedings of the Rockbridge Historical Society* 1 (1939–41): 31–33; Crenshaw, *Lee's College,* 61; Burton J. Hendrick, *The Lees of Virginia: Biography of a Family* (Boston, 1935), 392; Paul C. Nagel, *The Lees of Virginia: Seven Generations of an American Family* (New York, 1990), 184.

24. Dowdey and Manarin, *Wartime Papers,* 25, 769 [1st quote]; Lee to Francis H. Smith, July 4, 1864 [2nd and 3rd quotes], Mary Custis Lee to Francis H. Smith, Mar. 30, [1865] [4th quote], Sara Henderson Smith Papers, VHS; MacDonald, *Mrs. Lee,* 188; Couper, "War and Work," 34. Sara Henderson Smith is presumably the "Mrs. S." to whom Lee refers in his letter of July 4, 1864.

25. Robert E. Lee, Jr., *Recollections,* 204; Couper, "War and Work," 34, 36, 38 [1st quote], 39–40; Coulling, *Lee Girls,* 160; Mary Custis Lee to J. C. Derby, Jan. 20, 1869, Robert E. Lee Papers, Chicago Historical Society, Chicago; Mary Custis Lee to Gertrude Deutsch, Jan. 31, 1873 [2nd quote], Custis-Lee Family Papers, LC; MacDonald, *Mrs. Lee,*

Lee arrived in Lexington alone on September 18, 1865. There he found Elizabeth Randolph Cocke and some of her family, as well as two of his female cousins, and accompanied them to a nearby hot spring. This he had done many times before and would continue to do with Mary. As for the college, he convinced the trustees to cancel elaborate plans for his inauguration. He simply took an oath, participated in a prayer, and endured Brockenbrough's long speech to an audience composed primarily of faculty, students, and trustees. About fifty students were present by the opening day, October 2, and during the year another hundred or so registered, providing Lee with plenty of work and little time to soak.[26]

The trustees had promised to provide Lee with a residence, but there was some delay while a tenant was allowed to vacate and the home was refurbished. Lee spent his first night in Lexington with a professor at the college and then moved the next morning to the Lexington Hotel, where he roomed with Custis. His official residence was sparsely furnished, but Mary rectified that after her arrival. She got carpets and curtains from Arlington and other household items from her cousin Britannia Peter Kennon, Markie Williams' aunt who had rescued them after the Federals occupied the estate. The rugs had to be cut or folded, but with Washington's silver they provided a link to the hallowed past.[27]

17; Freeman, *Lee*, 4:242–43; Nancy S. Anderson and Dwight Anderson, *The Generals: Ulysses S. Grant and Robert E. Lee* (New York, 1988), 571.

26. Lee to Mary Custis Lee, May 8, 1861, Sept. 19, 25, 1865, De Butts-Ely Collection, LC; Dowdey and Manarin, *Wartime Papers,* 426–27; Winston, *Lee,* 369; Robert E. Lee, Jr., *Recollections,* 240–43, 274–79, 318–22, 359–62, 365–67; William F. Chaney, *Duty Most Sublime: The Life of Robert E. Lee as Told through the "Carter Letters"* (Baltimore, 1996), 162–65, 167–68; Lee to Edward Lee Childe, July 10, 1868, Robert E. Lee Papers, Jesse Ball Dupont Library, Stratford Hall, Va. [hereinafter SH]; Mary Custis Lee to Ann Atkinson, Aug. 8, 1869, Corcoran Papers, LC; Thomas, *Lee,* 376; Freeman, *Lee,* 4:229; Crenshaw, *Lee's College,* 148–49; Flood, *Last Years,* 99.

27. Robert E. Lee, Jr., *Recollections,* 190; Lee to Mary Custis Lee, Oct. 19, 1865, De Butts-Ely Collection, LC; MacDonald, *Mrs. Lee,* 211, 255; Fitzhugh Lee, *General Lee* (New York, 1894; reprint, Wilmington, N.C., 1989), 313; Dowdey, *Lee,* 288; Margaret Sanborn, *Robert E. Lee: The Complete Man* (Philadelphia, 1967), 122; Flood, *Last Years,* 95, 109; Coulling, *Lee Girls,* 160; Winston, *Lee,* 362; Mary Custis Lee to "My Dear Child," —— 25, 1866, Robert E. Lee Papers, William G. Perkins Library, Duke University, Durham, N.C. [hereinafter DU]; John W. Wayland, *Robert E. Lee and His Family* (Philadelphia, 1951), 28; Casdorph, *Lee and Jackson,* 406; Anderson and Anderson, *Generals,* 571; Freeman, *Lee,* 4:242.

Disaster nearly robbed the Lees of some of their most prized relics. Mary had cut many Arlington portraits from their frames in May 1861 and sent them to Ravensworth. She was not certain if they had survived, but after the war they were located and loaded on a canal boat for the trip to Lexington. Tragically, the vessel sank. Recovered and restored, the images graced the Lee's dining room. Among them were Charles Willson Peale's portrait of George Washington and another of Martha, both of which came from Mount Vernon, and the portraits of Lee and Mary done in 1838. Custis later gave many of these to the college.[28]

Lee became a good president. A Washington College historian later asserted that "The gift George Washington made in 1796 has probably been exceeded in importance to the school's development only by the appointment of General Lee to its presidency in 1865." Interestingly, Lee left decisions to his faculty after indicating the outlines of his program, much as he had done in the war. And he set an example by keeping a rigorous schedule as in wartime, rising early to attend chapel before going to his office. His hard work and flexible direction succeeded. By 1868, enrollment grew to 411, and the endowment increased by over $100,000 in his first year. Lee also expanded the curriculum, and Brockenbrough's law school was annexed in 1866.[29]

Lee renovated the campus as well. Under his supervision, the college gained a new chapel, president's home, and boarding house for students. The chapel was constructed in front of the main building, under the stony gaze of a statue of Washington. Some of the funds for it, and for Grace Episcopal Church nearby, were raised by selling images of George and Martha Washington. These were copied from the portraits in the Lees' home and were hand-tinted and autographed by Mary, whom a friend recalled as having developed a striking resemblance to Martha.

28. Mary Custis Lee to Benson J. Lossing, May 14, 1867, Mary Custis Lee to ———, May 22, 1867, Custis-Lee Family Papers, LC; Coulling, *Lee Girls*, 172; Robert E. Lee, Jr., *Recollections*, 354; Freeman, *Lee*, 4:382; Robert A. Brock, ed., *Gen. Robert Edward Lee: Soldier, Citizen, and Christian Patriot* (Richmond, 1897), 95, 104, 106, 145–49, 151, 156, 154; Anderson and Anderson, *Generals*, 571.

29. Thomas, *Lee*, 376–77, 383–84; Flood, *Last Years*, 105, 111–13, 133, 205–6; Crenshaw, *Lee's College*, 26 [quote], 150, 160–65, 170; Lee to Childe, Sept. 17, 1868, Lee Papers, SH; W. G. Bean, "Lee Talks Frankly of the War and His Final Months in Lexington," *Washington and Lee Alumni Magazine* 41 (Winter 1966): 2–9; Winston, *Lee*, 376; Freeman, *Lee*, 4:232.

Lee's office in the basement of the new chapel contained three pictures, one of which was a portrait of Washington. The trustees completed his new home in 1869 from a design Lee selected and modified. Of course, the Washington treasures went into the new house.[30]

Lee emphasized both "moral and intellectual culture" for students. Like Washington, Lee wrote a brief definition of what a gentleman should be. This became his blueprint for students. Among other rules, Lee insisted that they abstain from alcohol. His stand was reinforced by his own experiences, which differed from those of Washington. The first president was never publicly intoxicated, but he imbibed privately. Lee's temperance arose during his military career. As a young officer, he often served wine and liquor, but he grew concerned about friends and provided alcohol with decreasing frequency. Allegedly he carried a bottle of brandy to the Mexican War but returned it unopened. When he was superintendent of West Point, he served wine, and in Texas he sent "good liquor" to Nathan G. Evans, but he urged temperance. He was never seen with liquor during the Civil War or afterward, and he was stern with students who strayed under its influence. In honor of his rigid example, members of Kappa Alpha fraternity adopted Lee as their model when the fraternity was founded at Washington College.[31]

Despite his efforts, Lee could not avoid controversy. Race remained a troublesome issue as violence escalated throughout the South. In 1866, Lee prevented the lynching of a horse thief by an angry mob. Five students broke up a freedmen's meeting in Lexington in March 1867. One who drew a pistol and attacked a black man was dismissed, and the other four were reprimanded. Two years later, hearing that other pupils planned to disrupt a freedmen's meeting, Lee ordered students to leave

30. Thomas, *Lee,* 377–78, 384, 402; Winston, *Lee,* 377, 383–84; MacDonald, *Mrs. Lee,* 11, 225, 233; Sally W. Robins, "Mrs. Lee During the War," in Brock, *Gen. Lee,* 345–46; W. W. Scott, "Some Personal Memories of General Robert E. Lee," *William and Mary Quarterly* 6 [2nd Series] (Oct. 1926): 285; Fishwick, *Lee after the War,* 130; Chaney, *Duty Most Sublime,* 161; Flood, *Last Years,* 139; Robert E. Lee, Jr., *Recollections,* 353–54; Dowdey, *Lee,* 668.

31. Lee to B. T. Lacey, October 9, 1865 [1st quote], Robert E. Lee Papers, New York Historical Society, New York; Riley, *Lee after Appomattox,* 25; Thomas, *Lee,* 78, 150; Winston, *Lee,* 46; Lee to Nathan G. Evans, Aug. 3, 1857 [2nd quote], Gilder Lehrman Collection, Pierpont Morgan Library, New York; Flood, *Last Years,* 153–54; William C. McDonald, "The True Gentleman: On Robert E. Lee's Definition of the Gentleman," *Civil War History* 32 (June 1986): 118, 126, 136, 138; Freeman, *Lee,* 4:280–82.

any such gatherings alone. Meanwhile, in 1868 Lee faced a mob again when Brockenbrough's son was shot by a black man. Lee successfully demanded that the law should take its course, and he later blocked an effort to take the suspect from the jail. That same year Northern newspapers assailed Lee and the college when a former Federal soldier who moved to Lexington to build schools for freedmen was roughly handled by local youths and college students. Lee dismissed the latter, but this did little to stem the tide of condemnation.[32]

Lee urged cooperation and promoted education, but he refused to be a politician like Washington. In part this was because he did not consider himself worthy. As he asked Markie Williams on Washington's birthday in 1869, "Who can ever rival Washington in our esteem & affections?" The students were gathering in the new chapel that evening for the Washington Literary Society celebration, and Lee expected that "the speakers [would] recall for our edification his great example." Despite the ceremony, Lee wrote that the day depressed him because Americans no longer observed it with the same "delight" as in earlier times. He added, "It is still to me [a day] of thankfulness & grateful recollections, & I hope that it will always be reverenced & respected by virtuous patriots." Reviled as a traitor and a failure, Lee did not think of himself as a statesman like Washington and his generation.[33]

Lee rebuffed several offers to become involved in politics. During the war he spoke with Benjamin H. Hill about accepting a high civil office. Lee was adamant that he was not suitable, having been a military man for all of his adult life. When Hill reminded him of Caesar, Frederick the Great, and Napoleon, Lee recalled that all became dictators. When Hill noted Washington's dual role, Lee smilingly said "Washington was an exception to all rule, and there was none like him." Lee had not become involved when the legislature asked for his appointment as provisional governor of Virginia in 1865, and in 1866 when Brockenbrough asked if Lee would follow Washington's example and campaign for office, the former Confederate responded that he could not do so as a "soldier on

---

32. Thomas, *Lee,* 386–89; Flood, *Last Years,* 131–32, 151, 178–79, 181–83; Crenshaw, *Lee's College,* 150–55; Riley, *Lee after Appomattox,* 28–30; Freeman, *Lee,* 4:358–60. Charles B. Flood says that it was not Lee but another faculty member who stopped the lynching in the Brockenbrough case. See Flood, *Last Years,* 184.

33. Craven, *"To Markie,"* 84.

parole." In response to a demand for Lee as governor in 1867, Lee wrote that a candidate should be able to help his state, not have a past that would offend the national government. Lee considered that the Fourteenth Amendment settled the matter, and he ignored the call of newspapers in the North and South for his nomination to the presidency in 1868.[34]

Lee cultivated an image of political ignorance after the war, but in fact he had definite ideas about Reconstruction, all of them firmly rooted in the same reverence for the Revolutionary generation that he had before the war. He worried quite a bit; he told the mother of a student that his defeat and the plight of the postwar South so troubled him that he could not sleep. Lee fretted because he "revered the old Union that his father and his father's friends founded," and "he wanted to restore that Union as he had known and loved it." He remained a "devotee of the Union of Washington" and regarded the legal transformations of the war with great alarm.[35]

Lee's refusal to accept changes in federal authority did not lead him to oppose reunification. On the contrary, he stressed cooperation. To Letcher, Lee wrote that all Southerners should register and elect "wise and patriotic men" who would emphasize the "healing of all dissensions." He admitted to Maury, "We have certainly not found our form of Govt. all that was anticipated by its original founders." He added, "But that may be partly our fault, in expecting too much, & partly to the absence of virtue in the people." He still believed "that the Union, as established by our forefathers, should be preserved, and that the gov-

34. Hill, "Address," 495–96 [1st quote]; Lee to Brockenbrough, Jan. 23, 1866 [2nd quote], Lee Papers, W&L; James C. Young, *Marse Robert, Knight of the Confederacy* (New York, 1929; reprint, New York, 1932), 222–23, 303–4; Thomas, *Lee*, 385; White, *Southern Confederacy*, 447; Lee to Robert Ould, Feb. 4, 1867, Lee Letterbooks, De Butts-Ely Collection, LC; Lee to David S. G. Cabell, Feb. 25, 1867, Robert E. Lee Papers, University of West Virginia Library, Morgantown; James A. Baggett, "Origins of Upper South Scalawag Leadership," *Civil War History* 29 (Mar. 1983): 71; Jones, *Life and Letters*, 395–96; Crenshaw, *Lee's College*, 154–55; Flood, *Last Years*, 188–89.

35. Riley, *Lee after Appomattox*, 157; Coulling, *Lee Girls*, 167–68; Thomas, *Lee*, 381 [1st and 2nd quotes]; William E. Dodd, *Lincoln or Lee: Comparison and Contrast of the Two Greatest Leaders in the War between the States* (New York, 1928), 73 [3rd quote]; John E. Hobeika, *Lee, the Soul of Honor: An Appreciation by an Orientalist, with Additional Facts* (Boston, 1932), 251.

ernment as originally organised should be administered in purity and truth."[36]

Lee clung to the idea of limited central government, which he believed was what the Founding Fathers wanted, and thus was appalled at many Republican measures to promote Reconstruction. In 1866, he railed against the test oath in a letter to Reverdy Johnson. Called before the Joint Committee on Reconstruction, Lee insisted that he supported Andrew Johnson's policies, which restrained federal intervention. The spectacle of Lee confronting the Joint Committee led to some unsettling comparisons for many observers. Herman Melville mused,

> Who looks at Lee must think of Washington;
> In pain must think, and hide the thought,
> So deep with grievous meaning is it fraught.

Asked about Lee by the Joint Committee, District Judge John C. Underwood admitted, "[T]en or eleven out of the twelve on any jury, I think, would say that Lee was about equal to Washington." The mother of one of Lee's Georgia students assured Lee that he and Washington were "equally beloved and venerated by us all."[37]

Lee's meeting with congressional Republicans dismayed him. After returning from the Joint Committee interview, he wrote to John G. Walker, "The South, I fear, has yet to undergo much suffering; but I hope time will allay party rancour, and reason will at last resume her sway." He repeated the same ideas in a letter to Early. Concerning his own role, he wrote to James May, "I had no other guide, nor had I any other object, than the defense of those principles of American liberty upon which the Constitutions of the several States were originally founded; and unless they are strictly observed, I fear there will be an

36. Lee to Letcher, Aug. 28, 1865 [1st and 2nd quotes], Lee Letterbooks, De Butts-Ely Collection, LC; Lee to Matthew F. Maury, Sept. 8, 1865 [3rd and 4th quotes], Lee-Jackson Collection, W&L; Lee to Charles Chauncey Burr, Jan. 5, 1866 [5th quote], Lee Letterbooks, De Butts-Ely Collection, LC.

37. Lee to Reverdy Johnson, Jan. 27, 1866, Reverdy Johnson Papers, LC; Thomas, *Lee,* 382; Flood, *Last Years,* 124; William A. Bryan, *George Washington in American Literature, 1775–1865* (New York, 1952), 166; Herman Melville, *Battle-Pieces and Aspects of the War* (New York, 1866; reprint, New York, 1995), 232 [1st quote]; Richard Lowe, "Testimony from the Old Dominion before the Joint Committee on Reconstruction," *Virginia Magazine of History and Biography* 104 (Summer 1996): 384 [2nd quote]; Moger, "Letters to Lee," 63 [3rd quote]; Gallagher, *Confederate War,* 166.

end to Republican Government in this country." He added, "I have no influence, and do not feel at liberty to take a more active part in public affairs than I have done."[38]

An inquiry from British historian John Dalberg-Acton prompted an outburst after the Republican electoral triumph in the fall of 1866. Lee declared that the "consolidation of the States into one vast republic, sure to be aggressive abroad and despotic at home, will be the certain precursor of that ruin which has overwhelmed all those that have preceded it." Putting aside his dislike for Thomas Jefferson, he praised both him and Washington as leaders who had opposed "centralization of power." He believed this ideal was lost, and "the judgment of reason has been displaced by the arbitrament of war." Discussing President Johnson's troubles with his nephew Edward Lee Childe in January 1867, Lee described the president's role as completing the "avowed object of the war," which was the restoration of the Union with states' rights *"unimpaired."* For this, Lee noted, Johnson was threatened with removal, another step toward a dangerous concentration of power, contrary to the intent of the Founding Fathers.[39]

Passage of the Reconstruction Acts in 1867, which provided for military occupation of the South and a reorganization of its state governments, confirmed Lee in his opposition to Johnson's Republican opponents. He still stressed political cooperation, but he spurned James Longstreet's plea to endorse the Republican Party. Their focus on black suffrage further alienated Lee. He had been the first to join a black man at the communion rail at St. Paul's Episcopal Church in Richmond in June 1865 while other whites recoiled, but he told his cousin Thomas H. Carter to hire only whites because "wherever you find the negro, everything is going down around him." Allegedly Lee told William Preston Johnston shortly after the war that he wanted limited black suffrage, but when Lee spoke to the Joint Committee, he made clear his belief that blacks should not vote. He wrote to his youngest son in 1868, "I wish

38. Lee to John G. Walker, Feb. 27, 1866 [1st quote], Lee to Early, Mar. 15, 1866, Lee to James May, July 9, 1866 [2nd and 3rd quotes], Lee to Herbert C. Saunders, Aug. 22, 1866, Lee Letterbooks, De Butts-Ely Collection, LC; Jones, *Life and Letters,* 391–92; Freeman, *Lee,* 4:383.

39. Lee to Sir John Dalberg-Acton, Dec. 15, 1866 [1st–3rd quotes], Lee Letterbooks, De Butts-Ely Collection, LC; Lee to Childe, Jan. 5, 22 [4th and 5th quotes], 1867, Lee Papers, SH; Flood, *Last Years,* 143.

them no evil in the world. On the contrary, will do them every good in my power, & know that they are misled by those to whom they have given their confidence, but our material, social & political interests are naturally with the whites." In August, Lee and other Southern leaders signed a statement condemning black suffrage. Lee was pleased when it was well received.[40]

Many Southerners rebelled against Republican Reconstruction by joining the Ku Klux Klan and other groups, but Lee refused. He continued to believe that the country's ills could be cured within the system created by the Founding Fathers. He wrote to Annette Carter that the Southern states "must unite, not only for their protection, but for the destruction of this grand scheme of centralization of power in the hands of one branch of the Govt. to the ruin of all others & the annihilation of the Constitution, the liberty of the people & of the country." To George W. Jones, he wrote that if the "constitution & the Union established by our forefathers" were "restored," then "there will be no truer supporters of that union & that constitution than the Southern people." Regarding his violent past he wrote, "Every brave people who considered their rights attacked & their Constitutional liberties invaded, would have done as we did. Our conduct was not caused by any insurrectionary spirit nor can it be termed rebellion, for our construction of the Constitution under which we lived & acted was the same from its adoption & for eighty years we have been taught and educated by the founders of the Republic & their written declaration which controlled our consciences & actions." He fought to save, not destroy, the Founding Fathers' original plan.[41]

40. Lee to Robert Ould, Mar. 29, 1867, Lee to Raphael J. Moses, Apr. 3, 1867, Lee to Dabney H. Maury, May 23, 1867, Lee to James Longstreet, Oct. 29, 1867, Lee Letterbooks, De Butts-Ely Collection, LC; Robert E. Lee, Jr., *Recollections*, 168 [1st quote]; Lee to Robert E. Lee, Jr., Mar. 12, 1868 [2nd quote], De Butts-Ely Collection, LC; Lee et al. to William S. Rosecrans, Aug. 26, 1868, Lee Letterbooks, VHS; Jones, *Life and Letters*, 393–94; White, *Southern Confederacy*, 450–52; Winston, *Lee*, 371–72; Lee to Childe, Jan. 16, 1868, Lee Papers, SH; Stanley F. Horn, ed., *The Robert E. Lee Reader* (Indianapolis, 1949), 462; Flood, *Last Years*, 65–66, 195–96; Thomas, *Lee*, 382; U.S. House, *Report of the Joint Committee on Reconstruction, Part II*, 39th Cong., 1st sess., 1865, H. Rept. 30, serial 1273, 130, 134; William P. Johnston, "Memoranda of Conversations with General R. E. Lee," in Gary W. Gallagher, ed., *Lee the Soldier* (Lincoln, Nebr., 1996), 30.

41. Lee to Annette Carter, Mar. 28, 1868 [1st quote], Lennig Collection, W&L; Chaney, *Duty Most Sublime*, 146; Lee to Giles B. Cook, June 11, 1869, Lee Letterbooks, De Butts-Ely Collection, LC; Lee to George W. Jones, Mar. 22, 1869 [2nd–4th quotes], Lee

Lee opposed violence also because he continued to hope for peaceful reconciliation. In 1866 Early sent a draft of his memoirs to Lee, who then asked him to "omit all epithets or remarks calculated to excite bitterness or animosity between different sections of the country." A woman who lived near Lexington showed Lee a tree in her front yard that had been shattered by Union artillery. She expected that Lee would understand the emotions that had led her to preserve the tree, but he told her to cut it down. Asked to participate in erecting memorials at Gettysburg in 1869, Lee wrote that he would not because he thought "it wiser . . . not to keep open the sores of war, but to follow the examples of those nations who endeavoured to obliterate the marks of civil strife & to commit to oblivion the feelings it engendered." Lee also would not help raise a Confederate monument in Baltimore in 1866. Instead, he opined that it was better to aid in caring for the graves of the fallen. He set an example by giving money for moving Confederate dead from Gettysburg to Richmond.[42]

Lee's vision of reconciliation included a proper remembrance of history, especially the Revolutionary legacy. Toward this end, he worked to reclaim Washington relics taken from Arlington. He was perhaps alarmed when James D. McCabe, in an 1866 biography of Lee, reported that some Arlington treasures were "paraded in triumph in the salons of New York and Boston." Lee still had a few prized items. A young lady who visited the Lees at Lexington recalled the general rummaging through two trunks while Mary was looking "with distress" at some Washington letters and pictures. All of these were "faded and discolored" and even "moulded and almost defaced" from being buried. They had just been recovered, and Mary hoped they could be restored. Lee emerged with two of Washington's swords and another that had belonged to Light-Horse Harry. He explained the history of the Washington blades to his guest and said that he had kept one with him throughout the war.[43]

Papers, MOC; Dunbar Rowland, ed., *Jefferson Davis, Constitutionalist: His Letters, Papers, and Speeches,* 10 vols. (Jackson, Miss., 1923), 7:258 [5th quote]; Freeman, *Lee,* 4:265.

42. Lee to Early, Oct. 15, 1866 [1st quote], Early Papers, LC; Lee to D. McConaughy, Aug. 5, 1869 [2nd quote], Lee Letterbooks, Lee Family Papers, VHS; Lee to Mary E. Randolph, Mar. 8, 1870, Lee Letterbooks, De Butts-Ely Collection, LC; Jones, *Personal Reminiscences,* 257; Thomas, *Lee,* 384; Flood, *Last Years,* 136.

43. James D. McCabe, *Life and Campaigns of General Robert E. Lee* (Atlanta, 1866), 328 [1st quote]; Christiana Bond, "Memories of General Robert E. Lee," *South Atlantic*

Many of the Arlington treasures were lost forever, but Lee recovered a few. Most of the items that had value had gone to the Patent Office, whence they were forwarded to the national museum. S. B. Medlar arrived at Arlington in July 1864 as the superintendent of the national cemetery. He found a few moldy books, about a dozen paintings, including George W. P. Custis' huge battle scenes, and many empty picture frames. He was told by a former slave that many items had been taken by "soldiers and other persons seeking curiosities." Two years later, Lee sent a portrait of Washington, printed on satin in 1798, as a gift to a man who returned "three articles taken from Arlington during its occupancy by the U.S. Soldiers." Earlier, Lee accepted another writer's offer to return a ring and pin purchased from a Union soldier. The ring held hair from George and Martha Washington, and Martha had given it to Lee's father-in-law. The pin also contained the Washingtons' hair, and was given to Lee's wife by her mother. He recalled packing these in a "French rosewood dressing case with a leather cover." This had been taken to Edward C. Turner's home, which the Federals later occupied.[44]

Lee expanded his recovery work to include Washington items that had never been at Arlington. One of his greatest successes was the acquisition of a letter from Washington to the trustees of Washington College that had hung in the Washington Literary Society hall until Hunter's raiders took it. In July 1866, an attorney wrote to Lee that a former Federal lieutenant had the paper and wished to return it. Lee happily arranged for the transfer. Later in 1866, Lee accepted a copy of the *Ulster County Gazette* of January 4, 1800, which contained his father's resolution on the "event which produced more sadness than any other which befell this Country—the death of Washington." Another man wrote to Lee about a ring that he wished to return. The general replied that the ring was not his, but it was probably from the Washington fam-

Quarterly 24 (1925): 347–48 [2nd–4th quotes]; Flood, *Last Years*, 134; Long, *Memoirs of Lee*, 469.

44. Fitzhugh Lee, *General Lee*, 72; S. B. Medlar to James M. Moore, May 18, 1866 [1st quote], Enoch A. Chase Papers, VHS; William P. Snow, *Lee and His Generals: Their Lives and Campaigns* (New York, 1867; reprint, New York, 1982), 139; Robert E. Lee, Jr., *Recollections*, 337; Lee to Edward S. Hedden, Mar. 23, 1866 [2nd quote], Lee to John H. Gregg, Nov. 20, 1865 [3rd quote], Lee Letterbooks, De Butts-Ely Collection, LC; Moger, "Letters to Lee," 63–64.

ily, and he would make arrangements. Lee also agreed to act as broker for the return of a watch that belonged to the Washington family.[45]

Lee's pleasure at the recovery of Washington treasures was reduced by bitterness at failing to find more Arlington relics. When he was approached in 1866 by Robert W. Lewis, who offered to help recover items taken by Federal soldiers, Lee responded that it would be a troublesome task "and would not be attended by comparative good." However, he explained that he "would be glad to get" anything that came into Lewis' possession and could be returned without too much trouble. He grumbled in a letter to a friend that he did not know what had happened to many paintings left at Arlington. A report that Secretary of War Edwin M. Stanton had ordered the return of the Arlington furnishings held by the government in the fall of 1866 prompted a hopeful letter to a Virginia attorney, but the information proved to be false.[46]

Lee's hopes for the return of the Washington relics stored in the capital were unexpectedly resurrected in 1869. James May wrote to the Lees in January, suggesting that a note to outgoing President Andrew Johnson might secure what they desired. While his wife wrote to Johnson, Lee sent a letter to May thanking him for his kindness but reminding him that many objects had been taken by individuals and were "now scattered over the land." He added his hope that those who had them would "appreciate" these "silent monitors" and "imitate the example of their original owner," and thus the items would "accomplish good to the country." Thanks to the support of leading Democrats such as Jeremiah S. Black, the Lees were happily surprised when Johnson ordered the return of their property. A clerk inventoried the items, finding the Washington punch bowl and many other family treasures.[47]

45. Moger, "Letters to Lee," 63; Crenshaw, *Lee's College,* 221–22; James P. Rogers to Lee, July 15, 1866, Sam S. Mathers to Lee, July 30, 1866, Lee Papers, W&L; Lee to James P. Rogers, July 21, 1866, Lee to Mathers, July 21, 1866, Lee Letterbooks, De Butts-Ely Collection, LC; Lee to E. B. Cook, Nov. 26, 1866, Lee to Bushrod Johnson, Sept. 30, 1867, Lee Papers, MOC; Lee to P. C. Sutphin, Sept. 18, 1866 [quote], Lee Papers, LV.

46. Lee to Robert W. Lewis, Apr. 6, 1866 [quotes], Lee Letterbooks, Lee Family Papers, VHS; Tate, "Lee on Abandoning the South," 255–56; Lee to Mary E. Nealy, Oct. 1, 1866, Lee to Fisher, Oct. 20, 1866, Lee Letterbooks, De Butts-Ely Collection, LC.

47. Mary Custis Lee to Andrew Johnson, Feb. 10, 1869, Orville H. Browning to Mary Custis Lee, Feb. 24, 1869, Elisha Foote to Browning, Feb. 29, 1869, Chase Papers, VHS; Jones, *Personal Reminiscences,* 273; Mason, *Popular Life,* 341 [quotes]; Lee to Jeremiah S. Black, Jan. 13, 1869, Lee Letterbooks, Lee Family Papers, VHS; Lee to Browning,

Lee was cruelly disappointed when Congress forbade the return of the relics. Mary sent a petition demanding that they reconsider, but her husband morosely acquiesced. He wrote to May that he regretted the furor raised by his wife's inquiry. About the relics he declared, "I hope their presence at the Capital will keep in the remembrance of all Americans the principles and virtues of Washington." He repeated this in letters to George W. Jones and to a Kentucky congressman who had supported him, Thomas L. Jones. To the latter, he added that it was debatable whether keeping the articles or returning them would be more of an "insult, in the language of the Committee on Public Buildings, to the loyal people of the United States . . . but of this I am willing that they should be the judge; and since Congress has decided to keep them, she must submit." The items would finally be returned to the Lee family in 1903.[48]

Curiously, Lee was uninterested in his own relics or those of family members other than Washington. When a correspondent wrote that he had recovered a cane taken from Arlington that belonged to either Lee or his father-in-law, Lee responded that he would like to have it but added, "If the cane has any value in your eyes, as far as I am concerned, you are at liberty to retain it." Lee at one time had two pistols and a sash captured from a British officer and presented to Light-Horse Harry by a subordinate, but he gave these to the latter's son as a gift. When a man later wrote to Lee that he had two of his father's swords, Lee politely declined to pursue the subject, writing to him that he doubted if he could recognize the weapons, as he had not seen them since he was a child.[49] Lee's interest remained primarily in Washington relics as his contribution to a shared legacy for the nation.

As part of his role in preserving the legacy of Washington and the

---

Feb. 26, 1869, Robert E. Lee Letterbooks, Lee Papers, W&L; Robert E. Lee, Jr., *Recollections,* 337.

48. White, *Southern Confederacy,* 453; Lee to May, Mar. 12, 1869 [1st quote], Lee to George W. Jones, Mar. 22, 1869, Lee to Thomas L. Jones, Mar. 29, 1869 [2nd quote], Lee Letterbooks, De Butts-Ely Collection, LC; Freeman, *Lee,* 4:383–85; MacDonald, *Mrs. Lee,* 254; Robert E. Lee, Jr., *Recollections,* 337–38; Coulling, *Lee Girls,* 178; Flood, *Last Years,* 202; Winston, *Lee,* 384; Mason, *Popular Life,* 341.

49. Lee to Fred L. Cozzens, June 27, 1866 [quote], Jefferson Davis Collection, Howard-Tilton Library, Tulane University, New Orleans [hereinafter TU]; Robins, "Mrs. Lee During the War," 336–37; Sanborn, *Complete Man,* 2:310–11.

Founding Fathers, Lee became an author and editor. He believed that, as he wrote to a friend in 1868, "nothing is more instructive than the perusal of the deeds of men in other ages." This was a lesson he pressed upon his children even after they were adults. Mildred, for example, received a note admonishing her to "Read history, works of truth, not novels and romances." At that time, Lee was editing and writing an introduction to a second edition of his father's papers. C. B. Richardson had approached him, anticipating that such a work, with the imprimatur of Lee, would sell. Richardson also expected that such an effort would encourage Lee to write his own memoirs. He was doomed to disappointment on this issue, but Lee did work hard on the edition of his father's papers.[50]

Editing Light-Horse Harry's memoirs was hindered by the fact that Lee had lost his father's papers when Arlington was taken. He obtained some of his father's letters from his older brother, Charles Carter Lee, and William B. Reed, who wrote a biography of his own Revolutionary ancestor. He especially enjoyed writing to Reed about Washington's role in the attempted capture of Benedict Arnold and wrote that the Lee documents Reed had sent would be "doubly valuable to me, as relics of one whose memory I cherish & venerate, & as mementoes of your 'sincere regard.'" The revised memoirs Lee assembled included the text of several letters that focused on both Light-Horse Harry's and Washington's emphasis on morality and duty, and his biographical introduction avoided distasteful subjects and repeated "old family euphemisms."[51] In sum, Lee portrayed his father and Washington as models of virtue.

The task of editing made a scholar of Lee for the first time in years. Little remained of his Arlington library. Visitors to his office saw only two books on his desk: an Episcopalian *Book of Common Prayer* and a

50. Allen W. Moger, "General Lee's Unwritten 'History of the Army of Northern Virginia,'" *Virginia Magazine of History and Biography* 71 (July 1963): 342, 346–48; Lee to Henry I. Smith, April 8, 1868 [1st quote], Modern Ephemera Collection, Louisiana State Museum, New Orleans; Robert E. Lee, Jr., *Recollections,* 247–48 [2nd quote]; Lee to Charles Carter Lee, Aug. 18, 1865, Lee Papers, W&L; Lee to Charles Carter Lee, Mar. 29, 1866, Robert E. Lee Papers, Chicago Historical Society, Chicago; Crute, *Derwent Papers,* 23; Flood, *Last Years,* 75–77.

51. Lee to William B. Reed, Nov. 10, 1865, Lee Letterbooks, De Butts-Ely Collection, LC; Lee to Reed, Aug. 30, 1866 [1st quote], Davis Collection, TU; Thomas, *Lee,* 37 [2nd quote].

tattered copy of the *Meditations of Marcus Aurelius,* which his father had recommended and from which Lee could quote freely. The copy in his possession was a gift from translator George Long, who in place of a dedication included a statement declaring that if he dedicated it to any-one, it would be to Lee, "whose name seemed to me most worthy to be joined to that of the Roman soldier and philosopher." Lee expanded on his meager holdings by borrowing from the libraries of Washington Col-lege and the Franklin Society. In his footnotes, he cited the biographies of Washington by John Marshall, Jared Sparks, and Washington Irving, as well as Sparks's collection of Washington letters. He also drew upon David Ramsay's *American Revolution,* which included a "character sketch" of Washington; George W. P. Custis' *Recollections and Private Memoirs of Washington;* Henry Lee IV's book on Thomas Jefferson; and a handful of biographies of other Revolutionary figures.[52]

Lee's research did raise disturbing questions. He asked his brother Carter to clarify a reference in a biography of their father about his opposition to the Virginia nullification bills of 1798 and 1799, which were written by James Madison. He was disturbed that Light-Horse Harry had opposed this intervention of states' rights against an uncon-stitutional assertion of authority by the central government. After con-sidering the point and its clear implication for his decision in 1861, Lee wrote, "I do not wish to revive any partizan feelings, or to escalate party criticism against the book, or to stir up sectional animosity. . . . [I] there-fore think it best to say no more than to express our fathers [*sic*] senti-ments in the occasion & to explain his course."[53]

Despite Lee's efforts to produce a noncontroversial work, Richard-son became concerned that the political climate endangered potential sales. After a long delay, the volume finally appeared in late 1869, much

52. Winston, *Lee,* 382; Edward V. Valentine, "Reminiscences of General Lee," *Out-look* 84 (Dec. 22, 1906): 966; Henry E. Shepherd, *Life of Robert Edward Lee* (New York, 1906), 163 [1st quote]; Mason, *Popular Life,* 323; Riley, *Lee after Appomattox,* 147–48, 153; Lee to Augustus J. Requier, Sept. 5, 1866, Lee Letterbooks, De Butts-Ely Collection, LC; John E. Cooke, *A Life of Gen. Robert E. Lee* (New York, 1883), 492; Crenshaw, *Lee's College,* 74–75; Bryan, *Washington in American Literature,* 96–97 [2nd quote]; Franklin Society, Library Records, W&L; Washington College, Library Records, W&L; Henry Lee III, *Memoirs of the War in the Southern Department of the United States,* ed. Robert E. Lee (New York, 1869), passim.

53. Lee to Charles Carter Lee, Mar. 14, 1867, Lee Papers, W&L.

to Lee's pleasure. During the same time, Lee helped Mary in producing a revision of her father's papers. The Lees had only a few copies of the first edition, and she prized these as being "nearly all that [were] left to [her] from a house once abounding in relics of the Father of our country." With the few fragments left of the family's Washington papers, as well as the volumes perused by Lee, Mary and her husband were able to produce another literary addition to the Revolutionary legacy.[54]

Lee failed to complete his own memoirs, perhaps because he did not feel he compared well with his Revolutionary idols. He found an excuse not to write in the burning of his papers at Appomattox. Richardson provided some documents, but federal archivists would not. Lee wrote to many wartime associates, asking for records and explaining that he wanted to produce a correct account as a tribute to them. Many of them reported that they also had lost all papers; of those who sent recollections, many were unusable. Wade Hampton wrote candidly, "You must bear in mind, though, my dear General, that *I am not reconstructed yet,* and in what I shall write every word will be dictated by Southern feelings and come from a Southern heart." This was contrary to Lee's purpose; as he explained to his brother Carter, "I do not wish to add to the present excited feelings which rage in the country, but if possible to allay them." Hampton did note that Longstreet still spoke warmly of Lee, so Lee asked for and received some documents from him. They disagreed on politics, but as Lee declared, "I do not consider my partnership with him yet dissolved, & shall not let go him during life." As late as 1870 Lee wrote about completing his memoirs, as many asked him to do, but he never did.[55]

54. Lee to Charles Carter Lee, Dec. 22, 1868, July 8, 1869, Lee Papers, MOC; Flood, *Last Years,* 174–75, 223; Winston, *Lee,* 384; MacDonald, *Mrs. Lee,* 259–60; Mary Custis Lee to Richard M. Devens, Feb. 5, 1866 [quote], De Butts-Ely Collection, LC.

55. Connelly, *Marble Man,* 212; Moger, "Lee's Unwritten History," 342–47, 349–59; Wade Hampton to Lee, July 21, 1866 [1st quote], Wade Hampton Family Papers, University of South Carolina Library, Columbia [hereinafter USC]; Lee to Richard H. Anderson, July 31, 1865, Lee to Charles Carter Lee, Dec. 9, 1865 [2nd quote], Custis-Lee Family Papers, LC; Taylor, *Four Years,* 158–60; Lee to Walter H. Taylor, July 31, 1865, Lee Papers, LV; Walter H. Taylor, *General Lee: His Campaigns in Virginia, 1861–1865* (Norfolk, Va., 1906), 280–81; Craven, *"To Markie,"* 66; Lee to Beauregard, Oct. 3, 1865, Lee to Taylor, May 25, 1866, Lee Letterbooks, Lee Family Papers, VHS; Lee to Taylor, Dec. 28, 1866, Walter H. Taylor Papers, LV; Jones, *Life and Letters,* 390; Crute, *Derwent Letters,* 27; Jones, *Personal Reminiscences,* 182; Lee to Longstreet et al., Jan. 26, 1866 [3rd

In contrast to his conscientious research in editing his father's memoirs, Lee did not read most participants' accounts of the Civil War. As he confessed to Edward A. Pollard, "I have felt so little desire to recall the events of the war . . . that I have not read a single work that has been published on the subject." He also wrote to James D. McCabe, thanking him for his new biography, but explaining that he had been unwilling to read about himself. Lee appreciated the efforts of others and urged associates to write memoirs, but he would not assess his own participation. The exception was when he occasionally decided that his role had been misinterpreted. He wrote to A. T. Bledsoe, the editor of the *Southern Review,* to correct a claim that Jackson had made his flank attack at Chancellorsville of his own accord. He assured Bledsoe, however, that he had no further literary ambitions because he had "as yet felt no desire to revive [his] recollection of those events, and [had] been satisfied with the knowledge [he] possessed of what transpired."[56]

Lee steadfastly refused to cooperate with his biographers. To Pollard, he explained that no records could be found, that he was very busy, and that no one would be interested. Lee also warned that writing about the living was hazardous because "there are but few who would desire to read a true history of themselves." Lee was certainly not ashamed. Hampton recalled that after the war Lee said, "I did only what my duty demanded; I could have taken no other course without dishonor & if all was to be done over again, I should act precisely in the same manner." Lee may well have been pleased if he knew that Pollard wrote in an 1867 work that his character was "well-rounded and Washington-like." While Lee may have regretted his military education, as he told a Washington College student, he rebuked the same young man for saying that his time in the Confederate Army was wasted, saying that "However long you live and whatever you accomplish, you will find that the time you spent in the Confederate army was the most profitably spent por-

---

quote], Robert E. Lee Papers, United States Military Academy Library and Archives, West Point, N.Y.; Longstreet to Lee, Jan. 15, 1866, John W. Fairfax Papers, VHS; Lee to Early, Nov. 22, 1865, Early Papers, LC; Lee to Charles Carter Lee, Oct. 24, 1867, Lee Papers, MOC; Lee to Cassius F. Lee, June 6, 1870, Edmund J. Lee Papers, SH.

56. Lee to Edward A. Pollard, Jan. 24, 1867 [1st quote], Lee to James D. McCabe, Feb. 27, 1867, Lee Letterbooks, De Butts-Ely Collection, LC; John J. Bowen, *The Strategy of Robert E. Lee* (New York, 1914), 130–31 [2nd quote]; Riley, *Lee after Appomattox,* 159–60.

tion of your life." Lee did not regret his emulation of Washington, but he was disappointed with losing and so did not consider himself a worthy subject.[57]

Lee's belief that he was not a proper model also influenced his relationship with those who recorded his image. Photographer Michael Miley produced a few vivid pictures. One of these was the only postwar photograph of Lee in uniform astride Traveller, which was done at the general's request. Lee otherwise refused to wear a uniform for portraits, although he had pictures made of himself in civilian clothes to be sent to the many who asked for them. When Frank Buchser painted a portrait of Lee in 1869, the general wore a black suit. When Buchser protested, Lee agreed to put a uniform and sword on a table to be included in the picture. Edward V. Valentine worked with Lee on a bust at Lexington, and again Lee wore civilian clothes. One painter with whom Lee seemed pleased was William D. H. Washington, "a descendant of the Warner Washington who formerly owned Audley." Even then, Lee told Markie that he submitted to the ordeal for the sake of the artist, and because Mary pressed him to do so. Lee later recommended Washington to Superintendent Smith of the Virginia Military Institute, who commissioned portraits of himself and Stonewall Jackson.[58]

Having republished his father's memoirs and assisted in the enhancement of Washington's legacy, Lee spent a little time on his own past. When he traveled to Baltimore in 1869, he visited with Ulysses S. Grant in the White House. Their conversation was cordial, so Lee was outraged to read a hostile account of their meeting in the Baltimore *Sun,* which had earlier smeared him as a master who abused slaves. He retreated to the Alexandria home of Anna Maria Fitzhugh, where he

57. Lee to Pollard, Sept. 29, 1866 [1st quote], Lee Letterbooks, De Butts-Ely Collection, LC; Jones, *Personal Reminiscences,* 142, 166, 256; Hampton to J. William Jones, Jan. 2, 1871 [2nd quote], Hampton Family Papers, USC; Freeman, *Lee,* 4:315–16; Edward A. Pollard, *Lee and His Lieutenants* (New York, 1867), 37 [3rd quote]; Riley, *Lee after Appomattox,* 38–39 [4th quote]; Flood, *Last Years,* 104, 156.

58. Thomas, *Lee,* 403, 409; Flood, *Last Years,* 173, 220–21; Marshall W. Fishwick, *General Lee's Photographer: The Life and Work of Michael Miley* (Chapel Hill, N.C., 1954), 4–6, 8–9; Dowdey, *Lee,* 728; Lee to Martha C. Williams, Feb. 5, 1869 [quote], Gilder Lehrman Collection, Pierpont Morgan Library; Lee to Francis H. Smith, Sept. 22, 1868, Robert E. Lee Papers, Virginia Military Institute Archives, Lexington, Va. The Virginia Military Institute still has the Washington portraits of Lee, Smith, and Jackson.

found his brother Sydney Smith Lee and his family. Shielded from Baltimore "Philistines," the two brothers attended services together at Christ Church, where the memories of Washington and their own childhood were strong. Lee also visited with John Janney, who as president of the secession convention had given the command of Virginia's forces to Lee with a speech that recalled the heritage of Washington. Lee returned with Anna Maria Fitzhugh to Ravensworth, where he visited his mother's grave, then went to White House to see Rooney.[59]

Sadly, Smith Lee died in July 1869, prompting his younger brother to return to northern Virginia. He missed the funeral by one day, but stayed at Ravensworth and visited with Fitzhugh Lee, Smith Lee's son. As he had a few months earlier, Lee moved on to White House, where he served as godfather for his grandson when he was baptized as Robert E. Lee III in St. Peter's Church, where George and Martha Washington had attended services. Lee was fond of St. Peter's because of its link to Washington and contributed to its renovation after Federal troops had abused it. He was proud that the itinerant minister who preached there every fortnight stayed with Rooney each time, and he wrote that "It would be a shame to America if allowed to go to destruction." Lee took a similar interest in the development of Pendleton's Grace Church in Lexington, but St. Peter's was a bond with Washington.[60]

Lee's traveling taxed his health, which declined steadily. Pressed by family, faculty, friends, and doctors, he agreed to go south in the spring of 1870 with his daughter Agnes. The trip became a triumphal tour and an extended farewell. He visited the graves of his daughter Anne, at Warrenton, North Carolina, and of his father on Cumberland Island. He told his brother Carter that Agnes put "beautiful fresh flowers" on Light-Horse Harry's grave, adding, "I presume it is the last tribute of respect that I shall ever be able to pay it." In Savannah, he visited with

59. Thomas, *Lee,* 391, 403; Winston, *Lee,* 407–8; Lee to Samuel H. Tagart, May 3 and 18 [quote], 1869, Lee Papers, SH; Marshall W. Fishwick, *Virginians on Olympus: A Cultural Analysis of Four Great Men* (Richmond, 1951), 52; Philip Van Doren Stern, *Robert E. Lee, the Man and the Soldier: A Pictorial Biography* (New York, 1963), 233; Robert E. Lee, Jr., *Recollections,* 350–51, 362–64; Sanborn, *Complete Man,* 348; Freeman, *Lee,* 4:403–4, 520–21.

60. Thomas, *Lee,* 403; Robert E. Lee, Jr., *Recollections,* 350–51, 362–64; Sanborn, *Complete Man,* 348; Lee to Virginia Ritchie, Oct. 23, 1869 [quote], Lee Papers, LV; Flood, *Last Years,* 97; Lee to Charlotte Haxall, Aug. 9, 1869, De Butts-Ely Collection, LC.

Joseph E. Johnston, with whom he posed for pictures. His next stop was Charleston, where, as he had done during the war, he sat in the pew occupied by Washington at St. Michael's Church. He also tarried in Norfolk, where he visited Walter H. Taylor; at Shirley, his mother's old home; and White House, where he joined Mary. He even went to Romancoke, and was shocked by its decay.[61]

Lee made one last trip in the summer of 1870. He went to a doctor in Baltimore, then visited with Charles Henry Carter and his daughter, Annette Carter. He also talked with his cousin Cassius F. Lee and attorney Francis L. Smith about recovering Arlington, but they offered no hope. While in Alexandria, Lee visited two of his childhood homes. The occupant of the home on Orinoco Street where Lee's mother had lived as a widow had kept her bedroom just as Mrs. Lee did. He left Lee alone there, on his knees by her bed. Lee stayed at Ravensworth, whence bad health forced him to go home. He wrote to Custis, "I am very sorry not to have been able to have taken advantage of this vacation to talk to you all once more, for I feel that my opportunities of enjoying your company are becoming daily more precarious." Lee also declined an invitation to Mount Vernon, writing, "it is not in my power to visit a place where I have passed some happy days in my earlier life, & which from the virtues of its illustrious possessor is hallowed in the affections of the American people."[62]

After a detour to Hot Springs, Lee arrived in Lexington in time for school to open. Almost a year earlier, he had written to Childe, "You must remember your promise to return some day, & do not let it be distant, or you may find many missing." Lee knew his health was poor, and he may have recalled that many Lee men were not long-lived. He suffered a stroke on the evening of September 28, 1870, after he returned

61. Thomas, *Lee,* 37, 405–9; Robert E. Lee, Jr., *Recollections,* 401, 406–7; Flood, *Last Years,* 229, 234–37, 246; Shepherd, *Life of Lee,* 131, 221, 224–25; Stern, *Pictorial Biography,* 237; Maurine W. Redway, *Marks of Lee on Our Land* (San Antonio, 1972), 98; Lee to Mary Custis Lee, Apr. 18, 1870, Lee to Mildred Childe Lee, May 7, 1870, De Butts-Ely Collection, LC; Lee to Childe, June 3, 1870, Lee Papers, SH; Lee to Charles Carter Lee, Apr. 18, 1870 [quotes], Lee Papers, W&L.

62. Thomas, *Lee,* 409–10; Lee to Mary Custis Lee, July 15, 1870, De Butts-Ely Collection, LC; Flood, *Last Years,* 250; Winston, *Lee,* 410; Lee to Custis Lee, July 22, 1870 [1st quote], Lee Papers, DU; Lee to Ann P. Cunningham, July 20, 1870 [2nd quote], George B. Lee Papers, VHS; Chaney, *Duty Most Sublime,* 176–77.

home from a meeting in the chapel. He lived for two weeks, then died on October 12 without again speaking more than a few syllables. After lying in state, his body was buried in a vault beneath the chapel, where most of his family, including his father, would later be interred. Custis, who still taught at the Virginia Military Institute, was elected to succeed his father. At the same time, the name of the school was changed at the faculty's request to Washington and Lee College, a commemoration of how their "lives were so similar in their perfect renown."[63]

In death as in life, the names of Lee and Washington became linked. Lee would have protested the implication of equality, but he could not deny that he had striven to emulate the example of his father's Revolutionary commander. His disappointment with the result, defeat for his cause, was obvious to many who knew him well, but like Washington he continued to seek worthy roles. Lee in many ways became a statesman like Washington after the war, working for national unity. As a defeated leader, though, Lee did not receive the acclaim his mentor enjoyed, nor did he seek public office. Instead, he settled into the roles of educator and conservator, preparing young men for a future markedly different from the past whose relics he sought to preserve. For him, there was no irony in this. He had failed to achieve the standards of his idol, but Washington could be an important model for others.

63. Robert E. Lee, Jr., *Recollections,* 421–24; Lee to Childe, Nov. 17, 1869 [1st quote], Lee Papers, SH; Thomas, *Lee,* 411–16; Crenshaw, *Lee's College,* 175–76; Hume, "Cincinnati," 280; Jones, *Personal Reminiscences,* 465; *Southern Collegian,* Oct. 15, 1870 [2nd quote].

Epilogue

In the Shadow of Washington

More than a century after his death, Robert E. Lee remains in the shadow of George Washington. Those seeking to vindicate the Lost Cause made Lee the focus of their efforts and recalled his ties to Washington in an attempt to justify the Confederacy. The need for justification faded as the Civil War generation passed away, but comparisons of Lee to Washington persisted as Lee became a national, rather than regional, hero. Events during this century have altered most Americans' perceptions of revolutionary leadership, but many still compare the two Virginians in that Lee complements the ideal image of Washington that many Americans embrace.

Connections with Washington highlighted speeches about Lee after his death. Benjamin M. Palmer, a future president of the Southern Historical Society, said that Lee was "the second Washington," adding, "men scarcely speak of Lee without thinking of a mysterious connection that binds the two together." Henry W. Hilliard declared, "We place the name of Lee by Washington. They both belong to the world." William Preston Johnston said that Richard Wintersmith wrote, "When General Lee had been taken up to heaven, George Washington was relieved from the sense of an eternal loneliness." The greatest defender of the Lost Cause, Jubal A. Early, spoke at Washington and Lee College, asserting that "we may draw a parallel between General Lee and our great Washington in many respects." He added that Lee's military achievements eclipsed those of the latter. John E. Cooke, in an epistle attributed to an imaginary corporal, opined that "General Lee, to my thinking, greatly resembles" Washington. J. William Jones concurred that Lee "resembled" Washington on "many points."[1]

Newspapermen added their perspectives on the connection. The Richmond *Whig* had earlier declared that "our people love [Lee] as our fathers did George Washington." In October 1870 a writer for the Richmond *State Journal,* in an article reprinted in the Norfolk *Virginian,* admitted that he never admired Lee's military ability, but "He reminds us much of Washington in his career." A week later, the Virginia *Gazette* printed the request of the Washington College faculty that Lee's name be added to that of his idol in the name of their institution. Editors beyond Virginia agreed. The London *Standard* asserted that Lee had earned "as much confidence and esteem" from "his own countrymen" as Washington, and more "affection."[2]

John B. Gordon eulogized Lee in 1870 as a "patriot whose sacrificing devotion to his country ranks him with Washington." He expanded upon his later declaration in Jones's book that Lee was a "peer of Washington" to declare in his own memoir, "Unless it be Washington, there is no military chieftain of the past to whom Lee can be justly likened."

1. W. G. Bean, "Lee Talks Frankly of the War and His Final Months in Lexington," *Washington and Lee Alumni Magazine* 41 (Winter 1966): 3; "Tributes to General Lee," *Southern Magazine* 8, 10 (Jan. 1871): 14 [1st–3rd quotes]; William F. Chaney, *Duty Most Sublime: The Life of Robert E. Lee as Told through the "Carter Letters"* (Baltimore, 1996), 180; William P. Johnston, "Reminiscences of General Robert E. Lee," *Belford Monthly* 5 (June 1890): 85 [4th quote]; Jubal A. Early, "The Campaigns of General Robert E. Lee," in Gallagher, *Lee the Soldier,* 70 [5th quote]; John E. Cooke, *Wearing of the Gray* (New York, 1867; reprint, Bloomington, Ind., 1959), 354 [6th quote]; J. William Jones, *Personal Reminiscences, Anecdotes, and Letters of Gen. Robert E. Lee* (New York, 1874), 179 [7th and 8th quotes]; Gaines M. Foster, *Ghosts of the Confederacy* (New York, 1987), 50–51; Emily V. Mason, *Popular Life of Gen. Robert E. Lee* (Baltimore, 1870), 390. John E. Cooke, a veteran of the Army of Northern Virginia, compared many Confederates to Revolutionary leaders as part of his own effort to justify the Confederacy by equating it to the embattled American colonies in the eighteenth century. See Steve Davis, "John Esten Cooke and Confederate Defeat," *Civil War History* 24 (Mar. 1978): 66–83.

2. Clippings of Richmond *Whig,* Nov. 28, 186[?] [1st quote]; Norfolk *Virginian,* Oct. 15, 1870 [2nd quote], Virginia *Gazette,* Oct. 21, 1870, Louisiana Historical Association Collection, Howard-Tilton Library, Tulane University, New Orleans; "Tributes to Lee," 42 [3rd–5th quotes].

He was not the first of Lee's generals to include a comparison of the two leaders in memoirs. Richard Taylor in 1879 favorably compared Lee to Washington and declared that Light-Horse Harry Lee's eulogy for Washington in Congress "is now, by the united voice of the South, applied to his noble son." William R. Cox devoted the first few pages of a retrospective he wrote to an explication of what he believed were the similarities between the two men. When R. A. Brock published a list of those who surrendered at Appomattox, he included the assertion that Lee "is jointly enshrined in the reverential hearts of [Virginia's] sons with her Washington."[3]

Efforts by contemporaries to identify Lee with Washington climaxed with the dedication of Lee memorials as part of the Lost Cause movement. While organizing the Army of Northern Virginia Association, Henry A. Wise declared that it should be "like what the Cincinnati Society after the first American Revolution was to George Washington—full of affections and memories of which the great Chief was the centre." At the 1883 unveiling of Edward V. Valentine's recumbent statue of Lee at Washington and Lee, John W. Daniel, Early's adjutant, recalled that Lee was born in the same county as Washington and married the daughter of his adopted son. Lee, too, "reverenced" Washington "as his exemplar of manhood and his ideal of wisdom." Richmond residents in 1858 had dragged an equestrian statue of Washington to its pedestal beside their capitol; in 1890, they pulled a similar image of Lee to a base on Monument Avenue. Its unveiling included Washington's image in fireworks with the words "The First Rebel," while boys graced Washington's statue with a Confederate flag. Archer Anderson told the crowd that Lee was "Washington's personal representative" by marriage and "made Washington his model of public duty."[4]

3. "Tributes to Lee," 23 [1st quote]; Jones, *Reminiscences*, 347 [2nd quote]; John B. Gordon, *Reminiscences of the Civil War* (New York, 1903), 458 [3rd quote]; Richard Taylor, *Destruction and Reconstruction*, ed. Richard B. Harwell (New York, 1955), 113 [4th quote]; William R. Cox, "Washington and Lee—Appomattox Incidents," *Wake Forest Student* 27 (Jan. 1907): 330–38; R. A. Brock, ed., "Paroles of the Army of Northern Virginia. . . ," *Southern Historical Society Papers* 15 (1887): xxv [5th quote].

4. J. William Jones, ed., *Army of Northern Virginia Memorial Volume* (Richmond, 1880; reprint, Dayton, Ohio, 1976), 30 [1st quote]; "Unveiling of Valentine's Recumbent Figure of Lee at Lexington, Va., June 28th, 1883," *Southern Historical Society Papers* 11 (1883): 342 [2nd and 3rd quotes]; "The Monument to General Robert E. Lee," *Southern Historical Society Papers* 17 (1890): 248–59, 291, 305, 317 [4th and 5th quotes]; Foster, *Ghosts*, 100–101.

Virginia was not the only site of memorials that linked Lee to Washington. A statue of Lee in New Orleans was dedicated on Washington's birthday in 1884. That day, Charles E. Fenner told a large audience that "fate seems to have determined that this illustrious exemplar [Washington] should 'rain influence' upon Lee from every source." Because of this, Lee had accepted the first president as "the idol of his worship." After the turn of the century, Virginia chose a statue of Lee to stand by that of Washington in the national Capitol. Don P. Halsey explained, "there are no two great characters in history so much alike as Washington and Lee." Lee was chosen from among Virginia's "embarrassment of riches" because he was Washington's "peer, and the fittest of all her sons for this high distinction." Despite grumbling, Congress accepted this statement of the inseparability of the men. Ironically, this had been foreshadowed by Garnet J. Wolseley, noted British general and scholar. Years earlier, he wrote that Lee would "be regarded not only as the most prominent figure of the Confederacy, but as the great American of the nineteenth century, whose statue is well worthy to stand on an equal pedestal with Washington, and whose memory is equally worthy to be enshrined in the hearts of all his countrymen."[5]

The raising of statues of Lee prompted poets to compare him with Washington as well. The placing of the statue of Lee in Richmond inspired James B. Hope to write:

> I tell you Lee shall ride
> With that great 'rebel' down the years—
> Twin 'rebels' side by side!

More than a decade later, James R. Randall published an anthology of his work, which included "The Unconquered Banner," with the lines "The South is blameless, for she holds in fee / The stainless swords of Washington and Lee."[6] Similar sentiments had moved Virginia's leaders to insist that images of both men stand side by side in the national Capitol.

5. Charles E. Fenner, "Ceremonies Connected with the Unveiling of the Statue of General Robert E. Lee at Lee Circle, New Orleans, La., Feb. 22, 1884," *Southern Historical Society Papers* 14 (1886): 69 [1st quote], 72 [2nd quote]; Don P. Halsey, "Speech . . . on the Bill to Provide a Statue of Robert E. Lee to be Placed in the Statuary Hall in the Capitol," *Southern Historical Society Papers* 31 (1904): 95 [3rd–5th quotes]; Garnet J. Wolseley, "General Lee," in Gallagher, *Lee the Soldier*, 109 [6th quote].

6. Edwin A. Anderson et al., eds., *Library of Southern Literature* 17 vols. (New Orleans, 1907–1923), 6:2555 [1st quote]; James R. Randall, *Maryland, My Maryland, and Other Poems* (Baltimore, 1908), 47 [2nd quote].

Biographies comparing Lee to Washington appeared in tandem with the eulogies. Emily V. Mason in 1870 compared Lee's struggle in West Virginia to Washington's troubles at Boston. Cooke, in his 1871 study, recalled that Lee "seemed on all occasions to bear the most striking resemblance to the traditional idea of Washington." Judith W. Maguire in 1873 repeated William Preston's assertion that Lee was a "fit representative of his great prototype—General Washington." Within a few years, an English version of a French study of Lee by his nephew Edward Lee Childe, who had been raised in France, appeared. Childe asserted that Lee's marriage made him "in the eyes of the world . . . the representative of the family of the founder of American liberty." Attempting to explain Lee's failure in western Virginia, Childe wrote, "like Washington, he was ready to sacrifice his reputation rather than squander away men's lives in a useless attempt to keep a hostile district." Finally, Lee's simple manner and ability to command the devotion of his men "recalled, in an extraordinary manner, the traditional idea which we have of George Washington."[7]

Thanks in part to Lost Cause defenders' efforts to link the Confederacy with the legacy of the Revolution, comparisons of Lee to Washington did not decrease as the nineteenth century ended. Edmund J. Lee, a cousin of the general, published a biography of the family in 1892. In it, he included a letter from a Northern minister who wrote that while Lee was the "equal of Washington" as a soldier, it would be their "resemblance" in character that would fascinate future historians. James Ford Rhodes, in the third volume of his history of the United States, opined that "in all essential characteristics Lee resembled Washington." In a look forward, William P. Trent asserted in 1899 that Lee's "name will be more and more linked with that of Washington as time goes on." Henry E. Shepherd wrote in 1906 that Washington was Lee's "revered prototype." Lee's speech accepting command in April 1861 also recalled the "style of Washington" and even seemed to resurrect him to lead the South again. In 1907 Philip A. Bruce echoed Early's declaration: "No impartial mind can dwell upon General Lee's character without recall-

---

7. Mason, *Popular Life of Lee,* 88–89; Cooke, *Life of Lee,* 207 [1st quote]; Judith W. Maguire, *General Robert E. Lee, the Christian Soldier* (Richmond, 1873), 40 [2nd quote]; "Tributes to Lee," 4, 37; Edward Lee Childe, *The Life and Campaigns of General Lee,* trans. George Litte (London, 1875), 24, 57, 191 [3rd–5th quotes].

ing Washington's . . . [though] Lee possessed the greater military genius."[8]

Lee's ties to Washington fascinated early twentieth-century writers. Frederick T. Hill wrote that the careers of Washington and Lee were "astonishingly alike" because Washington was a "living presence" for Lee. Washington thus became Lee's "ideal of manhood upon which, consciously or unconsciously, he moulded his own character and life." Thomas N. Page declared that "One familiar with the life of Lee cannot help noting the strong resemblance of his character . . . to that of Washington, or fail to mark what influence the life of Washington had on the life of Lee." Wayne Whipple agreed that "there were a number of points of resemblance." Charles S. Farriss wrote that "No American was so like Washington as was Robert E. Lee." Edwin Wildman noted that "Lee grew up with a profound devotion to the principles of George Washington, whom, it has been claimed, he resembled in character, mould, and form of expression." Jennings C. Wise explained that Lee "more embodied than any other man known to history the spirit, the personality and all those things which entered into the character of Washington."[9]

As the midpoint of the century approached, the focus of many writers who linked Lee with Washington was not just how the former resembled the latter, but how Lee consciously imitated Washington. Historian William E. Dodd in 1928 accepted that Lee was the "heir of the Father of his Country." John E. Hobeika, an "Orientalist," concluded in 1932 that "All through his early life it seems that his feelings were actuated to emulate the great Washington." British scholar John F. C. Fuller in 1933 repeated Childe's claim that when Lee married, he became a "rep-

8. Edmund J. Lee, *Lee of Virginia, 1642–1892* (Philadelphia, 1895; reprint, Baltimore, 1983), 421, 425 [1st and 2nd quotes]; Foster, *Ghosts,* 120–21 [3rd quote]; William P. Trent, *Robert E. Lee* (Boston, 1899), 2 [4th quote]; Henry E. Shepherd, *Life of Robert Edward Lee* (New York, 1906), 34–36 [5th and 6th quotes]; Philip A. Bruce, *Robert E. Lee* (Philadelphia, 1907), 365–66 [7th quote].

9. Frederick T. Hill, *On the Trail of Grant and Lee* (New York, 1911), 7, 78–79 [1st–3rd quotes]; Thomas N. Page, *Robert E. Lee, Man and Soldier* (New York, 1911), 11 [4th quote]; Wayne Whipple, *The Heart of Lee* (Philadelphia, 1918), 75 [5th quote]; Charles S. Farriss, *The American Soul: An Appreciation of the Four Greatest Americans and Their Lesson for Present Americans* (Boston, 1920), 45 [6th quote]; Edwin Wildman, *Famous Leaders of Character in America* (Boston, 1922), 19 [7th quote]; Jennings C. Wise, *Robert E. Lee: Unionist* (Harrisburg, Pa., 1927), 3 [8th quote].

resentative of the family which had founded American liberty." William E. Brooks added another dimension, asserting that while "It has been pointed out again and again that in everything that was essential Lee resembled Washington," in fact Lee deliberately set out to be "Washington's spiritual heir."[10]

The watershed in Lee biographies came with Douglas S. Freeman's Pulitzer Prize–winning opus. Freeman wrote that in Light-Horse Harry Lee's home, where the future commander of the Confederacy was raised, "God came first and then Washington." Furthermore, Washington, "the embodiment of character" and Lee's "hero," became even more "real and personal in the environment of Alexandria." Lee "set himself to be worthy" of his Revolutionary ancestors, "precisely as he had made Washington his model, almost without being conscious of it." When he married Mary Randolph Custis, "he married Arlington as well," which deepened "his reverence for the Washington tradition." It naturally followed that while contemplating secession, Washington's "influence and the ideal were deep in his soul" because "Above his father and every other man he had always placed Washington." Writing literally in the shadow of Freeman, fellow Virginian Marshall W. Fishwick expanded upon his ideas in *Virginians on Olympus*. There he claimed that Light-Horse Harry's eulogy "For many Southerners, and most Virginians . . . no longer belongs to a Washington who made the most of victory, but to the son of Light-Horse Harry Lee, who made the most of defeat."[11]

Subsequent scholars distanced themselves from the Lost Cause but continued to note Lee's bond with Washington. Samuel Eliot Morison and Henry Steele Commager compared Lee to Washington in "simplicity and greatness." Clifford Dowdey said that Washington was not

10. William E. Dodd, *Lincoln or Lee, Comparison and Contrast of the Two Greatest Leaders in the War Between the States* (New York, 1928), 33 [1st quote]; John E. Hobeika, *Lee, the Soul of Honor: An Appreciation by an Orientalist, with Additional Facts* (Boston, 1932), 32 [2nd quote]; John F. C. Fuller, *Grant and Lee: A Study in Personality and Generalship* (Stevenage, U.K., 1933), 102 [3rd quote]; William E. Brooks, *Lee of Virginia: A Biography* (Garden City, N.Y., 1932), xiv [4th and 5th quotes]; Edmund J. Lee, *Lee of Virginia*, 206–7.

11. Douglas S. Freeman, *R. E. Lee: A Biography*, 4 vols. (New York, 1934), 1:22, 109, 169, 453, 4:496; Marshall W. Fishwick, *Virginians on Olympus: A Cultural Analysis of Four Great Men* (Richmond, 1951), 68.

a "remote historic figure" to Lee; instead, Lee became a "product of eighteenth-century Virginia's 'golden age' extended into the first quarter of the new century." Mary T. F. Cheek, director of the Robert E. Lee Memorial Association, agreed in her introduction to the published diary of Agnes Lee that Lee's "idol was George Washington." Nancy S. and Dwight Anderson went a step further and wrote that Lee "spent a lifetime emulating Washington and refuting . . . his father." This partial misstatement was corrected by biographer Emory M. Thomas: "Like his father, Robert Lee revered George Washington as model and hero." Echoing ideas discussed for over a century, Charles P. Roland wrote, "Lee's upbringing bore the impression . . . of one commanding figure beyond the family lines. This was George Washington." He added, "through Lee's marriage he became ever more strongly associated with the memory of the great American patriot, and perhaps in his own eyes Lee became Washington's living representative."[12]

Even those who were critical of Lee acknowledged his link to Washington. Lee's ablest critic, Thomas L. Connelly, declared in his seminal work, *The Marble Man,* that many key questions still remain unanswered because "the crucial element of personality has been absent in many biographies of Lee." To Connelly, the key to Lee was his religious fatalism, but he also pointed out that Lee "not only identified with Washington, but basked in the glory of the Washington heritage" that he obtained by marriage. In a later work coauthored with Barbara Bellows, Connelly repeated that, for Lee, secession was difficult and defeat was bitter because he "idolized George Washington."[13]

Lee never asked to be accepted as an equal of Washington, and he never believed that he had achieved that lofty plateau. To him, raised

12. Charles P. Roland, *Reflections on Lee: A Historian's Assessment* (Mechanicsburg, Pa., 1995), 4 [1st quote], 6 [7th quote], 8 [8th quote]; Clifford Dowdey, *Lee* (Boston, 1965), 34, 43 [2nd and 3rd quotes]; Mary Custis Lee De Butts, ed., *Growing Up in the 1850s: The Journal of Agnes Lee* (Chapel Hill, N.C., 1984), xi [4th quote]; Nancy S. Anderson and Dwight Anderson, *The Generals: Ulysses S. Grant and Robert E. Lee* (New York, 1988), 11 [5th quote]; Emory M. Thomas, *Robert E. Lee: A Biography* (New York, 1995), 79 [6th quote]; Edmund J. Lee, *Lee of Virginia,* 183–84.

13. Thomas L. Connelly, *The Marble Man: Robert E. Lee and His Image in American Society* (Baton Rouge, 1977), 171 [2nd quote], 198–99 [1st quote]; Thomas L. Connelly and Barbara Bellows, *God and General Longstreet: The Lost Cause and the Southern Mind* (Baton Rouge, 1982), 94 [3rd quote], 99.

within the traditions of Virginia's Revolutionary generation, the great Washington was an idol who set a standard to be emulated but that he never equaled. It became his deepest disappointment that his inspiration did not win independence for the new nation that depended upon him as earlier Virginians had relied upon Washington. In some small measure he atoned for this with his postwar work as president of Washington College, and he probably would have been pleased that some understood what he was trying to do as he struggled to regain lost Washington relics.

Ironically, what Lee never asked or accepted for himself has been bestowed upon him by a host of associates and writers who never met him. His efforts before the Civil War to keep the memory of Washington alive, and connect himself to it, drew some comments, but the connections became clear for many Confederates as he made his Army of Northern Virginia the focus of their war effort. The swelling tide of postwar Southern literature that accompanied the Lost Cause movement enshrined Lee as the equal of Washington, and that equation was not lost through the successive generations of revisionists and postrevisionists. Lee remains the dominant military figure of the Civil War, just as Washington remains the principal military figure of the American Revolution. Americans like their marble men, and Lee succeeded better than he knew in emulating the stony mentor that he never met.

Bibliography

UNPUBLISHED PRIMARY MATERIALS

Armes, Ethel. Papers. Library of Congress, Washington, D.C.
Barret, Mrs. Mason. Collection. Howard-Tilton Library, Tulane University, New Orleans, La.
Berkeley Collection. University of Virginia Library, Charlottesville.
Bigelow, John. Papers. Library of Congress, Washington, D.C.
Bixby, William K. Papers. Washington University Library, St. Louis, Mo.
Campbell, George W. Papers. Library of Congress, Washington, D.C.
Chapin, Henry. Papers. University of Virginia Library, Charlottesville.
Chase, Enoch A. Papers. Virginia Historical Society, Richmond.
Civil War Miscellany. Western Reserve Historical Society, Cleveland, Ohio.
Cooke, Philip St. George. Papers. University of Virginia Library, Charlottesville.
Confederate States of America, Army of the. Collection. William G. Perkins Library, Duke University, Durham, N.C.
Corcoran, William W. Papers. Library of Congress, Washington, D.C.
Crimmins, Martin L. Papers. Center for American History, University of Texas at Austin.
Custis-Lee Family. Papers. Library of Congress, Washington, D.C.
Davis, Jefferson. Collection. Howard-Tilton Library, Tulane University, New Orleans, La.
———. Papers. Robert W. Woodruff Library, Emory University, Atlanta, Ga.

De Butts-Ely Collection. Library of Congress, Washington, D.C.

Early, Jubal A. Papers. Library of Congress, Washington, D.C.

Fairfax, John. Papers. Virginia Historical Society, Richmond.

Franklin Society. Library Records. Washington and Lee University Library, Lexington, Va.

Gilder Lehrman Collection. Pierpont Morgan Library, New York.

Grant, Ulysses S. Papers. Library of Congress, Washington, D.C.

Gratz Collection. Historical Society of Pennsylvania, Philadelphia.

Hampton, Wade. Family Papers. University of South Carolina Library, Columbia.

Harrison, Burton M. Papers. Library of Congress, Washington, D.C.

Hartz, Edward L. Papers. Library of Congress, Washington, D.C.

Johnson, Reverdy. Papers. Library of Congress, Washington, D.C.

Kearny, Philip. Papers. New Jersey Historical Society, Newark.

Lee, Edmund J. Papers. Jesse Ball Dupont Library, Stratford Hall, Stratford, Va.

Lee, George B. Papers. Virginia Historical Society, Richmond.

Lee, Robert Carter. Papers. Virginia Historical Society, Richmond.

Lee, Robert E. Papers. Archives and Library Division, Mississippi Department of Archives and History, Jackson.

———. Papers. Center for American History, University of Texas at Austin.

———. Papers. Chicago Historical Society, Chicago.

———. Papers. Eleanor S. Brockenbrough Library, Museum of the Confederacy, Richmond.

———. Papers. Houghton Library, Harvard University, Cambridge.

———. Papers. Jessie Ball DuPont Library, Stratford Hall, Stratford, Va.

———. Papers. John Hay Library, Brown University, Providence, R.I.

———. Papers. Library of Virginia, Richmond.

———. Papers. Lincoln Museum, Fort Wayne, Ind.

———. Papers. New York Historical Society, New York.

———. Papers. Special Collections, Lehigh University, Bethlehem, Pa.

———. Papers. Special Collections, University of Texas at Arlington.

———. Papers. United States Army Military History Institute, Carlisle, Pa.

———. Papers. United States Military Academy Library and Archives, West Point, N.Y.

———. Papers. University of the South Archives, Sewanee, Tenn.

———. Papers. University of Virginia Library, Charlottesville.

———. Papers. University of West Virginia Library, Morgantown.

———. Papers. Virginia Historical Society, Richmond.

———. Papers. Virginia Military Institute Archives, Lexington, Va.

———. Papers. Washington and Lee University Library, Lexington, Va.

———. Papers. William G. Perkins Library, Duke University, Durham, N.C.

Lee Family. Papers. Virginia Historical Society, Richmond.

Lee-Jackson Collection. Washington and Lee University Library, Lexington, Va.

Lennig Collection. Washington and Lee University Library, Lexington, Va.

Longstreet, James. Letterbook. Center for American History, University of Texas at Austin.

Louisiana Historical Association Collection. Howard-Tilton Library, Tulane University, New Orleans, La.

Mackay-McQueen Family. Papers. Colonial Dames Collection. Georgia Historical Society, Savannah.

Mahone, William. "Memoirs." Typescript, n.d. United States Army Military History Institute, Carlisle, Pa.

McCabe, William G. Papers. University of Virginia Library, Charlottesville.

McDowell-Miller-Warner Family. Papers. University of Virginia Library, Charlottesville.

McGuire, Hunter H. Papers. University of Virginia Library, Charlottesville.

Modern Ephemera Collection. Louisiana State Museum, New Orleans.

Moses, Montrose J. Papers. William G. Perkins Library, Duke University, Durham, N.C.

Pendleton, William N. Papers. Southern Historical Collection, University of North Carolina, Chapel Hill.

Polk-Brown-Ewell Family. Papers. Southern Historical Collection, University of North Carolina, Chapel Hill.

Richey, Samuel. Collection. Walter Havinghurst Special Collections Library, Miami University, Oxford, Ohio.

Smith, Sarah Henderson. Papers. Virginia Historical Society, Richmond.

Taylor, Walter H. Papers. Jesse Ball Dupont Library, Stratford Hall, Stratford, Va.

———. Papers. Library of Virginia, Richmond.

Tucker, Beverly D. Papers. University of Virginia Library, Charlottesville.

United States Military Academy. Library Circulation Records. United States Military Academy Library and Archives, West Point, N.Y.

———. Post Orders. United States Military Academy Library and Archives, West Point, N.Y.

———. Superintendents' Letter Books. United States Military Academy Library and Archives, West Point, N.Y.

Venable, Charles S. Papers. Center for American History, University of Texas at Austin.

Washington College. Library Records. Washington and Lee University Library, Lexington, Va.

Wigfall, Louis T. Papers. Library of Congress, Washington, D.C.

PUBLISHED PRIMARY MATERIALS

Adams, Charles F. *Lee at Appomattox and Other Papers.* 2nd ed. Boston: Houghton Mifflin, 1903.

———. *Lee's Centennial: An Address Delivered at Lexington, Virginia, Saturday, January 19, 1907* . . . Boston: Houghton Mifflin, 1907.

Adler, Mortimer J., et al., eds. *The Annals of America.* 18 volumes. Chicago: Encyclopaedia Britannica, 1968.

Alexander, E. Porter. "Lee at Appomattox: Personal Recollections of the Break-Up of the Confederacy." *Century* 63 (March 1902): 921–31.

———. *Fighting for the Confederacy: The Personal Recollections of General Edward Porter Alexander.* Ed. Gary W. Gallagher. Chapel Hill: University of North Carolina Press, 1989.

———. *Military Memoirs of a Confederate.* New York: Scribner's, 1907. Reprint, Dayton, Ohio: Morningside Bookshop, 1977.

Alexander, Peter W. "Confederate Chieftains." *Southern Literary Messenger* 35 (January 1863): 34–38.

Allan, William. *Army of Northern Virginia in 1862.* Boston: Houghton Mifflin, 1892.

Anderson, Edwin A., et al., eds. *Library of Southern Literature.* 17 volumes. New Orleans: Martin & Hoyt, 1907–1923.

Andrews, Eliza F. *The War-Time Journal of a Georgia Girl, 1864–1865.* Ed. Spencer B. King. New York: D. Appleton, 1908.

Bean, W. G. "Lee Talks Frankly of the War and his Final Months in Lexington." *Washington and Lee Alumni Magazine* 41 (Winter 1966): 2–9.

Bond, Christiana. "Memories of General Robert E. Lee." *South Atlantic Quarterly* 24 (1925): 333–48.

Brock, R. A., ed. "Paroles of the Army of Northern Virginia. . . ." *Southern Historical Society Papers* 15 (1887).

Cathbert, Norma B. "To Molly: Five Early Letters from Robert E. Lee to His Wife, 1832–1835," *Huntington Library Quarterly* 15 (May 1952): 257–76.

Chamberlayne, John H. "Address on the Character of General Robert E. Lee." *Southern Historical Society Papers* 3 (1877): 28–37.

Cooke, John E. *Wearing of the Gray.* New York: E. B. Treat, 1867. Reprint, Bloomington: Indiana University Press, 1959.

Cox, William R. "Washington and Lee—Appomattox Incidents." *Wake Forest Student* 27 (January 1907): 330–38.

Craven, Avery, ed. *"To Markie": The Letters of Robert E. Lee to Martha Custis Williams from the Originals in the Huntington Library.* Cambridge: Harvard University Press, 1933.

Crimmins, Martin L., ed. "Robert E. Lee in Texas: Letters and Diary." *West Texas Historical Association Yearbook* 8 (1932): 3–24.

Crist, Lynda L., Mary S. Dix, and Kenneth H. Williams, eds. *The Papers of Jefferson Davis.* Volumes 7 and 8. Baton Rouge: Louisiana State University Press, 1991 and 1995.

Crute, Joseph H., ed. *The Derwent Letters.* Powhatan, Va.: Derwent Books, 1985.

Culberson, Charles A., comp. *The Greatest Confederate Commander.* Washington, D.C.: privately published, 1907.

Custis, George W. P. *Recollections and Private Memoirs of Washington.* Ed. Mary C. Lee. Washington, D.C.: William H. Moore, 1859.

Daniel, Frederick S. "A Visit to a Colonial Estate." *Harper's* 76 (March 1888): 517–24.

Davis, Jefferson. *The Rise and Fall of the Confederate Government.* 2 volumes. New York: D. Appleton, 1881.

———. *Robert E. Lee.* Ed. Harold B. Simpson. Hillsboro, Tex.: Hill Junior College Press, 1966.

Davis, Varina H. *Jefferson Davis, Ex-President of the Confederate States of America: A Memoir by His Wife.* 2 volumes. New York: Belford, 1890.

De Butts, Mary Custis Lee, ed. *Growing Up in the 1850s: the Journal of Agnes Lee.* Chapel Hill: University of North Carolina Press, 1984.

Denison, George T., Jr. "A Visit to General Robert E. Lee." *Canadian Monthly* 1 (March 1872): 231–37.

Dowdey, Clifford, and Louis H. Manarin, eds. *The Wartime Papers of Robert E. Lee.* Boston: Little, Brown, 1961.

Early, Jubal A. *War Memoirs.* Ed. Frank E. Vandiver. Philadelphia: Lippincott, 1912. Reprint, Bloomington: Indiana University Press, 1960.

Fenner, Charles F. "Ceremonies Connected with the Unveiling of the Statue of General Robert E. Lee at Lee Circle, New Orleans, La., Feb. 22, 1884." *Southern Historical Society Papers* 14 (1886): 63–102.

Fitzpatrick, John C., ed. *The Writings of George Washington.* 39 volumes. Washington, D.C.: United States Government Printing Office, 1931–1944.

Freeman, Douglas S., ed. *Lee's Dispatches: Unpublished Letters of General Robert E. Lee, C.S.A., to Jefferson Davis and the War Department of the Confederate States of America, 1862–65.* New York: Putnam's Sons, 1915.

Fremantle, Arthur J. L. *Three Months in the Southern States, April–June, 1863.* London: W. Blackwood & Sons, 1863.

Gallagher, Gary W., ed. "'We Are Our Own Trumpeters': Robert E. Lee Describes Winfield Scott's Campaign to Mexico City." *Virginia Magazine of History and Biography* 95 (July 1987): 363–75.

Gordon, John B. *Reminiscences of the Civil War.* New York: Charles Scribner's Sons, 1903.

Hairston, Peter W., ed. "J. E. B. Stuart's Letters to His Hairston Kin, 1850–1855." *North Carolina Historical Review* 51 (July 1974): 261–333.

Halsey, Don P. "Speech . . . on the Bill to Provide a Statue of Robert E. Lee to Be Placed in the Statuary Hall in the Capitol." *Southern Historical Society Papers* 31 (1903): 81–99.

Hill, Benjamin H. "Address . . . before the Georgia Branch of the Southern Historical Society at Atlanta, February 18th, 1874." *Southern Historical Society Papers* 14 (1886): 484–505.

Hood, John Bell. *Advance and Retreat.* New Orleans: P. G. T. Beauregard, 1880.

Horn, Stanley F., ed. *The Robert E. Lee Reader.* Indianapolis: Bobbs-Merrill, 1949.

Hoyt, William D., Jr., ed. "Some Personal Letters of Robert E. Lee, 1850–1858." *Journal of Southern History* 12 (November 1946): 557–70.

Imboden, John D. "Lee at Gettysburg." *Galaxy* 11 (April 1871): 507–13.

———. "Reminiscences of Lee and Jackson." *Galaxy* 12 (November 1871): 627–34.

Jenkins, John H., ed. *Lee on the Rio Grande: The Correspondence of Robert E. Lee on the Texas Border, 1860.* Austin: Jenkins Publishing Co., 1988.

Johnson, Robert U., and Clarence C. Buel, eds. *Battles and Leaders of the Civil War.* 4 volumes. New York: Thomas Yoseloff, 1956.

Johnston, William P. "Reminiscences of General Robert E. Lee." *Belford Monthly* 5 (June 1890): 84–91.

Jones, J. William, ed. *Army of Northern Virginia Memorial Volume.* Richmond: J. W. Randolph & English, 1880. Reprint, Dayton, Ohio: Morningside Bookshop, 1976.

———. "General Lee to the Rear." *Southern Historical Society Papers* 8 (1880): 31–36.

———. *Personal Reminiscences, Anecdotes, and Letters of Gen. Robert E. Lee.* New York: D. Appleton, 1874.

Jones, John B. *A Rebel War Clerk's Diary.* Ed. Howard Swiggett. 2 volumes. New York: Old Hickory Bookshop, 1935.

"Leading Confederates on the Battle of Gettysburg." *Southern Historical Society Papers* 4 (1877): 145–60.

Lee, Fitzhugh. *General Lee.* New York: D. Appleton, 1894. Reprint, Wilmington, N.C.: Broadfoot, 1989.

Lee, George T. "Reminiscences of General Robert E. Lee, 1865–1868." *South Atlantic Quarterly* 26 (July 1927): 236–51.

Lee, Henry, III. *Memoirs of the War in the Southern Department of the United States.* Ed. Robert E. Lee. New York: University, 1869.

Lee, Henry, IV. *The Campaign of 1781 in the Carolinas.* Philadelphia: E. Littell, 1824. Reprint, Spartanburg, S.C.: Reprint Company, 1975.

Lee, Robert E. "A Letter from Petersburg." *Civil War History* 3 (December 1957): 376.

Lee, Robert E., Jr. *Recollections and Letters of General Robert E. Lee.* New York: Doubleday, Page, 1904.

"Lee's Farewell to Texas, February 9, 1861." *Military History of Texas and the Southwest* 14 (1978): 244–45.

Long, Armistead L. *Memoirs of Robert E. Lee.* New York: J. M. Stoddart, 1886.

Longstreet, Helen D. *Lee and Longstreet at High Tide.* Gainesville, Ga.: privately published, 1904.

Longstreet, James. *From Manassas to Appomattox.* Philadelphia: Lippincott, 1896.

Lossing, Benson J. "Arlington House." *Harper's* 7 (September 1853): 433–54.

MacBride, Van Dyk. "The Autographed Field Letters of General Robert E. Lee." *The Stamp Specialist India Book.* New York: H. L. Lindquist, 1946.

MacNutt, Francis A. "A Lee Miscellany: Portrait of Mrs. Anne Hill (Carter) Lee." *Virginia Magazine of History and Biography* 33 (January 1925): 370–71.

Marshall, Charles. *An Aide-de-Camp of Lee, Being the Papers of Colonel Charles Marshall, Sometime Aide-de-Camp, Military Secretary, and Assistant Adjutant General on the Staff of Robert E. Lee.* Ed. Frederick Maurice. Boston: Little, Brown, 1927.

Mason, Emily V., ed. *The Southern Poems of the War.* 3rd ed. Baltimore: John Murphy, 1869.

Melville, Herman. *Battle-Pieces and Aspects of the War.* New York: Harper & Brothers, 1866. Reprint, New York: Da Capo, 1995.

Moger, Allan W., ed. "Letters to General Lee after the War." *Virginia Magazine of History and Biography* 64 (January 1956): 30–69.

"The Monument to General Robert E. Lee." *Southern Historical Society Papers* 17 (1890): 187–335.

Moore, Frank, ed. *The Rebellion Record: A Diary of American Events.* 12 volumes. New York: Putnam and Van Nostrand, 1861–1868. Reprint, New York: Arno, 1977.

Mosby, John S. *The Memoirs of Colonel John S. Mosby.* Ed. Charles W. Russell. Boston: Little, Brown, 1917. Reprint, Bloomington: Indiana University Press, 1959.

Myers, Robert M., ed. *The Children of Pride.* New Haven: Yale University Press, 1972.

Phillips, Ulrich B., ed. *Plantation and Frontier Documents: 1649–1863.* 2 volumes. Cleveland, Ohio: Arthur H. Clark, 1909.

Pollard, Edward A. *The Early Life, Campaigns, and Public Services of Robert E. Lee.* New York: E. B. Treat, 1871.

————. *Lee and His Lieutenants.* New York: E. B. Treat, 1867.

————. *The Lost Cause: A New Southern History of the War of the Confederates.* New York, E. B. Treat , 1867.

Preston, William. "Personal Recollections of General Lee." *Southern Magazine* 15 (September 1874): 605–36.

Rachal, William M. E., ed. " 'Secession is Nothing But Revolution': A Letter of R. E. Lee to His Son Rooney." *Virginia Magazine of History and Biography* 69 (January 1961): 3–6.

Randall, James R. *Maryland, My Maryland, and Other Poems.* Baltimore: John Murphy, 1908.

Reagan, John H. *Memoirs.* Austin: Pemberton, 1968.

Richardson, James D., comp. *The Messages and Papers of Jefferson Davis and the Confederacy, 1861–1865.* 2 volumes. Washington, D.C.: Government Printing Office, 1896–1899. Reprint, New York, Confucian, 1981.

Riley, Franklin L., ed. *General Robert E. Lee after Appomattox.* New York: Macmillan, 1922.

"A Robert E. Lee Letter to P. G. T. Beauregard." *Maryland Historical Magazine* 51 (September 1956): 249–51.

"Robert E. Lee: Portrait, Chronology, and Biography." *American Phrenological Journal* 40 (September 1864): 88.

Ross, Fitzgerald. *A Visit to the Cities and Camps of the Confederate States.* London: W. Blackwood & Sons, 1865.

Rowland, Dunbar, ed. *Jefferson Davis, Constitutionalist: His Letters, Papers, and Speeches.* 10 volumes. Jackson: Mississippi Department of Archives and History, 1923.

Schaff, Morris. *Spirit of Old West Point.* Boston: Houghton Mifflin, 1907.

Schiebert, Justus. *Seven Months in the Rebel States.* Trans. Joseph C. Hayes and William S. Hoole. Tuscaloosa: University of Alabama Press, 1958.

Scott, W. W., ed. "The John Brown Letters." *Virginia Magazine of History and Biography* 9 (April 1902): 385–95.

————. "Some Personal Memories of General Robert E. Lee." *William and Mary Quarterly* 6 [2nd Series] (October 1926): 277–88.

Shackelford, George G. "Lieutenant Lee Reports to Captain Talcott on Fort Calhoun's Construction on the Rip Raps." *Virginia Magazine of History and Biography* 60 (July 1952): 458–87.

Sibley, Marilyn M. "Robert E. Lee to Albert Sydney Johnston, 1857." *Journal of Southern History* 29 (February 1963): 100–107.

Simms, William G. "The Soul of the South: An Ode." *Southern Literary Messenger* 36 (February–March 1862): 101.

————, ed. *War Poetry of the South.* New York: Richardson, 1867.

Smith, James P. "With Stonewall Jackson in the Army of Northern Virginia." *Southern Historical Society Papers* 43 (1920): 1–295.

"The Spirit of 1861: Correspondence of General R. E. Lee." *Southern Historical Society Papers* 6 (1878): 91–94.

Stephens, Robert G., Jr., comp. *Intrepid Warrior: Clement Anselm Evans, Confederate General from Georgia.* Dayton, Ohio: Morningside, 1992.

Stiles, Robert. *Four Years under Marse Robert.* New York: Neale, 1903.

Tate, William, ed. "A Robert E. Lee Letter on Abandoning the South after the War." *Georgia Historical Quarterly* 37 (September 1953): 255–56.

Taylor, Richard. *Destruction and Reconstruction.* Ed. Richard B. Harwell. New York: Longmans, Green, 1955.

Taylor, Walter H. *Four Years with General Lee.* New York: D. Appleton, 1877. Reprint, New York: Bonanza, 1962.

———. *General Lee: His Campaigns in Virginia, 1861–1865.* Norfolk, Va.: Nusbaum, 1906.

"Tributes to General Lee." *Southern Magazine* 8 (January 1871): 1–46.

U.S. House of Representatives. *Report of the Joint Committee on Reconstruction, Part II.* 39th Cong., 1st Sess., 1866. H. Rept. 30. Serial 1273.

———. *Occupation of the "White House" in Virginia.* 37th Cong., 2nd sess., 1862. H. Exec. Doc. 145. Serial 1138.

———. *White House on Pamunkey River.* 37th Cong., 2nd sess., 1862. H. Exec. Doc. 135. Serial 1138.

"Unveiling of Valentine's Recumbent Figure of Lee at Lexington, Va., June 28th, 1883." *Southern Historical Society Papers* 11 (1883): 337–88.

Valentine, Edward V. "Reminiscences of General Lee." *Outlook* 84 (December 22, 1906): 964–68.

The War of the Rebellion: A Compilation of the Official Records of the Union and Confederate Armies. 130 volumes. Washington, D.C.: Government Printing Office, 1880–1902.

Wilmer, Joseph P. B. *Gen'l. Robert E. Lee: An Address Delivered before the Students of the University of the South, October 15, 1870.* Nashville: Paul & Tavel, 1872.

Wise, John S. *End of an Era.* Ed. Custis C. Davis. New York: Thomas Yoseloff, 1965.

Woodward, C. Vann, ed. *Mary Chesnut's Civil War.* New Haven: Yale University Press, 1981.

NEWSPAPERS

Charleston *Mercury,* 1862–1863.
Illustrated London News, 1864.
New York *Herald,* 1861, 1865.

Richmond *Dispatch,* 1862, 1865.

Richmond *Enquirer,* 1861.

Richmond *Examiner,* 1865.

Richmond *Whig,* 1862.

Southern Collegian, 1870.

BOOKS

Alexander, Holmes M. *Washington and Lee: A Study in the Will to Win.* Boston: Western Islands, 1966.

Ambrose, Stephen E. *Duty, Honor, Country.* Baltimore: Johns Hopkins University Press, 1966.

Anderson, Nancy S., and Dwight Anderson. *The Generals: Ulysses S. Grant and Robert E. Lee.* New York: Random, 1988.

Andrews, J. Cutler. *The South Reports the Civil War.* Princeton: Princeton University Press, 1970.

Arlington House: A Guide to Arlington House, the Robert E. Lee Memorial, Virginia. Washington, D.C.: U.S. Department of the Interior, 1990.

Armes, Ethel. *Stratford Hall: The Great House of the Lees.* Richmond: Garrett & Massie, 1936.

Benet, Stephen Vincent. *John Brown's Body.* New York: Farrar and Rinehart, 1941.

Beringer, Richard E., et al., eds. *Why the South Lost the War.* Athens: University of Georgia Press, 1986.

Bonekemper, Edward H. III. *How Robert E. Lee Lost the Civil War.* Fredericksburg, Va.: Sergeant Kirkland's, 1997.

Boritt, Gabor S. *Why the Confederacy Lost.* New York: Oxford University Press, 1992.

Bowen, John J. *The Strategy of Robert E. Lee.* New York: Neal, 1914.

Boyd, Thomas. *Light-Horse Harry Lee.* New York: Charles Scribner's Sons, 1931.

Bradford, Gamaliel. *Lee the American.* Rev. ed. Cambridge, Mass.: Riverside, 1929.

Breithaupt, Richard H., Jr. *Aztec Club of 1847, Military Society of the Mexican War: Sesquicentennial History, 1847–1997.* Los Angeles: Aztec Club, 1998.

Brock, Robert A., ed. *Gen. Robert Edward Lee: Soldier, Citizen, and Christian Patriot.* Richmond: B. F. Johnson, 1897.

Brooks, William E. *Lee of Virginia: A Biography.* Garden City, N.Y.: Garden City, 1932.

Bryan, William A. *George Washington in American Literature, 1775–1865.* New York: Columbia University Press, 1952.

Bruce, Philip A. *Robert E. Lee.* Philadelphia: G. W. Jacobs, 1907.

Casdorph, Paul D. *Lee and Jackson: Confederate Chieftains.* New York: Paragon, 1992.

Chaney, William F. *Duty Most Sublime: The Life of Robert E. Lee as Told through the "Carter Letters".* Baltimore: Gateway, 1996.

Childe, Edward Lee. *The Life and Campaigns of General Lee.* Trans. George Litte. London: Chatto and Windus, 1875.

Cohen, Lester H. *The Revolutionary Histories: Contemporary Narratives of the American Revolution.* Ithaca, N.Y.: Cornell University Press, 1980.

Connelly, Thomas L. *The Marble Man: Robert E. Lee and His Image in American Society.* Baton Rouge: Louisiana State University Press, 1977.

Connelly, Thomas L., and Barbara Bellows. *God and General Longstreet: The Lost Cause and the Southern Mind.* Baton Rouge: Louisiana State University Press, 1982.

Connelly, Thomas L., and Archer Jones. *The Politics of Command: Factions and Ideas in Confederate Strategy.* Baton Rouge: Louisiana State University Press, 1983.

Cooke, John E. *A Life of Gen. Robert E. Lee.* New York: D. Appleton, 1883.

Coulling, Mary P. *Lee Girls.* Winston-Salem, N.C.: J. F. Blair, 1987.

Crenshaw, Ollinger. *General Lee's College: The Rise and Growth of Washington and Lee University.* New York: Random, 1969.

Davis, Burke. *Gray Fox: Robert E. Lee and the Civil War.* New York: Rinehart, 1956.

Decker, Karl, and Angus McSween. *Historic Arlington: A History of the National Cemetery from Its Establishment to the Present Time.* Washington, D.C.: Decker and McSween, 1892.

Dodd, William E. *Lincoln or Lee: Comparison and Contrast of the Two Greatest Leaders in the War Between the States.* New York: Century, 1928.

Dowdey, Clifford. *Lee.* Boston: Little, Brown, 1965.

Durden, Robert F. *The Gray and the Black: The Confederate Debate on Emancipation.* Baton Rouge: Louisiana State University Press, 1972.

Escott, Paul D. *After Secession: Jefferson Davis and the Failure of Confederate Nationalism.* Baton Rouge: Louisiana State University Press, 1978.

Farriss, Charles S. *The American Soul: An Appreciation of the Four Greatest Americans and Their Lesson for Present Americans.* Boston: Stratford, 1920.

Faust, Drew G. *The Creation of Confederate Nationalism: Ideology and Identity in the Civil War South.* Baton Rouge: Louisiana State University Press, 1988.

Fishwick, Marshall W. *General Lee's Photographer: The Life and Work of Michael Miley.* Chapel Hill: University of North Carolina Press, 1954.

———. *Lee after the War.* New York: Dodd, Mead, 1963.

———. *Virginians on Olympus: A Cultural Analysis of Four Great Men.* Richmond: privately published, 1951.

Flexner, James T. *Washington: The Indispensable Man.* New York: New American Library, 1974.

Flood, Charles B. *Lee: The Last Years.* Boston: Houghton Mifflin, 1981.

Forgie, George B. *Patricide in the House Divided.* New York: Norton, 1979.

Foster, Gaines M. *Ghosts of the Confederacy.* New York: Oxford University Press, 1987.

Freeman, Douglas S. *R. E. Lee: A Biography.* 4 volumes. New York: Charles Scribner's Sons, 1934.

Fuller, John F. C. *Grant and Lee: A Study in Personality and Generalship.* Stevenage, U.K.: Spa, 1933.

Gallagher, Gary W. *The Confederate War.* Cambridge: Harvard University Press, 1997.

———, ed. *Lee the Soldier.* Lincoln: University of Nebraska Press, 1996.

Gerson, Noel B. *Light-Horse Harry: A Biography of Washington's Great Cavalryman, General Henry Lee.* Garden City, N.Y.: Doubleday, 1966.

Glatthaar, Joseph T. *Partners in Command: The Relationships Between Leaders in the Civil War.* New York: Macmillan, 1993.

Griffith, Paddy. *Battle Tactics of the Civil War.* New Haven: Yale University Press, 1989.

Hagerman, Edward. *The American Civil War and the Origins of Modern Warfare.* Bloomington: Indiana University Press, 1988.

Harsh, Joseph L. *Confederate Tide Rising: Robert E. Lee and the Making of Southern Strategy, 1861–1862.* Kent, Ohio: Kent State University Press, 1998.

Hattaway, Herman. *Shades of Blue and Gray: An Introductory Military History of the Civil War.* Columbia: University of Missouri Press, 1997.

Hendrick, Burton J. *The Lees of Virginia: Biography of a Family.* Boston: Little, Brown, 1935.

Hill, Frederick T. *On the Trail of Grant and Lee.* New York: D. Appleton–Century, 1911.

Hobeika, John E. *Lee, the Soul of Honor: An Appreciation by an Orientalist, with Additional Facts.* Boston: Christopher, 1932.

Jones, J. William. *Life and Letters of Robert Edward Lee, Soldier and Man.* New York: Neale, 1906.

Jordan, Ervin L., Jr. *Black Confederates and Afro-Yankees in Civil War Virginia.* Charlottesville: University Press of Virginia, 1995.

Lee, Casenove G. *Lee Chronicle: Studies of the Early Generations of the Lees of Virginia.* Ed. Dorothy M. Parker. New York: New York University Press, 1957.

Lee, Edmund J. *Lee of Virginia, 1642–1892.* Philadelphia: Franklin, 1895. Reprint, Baltimore: Genealogical Publishing, 1983.

MacDonald, Rose M. E. *Mrs. Robert E. Lee.* Boston: Ginn, 1939.

Maguire, Judith W. *General Robert E. Lee, the Christian Soldier.* Richmond: Woodhouse & Parham, 1873.

Mason, Emily V. *Popular Life of Gen. Robert E. Lee.* Baltimore: John Murphy, 1870.

Maurice, Frederick. *Robert E. Lee, the Soldier.* Boston: Houghton Mifflin, 1925.

McCabe, James D. *Life and Campaigns of General Robert E. Lee.* Atlanta: National, 1866.

McKinney, Tim. *Robert E. Lee and the Thirty-Fifth Star.* Charleston, W.Va.: Pictorial Histories, 1993.

McPherson, James I. *What They Fought For.* Baton Rouge: Louisiana State University Press, 1994.

McPherson, James M. *Battle Cry of Freedom: The Civil War Era.* New York: Oxford University Press, 1988.

———. *For Cause and Comrades: Why Men Fought in the Civil War.* New York: Oxford University Press, 1997.

McWhiney, Grady, and Perry D. Jamieson. *Attack and Die: Civil War Military Tactics and the Southern Heritage.* Tuscaloosa: University of Alabama Press, 1982.

Miers, Earl S. *Robert E. Lee: A Great Life in Brief.* New York: Knopf, 1956.

Mitchell, Reid. *Civil War Soldiers.* New York: Viking, 1988.

Nagel, Paul C. *The Lees of Virginia: Seven Generations of an American Family.* New York: Oxford University Press, 1990.

Nolan, Alan T. *Lee Considered: General Robert E. Lee and Civil War History.* Chapel Hill: University of North Carolina Press, 1991.

Oakes, James. *The Ruling Race: A History of American Slaveholders.* New York: Knopf, 1982.

O'Neill, Edward H. *A History of American Biography, 1800–1935.* Philadelphia: University of Pennsylvania Press, 1935.

Page, Thomas N. *Robert E. Lee, Man and Soldier.* New York: Charles Scribner's Sons, 1911.

Power, J. Tracy. *Lee's Miserables: Life in the Army of Northern Virginia from the Wilderness to Appomattox.* Chapel Hill: University of North Carolina Press, 1998.

Preston, Walter C. *Lee, West Point, and Lexington.* Yellow Springs, Ohio: Antioch, 1934.

Prussing, Eugene E. *The Estate of George Washington, Deceased.* Boston: Little, Brown, 1927.

Redway, Maurine W. *Marks of Lee on Our Land.* San Antonio: Naylor, 1972.

Rhodes, Charles D. *Robert E. Lee the West Pointer.* Richmond: Garrett & Massie, 1932.

Rister, Carl C. *Robert E. Lee in Texas.* Norman: University of Oklahoma Press, 1946.

Roland, Charles P. *Reflections on Lee: A Historian's Assessment.* Mechanicsburg, Pa.: Stackpole, 1995.

Royster, Charles. *Light-Horse Harry Lee and the Legacy of the American Revolution.* New York: Knopf, 1982.

Sanborn, Margaret. *Robert E. Lee: A Portrait.* Philadelphia: Lippincott, 1966.

———. *Robert E. Lee: The Complete Man.* Philadelphia: Lippincott, 1967.

Sears, Stephen W., ed. *The Civil War: The Best of American Heritage.* Boston: Houghton Mifflin, 1991.

Shaffer, Arthur H. *The Politics of History: Writing the History of the American Revolution, 1783–1915.* Chicago: Precedent, 1975.

Shepherd, Henry E. *Life of Robert Edward Lee.* New York: Neale, 1906.

Smith, Gene. *Lee and Grant: A Dual Biography.* Norwalk, Conn.: Easton, 1984.

Snow, William P. *Lee and His Generals: Their Lives and Campaigns.* New York: Richardson, 1867. Reprint, New York: Fairfax, 1982.

Speer, Emory. *Lincoln, Lee, Grant, and Other Biographical Addresses.* New York: Neal, 1909.

Stephen, Leslie, and Sidney Lee, eds. *The Dictionary of National Biography.* 22 volumes. London: Oxford University Press, 1917.

Stern, Philip Van Doren. *Robert E. Lee, the Man and the Soldier: A Pictorial Biography.* New York: McGraw-Hill, 1963.

Thomas, Emory M. *The Confederacy as a Revolutionary Experience.* New York: Prentice Hall, 1970.

———. *The Confederate Nation, 1861–1865.* New York: Harper and Row, 1979.

———. *Robert E. Lee: A Biography.* New York: Norton, 1995.

Trent, William P. *Robert E. Lee.* Boston: Small, Maynard, 1899.

Wayland, John W. *Robert E. Lee and His Family.* Philadelphia: McClure, 1951.

Weigley, Russell. *The American Way of War.* New York: Macmillan, 1973. Reprint, Bloomington: Indiana University Press, 1977.

Whipple, Wayne. *The Heart of Lee.* Philadelphia: G. W. Jacobs, 1918.

White, Henry A. *Robert E. Lee and the Southern Confederacy, 1807–1870.* New York: Putnam's Sons, 1897.

Wildman, Edwin. *Famous Leaders of Character in America.* Boston: Page, 1922.

Winston, Robert W. *Robert E. Lee: A Biography.* New York: Grosset & Dunlap, 1941.

Wise, Jennings C. *Robert E. Lee: Unionist.* Harrisburg, Pa.: P. & L., 1927.

Woodworth, Steven E. *Davis and Lee at War.* Lawrence: University of Kansas Press, 1994.

Wyatt-Brown, Bertram. *Southern Honor: Ethics and Behavior in the Old South.* New York: Oxford University Press, 1982.

Young, James C. *Marse Robert, Knight of the Confederacy.* New York: Henkle, 1929. Reprint, New York: Grosset & Dunlap, 1932.

ARTICLES

Adams, Charles F. "The Confederacy and the Transvaal." *American Antiquarian Society Proceedings* 14 (October 1901): 429–51.

Baggett, James A. "Origins of Upper South Scalawag Leadership." *Civil War History* 29 (March 1983): 53–73.

Bullitt, Thomas W. "Lee and Scott." *Southern Historical Society Papers* 11 (1883): 443–54.

Campbell, Edward D. C., Jr. "The Fabric of Command: R. E. Lee, Confederate Insignia, and the Perception of Rank." *Virginia Magazine of History and Biography* 98 (April 1990): 261–90.

Chessney, C. C. "Cooke's Life of General Robert E. Lee." *Edinburgh Review* 137 (January–April 1873): 363–98.

Connelly, Thomas L. "The Image and the General: Robert E. Lee in American Historiography." *Civil War History* 19 (March 1973): 50–64.

———. "Robert E. Lee and the Western Confederacy: A Criticism of Lee's Strategic Ability." *Civil War History* 15 (June 1969): 116–32.

Couper, William. "War and Work." *Proceedings of the Rockbridge Historical Society* 1 (1939–1941): 26–42.

Davis, Steve. "John Esten Cooke and Confederate Defeat." *Civil War History* 24 (March 1978): 66–83.

Dederer, John M. "The Origins of Robert E. Lee's Bold Generalship: A Reinterpretation." *Military Affairs* 49 (July 1985): 117–23.

———. "In Search of the Unknown Soldier: A Critique of the Mystery in the Coffin." *Virginia Magazine of History and Biography* 103 (January 1995): 95–116.

———. "Robert E. Lee's First Visit to His Father's Grave." *Virginia Magazine of History and Biography* 102 (January 1994): 73–88.

Drumm, Stella M. "Robert E. Lee and the Improvement of the Mississippi River." *Collections of the Missouri Historical Society* 6 (February 1929): 157–71.

Duncan, Richard R. "Marylanders and the Invasion of 1862." *Civil War History* 11 (December 1965): 370–83.

Ellis, Robert R. "The Lees at Fort Monroe." *Military Engineer* 42 (1950): 1–5.

Freeman, Douglas S. "Lee and the Ladies, Part II." *Scribner's* 78 (November 1925): 459–71.

Gallagher, Gary W. "The Army of Northern Virginia in May 1864: A Crisis of High Command." *Civil War History* 36 (June 1990): 101–18.

Hagerman, Edward. "From Jomini to Dennis Hart Mahan: The Evolution of Trench Warfare and the American Civil War." *Civil War History* 13 (September 1967): 197–220.

———. "The Tactical Thought of Robert E. Lee and the Origins of Trench Warfare in the American Civil War, 1861–1862." *Historian* 38 (November 1975): 21–38.

Hoover, Sallie W. S. "Col. John Augustine Washington, C.S.A." *Confederate Veteran* 34 (March 1926): 96–98.

Hume, Edgar E. "Light-Horse Harry and His Fellow Members of the Cincinnati." *William and Mary Quarterly* 15 [2nd Series] (April 1935): 271–81.

James, Felix. "The Establishment of Freedman's Village in Arlington, Virginia." *Negro History Bulletin* 33 (March 1970): 90–93.

Jones, Archer. "The Gettysburg Decision." *Virginia Magazine of History and Biography* 68 (July 1960): 331–43.

Jones, J. William. "The Friendship between Lee and Scott." *Southern Historical Society Papers* 11 (1883): 417–26.

Lowe, Richard. "Testimony from the Old Dominion before the Joint Committee on Reconstruction." *Virginia Magazine of History and Biography* 104 (Summer 1996): 373–98.

Luvaas, Jay. "Lee and the Operational Art." *Parameters* 22 (Autumn 1992): 2–18.

MacDonnell, Francis. "The Confederate Spin on Winfield Scott and George Thomas." *Civil War History* 44 (December 1998): 255–66.

———. "Reconstruction in the Wake of Vietnam: The Pardoning of Robert E. Lee and Jefferson Davis." *Civil War History* 40 (June 1994): 119–33.

McDonald, William C. "The True Gentleman: On Robert E. Lee's Definition of the Gentleman." *Civil War History* 32 (June 1986): 117–38.

Moger, Allen W. "General Lee's Unwritten 'History of the Army of Northern Virginia.'" *Virginia Magazine of History and Biography* 71 (July 1963): 341–63.

———. "The Value of a Portrait." *Civil War History* 3 (December 1957): 435–37.

Moore, R. Walton. "General Washington and Houdon." *Virginia Magazine of History and Biography* 41 (January 1933): 1–10.

Pohl, James W. "The Influence of Antoine Henri de Jomini on Winfield Scott's Campaign in the Mexican War." *Southwestern Historical Quarterly* 77 (July 1973): 85–110.

Reidy, Joseph P. " 'Coming from the Shadows of the Past': The Transition from Slavery to Freedom at Freedmen's Village, 1863–1900." *Virginia Magazine of History and Biography* 95 (October 1987): 403–28.

"Robert E. Lee: Virginia Chooses Her Leader." *Virginia Magazine of History and Biography* 30 (April 1922): 108–10.

Robert, Joseph C. "Lee the Farmer." *Journal of Southern History* 3 (November 1937): 422–40.

Templeman, Eleanor L. "Cincinnati Export Porcelain: The Washington and Lee Services." *Art & Antiques* 5 (January 1982): 74–79.

Thomson, J. Anderson, Jr., and Carlos M. Santos. "The Mystery in the Coffin: Another View of Lee's Visit to His Father's Grave." *Virginia Magazine of History and Biography* 103 (January 1995): 75–94.

Wyrick, Connie H. "Stratford and the Lees." *Journal of the Society of Architectural Historians* 30 (March 1971): 76–80.

REPORTS, THESES, AND DISSERTATIONS

Adams, Francis R., ed. "An Annotated Edition of the Personal Letters of Robert E. Lee, April 1855–April 1861." Ph.D. diss., University of Maryland, 1955.

Bailey, William W. "Robert E. Lee at West Point." Manuscript, n.d. United States Military Academy Library and Archives, West Point, N.Y.

Black, Robert K., ed. "Robert E. Lee, A Sesquicentennial Tribute: Ten Autograph Letters from Lee to his Closest Friend, John Mackay of Georgia, 1834–1843." Typescript, n.d. [1950] Rice Institute Library, Houston, Tex.

Manarin, Louis H. "Lee in Command: Strategical and Tactical Policies. . . ." Ph.D. diss., Duke University, 1965.

Wilson, Charlotte. "Robert E. Lee at West Point." B.A. Thesis, West Virginia University, 1941.

Index